Woodrow Wilson and the Press: Prelude to the Presidency

By
James D. Startt

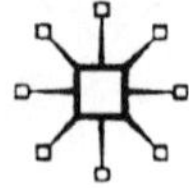

WOODROW WILSON AND THE PRESS: PRELUDE TO THE PRESIDENCY

First published 2004 by
PALGRAVE MACMILLAN™
175 Fifth Avenue, New York, N.Y. 10010 and
Houndmills, Basingstoke, Hampshire, England RG21 6XS
Companies and representatives throughout the world

PALGRAVE MACMILLAN is the global academic imprint of the Palgrave Macmillan division of St. Martin's Press, LLC and of Palgrave Macmillan Ltd. Macmillan® is a registered trademark in the United States, United Kingdom and other countries. Palgrave is a registered trademark in the European Union and other countries.

ISBN 1–4039–6372–X hardback

Library of Congress Cataloging-in-Publication Data
Startt, James D., 1932–
Woodrow Wilson and the press : prelude to the presidency / James D. Startt.
p. cm.
Includes bibliographical references and index.
ISBN 1–4039–6372–X
1. Wilson, Woodrow, 1856–1924—Relations with journalists. 2. Press and politics—United States—History—20th century. 3. Presidents—United States—Election—1912. 4. Governors—New Jersey—Election—1910. 5. United States—Politics and government—1901–1909. 6. United States—Politics and government—1909–1913. 7. Journalism—United States—History—20th century. 8. Presidents—United States—Biography. 9. Governors—New Jersey—Biography. I. Title.

E767.1.S73 2004
973.91′3′092—dc21 2003051736

A catalogue record for this book is available from the British Library.

Design by Newgen Imaging Systems (P) Ltd., Chennai, India.

First edition: January, 2004
10 9 8 7 6 5 4 3 2 1

Printed in the United States of America.

To Catherine, My Wife

Contents

List of Illustrations

Preface

Some nineteenth-century presidents tried to distance themselves from the press. Their twentieth-century counterparts, however, understood the danger of that type of self-imposed isolation. In the words of Woodrow Wilson, "The public man who fights the daily press won't be a public man very long."[1] Indeed, by the start of the twentieth century, the press had grown to gigantic proportions. Few people in the country were beyond its daily or weekly reach. With its mass circulating newspapers and periodicals and with its teeming specialized publications, the press had unprecedented means to sway public opinion, and public opinion had become a crucial factor in the nation's political culture. If the old partisan press characterized by newspapers tied to political parties was a thing of the past, the interest of the new independent press in politics remained alive. The press, however, was now a commercialized and popularized institution that focused on the personal qualities and actions of public figures as well as on issues. Modern presidents, as well as candidates for high office, attract this type of modern press scrutiny. They have to engage a vast independent press, and they have to reach a public that expects to receive news about their activities and policies. Therefore, their previous experience with the press, their ability to have constructive interaction with it, and their perception of its role in the nation's political culture are matters of importance in determining their potential for success or failure in office. It was a serious matter in the case of Wilson, who entered the presidency after only two years in politics and at a time when news from Washington was shifting its concentration from Congress to centering on the president.

Historians, however, have focused their studies on Wilson's press relations while he was president and have paid scant attention to them before that time. For the most part, following the leads suggested by Ray Stannard Baker in his early biography of Wilson and by Wilson's daughter Eleanor in her book, *The Woodrow Wilsons*, they trace her father's troubles with the press to incidents in which he became irritated with reporters while he was president-elect.[2] The resulting accounts portray him as having little experience with the press as well as little news sense. While there is some validity to that charge, it overlooks evidence that counterbalances it. The existing accounts also describe him entering the presidency disenchanted with the press and estranged from reporters.[3] However, when placed against the rich record that suggests otherwise, that is also an imperfect portrayal of him at this crucial point in his public career. Like many prominent men of his day, Wilson had his troubles with the press, with reporters in particular, and in some cases he could blame himself for them. Over the years, however, he received abundant favorable coverage in the newspapers and journals, and his association with journalists was often friendly and constructive.

Moreover, traditional accounts of his prepresidential public profile often suggest a flawed image of him. They picture him as an aloof and uncompromising man, even one with an ascetic personality, whose background as a college professor and then as a college president ill prepared him for coping with the realities of modern political journalism. These charges were a part of the press criticism raised against him, but they fail to capture the fullness of his public image that the press promoted. A few other observations about his relations with the press and with journalists and about his personality round out the traditional accounts of his early experience with them; however, these accounts fall far short of explaining either the range or the importance of his relations with the press. It was a vehicle of communication indispensable to his gaining political prominence. Fortunately, there is an extensive record to consult to explicate Wilson's prepresidential experience with the press and his associations with its practitioners, both of which were far more involved than is generally supposed. It is the intent of this book to explore that experience and those associations to balance traditional accounts of Wilson's early relations with the institution of the press.

From the earliest days of the republic, the press had been a major force in the life of the nation, but now with its technical and popular expansion, its force appeared amplified. The then current progressive impulse emphasizing participatory democracy and advancing the role of public opinion in politics further embellished that force as a political factor. Of course, force should not be equated with power, for other forces contributed to the shape and to the success or failure of public policies, to people's perception of public figures, and to the winning or losing of elections. Moreover, being the diverse institution that it is, the press in a free society never speaks with one voice. It is more appropriate to say that the press has influence rather than power. However, even its influence in politics is full of variables and difficult to quantify.

Franklin D. Roosevelt, for example, retained voter confidence despite widespread press opposition. On the other hand, the press was instrumental in forcing the resignation of Richard Nixon in 1974. However nebulous the effectiveness of its impact, it is clear that modern presidents and policymakers consider press influence a factor of prime importance. The efforts they make to manage it as well as their frequent criticism of how the media interprets their intentions and their positions only underscores the regard they have for the institution. Progressive era politicians never doubted that the press was influential in politics.

Journalists of the time held similar beliefs. The leading figures considered the affairs of state their business and perceived their institution, indeed their own work, to be linked to the center of democratic politics. They assumed that they were leaders of public opinion and that it was their duty to guide the public in accordance with their own political persuasions and preferences. They also assumed the responsibility of promoting candidates for office and claimed expertise in managing publicity on their behalf. As an institution, the press in Wilson's time was a many-sided enterprise, as capable of aggressive, sometimes unethical, oppositional journalism as it was of serving the public good. Upon entering politics, he had to engage its full force, but his ideas about it as an element of politics and his personal experience with it long predated that time in his life.

The press was a part of Wilson's life from the time he edited his college newspapers until he went to Washington in 1913. Sometimes he contributed to it, particularly as a literary journalist, while at other times he was the subject of its attention. His newsworthiness grew during the years he spent as the president of Princeton University, then as the governor of New Jersey, and later as a presidential candidate. From the time the opponents of his reforms at Princeton used the press at their disposal to attack him until his election as president of the United States, he was the target of biting, sometimes brutal, criticism in the press. However, he also had his champions among the journalists. But for their support, he would never have reached the White House. Consequently, the public image the press projected of him was varied. So, too, was his association with journalists. It can be traced back to the time he was a young man, and as he became interested in a political career, that association acquired added importance. As for the widening press attention accorded him, Wilson encouraged it through his association with individual journalists who wished to promote him and by his performance as a public speaker. Both of these aspects of his relations with the press are stressed in this book.

The story of Wilson's prepresidential relations with the press, broadly interpreted, deals with a vital dimension of his life during his ascendancy first as a public and then as a political figure. It provides an entrance to his thinking about the press as it surfaced in his formal and informal writings and commentary. It also affords the opportunity of seeing how politically minded, Progressive era journalists conducted themselves and how the press performed as presidential campaigns transformed after 1896 to acquire their modern form. The special interest press has a significant place in this account of Wilson's early press relations, for without knowledge of how these newspapers perceived him in 1912, it is impossible to grasp the diverse image the nation had of him when he entered the White House. His campaigning in 1912 also provides an introduction to how he related to the new film and recorded sound media. Some giants of journalism history like the ever controversial William Randolph Hearst and the pontifical E. W. Scripps also have an important place in this book, along with a number of other notable journalists, but most of all it focuses on Wilson's varied experience with the press during the years when he formulated and began to put into practice his ideas about it.

ACKNOWLEDGMENTS

One cannot write history without the collaboration of many people, and it is a pleasure to recognize those who aided me in researching and writing this study. I am in the particular debt of two historians—Gordon W. Prange and Arthur S. Link. Professor Prange was not only an inspiring teacher but also a mentor who conveyed to me, and to many other graduate students at the University of Maryland, the value and fascination of historical research. He first interested me in the subject of Wilson and the press and continued to encourage me in all of my work until his death in 1980. I knew Professor Link only through his monumental works on Woodrow Wilson, but anyone who chooses to study and to write about Wilson will be in debt to his standard-setting scholarship and to the many leads to additional related topics that it affords. That is most true in my case.

Valparaiso University has supported this study in many ways. I wish to thank its Committee on Creative Work and Research for the support it gave for my original proposal to begin this study in 1988 and for the ensuing Research Leave of Absence it granted me. President Alan Harre, Provost/Vice President Roy A. Austensen, and Dean Albert Trost have been generous in offering me encouragement in my work. I wish to thank them especially for my appointment as a Senior Research Professor. Nothing has facilitated the writing of this book more than the benefits of holding that position.

I have been fortunate throughout the course of researching this book to have had the assistance of numerous librarians, curators, and archivists. They all have my appreciation, and I wish to thank the following in particular: Madeline F. Matz and Rosemary C. Hanes at the Motion Picture, Broadcasting, and Recorded Sound Division at the Library of Congress; Christine W. Kitto and Daniel J. Linke at the Seeley G. Mudd Manuscript Library, Princeton University; Thomas P. Ford and Leslie A. Morris at the Houghton Library, Harvard University; James Marshall and Michael W. Lora in the Local History Department at the Toledo Lucas County Public Library; Melanie Yolles at the

New York Public Library; Adam Erik Batkay at the New Jersey Historical Society; George W. Bain at the Vernon R. Alden Library, Ohio University; and Ken Tilly at the State of Alabama's Department of Archives and History. Wendy M. Nardi, the curator of the Trentoniana Collection at the Trenton Public Library went out of her way to assist me when I visited there. During my numerous visits to the Library of Congress, I have valued the efficiency of the staff in its Manuscript Division and wish to express my thanks for their help. Closer to home, the staff of the Moellering Library at Valparaiso University has always been helpful and cheerful in responding to my requests, and they have my sincere thanks for their assistance.

I am indebted to my friends in the American Journalism Historians Association, who have helped and encouraged (sometimes unknowingly) my work. For sharing their knowledge of journalism with me and also for their exemplary congeniality, which has always made our conversations about history a genuine pleasure, I extend my sincere appreciation.

Although it is never possible to acknowledge fully the sustaining support of those nearest you, I want to recognize the special contribution my children James and Jennifer and their spouses Rebekah Rast and Donald Sipe made to this book. Their curiosity about its subject and its progress have been invaluable, and the perceptive questions they have raised about it have often prompted my own reflections. There is, moreover, no substitute for the contribution that ongoing dialogue about the past makes to the writing of history, and that they have provided. I reserve my deepest thanks, however, for my wife Catherine. Her unfailing help, sound advice, and enthusiasm for my work have been sources of continuing encouragement for me, and it is to her that I dedicate this book.

Chapter 1
Early Encounters with Journalism

Long before he entered politics in 1910, Woodrow Wilson was a man of letters and an orator of uncommon ability. His writing and speeches brought him early press attention and public stature. It was also during his early career, even before he became president of Princeton University in 1902, that he developed his basic views about public opinion and democratic government as well as the intention to exercise an influence in national political life. While yet a student, he explained his goals to Ellen Axson, his future wife. "I have a passion for interpreting great thoughts to the world; I should be complete if I could inspire a great movement of opinion, if I could read the experiences of the past into the practical life of men of today and so communicate the thought to the minds of the great mass of the people as to impel them to great political achievements."[1] This was heady speculation for a young man, but he pursued it with rare determination. His interest in public opinion, national political life, and the art of communication, all factors that led him to take the press into account, long predated his entrance into politics. In fact, during those early years, he associated with journalists and journalism to a greater degree than is normally supposed.

It is customary, however, to perceive Wilson's life prior to 1902, as that of a southerner. Born in Staunton, Virginia in 1856, he spent his youth there and in several other southern states—Georgia, South Carolina, and North Carolina. He began his undergraduate education at Davidson College in North Carolina and completed it at the College of New Jersey (Princeton University) in 1879, after which he attended the University of Virginia's law school for a year. In 1882 he was admitted to the state bar of Georgia, but turned away from law to study for a Ph.D. at Johns Hopkins University. Gaining his doctorate there in 1886, he began his teaching and publishing career at Bryn Mawr College. In 1888 he accepted the endowed Hedding Professorship of

History and Political Economy at Wesleyan University in Connecticut, and two years later he returned to Princeton to occupy its chair of Jurisprudence and Political Economy. There, as a distinguished teacher and scholar, he remained until 1902.

The man whom the press would sometimes label naive was, in fact, complex. Throughout his life he felt a kinship with his Scotch and Scotch–Irish heritage. Stockton Axson, his brother-in-law and friend, claimed that his Scottish lineage was at the root of Wilson's caution in human relationships.[2] Wilson preferred association with a few intimate friends and family to that of a public social life. Journalists would often interpret him as aloof and cold, suggesting the Scotch austerity, but he also had a lighthearted side from his "Irish blood." At home he was spontaneous with his family, often reciting doggerel and limericks, telling stories, and singing and dancing with his daughters, his hat tilted to one side.[3] Although journalists rarely saw this side of him, he could reveal his lighter side to small groups of reporters. Contrary to the image of him that often appeared in the newspapers, he was warm and considerate in the small circle of those familiar to him.

Even his religious convictions and his southern origins could cause confusion about him. Wilson had a deep Presbyterian faith, but was hardly the "Presbyterian priest" some of his critics accused him of being. He believed that individuals had a personal relationship with God, that there was sustaining power in prayer, that the Bible was the "Magna Charta of the human soul," and that God's providence ordered human affairs.[4] Yet, he took little interest in theological doctrines and disputes, and despite some charges to the contrary that would later appear in the press, he was tolerant of other religious persuasions. He also believed that individuals should carry out God's will by means of service to society, an idea that would set him at odds with journalistic practices he would encounter in public life. As for his southern origins, he felt a kinship with the area of his youth. His young wife acknowledged this when she wrote to him, "I do believe you love the South, darling—that she hasn't a truer son, that you will be, and are, an infinitely better, more helpful son to her than any of those who cling so desperately to the past and old prejudices. I believe you are her *greatest* son in this generation and also the one who will have the greatest claim on her gratitude."[5]

Still, as his foremost biographer Arthur S. Link pointed out, Wilson was anything but southern in many of his actions. Although southerners were numerous at Princeton when he was a student, he made no lifelong friends among them. None of his student essays concentrated on the South. After his marriage to Ellen Axson, he tried to purge his and his wife's speech of traces of a southern accent. Rather than from the South, much of the inspiration for his early political essays came from British sources, from Walter Bagehot and Edmund Burke in particular.[6] Moreover, he spoke of Daniel Webster, as "the noble Webster," and of Abraham Lincoln as the personification of the American spirit. In one of his early essays, he wrote, "I yield to no one precedence in love for the South. But *because* I love the South, I rejoice in the failure of the Confederacy."[7] Victory in the Civil War, he claimed, would have been disastrous for the South. While it is true that southern propriety and courtesy were innate parts of his demeanor, it is also true that his outlook as a young scholar was progressive and national.[8] Yet, southern editors who were instrumental in his political ascendancy claimed him as one of their own.

Finally, it bears mentioning that his opinions would evolve over time. Some of his later opponents in the press would find that an inexcusable trait. He also had little use for detailed knowledge about certain subjects like economics, which he would dwell on in his rise to national prominence. He was more interested in large ideas. That tendency also occasioned editorial criticism in years to come. Understandably, journalists would find him a difficult person to cover and interpret, yet during his early years, he was more interested in their craft than they expected.

I

The several-sided association Wilson had with journalism prior to 1902 ran throughout his early career. Antecedents for it can be found in his family history. His paternal grandfather, James Wilson, migrated from Ulster in 1807, settled in Philadelphia, and worked for William Duane, whose *Philadelphia Aurora* was an outspoken publication of the early republic. Later, in 1815, Wilson moved west, first to begin his own paper in Ohio, the *Western Herald and Steubenville Gazette*, and in 1832, to establish the *Pennsylvania Advocate* in Pittsburgh.[9] James and his wife Anne Adams, also an able publisher, had ten children, seven of them boys. Their father taught all of the boys the printer's trade.[10] The eldest, William Duane, settled in Chicago where he briefly published the *Dollar Weekly*, became owner and editor of the *Chicago Tribune* (1852–53), and for a while published another daily, the *Courant*. He moved to Iowa, served as secretary to the Agricultural College and later as editor of the *Iowa Homestead and Farm Journal*. Another son, Robert, took over the Steubenville paper in 1838 and later, in 1856, purchased the *New Lisbon Buckeye State* and published it until his death in 1863.[11]

The youngest son, Joseph Ruggles, was Woodrow Wilson's father. As William Allen White once observed, the printing office was his "boyhood home," and it was there that he earned his keep until leaving for college. For a while prior to that he published his own boy's paper.[12] Later in life, after he gained recognition as a Presbyterian minister, Wilson's father edited the *North Carolina Presbyterian*, from 1876 to 1877. For a brief time, Woodrow helped his father edit that newspaper.[13] Considering Wilson's close relationship with his father, it is probable that informed references to journalism entered their conversations.

Wilson had yet other family connections with journalism. An uncle on his mother's side taught in succession at Oglethorpe University, Columbia Theological Seminary, and at South Carolina College (now the University of South Carolina), where he also served as president from 1891 to 1897. For years prior to his presidency, he was editor and publisher of the *Southern Presbyterian*. Upon his death in 1907, Wilson called his uncle "one of the noblest men" he had ever known and wrote of him: "It pleases me to think of the gracious and helpful influences he has brought into the life of a nephew who never told him how much he owed to him."[14] Wilson's younger brother Joseph R. Wilson, "Josie," was editor of the *Clarksville* (Tenn.) *Leaf-Chronicle* from 1895 to 1904 and after that on the staff of the *Nashville Banner* until going to Baltimore to pursue business in 1913.[15]

Wilson's acquaintance with journalists extended beyond his own family. His close friend while a student at Princeton was Robert Bridges who, upon graduating from Princeton, distinguished himself as an author, poet, and journalist. Early in his career he worked for the *Rochester Democrat and Chronicle* and the *New York Evening Post* before moving to positions with several periodicals. He became assistant editor at *Scribner's Magazine* in 1887, and in 1914 became its editor. After the two young men left Princeton, they corresponded regularly and met whenever possible. Wilson paid close attention to the career of his "most intimate friend," and even offered his advice on Bridge's early career moves.[16] Also among his Princeton friends were Frank P. Glass, who became an Alabama newspaperman and George S. Johns, the long-time editor of the *St. Louis Post Dispatch*. In 1882, Wilson began an association with Walter Hines Page, then associated with the *New York World*. He had come to Atlanta, where Wilson practiced law, to cover the proceedings of the Tariff Commission meeting there. Within a few years, he would become a successful magazine editor, and, as such, he was instrumental in getting Wilson to contribute to his publications.[17] Years later Page played a major role in Wilson's entrance into politics.

Throughout these years, Wilson formed relations with established journalists and with young men entering the field who were destined to make a mark in it. At Johns Hopkins he became a student in Herbert Baxter Adams' Seminary (seminar) of History and Politics. The seminar became famous for the succession of young scholars, like Wilson, who went on to distinguished careers in various academic disciplines.[18] Adams frequently invited quests to speak at the seminar and among them were journalists. One such guest was Talcott Williams, managing editor of the *Philadelphia Press*. Wilson's acquaintance with him lasted for many years subsequent to their meeting there. Another guest, John C. Rose, was an associate editor of the *Baltimore Sun* and consultant for the *Nation*. Professor Adams called him the "Baltimore Gladstone." Rose's expertise in statistics impressed Wilson, who felt that the editor's presentation was one of the best he had heard at the seminar.[19] A fellow student of Wilson's in the seminar was Albert Shaw, who afterward had a notable career as a scholar and, in particular, as the editor of the *American Review of Reviews* from 1891 to 1920. Wilson and Shaw's correspondence reveals once again, Wilson's discerning judgment about various journal publications.[20] It was also at Johns Hopkins, where he returned each year from 1888 to 1898 to present a five-week-long series of 25 lectures, that he met Charles Grasty and Fabian Franklin, respectively the manager and the editor of the *Baltimore News*. They were among Wilson's staunch supporters when he sought public office, and they are indicative of his widening circle of journalistic acquaintances.

However impossible it may be to identify every member of that circle, one additional publicist, George Harvey, deserves mention. As of 1899 he was the owner and editor of the *North American Review* and president of Harper and Brothers publishing house, which had recently published Wilson's biography of Washington. Two years later he also assumed the editorship of *Harper's Weekly*. Desiring to keep well-known writers with Harper's, he asked Wilson to write a general history of the United States. That resulted in Wilson's *A History of the American People*, serialized by *Harper's Magazine* prior to its publication as a complete work in 1902. Early in that same year, Harvey urged Wilson to write a volume for Albert Bushnell Hart's "American Nation Series" that Harper's was planning.[21] Wilson rejected that offer, but thus began his association with Harvey. At first it was a formal publisher–author relationship, but one destined to have great consequence in Wilson's later political ascendancy.

II

The fact that Wilson had a number of relatives who were journalists and came to know various others fits into a larger context of interest and activity. His personal correspondence indicates that he read periodicals like the *Edinburgh Review* and the *Nation* in his late teens and he broadened that habit throughout his college and teaching years.[22] Nor did newspapers escape his attention. "Spent the morning studying mathematics & reading the New York Herald," he noted in a typical diary entry while a student at Princeton.[23] Vacationing in western Virginia in 1880, he wrote to a friend that he was idling away his days reading scarcely more than "a few newspapers which a tardy semi-weekly mail brought, with news that was stale to the outside world, no doubt, but was new and eagerly devoured by our party."[24] A year later, while planning to settle in Atlanta, he told Robert Bridges, "I am particularly glad that the *Atlanta Constitution* is prominent among the leading advocates of these old principles [honestly held political opinions and interest in broad political movements rather than party intrigues] made new and fitted to a reforming society."[25] Such comments reveal how eagerly Wilson read newspapers. His wife, whom he claimed was his "counselor" in all matters, shared that interest. For instance, while visiting relatives, she wrote to him in reference to a disputed election in Kentucky, "I wonder what you and the 'Times' think about the situation there. How I have wished all week for the New York papers."[26]

Wilson's interest in journalism was more than cursory. In 1876 while helping his father with the *North Carolina Presbyterian*, he wrote a series of articles for that journal. They represented an effort to apply Christianity to everyday life and to make applied Christianity a source of human progress.[27] The youthful Wilson, then a student at Princeton, followed these initial publications with many others. At Princeton he became associated with the *Princetonian*, the student newspaper, first as a member of its board, then as joint managing editor, and finally as managing editor. His fellow editors recalled his commitment. As one of them put it, he "formulated politics; he was the chief. He would come around to me and say that he would like me to write on such and such. If he did not like what I wrote, it would not go in. . . . He was boss and deserved to be. He ran a good paper. I can remember him now running around with a memo pad, taking shorthand notes; he worked hard."[28]

During his time as editor, Wilson wrote most of the editorials, many news articles, commentaries and summaries of other student publications, and occasional book reviews.

He said his intention was to make the *Princetonian* "a medium for a bold, frank, and manly expression of College opinion."[29] His criticism of college authorities and administrative practices indicates he was serious about that intention. His editorials often targeted sports and he campaigned for upgrading the baseball and football teams. He championed improved organization, sound leadership, systematic practice, adequate financial support, and disciplined players. When Princeton's football team went undefeated in 1878, Wilson could feel he had contributed to that success not only through his editorials but also as one of the five directors of the Football Association, a position that placed him in charge of the team's practical business and involved him in coaching.[30] Long after his graduation, he was often the main speaker at the *Princetonian* Board's annual banquets, and when the newspaper incorporated in 1910, he purchased five shares of its preferred stock.[31]

It is also clear that after graduating from Princeton he thought about a career in journalism. As he confided to Robert Bridges, "I could wish to be a journalist myself if such a place [a position on the *Nation*] were open to me."[32] In fact, Wilson began to contribute to the press of the day in various ways. His publications in those years were part of an effort to define himself. "My *end*," he confided to Bridges, "is a commanding influence in the councils (and counsels) of my country—and *means* to be employed are writing and speaking."[33] While in college he had published essays on Otto von Bismarck and William Pitt the Elder in the *Nassau Literary Magazine*, the student monthly at Princeton, as well as a lengthy article, "Cabinet Government in the United States," in the *International Review*.[34] Now he published several more essays on two of his favorite British political leaders, John Bright and William Ewart Gladstone.[35] Then he tried producing some items of a strictly journalistic nature.

He began by sending three articles on education to his hometown paper, the *Wilmington* (N.C.) *Morning Star*. Unfortunately, the editor gave Wilson no credit for those contributions, publishing them in his own editorials with only minor revisions.[36] Wilson felt slighted and even more so when the editorials were praised across the state. Venting his frustration, he told Robert Bridges that the editor was an "exceptional ass" who produced a "puerile and picayune" newspaper.[37] A year later Wilson published three letters in the *North Carolina Presbyterian* under the pseudonym "Anti-Sham" in which he attacked that editor for endorsing speeches made by visiting Catholic prelates supporting the installation of a new bishop in Raleigh.[38] They occasioned angry rejoinders from Catholics living in Wilmington, but Wilson treated the entire matter as "an amusing passage at arms" and "a good chance to exercise myself in satire and ridicule."[39] Be that as it may, his more serious efforts in journalism led in other directions.

During the next several years, while engaged in a brief legal career in Atlanta, he published some lengthy articles with the *New York Evening Post* based on various political, cultural, and economic conditions in the New South. One article, "New Southern Industries," proclaimed that a new generation was guiding southern fortunes and was determined to advance industrial development of the region. It endorsed the policies associated with the New South Movement that, despite the ambiguity associated with that term, tried to inspire an acceptance of a new economically diversified and industrial South with its sectional differences reconciled. It was an optimistic movement and Wilson's article reflected that optimism. In another article, he took to task Georgia's convict labor system arguing that "the system is quite incompatible with the modern ideas of the duty which society owes to the criminal classes."[40] Journalism was again igniting his reform impulses.

"I so love to write," he told Bridges, "that I sometimes imagine that I would be happy and useful on the staff of some such paper as the *Nation*. . . ."[41] Twenty-six years old at the time, he gave up law and turned to graduate studies at Johns Hopkins. "I want to make myself *an outside force in politics*," he explained to Bridges. "No man can safely *enter* political life nowadays who has not an independent fortune, or at least independent means of support: this I have not: therefore the most I can hope to become is a speaker and writer of the highest authority on political subjects."[42]

Although he can be found calling these years "the age of journalism," his experience as an occasional correspondent left him ambiguous about the field.[43] "As for newspaper correspondence," he wrote to Ellen Axson,

> the more I think of it the more I question its being the ideally desirable thing. The best newspaper in the country when at its best would scarcely want to print letters embodying strictly scientific study of institutions and, however that might be, what would lie beyond in the way of a career? The work would be thoroughly congenial and helpful from the first, but I should not want to keep at it indefinitely. . . . There is no other field of journalism that I care to enter ever. I decided *that* before I left the law, and have seen no reason to alter the decision. When the correspondence vein was worked out, where would I open a mine next?[44]

He was, in fact, specific about what he hoped to achieve at Johns Hopkins. "The *object* for which I came to the University," he told Ellen, was "to get a special training in historical research and an insight into the most modern literary and political thoughts and methods, in order that my ambition to become an invigorating and enlightening power in the world of political thought and a master in some of the less serious branches of literary art may be more easy of accomplishment."[45]

Wilson achieved a record at Johns Hopkins, both in and beyond his classes, that any aspiring teacher would envy. Professor Adams claimed that he was "the ablest student he ever had" (even if Wilson was less than appreciative of the Germanic form of scholarship favored by Adams).[46] Wilson was only at Johns Hopkins for two years, but during that time he wrote and published his much acclaimed *Congressional Government*, the book that established his reputation as a political scientist. Amid his busy life at the university, he somehow found time to write a few articles for New York newspapers. Robert Bridges asked Wilson to send him occasional items for the *Evening Post*. Since Johns Hopkins, only recently founded in 1876, was already assuming leadership among American universities that stressed graduate education and research, reports on happenings there were newsworthy. Wilson accepted the offer to become, as he termed it, the "Johns Hopkins correspondent of the *Post*" and said he would "send a few notes weekly."[47] Although he was too ambitious with that promise, he did manage to send Bridges three monthly "newsletters" before the weight of his academic work forced him to have a classmate continue the correspondence with the *Post*.[48]

The following year, William F. Ford, editor of *Bradstreet's*, a quality journal of finance and public economy, invited Wilson to write an article on "congressional matters."[49] After he responded with an article, "Congressional Government in Practice," Ford asked him if he would assume "the position of Washington correspondent for a New York newspaper" if that newspaper "would stand for something far beyond the present newspaper methods."[50] Wilson turned down that offer, and thus set forth on an academic career. Success followed success for him. Apart from becoming one of the most popular and brilliant teachers of his generation, he achieved a prodigious record as a publishing scholar, producing nine more volumes and over 30 articles by the time he became president of Princeton in 1902.

III

During this intense period in which his achievement as a scholar and teacher peaked, he also pursued a busy supplementary career, as he called it, of public lecturing and popular writing. Both help to explain the growth of his reputation prior to his Princeton presidency. By the time he left college, for instance, Wilson's interest and ability in public speaking was obvious. His major interest at Davidson College was oratory. At Princeton he formed the Liberal Debating Club and gained the reputation as a skilled speaker and debater on campus. Later, while at the University of Virginia, he became a star of the Jefferson Society, a literary and debating group. Responding to demand, the society opened its doors to outsiders for the first time to hear him deliver a speech on John Bright, the famous English orator and liberal.[51] Wilson became a student of oratory. He studied the speeches of Daniel Webster and of his favorite English statesmen, practiced wherever and whenever he could, and often commented on the subject in his correspondence. It should be, he said, "the art of persuasion, the art of putting things so as to appeal irresistibly to an audience. And how can a teacher stimulate young men to study, and how can he fill them with great ideas and worthy purposes, how can he draw them out of themselves and make them to become forces in the world without oratory?"[52] He exemplified his own advice. As one of his professors at Johns Hopkins remembered, no one could match Wilson in debate and oratory except its president, Daniel Coit Gilman.[53]

He was a speaker in demand already in the 1890s. Aside from his numerous presentations in and around Princeton and frequent after-dinner speeches for Princeton alumni groups, he delivered over 100 public addresses between 1890 and 1902. He spoke to groups at various colleges and to bar associations, he was a commencement speaker in demand, and he often addressed lyceum clubs and church groups. His repertoire of speeches included "Leaders of Men," "Patriotism," "Democracy," and others about history, government, and education. Up and down the east coast, newspapers such as the *Boston Herald*, the *Philadelphia Inquirer*, the *Baltimore Sun*, and the *Washington Post* reported and praised his speeches. Reports in other newspapers were no less complimentary when he ventured farther south or west. Sometimes they provided lengthy summaries of what he said, sometimes long extracts. As the big metropolitan papers prominently reported his speeches, he gained the reputation as one who spoke with authority. In a typical comment, the *Indianapolis News* described him as "exceptionally brilliant and forceful" with a platform manner that combined "strength, wit, dignity, and marked personal charm."[54]

None of Wilson's speeches was more important to him than one he gave in 1896 at Princeton for its one hundred and fiftieth anniversary.

His speech, "Princeton in the Nation's Service" caught the attention of the national press. It was extracted in numerous newspapers and journals and sometimes reproduced in full text, thus heightening interest in his subsequent speeches and writings. His Princeton address underscores the point that he spoke to sophisticated audiences in his major speeches. Not until 1896, when he spoke before a large civic meeting at the Baltimore Music Hall, did he depart from that practice. Theodore Roosevelt was the featured speaker on that occasion, but according to the *Baltimore Sun*, "laughter," "cheers," and "applause" interrupted Wilson's speech more than any other.[55] Wilson knew how to adapt a speech to an audience.

A similar flexibility appeared in his writing. While still producing scholarly studies, he turned to writing popular historical and biographical works and a variety of essays—essays that found their place in the genre of literary journalism. He wrote them for the general, educated public, and he published them mainly in the *Atlantic Monthly*, the *Century Magazine*, and the *Forum*.[56] They were magazines that ranged between the more serious learned journals and the mass circulating, low priced popular magazines, which were growing and changing periodical publication. The type of magazines in which he chose to publish had a long history as literary reviews and held an important position in the nation's literary culture.

Toward the end of the nineteenth century, these monthly magazines became livelier in appearance and more general and practical in content. They represented literary journalism of an increasingly practical bent. This was even true of the *Atlantic Monthly*, a bastion of tradition. When the *Forum*, a new monthly, first appeared in 1886, it declared itself "preeminently a *public* magazine, a medium for discussion, sanely and seriously, of all vital questions."[57] The *Forum*'s innovative editor in the early 1890s was Wilson's old Atlanta acquaintance, Walter Hines Page, who now urged Wilson to write for monthly magazines.[58]

This opportunity appealed to him. These magazines paid well and he recognized the attention such publications attracted. Wilson spoke of the "popular notice" the *Forum* offered its writers and told Page, "I have been little less than astonished at the number of persons I seem to have reached in the papers I have written for it within the last two years."[59] Although he continued to publish in the *Forum*, he placed even more articles with the *Atlantic*, which Page had joined in 1895.

He wrote about a number of topics in these monthly magazines. In particular, he developed lengthy commentaries on literary style, on history and biography, and on American ideals and politics.

His interpretation of a proper literary style reveals his intent in promoting a narrative form capable of attracting attention and inspiring imagination. A writer, he said, must remember "he is writing, not to describe, but to make alive."[60] Great writing, whether fictive, historical, philosophical, or political, should contain "the colors of life," contain imagination and spirit as well as analysis, for it had to attract the "general public" to contemplate the truth within it.[61] He favored historians who "stand in the midst of old letters and dusty documents . . . [and] see a distant country and a far away people before their very eyes, as real, as full of life and hope." History *had* to embrace art, for it was "as bad to bungle the telling of the story as to lie, as fatal to lack vocabulary as to lack knowledge."[62]

His emphasis on imagination and spirit in historical writing is significant. It led him to concentrate on the commanding themes of the nation's growth and promise. To him its course was a dramatic story, distinct from that of Europe. Wilson found the genius of our nation in the spirit of its western growth. The unfolding of the frontier had set the pace, and now that the epic of the nation's western movement had ended and Americans had to live as neighbors in closer proximity to one another, he searched for its meaning, for its moral. Seeing little of the flaw of the frontier spirit, he concentrated on its perceived greatness. "Let us resume and keep the vision of that time: know ourselves, our neighbors, our destiny, with lifted and open eyes: see our history truly, in its great proportions: be ourselves liberal as the great principles we profess . . .," he extolled. " 'Tis thus we shall renew our youth and secure our age against decay."[63] He also used the tool of biography to search for what he termed "our canons of Americanism." He found their embodiment in Abraham Lincoln, in his "genius for things American." Wilson claimed that Lincoln was the sum of the entire country, a man "instinctively for the Union; a man of the common people, he deemed himself always an instrument, never a master."[64]

These essays reveal Wilson's fundamental idealism. Through history and biography he dramatized and personalized national virtues and achievement. The essays show an unmistakable belief in progress and the linking of progress with national purpose. They also contained ideals that unite society, that connect leaders and people while transcending sectional and social distinctions. Wilson praised democracy and claimed it was "a principle with us, not a mere form of government." To keep the principle alive, "We must learn what we can, and yet scrupulously square everything that we do with the high principles we brought into the world: that justice may be done to the lowly no less than to the great; that government may serve its people, not make itself their master,—may in its service heed both the wishes and the needs of those who obey it; that authority may be for leadership and not for aggrandizement; that the people may be the state."[65] In these essays, he often turned to the place and quality of leadership in the country and urged that a way be found to make it efficient, to produce a leader conscious of the responsibility of their position and able to "command the ear of both Congress and the country." Such men could only be found by "constructive choice" rather than by existing methods of "compromise and barter." Obviously displeased with the low state to which our institutions of government had fallen in recent years, Wilson urged change. "Once more," he wrote, "is our problem of nation-making the problem of a form of government. Shall we show the sagacity, the open-mindedness, the moderation, in our task of modification, that were shown under Washington and Madison, . . . in the task of construction?"[66] Wilson wrote to inspire people to noble action. He was attempting to apply lessons from the nation's history, as he perceived it, and from his knowledge of the workings of government to contemporary national circumstances—attempting to become "an outside force in politics."

When considering Wilson's literary journalism, it is instructive to recall the high regard he had for Walter Bagehot, one of Victorian Britain's most versatile men of letters. "He was not a literary critic in the academic sense of the term, nor a political economist, nor an historian. He was all of these and none of them," writes one of his biographers.[67] As editor of the *Economist*, he was as at home in the deeper questions of political philosophy as he was in the intricacies of currency and finance. While lecturing at Johns Hopkins in the 1890s, Wilson earned the epithet, "The Walter Bagehot of America."[68] He often cited Bagehot in his writings, referred to him as his "master," and made him the subject of an address, "A Literary Politician," which became part of his repertoire of lectures and later one of his finest essays. By "literary politician" he meant someone who "has the genius to see deep into affairs, and the discretion to keep out of them, . . ." Life for Bagehot, Wilson wrote, was "dramatic, full of fierce, imperative forces."[69]

Bagehot inspired Wilson's first book, but in "A Literary Politician" a more intimate inspiration can be detected. Wilson concluded it with this thought:

> Had I command of the culture of men, I should wish to raise up for the instruction and stimulation of my nation more than one sane, sagacious, penetrating critic of men and affairs like Walter Bagehot. . . . It is

> necessary to stand with the poets as well as with lawgivers; . . . with the merchant and the manufacturer as well as with the closeted student; . . . in the midst of thought and also in the midst of affairs, if you would really comprehend those great wholes of history and of character which are the vital substance of politics.[70]

In his commentary on Bagehot, Wilson, the scholar, the author of acclaimed books on government and history (*Congressional Government, The State*, and *Division and Reunion*), an inspiring orator, and now the literary journalist, revealed something of what he was striving to be.

IV

With his interest in the nature of movements and institutions, it was natural for Wilson to turn his mind to thoughts about the press and its role in politics. During the 1880s and 1890s the press was undergoing a transformation. Broad news coverage, commercial enterprise, and political independence characterized its new identity. With its modernization came the advent of the New Journalism and all of its brash, sensational, and slanted news content as well as its brazen style. Evidence of Wilson's awareness of this phenomenon as well as his thoughts about the political role of the press can be found both in his letters and in his formal writings.

His letters reveal his preferences about the press as well as his cognizance of the narrative and technical devices associated with the New Journalism. However, his correspondence shows he favored a more dignified form of journalism.[71] "Big-type, *semi-headings*, like all other sensational mechanical tricks" robbed journalism of its "air of sincerity," he claimed.[72] By contrast in his favorite newspaper, *The Times* of London, which he read regularly as a college student and whose weekly edition he later subscribed to, he found a "splendid monument of talent and industry."[73] With its exhaustive reports of political news and speeches, its thorough financial and economic news columns, its extensive foreign correspondence and editorials, and its reputation as a trustworthy newspaper of record, it is easy to understand why Wilson favored it. It is also clear that he tried to grasp the political role of the press, a topic he returned to several times in his various writings.

He first considered it in his *Congressional Government.* Bearing in mind the role the press would play in his later political career, the influence he attributed to it at this point is interesting. "The utterances of the Press," he wrote, "have greater weight and are accorded greater credit, though the Press speaks entirely without authority, than the utterances of Congress, though Congress possesses all authority. . . . The editor directs public opinion, the congressman obeys it." He went on to lament the fate of political orators at the hands of the press.

> Speaking . . . without authority, the political orator speaks to little purpose when he speaks about legislation. The papers do not report him carefully; and their editorials seldom take any color from his arguments. The Press, being anonymous and representing a large force of inquisitive newshunters, is much more powerful than he chiefly because it *is* impersonal and seems to represent a wider and more thorough range of information. . . . And besides, it is almost everywhere strong enough to deny currency to the speeches of individuals whom it does not care to report. It goes to its audience; the orator must depend upon his audience coming to him. . . . There is no imperative demand on the part of the reading public in this country that the newspapers should report political speeches in full. On the contrary, most readers would be disgusted at finding their favorite columns so filled up. By giving even a notice of more than an item's length to such a speech, an editor runs the risk of being denounced as dull.[74]

Was there no hope for the political orator? Only when he combined "genius and authority," wrote Wilson. He cited William Ewart Gladstone, Britain's Grand Old Man of politics, as an example of someone who demonstrated how an orator of genius and authority could exert leadership over opinion.[75]

Later he explored the role of the press in a democratic society in his essays and in his manuscript "The Modern Democratic State." He began writing the latter in 1885 and returned to it off and on through the 1880s and 1890s. Although it remained unpublished, it provides insight into his thinking, for it became, as Arthur S. Link and other historians claim, "the foundation" even the "ideological framework from which Wilson never seriously deviated."[76] In this manuscript, when his thought turned to the "diffusion of enlightenment among the people," it also turned to the subject of newspapers. They spoke, he observed, in many and diverse voices, and they could "confuse and paralyze" an individual's mind "with their myriad stinging lashes of excitement." "Newspapers stream light about" providing "countless things to look at." But do they clarify vision? "Activity of mind is not strength of mind," he cautioned. However, he admitted that newspapers performed a service for democracy. Despite their multiple opinions and lack of common voice, their "aggregate voice thunders with tremendous volume; and that aggregate voice is 'public opinion.'" Wilson explained that "we all allow the greatness of the press without thinking of it." Along with the telegraph and the railway, it was transforming national political life. From all parts of the world, it delivered news "within a limit of two days time." He continued by arguing that the newspaper press was a "type of democracy." When considered in toto it contained "every topic reduced to a common standard of news; [with] everything noted and argued by everybody."[77]

Nor did the negative potential of the modern press escape his attention. He admitted that newspapers "may often be misdirected or unhealthful, may sometimes be only feverish and mischievous, a grievous product of narrow information and hasty conclusion." Yet, he deemed the newspaper press a "growing and potent activity" that marked "the initial stages of effective thought."[78] At a time when criticism of the press was growing, he chose to side with those commentators on the institution who stressed its positive role.

It is possible to detect a connection between Wilson's commentary on the press and his own work in journalism. In both cases, he viewed the press as an instrument that could be used for the betterment of society. His first articles in the *North Carolina Presbyterian* dealt with Christianity as a source of progress. As editor of the *Princetonian* he campaigned for improvement of campus social and cultural life and for a higher quality sports program. The best of his newsletters dealt with either needed reforms or with new developments in industry and in university life. Writing for prestigious monthly magazines in the 1890s, he explored literary style, history, biography, politics, and government to explain the importance of seeing the "permanent element in things—the acts which display the veritable characters of men" and to praise the principles of democracy along with great figures who personified them.[79] There was a motif in these articles, which revealed the belief that literary journalism, when taken to include the scope of his contributions to that genre, had a role to play in promoting the public good. Could the same be said about his perception of the political press?

He did, in fact, comprehend a great deal about the role of the press in politics. His understanding of it was elitist, but he perceived the press in general as a force in interpreting public opinion and in the reform of society. Given his belief in ordered progress and his serious temperament regarding political life, it comes as no surprise that he disdained the New Journalism, which, along with the rest of its popularizing and sensational tactics, was pushing the "human interest factor" into political journalism. That style of journalism also had its serious side, and in the hands of its major promoter Joseph Pulitzer, it could be earnest and honest in its support of good causes. Nevertheless, such popular journalism, with its tendency to personalize and sometimes trivialize political news, did not appeal to Wilson. He preferred newspapers like the *New York Evening Post* and the quality periodicals, publications that the college educated and professional classes favored. His own serious disposition in matters of news and politics helps to account for his preference for the publications of the quality press, and it doubtless also reflects the preferences of the journalists with whom he associated. They were, in the main, friends, classmates, and editors of esteemed newspapers and magazines. Regardless, Wilson formed his fundamental ideas about the press in the 1880s and 1890s.

His thoughts on the press were not the only aspects of his early encounters with journalism and journalists that would continue long into the future. By this time, he had demonstrated his ability to attract favorable notice in the press, and the expanding attention the press would subsequently accord him would be a major factor in his rise to elected office. Midway through the 1890s, his brother Joseph commented that Wilson "had a wide association with journalists."[80] That association, composed of only a few friends at first, expanded as his career as scholar, public speaker, and literary journalist advanced. Nothing would be more important to Wilson's political ascendancy than this association as it grew in forthcoming years.

Chapter 2
The President of Princeton and the Press, 1902–10

The year 1902 represented a watershed in Wilson's life. Up to this point, he had been accumulating knowledge, refining his ideas, and developing and practicing his skills as a scholar, writer, and public speaker. From this point on, he would spend the rest of his active life in positions of leadership. At each stage, as the chief executive of a university, of a state, and finally of the nation, he would engage an ever widening public and, in the process, have an increasing involvement with the media. Starting in June 1902, upon assuming the presidency of Princeton University, his newsworthiness increased, gaining him the distinction as one of the country's foremost educational spokesmen.

Within a few years, he also became the subject of speculation in the press about the possibility of his candidacy for high political office. That speculation was not left to chance. A handful of journalists, who would play important roles in his future, nurtured it. However, since his presidency of Princeton University was the commanding center of his work for the immediate future, it deserves attention before his political ascendancy can be considered. The eight years Wilson spent as Princeton's president were among the most important in his life. They were years in which he began to have a new type of relationship with the press. It now took an interest in him as a leader whose policies and statements made news. The way in which the press treated that news became a source of both gratification and annoyance to him.

I

Wilson's election as the thirteenth president of Princeton University, the first layman to hold that position, was a landmark event in its history. American colleges and universities had been undergoing a transformation for a generation and a new order of higher education was emerging.

In contrast to the narrow sectarianism and strict classical curriculum characteristic of its mid-nineteenth-century counterpart, the new order was more democratic, secular, technical, and scientific, and more attuned to the industrial, urban, and international realities at work changing society.

The response that Princeton would make to the new trends in higher education was a major, but not the only, challenge the incoming president would face. Despite the age and prestige of the university, its academic standards had become lax and would have to be raised; its graduate and professional schools had to be expanded; new faculty, recruited; new buildings, constructed. The curriculum needed upgrading as did the quality of campus life. Finally, none of these improvements would be possible without a dramatic increase of the university's endowment.[1] Consequently, its Board of Trustees, believing that Princeton needed more energetic leadership, turned to the 45-year-old Wilson to move Princeton forward. Not only was he the most popular professor at the university and a faculty leader, but he was also someone the trustees had already turned to for advice on administrative reorganization.[2] His association with Princeton's alumni was excellent, and his reputation reached far beyond Princeton's own and extended community. He was a scholar with expertise in the fields of government, administration, and political thought, and the reputation he had acquired by his writing and lecturing was enviable. Both now and later in his career, his oratorical ability must be taken into account, for it helped to attract the press to him.[3]

The subject of many of his important addresses was the purpose of a college education. He believed it should promote subjects collectively known as "general training," "liberal culture," or the "liberal arts" (the term "humanities" was rarely used then). The aim, he said, was to produce "something more than excellent servants of a trade or skilled practitioners of a profession. It should give them elasticity of faculty and breadth of vision, . . . [and an] appreciation of the best achievements of men and the best processes of thought since days of thought set in." He felt that higher education should deal with the "spirits of men, not with their fortunes," and that, in this manner, colleges could offer a preparation for service to society.[4]

People who knew him also knew of the loyalty he felt toward the university. Among them there was widespread confidence in his ability to lead it to new and more prestigious heights. Time would vindicate their confidence in him. Under his leadership, during the next eight years, Princeton became one of the most talked about universities in the country. Of course, his colleagues as well as his supporters among the alumni shared in the university's advance at this time, but Wilson's leadership was always present. His Princeton, with all of its physical growth, academic experimentation, new programs, expanded influence, and sometimes bitter and prolonged fights about yet additional reforms, captured public attention and became an engaging subject for the press. Several of those struggles, those in which Wilson fought with all his intensity and strength and ultimately lost, became in the hands of the press, extensions of reforms progressives were battling to achieve in the public realm.

Beginning with the announcement of his election as president of the university, the press wrote a rash of articles about him that his wife had every right to call "wonderful."[5] The *New York Times*, the *New York Tribune*, and the *New York Sun* featured the announcement as front-page news worthy of a full column or even longer reports and devoted lengthy editorials to the news. In a typical response to the announcement, the *Times* editorialized, "The new President is a man of distinction. . . . Under his direction a new life, a higher fame, and a greater usefulness to the youth of the Nation and to the Nation itself await the university."[6] A number of editors wrote to Wilson offering their personal congratulations and their confidence in the promise of his success. In acknowledging those letters in the gracious style that many journalists would come to recognize in years to come, Wilson conveyed a sincere appreciation of their support. It can be seen in his reply to a letter from one of the *Evening Post*'s editors. "If anything could make a man fairly believe in himself," he wrote, "it would be the support of such men as yourself and of such real friends of education as the 'New York Evening Post.' You have given me a great deal of pleasure and a great deal of courage."[7] Press response was by no means limited to New York City newspapers, which might be expected to take a particular interest in the affairs of the nearby university.

From Boston to New Orleans, newspapers throughout the East and South took notice of his election.[8] "A Southerner to preside over a great Northern school," proclaimed the *Charlotte Observer*, and a writer of one of the *Atlanta Constitution*'s commentaries concluded, "The phenomenal success of Princeton's new president should inspire Georgians with renewed hope, energy, and determination."[9] In some cases the enthusiasm the southern editors conveyed in their commentary exceeded their attention to accuracy. The *Nashville American*, for instance, stated that Wilson spent his youth and early manhood in Clarksville, Tennessee, while the *Richmond Times* declared he was not only born but also raised in Virginia.[10] "It is very flattering to think there should be a competition between different places to claim my boyhood," Wilson said when a friend called these inaccuracies to his attention.[11]

He could not, however, bring himself to treat another published opinion about him in a similar lighthearted manner. An article in *Popular Science Monthly* that Robert Bridges had brought to his attention clearly irked him. The editor of that journal had written that science at Princeton would prosper no better under Wilson than it had under his predecessor, quoting a passage from a speech Wilson had delivered six years before to prove his point. In that passage Wilson had stated, "I am much mistaken if the scientific spirit of the age is not doing us a great disservice, working in us a certain great degeneracy. Science has bred in us a spirit of experimentation and a contempt for the past."[12] Wilson's dislike of the role science was coming to play in higher education was well-known among those people who followed the current debate over the purpose of a university. He believed that the scientific method was harmful to the study of the humanities. Nevertheless, he gave due credit to science, and in the very speech quoted in the article he stated, "No man more heartily admires, more gladly welcomes, more approvingly reckons the gain and the enlightenment that have come to the world through the extraordinary advances in physical science. He would be a barbarian and a lover of darkness who should grudge that great study any part of its triumph."[13] Yet, the editorial in *Popular Science* omitted those comments and publicized the ones that portrayed Wilson as an enemy of science. After reading what the editor had to say, Wilson wrote to Bridges, "The contemptible creature . . . [the editor] has begun his quotation from me this time as he did the last, in the middle of a paragraph; has left out the whole strong eulogy of science; and has misrepresented me just as much as possible. I have a mind . . . to tell him just what I think of him. . . . I [would] like to know what the cur is about."[14]

It was, however, the *New York Sun* that took the greatest exception to generous press response to Wilson's election. Spurred on by the receipt of an anonymous letter asserting that the trustees had forced the retirement of Rev. Francis L. Patton, the former president, because he was hindering Princeton's progress, the *Sun* ran a series of articles and editorials describing his resignation as a move made to save the university from ambitious individuals who were aspiring to his position. It argued that several faculty-trustee "cliques" at Princeton were "intriguing" to have him removed and then to control the succession to the presidency.

To defeat this "adroit minority" of "mischief makers" and to preserve Princeton's dignity and integrity, he suddenly resigned and suggested Wilson as his successor. By employing the language of intrigue about "the Clique of the Ambitious" and by using headings like "A NARROW Escape for Princeton" and "THE GAME DR. PATTON BEAT," the *Sun* sensationalized the story, which by implication suggested that Wilson, who had maintained an uncustomary silence in recent faculty debates, was the beneficiary of Patton's maneuver, which he certainly was.[15] There were elements of truth in the *Sun*'s series. Some faculty and board members had grown impatient with Dr. Patton's leadership, and his resignation did come as a surprise, although it appears that he had been contemplating it for some weeks. Moreover, when, upon announcing his resignation, Patton immediately proposed Wilson to succeed him, the trustees suspended the bylaws requiring an interval of at least one day before electing a successor and unanimously elected Wilson president. Whether or not there was any credence to the plotting implied in the *Sun*'s reports remains unknown, but the sensational manner in which they were presented attached an aura of collusion to a transfer of power that could be otherwise explained.[16]

The *Princeton Alumni Weekly* could not allow the *Sun*'s charges to go uncontested. In an extended article, its editor, Jesse Lynch Williams, labeled them "inaccurate and misleading." Of course, there had been differences of opinion among the faculty, and the recent faculty debates about changing the university's curriculum had been spirited, he argued. But that was common to all universities and no Princeton faculty member who failed to "stand up for his opinions on important matters and fight for them if necessary" could expect the respect of his colleagues. These differences of opinion, however, could not explain Patton's resignation any more than they could support the idea that Wilson was elected "to foil a clique that was endeavoring to run in" its favorite candidate. Nor were trustees members of such a clique. Williams pointed out that after Wilson had been nominated, no other names were put forward when the floor was open to "any other nominations." Wilson was the logical choice; Patton retained the high regard of the faculty; there was "nothing revolutionary about it."[17]

The overall press response to the announcement of Wilson's election can be seen as part of a larger reaction that came from a number of quarters. Friends, relatives, colleagues, clergymen, professionals and businessmen, scholars and presidents at other universities, extended generous congratulations to him at this juncture. The President of the United States wrote saying, "As an American interested in that kind of productive scholarship that leads to statesmanship, I hail your election as President of Princeton, and I count myself fortunate in having the chance to witness your inauguration."[18] President Roosevelt's other correspondence at the time reiterated that sentiment. "Woodrow Wilson is a perfect trump. I am overjoyed at his election," he stated in one letter and in another, "I have long regarded Mr. Wilson as one of the men who had constructive scholarship and administrative ability."[19] The promise for Princeton with Wilson at the helm implied in Roosevelt's comment and in many others, both private and public, was no less apparent in the responses to his inauguration five months later.

That event was, as his brother-in-law and close friend Stockton Axson recalled, "one of the most impressive college functions which up to that time had been held in America."[20] The main feature of the news reports and of the editorial commentary about the event was Wilson's inaugural address. Delivered before an audience that included prominent educational figures in the country, a sense of importance preceded it. In the address, "Princeton for the Nation's Service," he envisioned a university in which the traditional forms of knowledge would reside in association with subjects reflecting the spirit of the new age. More than in his previous speeches, he stressed that science and mathematics would occupy an important place in a curriculum that would allow some election of subjects. The university would have a graduate college, and it would be "a college of residence." His two favorite ideas defined the core of the address: the ideal of the university as preparation for service, as he perceived that term, and the place of the liberal arts at the heart of the university.[21]

Moderately conservative in content and inspiring in tone, his address won immediate acclaim. When President Roosevelt read it, he wrote to Wilson, "As a decent American I want to thank you for it."[22] At a time when many people thought that some of the educational reforms (e.g., those for shorter courses, more utilitarian subjects, and expansion of the elective principle in curriculum design) were too radical, Roosevelt was expressing that concern as well as his own love of literature and writing. A similar reaction to the address echoed through various newspapers. The *Boston Evening Transcript* cited his speech as an example of "careful conservative progress" and the *Philadelphia Press* labeled it "the beginning and the end of the full wisdom of higher education."[23] Wilson had struck the golden mean in his address and had done so with exceptional literary grace. The notice it attracted placed Princeton in the forefront of what was and would continue to be newsworthy about higher education.

Throughout his presidency of the university, Wilson continued to make his views on higher education known to the public by means of both pen and platform. He addressed them in articles appearing in the *Daily Princetonian, Harper's Weekly*, and the *Independent*. His major articles on education, "The Personal Factor in Education," "My Ideal of the True University," and "What Is College For?" appeared in *Youth's Companion*, the *Delineator*, and *Scribner's Magazine*.[24] Occasionally he granted interviews on educational matters to reporters representing important newspapers.[25] But the most consistent means he used to publicize his views was the lecture platform. Aside from his numerous speeches to alumni groups around the country, he delivered dozens of addresses about education at schools and universities, teachers' and bar associations, and at university and civic clubs throughout the East. His typical topics were "the Meaning of University Education," "the University and the Nation," and "Liberal education." Like the Phi Beta Kappa address he delivered at Harvard in 1909, his speeches on education were well reported and often the subject of generous editorial commentary. That platform–press interaction would become a strong asset in his future positions of leadership. At the present, however, the press placed its main focus on the efforts made during his administration to implement changes at Princeton.

II

During the eight years Wilson served as Princeton's president, press reports conveyed the sense that Princeton was on the move. As one publicist put it, Princeton was "the most interesting American university to study just now." "To find anything equal to it," he wrote, "we must go back fifteen years to the time when [William Rainey] Harper built the new University of Chicago out of the ruins of the old, or forty years ago when [Charles William] Eliot took hold of Harvard."[26] Enthusiasm at and about Princeton ran high as the transformation of the university proceeded and the faculty, trustees, and alumni claimed Wilson was "Princeton's most valuable asset."[27] Press interest focused on the major reforms initiated during his administration. They were four in number. The first two concerned the curriculum and an innovative experiment in student–faculty relations; the last two, residential life and the building of a graduate school. Not only did the press serve as a medium of news about these reforms, but it also became a means of publicity that both Wilson's supporters and opponents used. Wilson also learned that greater press scrutiny, in some instances, invited criticism of him.

Little of that criticism appeared in the press's treatment of the reforms enacted during the early years of his tenure. It took two years to reconstruct the university's curriculum. By 1904, Princeton's students had a course of study that would become standard in many other colleges. It offered students an alternative to the free election system of course selection, which other colleges had introduced and which was attracting increased criticism, by providing for a largely prescribed curriculum during the first two years of college followed by more elective courses, within a field of concentration, for the last two years. Courses taken in the first two years would be of a general nature; those in the last two years, more specific. To accompany this redesigned curriculum, Wilson also introduced the first real organization of departments at the university.[28] One year after the new curriculum went into effect, he proposed a second reform, a preceptorial system, and hired 45 young scholars to launch the program. These preceptors were assigned a small group of students and, as Wilson described their duties, were to serve as their "guides, philosophers, and friends".[29] The idea behind this system was to break down the formality of large lecture classes and to have the preceptors, meeting with groups of four or five students at a time, inspire the students' interest in their studies.

While implementing these two major reforms, Wilson worked to improve the university in other ways. Entrance requirements were raised; academic standards and student behavior, improved; and distinguished scholars, hired. Despite his own championing of humanities, he did not neglect the sciences. They were upgraded and provided with new laboratory buildings. Wilson felt that the reforms had produced a "manifest improvement" in the intellectual life of the university and believed it was progressing toward a position of "highest distinction" among the country's best colleges.[30]

According to the favorable notice Princeton received in the press, many observers beyond the university shared Wilson's enthusiasm for the changes underway there. "Keep your eye on Princeton," a writer in the *Independent* exclaimed in conclusion to his article on these reforms.[31] That opinion echoed throughout the attention the press devoted to higher education. It reduced "chaos to order," the *New York Times* commented in its representative response to Princeton's new curriculum while speculating quite correctly, that it might become a model for other colleges to follow.[32] The introduction of the preceptorial system won even more press notice as editors and writers greeted it as an idea that attracted "the attention of the educated world."[33] Later articles reporting on the success of the system were no less complimentary. As the interest of the press and the informed public grew in developments in higher education, one writer was not exaggerating when he wrote that the preceptorial system, which experts in education were closely watching, had "incited the intelligent curiosity of college men everywhere."[34] The articles were often as much about Wilson as they were about the reforms. As a result, one young journalist, who met him for the first time in Chattanooga in 1906, later recalled, "I didn't know much about anything in the academic world at that time—in fact, I knew nothing—but I knew Woodrow Wilson by reputation."[35] During the next several years, interest in Wilson would mount, but even the growing stature of the man could not guarantee the success of the subsequent major changes that he hoped to make at Princeton.

Toward the end of 1906, he promoted another major reform. Known as the Quadrangle (or Quad) Plan, it involved transforming the organization of university life. Rather than fraternities, Princeton had eating clubs for which only juniors and seniors were eligible. Located in splendid buildings along the town's Prospect Street, the clubs attracted two-thirds or more of the upperclassmen. Competition for election into a club could disrupt friendships, and some students, failing to gain election, left the university. The exclusiveness of the clubs became more severe when a network of freshmen and sophomore feeder clubs sprang up. Membership in the latter might even be determined by seniors in preparatory schools that traditionally sent large numbers of their graduates to Princeton. The entire system was "the most pernicious and evil influence in the university," the *Daily Princetonian* claimed.[36]

Wilson agreed. He believed that they created an anti-intellectual environment and were obstacles to the greater social coordination of college life that he was trying to foster. Borrowing from the residential arrangements practiced at the great English universities, he thought his Quad Plan could solve the problem. It involved turning the existing clubs into quadrangles by constructing dormitories onto their present buildings. All of the undergraduates, including members from every class, would eat and lodge in one or another of the quadrangles. Under the direction of a faculty member, the students in each building would regulate their own affairs. Wilson presented the plan to the trustees, and they responded to it favorably by authorizing him to proceed with its development. Many faculty members, alumni, and parents added their approval to that of the trustees, after the *Princeton Alumni Weekly* reported the plan on June 12.[37]

When the Associated Press circulated news of the Quad Plan, it attracted the attention of eastern metropolitan newspapers and some national journals. Most thought well of it. Newspapers, like the *New York Evening Post*, called it a "praiseworthy" democratic reform, while the *Literary Digest* described it as a plan "TO NURTURE COLLEGE DEMOCRACY" to its large national readership.[38] However, some, like the *Hartford Daily Courant* and the *New York Tribune*, were quick to report the comments of individual students and faculty members, who disparaged the proposal, while the *Hartford Times* editorialized that it was a "blow at individual freedom" that was arousing the "wrath" of the students and some alumni.[39]

An interesting aspect of the press responses was the way in which many editors interpreted it as a democratic measure. Even editors who knew Wilson, like his old friend Albert Shaw, praised the plan as a democratic measure.[40] George Johns of the *St. Louis Post-Dispatch*, Wilson's friend since their student days together at Princeton, wrote to congratulate him on his plan for democratizing Princeton. Johns, a well-known public speaker in St. Louis, told Wilson that it was the growth of the club system at Princeton that moved him two years before to make a speech at an alumni luncheon about "the necessity of maintaining equality in the university, and the danger of driving away young men of moderate and little means by the growing distinctions of wealth and social position, . . ." His editorial on the plan reflected these thoughts, which he assumed Wilson shared.[41] Wilson, however, did not envision it as democratic in nature. From the first he insisted that his proposal was academic, for "the reorganization and revitalization of the University as an academic body, whose objects were not primarily social but intellectual."[42] But there was more than enough in the language of the announcement of the plan and in Wilson's subsequent explanation of it to mislead the editors. What were they to think he meant by terms like "social coordination" that he used in those explanations? As controversy about the plan grew, both its detractors and its defenders exploited it as a proposal for greater democracy.[43]

Indeed, the controversy over the plan became bitter as Andrew F. West, the Dean of the Graduate School, Jesse Lynch Williams, who was still connected with the *Princeton Alumni Weekly*, and a few others engineered resistance to it.[44] The *Weekly*'s role in this and other university issues was crucial. It not only reached the alumni, who exerted influence on the Board of Trustees, and provided alumni and others a forum to express their opinions, but it also was a source of information for the public press. In September 1907, the *Weekly* opened its columns to views on the Quad Plan, but the letters selected for publication made it clear that it was aligned against Wilson.[45] Although he retained support for the plan from most of the faculty, opposition to it among the trustees and alumni reached serious proportions by the time the trustees met in the fall. Consequently, at their October 17 meeting, they voted to withdraw the approval of the plan, which they had given in June. Although they also voted permission for Wilson to continue to try to persuade the Princeton community of the merits of the scheme, their vote spelled its de facto end.

The trustees saw little alternative to the action they took. Aside from the fact that it divided the Princeton community, there was concern that the plan weakened their previous commitment to Dean West to build a graduate college. He had important allies among the trustees, including Grover Cleveland. The plan would be costly, and Princeton was already running a deficit. To make matters worse, most of the trustees were men of wealth who were concerned about the stock market decline and business failures that led to the Wall Street panic of 1907 only a few days after their meeting. Moreover, the secretary of Princeton's fund-raising operations, who opposed the plan, informed a trustee that there had been thousands of cancellations since the announcement of the plan. There was also a feeling that Wilson had mismanaged the plan's development and direction. He had failed to consult the faculty before presenting it to the trustees; and he had assumed an intransigent position by refusing any compromise in defending it.[46] The board's withdrawal of its sanction of the plan was a crushing blow for him, yet he decided to push on with his effort to win support by means of a tour to speak at various alumni meetings. When that failed to mollify the trustees, Wilson knew that his opponents had prevailed. "They are fighting me on the basis of privilege, and privilege never yields," he told his brother-in-law.[47] Furthermore, he knew he had to raise the money for it, over three million dollars, but no donor could be found to make that sort of contribution.

III

In the wake of the rejection of the Quad Plan, the debate over building a graduate residential college emerged as the leading issue at the university in 1908. The ensuing struggle, Wilson's last one as president of Princeton, was no ordinary dispute over policy or planning. To the contrary, the most authoritative scholar on Wilson's academic career claims it was "one of the most bitter and complex rows in all academic history."[48] As it gained precedence in the university's life and politics, both press and public found it an engaging issue. Wilson's chief opponent was Dean West, popular with the alumni and a powerful university figure who had the support of a bloc of trustees. Various subcurrents, personality clashes, shifting positions, and concealed motives gave a labyrinthian quality to the struggle that few people, apart from those immediately involved, understood. At bottom it was a contest over control of the graduate college, but the most visible issue was about where it would be located. Wilson, in keeping with his idea of an integrated university, wanted it built near the center of the campus; Dean West preferred a site on the university-owned golf links removed from campus. Wilson thought this plan would disconnect it from the university.

The controversy came to a head in 1909. It was then that William Cooper Procter, a wealthy alumnus and close friend of Dean West, offered Princeton $500,000 for the graduate college if the trustees would match that amount and build it away from the center of campus. With battle lines drawn in the faculty and among the trustees between Wilson's and West's supporters and with old friendships dissolving as colleagues joined one side or the other, the dispute acquired crisis proportions. Moses T. Pyne, a wealthy alumnus, a power at Princeton, a supporter of West, and chairman of the trustee's committee on the graduate school, lost confidence in Wilson's ability to govern the university following his poor performance at a recent board meeting. Pyne even proposed a plan to his allies to remove the president from office. The plan never materialized, but feelings ran high with the approach of the board meeting on February 10, 1910, at which the trustees were to decide whether or not to accept Procter's offer. Before they could meet, the controversy took a dramatic turn. On February 6, disturbed by how Wilson and his associates had dealt with his offer, Procter withdrew it. Four days later the trustees voted in favor of Wilson's preferred location for a graduate college building.[49] The crisis appeared to be over; the issue, resolved.

In fact, its stormiest period was only beginning. What had largely been a university affair now became a prominent item in the public press. "It has roused the whole country to curiosity," exclaimed the *Boston Evening Transcript*, and there was an element of truth in its flamboyant exclamation.[50] Why did this internal dispute at an exclusive college gain such press attention? The answer leads to Wilson's opponents who tried to discredit him on this issue and, in some cases, to force his resignation. They used publicity to gain support for their cause. Already by the end of January, some of Wilson's supporters were complaining about his opponent's use of the *Princeton Alumni Weekly* in this manner. As one pro-Wilson trustee, a member of the Graduate

School Committee, protested:

> The thing that irritates me beyond endurance is the small and sharp politics in which the opposition has indulged in trying to influence the Board and the alumni against Wilson and his ideas. . . . Most of all I am irritated at the way in which the Princeton Alumni Weekly is used after each meeting of the Board or when an issue is up, to give publication to the opposition's interpretation of the situation, [and] to print letters which, however they may have been addressed to individuals, were intended for the consideration of the Board. All these things seem to show a desperate determination to break down Wilson and his supporters by creating . . . a sentiment they cannot resist.[51]

The authors of the letters referred to in this comment knew that such conspicuous publicity in a publication the New York newspapers routinely scanned would attract the notice of the public press—which it did.

Nothing was left to chance. Based on "special dispatches" received, the *New York Herald* began a series of four articles on the controversy. The series ran from January 27 to January 30 and conveyed the impression that the university was experiencing a serious conflict in which there was an almost full break between Wilson and the alumni. "DR. WILSON FACES TURNING POINT IN PRINCETON'S LIFE—Sensational Developments Expected," was the heading for the *Herald*'s January 29 article, which for the first time traced the graduate college debate to differences between Wilson and the alumni over the Quad Plan. Wilson published a denial of that inference, but the very suggestion that the present debate was an outgrowth of the previously defeated Quad Plan, which was untrue, could only rekindle old anti-Wilson anxieties. When viewed together, the articles favored Wilson's opponents, and reflected "inside" information.[52] Aimed to alert alumni to action and to arouse public interest in the issue, the series achieved its purpose, but the outcome was not that which was anticipated.

One person who sensed the need to have the other side of this issue disclosed was Henry B. Brougham, a *New York Times* editor. He wrote to Wilson, "If the Times can help you editorially in your efforts to organize the college life at Princeton in a different spirit and for a different purpose than the spirit and purpose fostered there by tradition, it is at your service." Brougham then asked Wilson for his "editorial guidance in this matter" so that the editorial he planned to write about it would have "an authority that comes from a good understanding."[53]

Wilson's response to this request raises some ethical questions. Brougham's letter arrived at an opportune time for him. He was unable to speak out on his own because of a pending meeting of a committee that the trustees had appointed to meet with Procter in hope of reaching an acceptable settlement with him. Nevertheless, he immediately replied by sending the editor a copy of a report prepared by four of his colleagues that he planned to read to the trustees—one that he considered "private and confidential." In his cover letter, he told Brougham that his ideals about the location of the graduate college were those "of genuine democracy" as opposed to those of "social exclusiveness," and he remarked that, "the great newspapers of the country can do an immense service now in helping to put the places where the young men of the country are trained upon a basis of sound democracy and genuine work again."[54] Consequently, Wilson not only provided private information intended for use in a private meeting for the editorial but also, by casting it as a battle for democracy, distorted the position of his opponents. The graduate school debate had hardly centered on the issue of democracy vs. exclusion. Nevertheless, Wilson had come to believe that the issue did involve a democratic principle. It might also be added in regard to his tactics in this case that his opponents were no strangers to *sub rosa* maneuvers in their efforts to defeat him, or even to force him from office.[55]

When the editorial appeared on February 3, it left no doubt about its interpretation of the crux of the controversy. "At Princeton," it began, "the scene of a battle fought a century and a third ago for the establishment of American democracy, is in progress to-day. . . ." Continuing, it incorporated the basic arguments and some of the language Wilson used in his letter to the editor, and it also exaggerated the democratic line of argument to the degree that the debate about the graduate college became a matter of national concern. "The Nation," the editorial declared, was "aroused against special privilege" which, in turn, was "sheltered by a great political party." Then it asked if Princeton and other universities would allow such an influence to corrupt their institutions, "to bend and degrade them into fostering mutually exclusive social cliques, stolid groups of wealth and fashion, devoted to nonessentials and the smatterings of culture?"[56] One of the leading opponents of Wilson, Jessie Lynch Williams, the former editor of the *Princeton Alumni Weekly* and now chairman of its Executive Committee, used the *Weekly* to denounce the *New York Times* article as an "indecent exposure of our Alma Mater's linen to public view." He then explained at length how the *Times* and other newspapers following its lead had misinterpreted the entire dispute. Although neglecting to mention the role of the *Weekly* and that of the *New York Herald* in publicizing the issue, he was correct in concluding that "since the publication of the *Times* editorial . . ., many other editorial pages throughout the land have echoed the same grave warning against the bribe of gold."[57]

Meanwhile, Moses T. Pyne and others wrote to the *Times* repudiating its editorial. There was nothing exclusive about the intent of Procter's grant. It was to be used for scholarships and for buildings large enough to house all the graduate students who wished to live there, Pyne argued. In another case, an anonymous alumnus went to great lengths in a letter to the *Times* to argue that the charge that the gift would foster privilege at the expense of democracy was unfounded and called upon Wilson to deny it "authoritatively."[58] The publication of the repudiations, however, did little to quell the now aroused interest of the press, for as Brougham told Wilson, "The issue at Princeton is in a peculiar sense a public issue, concerning vitally the interest of higher education in this country."[59]

Numerous newspapers proved the correctness of Brougham's comment when the trustees upheld Wilson's position on the graduate college a few days later following Procter's withdrawal of his gift. Editors throughout the East and beyond hailed the trustee's action as a victory for democracy and Wilson as the president who, in the spirit of democracy, had rejected a $500,000 gift for his university.[60] Wilson felt relieved and vindicated by the way in which the dispute had ended, and set off to Bermuda for a short rest. When he returned, however, he found that the embroilment was, in some respects, worse than when he left.

His opponents among the trustees and the alumni, particularly those in New York and Philadelphia, refused to consider the issue resolved. Publicity about it continued with the *Alumni Weekly* at the storm center. Week after week, proponents on both sides of the controversy published lengthy, in many cases documented, accounts favoring their position in the *Weekly*. Some of the writers preferred to state their case in the form of letters to the editor, either in the *Weekly* or in the public press. Reports, editorials, letters, and anonymous statements about the controversy continued to appear, as one observer said, "in public prints near and far thruout the country."[61] The debate also continued by means of another medium, the advocacy pamphlet—one of the oldest forms of publicity known to journalism.

This pamphlet literature can serve as a weather vane of the direction the debate was taking. Proponents of both sides of the controversy wrote the pamphlets, but from the start it became apparent that Wilson's opponents were more determined to utilize them. They published more of them and used more aggressive argumentation in presenting their cases. For instance, Dean West compiled one pamphlet, *Princeton University: The Proposed Graduate College, Record of the Project from 1896 to 1910*, on January 29, which, despite its objective format, discredited Wilson. By April 1, the anti-Wilsonians had four more pamphlets in circulation as opposed to at most two that could be called pro-Wilson.[62] Printed for alumni and, in some cases for student consumption, they found their way into the public press. The *New York Times*, for instance, published an article about one anonymous pamphlet, *The Phantom Ship*, which argued that at bottom the graduate college controversy was about resurrecting the Quad Plan. It quoted an alleged statement by an unnamed "pro-quad Trustee" saying in effect that if the "gift were declined or withdrawn, . . . Princeton in ten years would be in full operation under the 'quad system.' " That, the pamphlet argued, would commit Princeton to a "failed experiment" and leave the university "heavily in debt and with division and discord in [its] Faculty, Trustees, and alumni." This argument, though specious since it had not been part of the case for or against the Procter gift and since Wilson had avoided referring to it during the debate, could reenergize the sharp opposition of some alumni to the Quad Plan and direct it toward the present issue. By publicizing such arguments and charges, Wilson's opponents hoped to influence trustees to reopen negotiations with Procter and have new members, like Adrian Joline, well-known for his opposition to Wilson's plans, elected to the board.[63]

The tide of alumni opinion appeared to be running against the president. His most adamant opponents raised the banner, "Wilson must go," and believed his resignation was a distinct possibility.[64] Princeton alumni in Cincinnati believed he might even resign by the end of February.[65] Wilson, however, regained the advantage by making a "swing around the circle" to overcome alumni opposition. Starting in Baltimore, he moved on to Brooklyn, Jersey City, and St. Louis. Everywhere he spoke in a conciliatory manner stressing the recent achievements, physical growth, and rising prestige of the university and crediting it all to collective effort. When addressing the circumstances surrounding the graduate college controversy, he placed the entire matter in a broad and positive perspective, and he framed his comments on the subject in appreciative, if general, language. No mention of personalities entered his explanation of that issue.[66]

Wilson had reason to feel encouraged by his reception at these alumni meetings, particularly the one in St. Louis. There he concluded his comments about the graduate college by recommending the entire matter be placed before the faculty and pledging his full cooperation with their verdict even if they decided against him.[67] Procter was also at the St. Louis meeting, and he and Wilson took the opportunity to discuss the lingering issue. The outcome of this and other conversations Procter had there indicated that a solution to the problem was possible. He said that he agreed with everything Wilson had said in his speech and gave intermediaries the impression that he would renew his offer if a compromise could be found.[68] Also, by this time, Princeton alumni sympathetic to Wilson's achievements and position had checked the publicity campaign of the anti-Wilson alumni by means of publications of their own.[69] For the second time, victory seemed attainable.

Once again, however, it eluded him. Early in April he had ventured into the citadel of his most caustic alumni opponents, the Princeton Club of New York, to deliver a speech largely devoted to explaining the graduate college controversy, as he said, "stripped of all personalities."[70] "The tension that evening was indescribable," wrote David Lawrence who, as a student, had known Wilson, and who covered Princeton affairs for the Associated Press. "Never in his later career did Woodrow Wilson face an audience more hostile to him."[71] Worse yet, before the speech began, a sarcastic, unsigned, anti-Wilson pamphlet, *Cheer Up*, circulated among the alumni. The president spoke with sincerity, Lawrence said, even with eloquence, but failed to engender enthusiasm for his position. After remaining unresponsive during the speech, the audience dispersed with only a few discernible hand claps.[72] A week later on April 14 the trustees rejected a resolution proposing that the faculty be requested to express themselves about the "character, methods, and administration" desirable for the graduate school.[73] Wilson believed the faculty would support him, and the trustees' rejection of the resolution was a severe blow to his hopes to have the issue resolved as he wished.

Two days later he arrived in Pittsburgh to address a friendly group of alumni. He appeared visibly dejected.[74] Having been subjected to great pressure for months and having carried his struggle with the trustees so close to victory, he now realized that the opposition to his hopes for the graduate school was far from defeated. The Pittsburgh alumni, however, greeted him with a standing ovation. Perhaps that gesture of appreciation helps to explain what followed, or perhaps recent frustrations with the trustees and with other alumni weakened his power to restrain his inner feelings, including his growing conviction that the democratic spirit was, indeed, present in the causes he championed at Princeton.[75]

Regardless, he addressed the Pittsburgh alumni in a manner they little expected. Gone was the conciliatory tone of his previous speeches. Wilson's words were intemperate, even confrontational. First he attacked the trustees. Because of their recent action, he said he did not know what opinion they held in regard to the graduate school, and therefore he felt left in a position of "splendid isolation." The longer he spoke, the more he lost control of measured expression. For some reason, he used the Protestant churches as an example to explain what was happening at Princeton. They paid "more regard to their pew rents than to the souls of men," he charged. And so it was with colleges like Princeton. They sought the support of "the classes," of "wealth," and disparaged the "service of the people." Lincoln, he declared, would have been less fit for office had he attended college. There he would have been led, like others, to forget his "common origins" and "universal sympathies" in favor of class, and "no class can serve America." Then he returned to the strife at Princeton. "Will America tolerate the seclusion of graduate students?" Obviously not. "Seclude a man from the rough and tumble of college life" and the nation will brand him with its "contemptuous disapproval," he announced, while declaring he would use all his power to achieve "an absolutely democratic regeneration of spirit" in any college with which he was connected. He then invited the alumni to make a similar commitment.[76]

At the end of his remarks, the audience sat in silence, but many eastern newspapers were quick to voice their reaction to it. The *Pittsburgh Dispatch* headed its report on the speech "DISASTER FORECAST BY WILSON," while the *New York Tribune* declared on its front page, "DR. WILSON AN ALARMIST."[77] Some editors characterized the speech as rash or self-serving; others were more understanding with their comments, even if they took exception to some of Wilson's statements.[78] A few journalists of strong progressive persuasion found it an inspiration, and the noted muckraker David Graham Phillips considered it as proof that Wilson was leading Princeton away from the "mockery of medievalism."[79] Nevertheless, Wilson's opponents could find ample unflattering reports and editorials on the speech to use to their advantage by printing excerpts from them in yet another anonymous hostile pamphlet, *That Pittsburgh Speech: and Some Comment*, which they distributed widely.[80]

Wilson realized the damage he had done to his own cause. "I spoke too soon after a meeting of the Trustees at which the majority vote seemed to me to create an impossible situation; but that is only an explanation of my stupid blunder, not an excuse for it," he wrote to one correspondent, adding, "I shall try to remedy the situation, but by more just exposition of the matter."[81] He began with a conciliatory speech to the Chicago alumni on May 12, but little time remained to settle the issue. One week later a wealthy alumni, Isaac Wyman, died leaving his entire estate of several million dollars for a graduate school at Princeton along the lines that West, who had secured the bequest, favored. Wyman's will even named West an executor of the estate. What Wilson's foremost biographer labeled "The Battle of Princeton" ended as the board accepted a renewed offer from Procter, made after he was informed of the Wyman bequest, and as Wilson accepted defeat with good grace.[82]

IV

During his eight years as Princeton's president, Wilson grew in stature, and the attention the press gave him helps to account for his enhanced public recognition. He had reason to be pleased with the mainly favorable response that the press accorded his university activities, his educational writings and speeches, and his occasional interviews. Of course, the way in which his opponents used the *Princeton Alumni Weekly* to discredit him during the latter years of his tenure had to be a disappointment to him, but with few exceptions the public press had favored him and his educational endeavors. In the stormy graduate college debate it supported his cause in most cases. Regardless, he felt justified in complaining about how particular press reports misinterpreted his position. Many public figures at the time voiced similar complaints. Nevertheless, they are indications of his evolving attitude toward the press. Already in 1904, well before the issues of the Quad Plan and the graduate college emerged, he consoled one of his colleagues, upset by the way reporters distorted the intention of his comments, by saying, "I have suffered so many unspeakable things from reporters myself that I am not likely to take their word too seriously with regard to others."[83]

Although he once said that he made it a "rule never to take exception to newspaper interviews or to attempt to correct impressions that may have been made by them," he broke that rule at times.[84] On at least one occasion, he published a complete denial of an interview, as he did with this statement in the *Daily Princetonian*: "I drop you a line to say that the alleged interview with me printed in this morning's Philadelphia Press, is an absolute fabrication. I had an interview with a representative of that paper, but said to him nothing even remotely resembling what he reports me to have said."[85] On another occasion, he took issue with the *Springfield Republican*'s editorial on his Phi Beta Kappa address at Harvard. In his remarks he suggested ways, other than by compulsion, to have students acquire "the spirit of learning," but the *Republican*'s editor criticized him for overlooking "the old fashioned idea that it is work that makes men as well as cities and empires."[86] Wilson wrote to the editor saying that he took for granted the idea that "hard and consistent work" was necessary for disciplined learning, but, while he thought he had made that clear in the address, he was exploring additional means that would relate learning to life. He had a point, but it could have been missed in hearing the address. No matter, the editor had cited what he thought was a lapse in Wilson's reasoning and embellished his remarks on that perceived shortcoming.[87] About this same time, the *Princeton Alumni Weekly* began an interview article on one of Wilson's recent speeches by saying that "President Wilson's speeches have been so frequently misrepresented that the *Weekly* took it for granted that the startling statements [from this speech] reported in the newspapers to have been . . . taken out of context." Then it quoted Wilson's own reasons for being "extremely mortified" by being so misrepresented.[88]

His explosive speech in Pittsburgh discussed earlier was certain to raise questions even among friendly editors. Wilson had a poor position to argue in this case, but he fended off criticism in the New York and Philadelphia newspapers. To the editor of the *New York Evening Post* he tried to explain that he had no intention of overlooking the value of "culture" and "intellectual power" in that speech. "Unfortunately," he said, "my mind is a one-track affair on which I can run only one through train at a time. . . . I beg that you will not believe, that because I seem incapable of stating more than one side of a question in any one speech, I do not know and appreciate the other side." It was a weak argument, and when the *Post* printed Wilson's letter it editorialized, "It is precisely because he is the very kind of man who inherently stands for the value and dignity of learning and culture that we regretted to see him, whether consciously or not, adding force to a current that sets strongly against the upholding of learning and culture in their rightful position."[89]

Wilson also complained to the editor of the *Philadelphia Press* claiming its article on the speech had "seriously misinterpreted" the entire "tone and attitude" of what he had said. The editor answered him at length saying he was unable to discover any interpretation of tone and attitude in the article, which only quoted Wilson's own language, and the fact that the speech had "startled its hearers." Wilson claimed that "the dispatch . . . [was] entirely without foundation and fact." However, the editor responded by pointing out that a "number of Princeton men who attended the dinner, consented to be quoted, some by name and some anonymously in regard to the speech," and he concluded that their comments ran parallel to the words the reporter used in the article. Endeavoring to be as fair as possible, the editor said he would conduct a "thorough investigation" of the article before printing anything more about it. As it turned out, the reporter who produced the dispatch had been told by his chief to make additional inquiries about the accuracy of the report before sending it. He did that and even claimed Wilson himself had verified the quoted passages in the presence of Warren Seymour, who had been the toastmaster at the Pittsburgh meeting. Consequently, the *Press*'s editor assured Wilson that his newspaper always tried to present both sides fairly in its news columns and to reserve interpretation for its editorials. Nevertheless, since Wilson had claimed that he had not been asked if he were properly quoted, the *Press* would open its columns for any statement he cared to make about this matter. The editor added that if an error had occurred he would accept Wilson's "statement that the quotation in question was incorrect," but any error in the article was due to the "imperfections of newspaper reporting" rather than to a "lack of diligence."[90] His convincing responses to Wilson's charges, plus the fact that the *Press*'s article, which a news service supplied, agreed with other news reports about the speech sent by other news services, suggest the weakness of Wilson's complaint. An honest and diligent editor held the high ground in this instance.

Of course, Wilson could be high-minded, even inspiring, and these were qualities that made him attractive to many journalists. They perceived him as a fighter trying to advance the line of democracy in college and some joined the ranks of his devoted followers at this time. For example, Ellery Sedgwick, of the *Atlantic Monthly*, later recollected his first encounter with Wilson. It was at the time of the Quad fight, and Sedgwick claimed that "to this day I recall the experience minute by minute." Wilson was speaking to a hostile audience at a New York dinner, and he spoke with eloquence, passion, and convincing argument. He went home, Sedgwick remembered, a "burning disciple," and declared to his wife, "I have been listening to a great man. I know it! I know it! Wilson will be famous."[91] Enthusiasm aside, his reaction expressed a sentiment that an increasing number of journalists could share.

Chapter 3
Advent of a Public Statesman, 1906–10

At the peak of his campaign for the presidency in 1912, Wilson said he regretted not having entered politics earlier, at the point when the progressive spirit was just beginning to awaken the nation.[1] That thought reflected his latent interest in a political career. As a college student, he would jest with friends about meeting them someday in the Senate where they could continue their debates, and as a young man he spoke of his "first-primary-ambition" being to take an "active, if possible a leading, part in public life."[2] Upon witnessing a session of Congress in 1898, he told his wife, "The old longing for public life comes on me in a flood."[3] A few years later, he confided to a friend, the historian Frederick Jackson Turner, "I was forty-five three weeks ago, and between forty-five and fifty-five, I take it, is when a man ought to do the work into which he expects to put the most of himself. . . . I was born to be a politician and must be at the task for which, by means of my historical writing, I have all these years been in training."[4]

Subsequently, Wilson gained prominence while serving as Princeton's president, evidenced by the attention the press accorded him in that capacity, and by 1910 he had acquired a reputation as a public statesman. More and more, newspapers described him as "eminent" or "prominent" in their reports of his speeches and other activities as his commentary and analysis of public affairs grew more frequent. Coupled with his achievements at Princeton, and the battles he waged there, this other side to Wilson's life has to be kept in mind when contemplating his entrance into politics in 1910. His decision in the summer of that year to become a candidate for the governorship of New Jersey was a personal one, hesitantly taken. It was not, however, an isolated act. The press attention accorded him for years, the manner in which some journalists had promoted his candidacy since 1906, and the more recent speculation about and enthusiasm for his possible candidacy provided a context for his decision. So too, did the prevailing political environment.

An interesting aspect of the progressive movement was its emphasis on newness. Progressives were confident that they were building something new. As Richard Hofstadter once pointed out, the titles of major books of the time like Herbert Croly's *The Promise of American Life*, Walter Weyl's *The New Democracy*, and William Allen White's *The Old Order Changeth* suggested that "something new and hopeful was being created."[5] That mood propelled a new generation of leaders into politics. Like the Progressive era muckrakers, who animated the journalism of the era, they were men in their thirties or forties (e.g., Hiram Johnson was 34 in 1900; Robert M. LaFollette, 45; Theodore Roosevelt, 42).[6]

It is only necessary to read the many complaints about political corruption at the national level that appeared in the press at this time to appreciate why the way was opening for new people to enter politics. As James Kerney, editor of the *Trenton Evening Times*, wrote in retrospect, "for some years the big magazines of the country . . . had been cultivating a demand for men of higher intellectual and social eminence in public life."[7] The *Atlantic Monthly*, *Century*, *Harper's*, *Scribner's*, and *World's Work* were among the magazines advancing that idea, and it was to Wilson's advantage that he had contacts with their editors and friends who held editorial positions. In addition, during the first decade of the new century many journalists, who knew him only by reputation, came to believe that Wilson deserved a place in the front rank of this new generation of political leaders.

I

To appreciate the interest journalists took in him as a spokesman on national affairs, recall his reputation as a public speaker. Wilson had the remarkable talent to compartmentalize his activities, and even during the stormiest years of his tenure as Princeton's president, he mounted the public platform time and again to address audiences on topics other than education. According to the surviving record he gave about 290 public speeches (approximately 36 each year) while he held that office. Some, of course, were to alumni groups, and others were delivered in his capacity of representing his university at ceremonial affairs at other colleges. He also spoke on a number of topics of general interest and on others targeted for specific religious, civic, or professional audiences.[8] Some of his speeches were inspirational; others were historical; others yet were patriotic. He liked to establish relationships between individual groups and the wider community in his speeches, as can be seen from these titles: "The Minister and the Community," "The Banker and the

Nation," "The Business Man and the Community," "The State and the Citizen's Relation to It," and "The Lawyer and the Community." As historian John M. Mulder concludes, Wilson became "the moralizer of American life."[9] He carried his message of personal responsibility and public service to all types of audiences. Sometimes he spoke on particular national and civic problems in political addresses, and, at one point he delivered a series of eight lectures on constitutional government at Columbia University.[10] The newspapers followed these speeches and reported them with generous tributes to the speaker.

He became one of the most accomplished public speakers of his generation. Report after report about his speeches in newspapers throughout the eastern half of the country made it clear that he was polished and persuasive. The press described him as "forceful," "witty," and "stimulating," as a southerner who had acquired national stature. Following an address on "Americanism" in Charleston, South Carolina in 1906, the editor of the *News & Courier* told Wilson that his was the best speech heard there "for many years." "The whole town," he said, was still talking about it.[11] Ray Stannard Baker, the muckraker and future Wilson biographer, observed that Wilson's speeches during these years were filled with "peculiar power and passion" and "made him everywhere converts and followers."[12]

Even as a busy university chief executive deeply immersed in his institution's politics and determined to frequent the lecture circuit, he found time to revive his old role in public affairs as a literary journalist. Notably, he produced four essays, "Politics (1857–1907)," "The State and the Federal Government," "The Tariff Make-Believe," and "Hide and Seek Politics," that appeared in the *Atlantic Monthly* and the *North American Review* between 1906 and 1910. In them he applied his knowledge of the past to current problems. More important, in 1908, he published *Constitutional Government in the United States* based upon the eight lectures he delivered at Columbia University the previous year. With this book, which would be his last, he again produced a sound work in political science, one that updated his *Congressional Government*, written more than 20 years earlier. *Constitutional Government* was an able effort to explain how the federal government functioned, and reviewers were quick to notice that it was a "popular treatise" intended for general readers. Wilson's reputation as an authority on the workings of government and as a spokesman engaging the national political culture, plus his stature as Princeton's president, led many journalists in time to perceive him as a fresh political personality.

Interest in his entering politics, even in his becoming a possible presidential candidate, surfaced early in the decade. In 1902 a letter appeared in the *Indianapolis News.* Written by "An Old-Fashioned Democrat," it suggested that the Democratic party give serious attention to Wilson for its presidential nominee in 1904. The writer, later discovered to be a local journalist, said he did not know Wilson; he had only heard him when he spoke a few days before in Indianapolis. Yet based on his impression of him at that time, he believed him to be the new type of man needed for the presidency, "a man of ability and character" who had a "conviction of the truth of Democratic principles" and "a man of affairs, a scholar, a patriot, and a man whose very presence inspires enthusiastic devotion."[13] This tribute alone would be insignificant were it not for the fact that it prefigured similar suggestions that journalists would make in forthcoming years. In 1906, for example, the well-known journalist and political scientist Henry Loomis Nelson offered a long appraisal of Wilson in the *Boston Herald* citing him as a high-minded man who had not "made a business out of politics." The mere mention of Wilson's name, Nelson wrote, indicated that some people were considering "reforming the character of our politicians by putting superior men in service."[14] Nelson's article became part of the first serious, coordinated effort to publicize and promote Wilson as a presidential candidate in 1908.[15]

As his frustrations in the Princeton presidency grew, there were indications that he contemplated entering politics. "Things have come to a turning point with me," he wrote to a correspondent in 1908. "If I cannot do this [restore the old 'democracy of spirit and action' at Princeton], I must turn to something else than mere college administration."[16] No doubt he was encouraged toward his decision by the numerous favorable comments about him appearing in the press. As one newspaperman put it after listening to a Wilson speech, "Pity that so able a man is not in the political world" and in it as a "man of leading."[17] The comment is typical of many others that can be found among the newspaper clippings in Wilson's personal papers. This much is clear. By 1908, when a movement, mainly by journalists, to wrest the Democratic presidential nomination from William Jennings Bryan failed, Wilson's political star was rising. He addressed political issues more and more in his speeches, and his major addresses like "The Banker and The Nation," delivered in Denver at the annual convention of the American Bankers' Association, became front page news. When the Short Ballot Association was launched in New York in 1909, Wilson took a position on its advisory board. By 1910 he was president of that association and moving ever closer to a political career. However, any account of his entrance into politics invariably leads to George Harvey, one of the era's most colorful journalists.

II

No one with knowledge of early twentieth-century journalism and politics would deny Colonel George Brinton McClellan Harvey his rightful place among the era's prominent political publicists. Fascinated with journalism, the Vermont-born Harvey began to practice the craft early in life. At twenty one, he advanced his promising career by moving to New Jersey to become managing editor of the newly launched New Jersey edition of Joseph Pulitzer's *New York World.*[18] A close student of New Jersey politics, he served on the governor's staff with the rank of colonel—a title he retained for the rest of his life. In 1891, when Pulitzer appointed him managing editor of his flagship newspaper in New York City, Harvey ascended to one of the premier editorial chairs in American journalism. His fascination with national politics led him to play a major role in Grover Cleveland's election to his second term in the White House. In the mid 1890s, Harvey left journalism long enough to make a substantial fortune by his investments in electric railways and other business enterprises. This interlude led to a close association with the financier William C. Whitney and friendships with others like Thomas Fortune Ryan and J. P. Morgan—relationships that would have an indirect impact on Wilson's quest for political office years later. Harvey's main interest, however, remained in journalism. When the opportunity to purchase the *North American Review* occurred in 1899, he seized it, and displaying his customary vigor, he assumed multiple positions at this time. Along with acquiring and editing the distinguished old *Review*, he became the head of the prestigious publishing house, Harper and Brothers, and shortly thereafter the editor of the lively conservative periodical, *Harper's Weekly*.

It was, however, the character of the man and his journalistic style that made Harvey a formidable publicist. He was a Democrat, and by persuasion a conservative and spirited partisan. His friends likened him to Junius, the eighteenth-century British writer who combined engaging style and scornful invective in a famous series of political articles in London's *Public Advertiser*. Opponents considered him a political intriguer who, as some of them claimed, was capable of strutting while sitting down. Some even considered him a "political roughneck."[19] As editor of the *North American Review* and *Harper's Weekly*, his writing was clear, powerful, and often trenchant. Although circumstances denied him a college education, it was a tribute to his prodigious writings that he received honorary degrees from Dartmouth College, Middlebury College, the University of Vermont, Erskine College (S. C.), and the University of Nevada. William and Mary College, where Phi Beta Kappa, the oldest Greek-letter society in the United States had been founded in 1776, awarded him an honorary membership in that premier honor society.[20]

As mentioned earlier, Harvey's acquaintance with Wilson began several years before when Harvey became president of Harper and Brothers, the publisher of Wilson's latest books. Upon attending Wilson's inauguration as president of Princeton, Harvey was so impressed by the scholar–administrator that he began to think of Wilson not only as a university president but also as a potential candidate for the presidency of the United States. Once aroused, his interest in Wilson's possible candidacy grew.

While president of Princeton, Wilson signaled his interest in politics a number of times. Almost until the end those signals were tentative and without commitment, but they tantalized some of the journalists. For instance, in the wake of Alton B. Parker's defeat as the Democratic candidate for the presidency in 1904, Wilson delivered an important speech, "The Political Future of the South," to the Society of Virginians in New York City. By nominating Parker, the Democratic party had turned away William Jennings Bryan, its standard bearer in 1896 and 1900, but Wilson contended that the radicals and populists in its midst had kept it from victory in the recent election. Consequently, he believed that the South should take the lead in restoring moderation in the party. "The country as it moves forward in its great material progress," Wilson proclaimed, "needs and will tolerate no party of discontent or radical experimentation; but it does need a party of conservative reform, acting in the spirit of law and ancient institutions." His speech, with all of its implications favoring a limited government, struck a receptive nerve in the audience. The speech received "one of the most remarkable demonstrations of approval that has been manifested at a public dinner in this city for a long time," commented the *New York Sun*.[21] It would appear that Wilson was positioning himself as a political conservative and that was most pleasing to Democrats like Harvey, who were hopeful of finding someone whom conservative, Grover Cleveland Democrats could support.

There was good reason for them to have perceived him in this manner, for his "The Political Future of the South" speech was a clear repudiation of William Jennings Bryan's leadership of the Democratic party. Moreover, there was much in Wilson's background, in his speeches and writings, that underscored his conservatism.[22] It should be remembered, however, that it was of the Burkean variety. Wilson admired the writings and oratorical style of this great eighteenth-century Anglo-Irish writer–statesman, and in 1893 he called Edmund Burke his "master."[23] Burke, of course, was no standpat conservative. His belief in tradition, for instance, found its balance in his value of practicality. He believed that political institutions were organic, or evolving, entities forged by history. Burke disclaimed abstract theorists and was famous for his stand against the French Revolution. So it was with Wilson. He reread Burke in the 1890s, a turbulent decade for the nation, and in his lectures denounced radical theories of government and popular excesses in political life and referred to him as "the apostle of the great English gospel of Expediency."[24] His reference to "Expediency," in a political sense, suggests prudence, practicality, and a willingness to accommodate one's actions to realities. Wilson placed Burke, an antirevolutionary who supported most major political reforms of his day, in the company of "every real liberal man in England. . . ."[25] Accordingly, in 1904 Wilson was, like Burke, a moderate conservative with an enthusiasm for reform.[26] His conservatism represented a desire to temper the political movement of the time with the principle of ordered progress. It is difficult to say how well the journalists understood the premises beneath Wilson's statements, but some key conservatives among them believed he was sound enough in his political principles to be a candidate they could support.

That was the case with George Harvey. A little over a year later, he made his first move to launch a Wilson movement. On February 3, 1906, at the Lotos Club dinner in Wilson's honor, Harvey suggested Wilson's nomination for President of the United States. Subsequently, his *Harper's Weekly* carried a full front page picture of Wilson in its March 10 issue along with Harvey's own Lotos Club speech. Then the article cited favorable press responses to the idea of a Wilson candidacy from various southern newspapers.[27] Three weeks later the *Weekly* published yet more favorable press commentary from across the country. Some were Harvey inspired, including the previously cited Henry Loomis Nelson article in the *Boston Herald*.[28] Regardless, the Wilson "candidacy" articles continued to appear in the *Weekly* through June.

Harvey also brought his *North American Review* into line behind Wilson. He wrote a lead editorial advocating Wilson in its April issue and had one of his writers contribute a long article on the Democratic candidates surveying each section of the country in search of the right Democratic candidate for 1908. In the end, it settled on Wilson. Depicting him as a distinguished person of "exceptional popularity" known to "a multitude of thoughtful readers" and "worthy of Virginia's noblest traditions," the article concluded with a flourish.

> The country needs relief from the strenuous and histrionic methods of Federal administration now exemplified in the White House. It needs a man who is a genuine historical scholar, and who has conclusively proved himself a competent executive. It needs a statesman of breadth, depth and exceptional sagacity; an idealist, who, at the same time, shall be exceptionally sane. . . . It needs a man whose nomination would be a recognition of the South, which the South nobly deserves, and whose election would be decisive proof of the union. . . . Such a man is Woodrow Wilson of Virginia and New Jersey. We add that he is a Democrat, and of course a tariff-revisionist. In a word he meets all the exigencies of the situation.[29]

The author, Mayo W. Hazeltine, who signed himself "a Jeffersonian Democrat," allowed his enthusiasm to exceed his reason by arguing that Wilson was a "conclusively proved" executive and a "statesman of breadth, depth and exceptional sagacity," for he had not yet had the opportunity to demonstrate these qualities in a manner normally expected of a candidate for the country's highest office. Regardless, Harvey had launched a trial balloon, and it caught the attention of the mass circulating *Literary Digest*, which devoted a prominent article, "A College President for the White House" to Harvey's Lotos Club speech and the ensuing press commentary about it, thus publicizing Wilson for a large and popular readership.[30]

In the midst of all of this speculation, Wilson delivered another important political speech. Addressing the annual Jefferson Day Dinner of the National Democratic Club of New York on April 16, 1906, he lauded Jefferson's championing of individualism. He contended that the country needed no new program, only "a new spirit" of responsible individualism. Speaking of the current "contest between capital and labor," he cautioned: "Capital will not discover its responsibilities if you aid it. Labor will not discover its limitations and ultimate conditions if you coddle it." If either side used unfair advantage in the contest, there was the law to serve as umpire. His challenging the need for greater government regulation pleased the more than 400 guests there including many of the leaders of the conservative wing of the party. Bursts of applause interrupted his presentation.[31] Though political, the speech did not mean that Wilson had decided to run. That decision was yet far off, and his physical health ruled out a possible move into politics at this time. One morning in May he woke up unable to see with his left eye. Diagnosed as the result of hypertension, it forced Wilson to clear his schedule for a complete rest in the months ahead.[32] By the end of June, he had recovered sufficiently to spend the next three months of his recuperation in England's Lake District, one of his favorite spots in the world.

While Wilson was in England and without his knowledge, Harvey schemed to involve him in politics. He began working through New Jersey Democrats to have Wilson nominated for the U.S. Senate. At first, upon arriving home from England, Wilson was somewhat drawn to the idea, but he soon had second thoughts and withdrew from the contest. This turn of fortune failed to discourage the irrepressible editor. He now focused his attention on grooming Wilson as a candidate for the presidency in 1908, though the election of 1912 was his real target. Even before that, the New Jersey governorship could be contested in 1910.

From 1906 on, Harvey worked both in print and in private to promote the possibility of Wilson's presidential candidacy. He informed Wilson of important men who had responded favorably to that idea, men like bankers August Belmont and Dumont Clarke, the financier Thomas Fortune Ryan, and prominent journalists, Adolph Ochs, proprietor of the *New York Times*, Charles Miller, *New York Times* editor, Henry Watterson, editor of the *Louisville Courier-Journal*, and Major James Calvin Hemphill of the *Charleston News & Courier*. He also made reference to William Mackey Laffan, publisher and editor of the *New York Sun* who, after a visit to the nation's capital, told Harvey of the considerable speculation including some "apprehension in official circles" about the idea that was present in Washington. It is not surprising that Laffen himself was noncommittal about the idea, for his *New York Sun* was one of Wilson's most persistent critics. Only a few days before it had editorialized that Wilson was impractical and "plainly disqualified" to be the Democratic nominee.[33]

Nevertheless, Harvey continued to forward Wilson's prospective nomination throughout the following year. He assigned one of his writers, William Inglis, to become his "first lieutenant" in the publicity campaign for Wilson and instructed Inglis to give it his best thought and let it consume all his energies. At first Inglis had doubts about the assignment, but Harvey's spirited belief in Wilson's candidacy infected him, and once he began working on the campaign, his enthusiasm never wavered.[34]

It would help to have Wilson meet some of the influential men Harvey had mentioned in his correspondence, and conversely, to afford them the chance to scrutinize him. With this thought in mind, Harvey initiated a private dinner meeting at Delmonico's in New York for Wilson and the ultraconservative William Mackey Laffan, Thomas Fortune Ryan, and Dr. John Wyeth, president of the Southern Society of New York, who had arranged it. The atmosphere was congenial, and Wilson was talkative and relaxed. However, on March 19, four days after the meeting, Laffen's *New York Sun*, responding to comments Wilson had made the previous evening at a gathering of the South Carolina Society of New York, charged him with uttering the "NOTIONS OF A MOLLYCODDLE." Portraying his comments on labor unions and on tax reform as "hopeless," the article offered a devastating indictment of the Princeton president as someone who was aloof from the economic realities of the world. His speech, the editorial announced, "smells of the lamp and betrays the student of history, which are the well-known characteristics of the mollycoddle. It bears all over it the particular brand of the mollycoddle, . . . [his need to criticize] the deeds that others do. . . ." Not satisfied to leave it at that, the editorial concluded, "Truly, the college professor to-day endeavoring to illuminate the path of the future by the light of his researches into history and human experience is a melancholy spectacle."[35]

There did not appear to be much room for Wilson to continue in dialogue with men like those who controlled the *Sun*. Yet, there are no straight roads in politics. After the Delmonico's dinner, Dr. Wyeth suggested that Wilson write a summary of his political views to Ryan and Laffen.[36] Thereupon Wilson produced a statement entitled "Credo." It was bound to please conservatives. In it Wilson declared, "There is no such thing as corporate liberty or corporate morality: only the individual can be free or moral." He recognized "great trusts and combinations" as necessary to modern business and largely honest and legal in their transactions. Their methods were "for the most part sound and unobjectionable; . . ." Moreover, in cases where they did engage in transactions prohibited by law they should be punishable by law. Government regulation could not remedy their transgressions.[37] When wrongdoing occurred the responsible individual, not the corporation could be punished. This line of argument was typical of the message that Wilson delivered in numerous speeches, articles, and interviews in the year following the Delmonico meeting.[38] The bold educational reformer appeared less bold as a political reformer, and his words appeared to satisfy Ryan and Laffen. Ryan helped to finance Wilson's gubernatorial campaign three years later, and the *Sun* supported Wilson, even for a while after Laffen's death in 1909.[39]

Once the conservative democrats whom Ryan and Laffen represented were reassured about Wilson, Harvey could resume his campaign to have Wilson nominated in 1908. Despite the slim chance of having that succeed, publicity about Wilson now would help him compete for the New Jersey governorship in 1910, and if he could win that office, he would be in a position to make a serious run for the presidency in 1912. Harvey was a good friend of his former boss, Pulitzer, the restless press lord. Pulitzer had already become interested in Wilson as a possible presidential candidate, as a southerner who could carry New Jersey and New York.[40] Now Harvey suggested that Pulitzer's *World*, the leading Democratic newspaper in the country, should come out for Wilson. Hoping to find an alternative to a third nomination of William Jennings Bryan, whom Pulitzer deemed hopeless, the publisher agreed, but with one reservation—he would print an editorial in favor of Wilson if Harvey would write it. The editorial, appearing in the *World* on January18, 1908, was a major triumph for Harvey's publicity campaign, and it initiated more speculation in the press about Wilson's candidacy. Placing scruples aside, Harvey even quoted his own article in a subsequent article in his *Weekly*, citing only the *New York World* as a source.[41]

The intrepid editor had one remaining preconvention promotion to make for Wilson. Shortly before the Democrats met in Denver in July, he had Mayo W. Hazeltine write another article extolling his candidate. Again it appeared in the *North American Review*, and stressed Harvey's common theme that it would be expedient to have a nominee with both a southern and a national outlook. Such a man, the article claimed, could be found in Woodrow Wilson, who ranked among the "great captains of higher education." Hazeltine now toned down the previous superlatives he used when writing as "a Jefferson Democrat" claiming that Wilson had great natural ability, distinguished experience, and, due to his study of politics and history, a grasp of fundamental political principles and "primary truths." Thoughtful readers knew and respected him through his writings. Although Hazeltine held that Wilson had "exceptional popularity" without defining the limits of that popularity, he made a creditable case for Wilson, claiming that, in practical terms of political arithmetic, he could win support in both southern and northern states and in enough other states to win a majority of electoral votes.[42]

Despite Harvey's publicity campaign, Wilson believed he had "not a ghost of a chance of defeating Bryan" at the Denver convention.[43]

He was vacationing in Britain when the Democrats convened. Some newspapers mentioned that he might be nominated for vice president on a ticket with Bryan. Wilson refused that idea outright before he sailed for England, and left instructions with his brother-in-law, acting as his political agent at home, to stop such a move should it occur. Regardless, Bryan controlled the convention, and the delegates nominated him on the first ballot, giving him a third chance to win the highest office in the country. Once again, however, his personal popularity proved insufficient to defeat a Republican opponent, in this case William Howard Taft. But Taft floundered during his first year in office and then faced a serious challenge from progressive Republicans as well as from Theodore Roosevelt, who became politically active again after 1910. In the years following Bryan's defeat in 1908, the Democrats had reason to hope for better fortune in the near future. More than ever, the way opened for new Democratic leadership, and Harvey's plans for Wilson seemed to be progressing a pace.

III

However, in the several years before the gubernatorial contest of 1910, Wilson's political ideas began to move toward a more progressive position. Given the temper of the progressive-reformist spirit of the time, some publicists thought they needed to evolve farther. For instance, in response to a Wilson speech opposing the idea that state and federal governments use commissions to regulate corporations, the *Chicago Tribune* charged that he was not as progressive as the public whose interest he hoped to advance.[44] It had a point about Wilson's resistance to business regulation by this means. That could be a deceptive point, for in other ways, he came to question the conservatism that many of his supporters held dear. During the struggle over the Quad Plan at Princeton, Wilson had maintained that his purpose was "academic," but it was that struggle that encouraged his more spirited commitment to democracy. His brother-in-law once observed that when "Wilson realized the character of the forces that were opposing him, all of the democracy that was in him latent, as well as conscious, leaped into flame. He had always been a democrat, but now he had become a fighting democrat, and when the story of this great democrat is told in great detail we must go back to Princeton in 1907 for the epochal moment of its development."[45]

The change now apparent in Wilson can be seen in the role he assigned to citizens in his *Constitutional Government* (1908). As opposed to the attentive but passive role he gave them in his older *Congressional Government*, he now depicted them as a more active force in politics. Thus public opinion acquired a more compelling role in government and the president a much more forceful role in leading it, for he was the only elected representative without a particular constituency and one who identified with no special interest. He represented the "whole people" and could mobilize them behind him. "The President is at liberty, both in law and conscience," Wilson wrote, "to be as big a man as he can. His capacity will set the limit. . . ."[46] Wilson, in fact, was providing justification not only for the growth of national as well as presidential power but also for the greater role in public affairs for the press. In a country the size of the United States, no other current medium reached so many people. None could match it as a mass communication vehicle to mobilize public opinion.

Interestingly, in *Constitutional Government*, he argued that radical changes, which had drawn the nation together, had occurred since the writing of the Constitution. The nation had acquired a "common consciousness" as a result of sweeping changes in communications and economic life. "The copper threads of the telegraph run unbroken to every nook and corner of the great continent, like nerves of a single body, transmitting thought and purpose with instant precision," he reasoned. "Railways lie in every valley and stretch across every plain. Cheap newspapers make news of every country-side the news of the nation." Modern industrial organization, moreover, was oblivious to state boundaries and swept "from state to state in currents which can hardly be traced for number and intricacy."[47] The resulting national integration allowed a modern president to mobilize public opinion, but how could that be achieved? Of course, by means of presidential messages and oratory, and also through the medium of the press.

There were, in fact, indications that Wilson was expanding his interest in the press. Early in his Princeton presidency, friends and associates often sent him newspaper clippings in which he was featured. He also subscribed to professional clipping services and, consequently, had access to a systematic compilation of press reports and commentaries about his speeches and his public acts.[48] Moreover, from 1907 on, his complaints to editors about his statements being misrepresented became more frequent in relation to his speeches on public affairs as well as those on education. Two pronounced cases in which he took issue with newspapers about their misleading reporting of his commentary on public affairs occurred with the *New York Times* and with several Denver newspapers. In 1907, Wilson granted a long interview to the *New York*

Times on present political and economic affairs but afterward complained to the editor that the way in which it was reported created "false impressions." He protested that the interview "heightened the color" of his views and that its headline, which referred to his "Scathing Arraignment of Political and Industrial Conditions," was misleading. An examination of the text shows that Wilson had reason to complain, and in this case the editor permitted him to publish a subsequent letter in the newspaper to correct alleged inaccuracies.[49]

The trouble with reports in the Denver newspapers occurred a year later. As the presidential election of 1908 neared, Wilson made an important public affairs speech addressing the annual convention of the American Banker's Association in Denver. It was a progressive speech both in tone and substance in which he warned bankers that they were isolated from their communities. There had been an "extraordinary awakening . . . in recent years . . . with regard to the moral obligations involved in business," and as a result there was "a general feeling in this country that there is a difference between the general interest and the interests recognized by those who handle capital," he told the bankers. Alerting them to the idea that the people of the country regarded banks as institutions "belonging to some power hostile to them," he urged the bankers to get closer to the people, serve their needs, and aid the plain man.[50] Perhaps, he suggested, the establishment of inexpensive branch banks would be a move in that direction. The speech was tactfully presented and often interrupted by applause and laughter. It was widely reported and an abstract of it even appeared in the *Congressional Record*. However, Wilson had reason to feel misrepresented by the leading Denver newspapers when they covered it with headlines saying he told the bankers they must accept "Regulative Legislation" and that he condemned "Postal Banks"—since he made neither of these claims in the speech.[51] Those alleged statements had political implications, and he had no recourse other than to issue a public denial of having made them.

Such misrepresentations were a common occurrence. Even President Theodore Roosevelt, with all of his publicity management and media skills, complained about "lies" in newspapers regarding him and said that journalists responsible for them were a "potent force for evil in society."[52] James Bryce, the renowned student of American character and institutions who was then the British Ambassador in Washington, made a study of the American press and concluded that fabricated news reports were common in this country's newspapers.[53] Wilson, therefore, was in good company in voicing complaints about such misrepresentations, and it should not be forgotten that the coverage the press accorded him was decidedly favorable. Moreover, the press attracted his attention in other ways as well.

The clearest indication of his interest in the press can be found in his general references to it. They show his awareness of the prevailing trends of journalism such as the ascendancy of news over editorial matter, the impact of modern communication technology on newspapers, and the international outreach of news. He was also aware of the growing body of press criticism that called attention to the irresponsible actions of reporters, to the perils that sensational journalism posed for the public good, and to the reckless excesses that had crept into the work of some of the muckrakers. In 1906, for instance, *Cosmopolitan* magazine published a series of exposures by David Graham Phillips entitled, "The Treason of the Senate," in which he accused a number of conservative senators of being in alliance with business "Interests." This angered President Roosevelt into charging that writers who went this far in their effort to expose corruption reminded him of a character in John Bunyan's *Pilgrim's Progress*, "the man with a muck-rake," who only looked downward and failed to "look upward to the celestial crown above."[54] Just a few days after this speech, which fixed the label "muckrakers" on the exposé journalists, Wilson commented on the subject. With the "Treason of the Senate" series in mind, he told a group of Princeton students interested in journalism that they should avoid distorting facts, "a habit into which many newspapers have fallen." "This ferocious criticism of the Senate," he said, was "manifestly unfair." "What is needed for the education of a man for Journalism," he urged, "is a broad and liberal education. A journalist must be educated to see at a glance all phases of a subject." This was the course that students should follow if they hoped to serve the "welfare" of the nation through journalism.[55]

The same theme of journalism as a form of public service also appeared in his comments to professional journalists. He addressed the subject before a group of newspaper publishers and members of the Associated Press in 1910. Observing that people's awareness was growing about who owned the organs of the press and even about their chief editors, Wilson told them the time had arrived for a "grand reassessment of character and motive" of men who were now being judged in "the court of public opinion." He ended with an invitation for journalists to join the ranks of those seeking, unlike some irresponsible reformers, the genuine betterment of the country. For a journalist the question should be, "Is he serving himself, or is he serving the public interest?"[56] Wilson's advice was, of course, an extension of the public philosophy he had preached for years.

His statement indicates how he positioned himself regarding one of the major criticisms of the press—charges of its commercialization. The argument ran that in too many cases publishers pursued profits at the expense of the needs and expectations of democracy and resorted to practices, however disreputable, that sold newspapers and attracted readers and advertisers. In fact, at the very time Wilson was addressing this subject, the journalist Will Irwin was conducting an investigation of the press that consumed more than a year and resulted in a 15-part series, "The American Newspaper: A Study of Journalism in its Relation to the Public." *Collier's* published the series, which became a classic statement in the history of press criticism, and in it Irwin attacked newspapers for serving wealth, suggesting that many of the failures of newspapers could be traced to their commercialization.[57] While he admitted that respectable and sincere newspapers still existed, he spent most of the series exposing shortcomings of early twentieth-century newspapers. In the end, he concluded that the press lagged behind the "thought of the times" and hoped that journalism was entering a new era of greater honesty and ethical intent.[58] As an experienced journalist, Irwin spoke with greater expertise than Wilson, but both men in the end advanced the same sentiment: many newspapers and the men behind them needed to abandon their errant ways and adhere to the spirit of the age.

Perhaps Wilson's most interesting reflection on the press dealt with the provincialism of American newspapers. His own travels around the country and his observations about *The Times* (of London), a national newspaper like the other large and influential London papers, led him to conclude that the American press was localized and hampered by that fact. He contended that even in the great metropolitan dailies of this country, local news crowded out national news, even Associated Press dispatches that carried national and international news fell victim to this tendency. While his line of argument failed to consider the expansion of news sources both in Washington and abroad, as well as the growth of press associations and syndicated services, not to mention the current appearance of widely circulating new popular magazines that made a national impact, it did make a point. Considering the steps he later took during World War I to create a form of national journalism, his reflections at this time suggest that this was a matter that long engaged his thought.[59]

The idea of a national newspaper became the subject of several of Wilson's public statements.[60] On one occasion, he even promoted a publication of that type. Contacting his old friend Robert Bridges, he asked: "If you had an opportunity to buy an established newspaper in the South, say at Baltimore, and desired to find a man to act as editor . . . , who could give the paper a character which would make it deserve national attention and be calculated to widen its interest in all national matters and attract the attention of thoughtful people everywhere, . . . whom would you choose?" Wilson made the inquiry on behalf of someone else whose name he could not indulge but someone whom he "should like very much to assist in this important choice."[61] Although the scheme came to naught, it does show that Wilson had more than a theoretical interest in the press, and that he was sensitive to the role it played or failed to play, as a disseminator of public policy and as an organic element in shaping public opinion.

IV

More pronounced than the growth of Wilson's interest in the press was the attention the press was giving to him as a public figure. As this sampling of headlines of news articles about him shows, the newspapers considered him someone who was more than an authority on higher education and scholarly subjects.

> " 'PRESIDENT BIGGER THAN HIS PARTY'
> Office Has Far Outgrown Original Limits Says Woodrow Wilson"
> (*New York Herald*, 15 March 1907).
>
> "ENTIRELY POSSIBLE TO CURB TRUSTS—
> WOODROW WILSON"
> (*New York World*, 3 Apr. 1908).
>
> "A CHANCE FOR THE DEMOCRATS. WOODROW WILSON COMPARES ITS STAND WITH THAT OF PARTY IN POWER. WARMS UP ON TARIFF QUESTION"
> (*Newark Evening News*, 30 Oct. 1909).[62]

Wilson's private correspondence provides further evidence of the press's mounting interest in him as an authority on public affairs. For instance, in a typical message, a Joliet newspaperman H. E. Baldwin wrote to Wilson: "As one of the guests at the recent banquet of the American Newspaper Publishers' Association and Associated Press, I wish to express my sincerest appreciation of the sentiments you expressed on that occasion and upon others before and since. . . . The common-sense view expressed by you cannot fail to bring the proper equilibrium in dealing with these great public questions."[63] After listening to that same speech the *New York Times*, H. B. Brougham wrote to

Wilson: "I . . . congratulate you upon your philosophic insight and ability to speak at once the words that are needed."[64] Echoes of these sentiments were becoming common, particularly among New York and New Jersey journalists.

Nevertheless, two questions persisted about Wilson as a possible Democratic candidate. First, was he a conservative or a liberal, and second, was he interested in running for the governorship? At times Wilson seemed to question himself about the former. "I never know whether to describe myself as a liberal or as a conservative," he reflected in one of his speeches in 1909. "I believe that many of the alumni of Princeton would now describe me as a radical; yet I deem myself a conservative, for I believe that life is the only thing that conserves, and life is the only thing that does not stand still or retrogress. Progress, therefore, is part of the essential process of conservation."[65] However Burkean that self-analysis may have been, it was an effort to align himself with the forces of change. Increasingly, his public pronouncements on political as well as educational matters acquired a progressive tone. "No one now advocates the old *laisser faire* . . . or questions the necessity for a firm and comprehensive regulation of business operations in the interest of fair dealing, . . ." he told a New York audience.[66] He was distancing himself from his previous opposition to the regulation of business, and in general, was assuming a position on the progressive side of politics. Indeed, he went so far as to declare, "We live in an age in which old things are passing away, in which all things are under scrutiny, in which the renaissance of government by opinion and the general interest is as plainly forecast by every sign of the times as it was in the period preceding the French Revolution."[67] More and more, he punctuated his speeches with references to "the revival of popular politics," and to the fact that "*we*" Democrats have an "abiding confidence in the people" as he criticized "the interests" and urged the establishment of "leadership" mindful of the public good.[68] Wilson was emerging as a spokesman for moderate progressivism, and with the press coverage he received, his public statements began to attract the interest of a wider circle of journalists.

Among them was Henry Eckert Alexander, the editor and publisher of the *Trenton True American*. "More and more I am convinced that the Democracy of New Jersey, *without any encouragement whatever from you*, will turn to you for leadership in the coming campaign," he told Wilson. "You will be nominated and elected Governor of New Jersey. . . ."[69] Although a newcomer to New Jersey journalism, Alexander became an enthusiastic Wilson champion and for a while a political advisor. He was an experienced editor and publisher from the Midwest, who in 1908 purchased the venerable *Trenton True American.* As late as the 1890s, the *True American* had the largest circulation among Trenton's four major newspapers, but it was in decline when Alexander bought it.[70] Its problems began in 1896 when, breaking with its Democratic tradition, it supported William McKinley for president—a decision that cost it at least 500 subscribers and much goodwill in the city. Alexander hoped vigorous journalistic enterprise could reverse its decline.[71] One means he employed to reinvigorate the *True American* was to place its weight behind an electable Democratic candidate for governor. Alexander first approached Wilson with this idea late in 1909. A few months later, he became convinced that Wilson could win the governorship, and with the national attention that would bring, along with support from the South, he could also win the Democratic nomination for the presidency in 1912.[72] He may have been the original New Jersey editor to promote Wilson, but others soon followed. Nevertheless, the strategy they mapped out for Wilson to carry him from Trenton on to Washington was that which Harvey had developed.

Harvey, in fact, had already announced that strategy to the public. On May 15, 1909, his lead editorial comment in *Harper's Weekly* stated, "We now expect to see Woodrow Wilson elected Governor of the State of New Jersey in 1910 and nominated for President in 1912 upon a platform demanding tariff revision downward."[73] Undeterred by Wilson's increasing identification with progressivism, the conservative editor continued to publicize Wilson's candidacy in his *Weekly*, and as was his habit, by private means as well. In January 1910, Harvey met with the New Jersey Democratic leader James Smith, Jr. to interest him in Wilson's candidacy. A colorful and influential Irish American politician, Smith had risen through the ranks of Newark politics to serve as U.S. Senator from 1893 to 1899. As the controller of the Essex County political machine, he was not only the political master of New Jersey's most populous county, which included Newark, but also the most powerful politician in the state. His nephew James R. Nugent, moreover, was chairman of the state's Democratic committee and usually followed his lead in politics. Smith had yet another political asset—his views were heralded in his own *Newark Star*. In terms of personal choice, Smith favored Wilson, but he had doubts about the support Wilson might receive from rank and file Democrats in the state. However, after making appropriate inquiries, he believed that the party regulars could be won to Wilson's cause.[74]

Would Wilson consent to run for the governorship, even with Smith's powerful machine behind him? Harvey set about to force its resolve, and he acted none too soon. Growing numbers of New Jersey Democrats were considering supporting Frank S. Katzenbach of Trenton who had waged a strong campaign for the governorship in 1907 and whom many party workers felt deserved another chance. Smith was also worried about how Wilson would act, if elected, toward his own organization. Would he build up a rival one of his own? Working through intermediaries, Smith sought Wilson's answer to that question, and he was satisfied when the potential candidate responded that he would not consider assembling a personal machine so long as the existing organization was willing to support policies to reestablish the state's reputation and that would be his attitude as long as he remained "absolutely free in matter of measures and men."[75] All that remained was to have Wilson commit himself. Consequently, Harvey arranged a meeting for June 26 at his New Jersey home for Wilson to confer with Smith, and his friend, the *Louisville Courier Journal*'s Henry Watterson, whose editorial pen Democrats near and far respected. The meeting, which Harvey's lieutenant William Inglis also attended, went well, yet Wilson declined to commit himself. Meanwhile, as speculation about his candidacy appeared in the press and reports of these private meetings leaked out, journalists scurried to discover his intentions.[76]

Even Harvey had difficulty in determining them. If he could arrange to have the nomination offered to him "on a silver platter" with no pledges of any sort and without any effort on his behalf, what would Wilson's attitude be, the editor had asked Wilson back in January. Wilson's response was that, under those conditions, he would give it serious thought. It was not, however, until the first week in July that Wilson told Harvey and Smith he would accept the nomination under the conditions the editor had specified.[77] Wilson still hoped to remain silent in public about his decision, for as he told the *World's Work* editor, "to go into print now would seem like trying to draw opinion to myself."[78] That was an impossible strategy, and Wilson was naive to think that the news could be kept from a press already discussing the possibility of his nomination.

Politics being what they are, once made, his decision would become news. Nevertheless, Wilson was "astonished" on July 7 when a reporter from William Randolph Hearst's *New York American*, told him that he had learned "from Wall Street" sources most of what had transpired regarding his nomination. He wanted to know if Wilson had been won over by "the Interests." Wilson's response that his proposed candidacy was informal, and that he "was in no sense a candidate," failed to convince the inquiring reporter.[79] The next day the *American* ran a front page article headlined, "**WALL ST. TO PUT UP W. WILSON FOR PRESIDENT.**" It spelled out how Wilson was being forwarded for the governorship in preparation for a run for the presidency by Harvey, Smith, and others whom Smith had contacted, and it underscored the Wall Street connections of these men.[80] Newspapers friendly to Wilson labeled the article an "ATTEMPT TO DISCREDIT WOODROW WILSON" and on July 9, Alexander's *Trenton True American* came out with an editorial, "FOR GOVERNOR OF NEW JERSEY—WOODROW WILSON," which simply brushed aside the *American's* charges and presented Wilson as a high-minded candidate, free of alliances with either "corporations or politicians," immune from "factional associations," and as one whose competence for the office was matched by the confidence the people would have in him. "I have seen a great deal of favorable comment" on that editorial, Alexander told Wilson, and he said he had even sent it to Republican editors, who greeted it "with great favor"—except those "Republicans of the machine type." In subsequent issues, Alexander began to publish excerpts urging Wilson's nomination taken from other New Jersey papers.[81] Still Wilson made no public announcement about his intentions.

However, when the *New York World* reported, as a result of a July 12 meeting of Wilson, Harvey, and New Jersey Democratic party leaders, that Wilson was a candidate for the governorship, he felt his hand had been "forced." He then contacted the *Trenton True American* and the *Newark Evening News* with the message that if it were true that "a decided majority of the thoughtful Democrats of the State" wished to have him accept the nomination, he would consider it his duty "as well as his honor and privilege, to do so."[82] No editor was more pleased with the announcement than Alexander who wrote to Wilson, "Your 'statement' was exactly the thing. In my opinion it prepares the way for your unanimous nomination and election and then! It means a political revolution in New Jersey and every man who has any political sense understands it." The feisty and reform-minded editor added, "I have been testing sentiment. It can be shaped into something tremendous for you and your ideals." He wrote to Wilson again the next day reporting more favorable responses to his announcement. "It is refreshing to find that in spite of the opposition of the political crooks and time-servers, the people are rising to the occasion. Party lines are ignored in the demand for such a candidate [as Wilson]," he said, adding this afterthought. "My paper is read every day in the homes of 700 clergymen in New Jersey. That ought to count for something."[83]

Not every Democratic editor shared Alexander's enthusiasm for Wilson. Two of the leading progressive Democratic newspapers in the state, the *Hudson Observer* of Hoboken and the *Trenton Evening Times*, immediately came out against his nomination on the grounds that it was engineered by big city bosses and by the powerful financial and big business interests of New York City. The *Observer* even charged that Wilson allowed himself to "be used as a catspaw, to serve the purpose of the bosses" in frustrating reform.[84] Despite the influence they wielded, these newspapers were exceptional, for newspapers throughout the state and in nearby metropolitan areas lauded Wilson's candidacy as means to revive the Democratic party in the state and to upgrade the level of politics.[85] The editor of the national weekly, the *Nation*, caught that sentiment when writing in private to Wilson, "Believe me, nothing has so inspired and invigorated us here in the office for a long time as the prospect . . . of battling for you for the Governorship of New Jersey."[86]

The nominating convention would not be held until September 15, and Harvey advised Wilson to say as little as possible during the summer. He would manage the political negotiations, which he assured Wilson were going well with "no breaches in the walls."[87] Now convinced that there was a genuine and popular demand for him, Wilson followed Harvey's advice, despite the fact that the *Hudson Observer* and the *Trenton Evening Times* continued to wage a campaign against his nomination and despite being, as he said, "more or less pursued by reporters."[88] Only on a few occasions did he stray from his intention to remain silent until the convention. When Harvey suggested "it would be a good idea to scatter a sort of character sketch of yourself amongst the small country weekly papers of the state" because "we have all sorts of folk in Jersey, and I dare say that there is in the minds of some of the backwoodsmen an impression that you are a man who makes whiskey or sewing machines," Wilson agreed to see Harvey's lieutenant Inglis to compile such a sketch. He already had allowed Anne McIlvaine, a personal friend, a Trenton woman who was active in civic affairs, to interview him for a similar sort of sketch and felt her article "promised to be a very clever and effective thing." As it turned out, Inglis's sketch was a disappointment. In the judgment of Henry E. Alexander, it failed to tell if Wilson "ever had an idea about God, man, or the Devil." However, McIlvaine's piece, "Woodrow Wilson's Home Life," that the *Trenton Evening Times* published, was more on the mark, plus she had additional material to pass on to Alexander, which he deemed "far more suggestive" and substantive than Inglis's. Regardless,

Alexander took material from both interviewers for an article, "A Plain Man of the People," for 48 other newspapers to use.[89]

Another instance in which Wilson broke his silence was of greater consequence. It concerned charges that he was unfriendly to organized labor, justified in part by statements he had made in his speeches. In one such well-publicized speech in 1909 he claimed that "in some trades and handicrafts [unions] no one is suffered to do more than the least skillful of his fellows can do within the hours allotted to a day's labour, and no one may . . . volunteer anything beyond the minimum."[90] It was not the first time he had made such a claim, and on this occasion a number of union members informed him of his errant views on the functioning of unions. Wilson was, by his own admission, "a fierce partizan of the Open Shop and everything that makes for individual liberty," and in reply to the complaints unionists made of his charges against their organizations in 1909, he could only cite as his source the fact that he was "in constant contact with those who do employ labor on a great scale."[91] That was insufficient to mollify some local labor leaders troubled by the news that he would stand for the governorship. Accordingly, when the New Jersey State Federation of Labor met on August 16 in Newark, it passed a resolution urging organized labor to oppose his candidacy because of his previously made "unfair and misleading" statements, which were unworthy of an aspirant for public office.[92] A week later Edgar R. Williamson, the editor of the *Labor Standard* of Orange, New Jersey asked Wilson to set forth his views on labor unions. He seized that opportunity and responded through the medium of the press with an open letter published in the *Labor Standard* and subsequently in the *Trenton True American*.

The letter is interesting for several reasons. First, in an effort to place his comments in perspective, he charged that some newspapers had made "gross misrepresentations" of his views. Given his past experience with how the press interpreted his comments, it is not surprising that he offered this explanation again in this case. There was even an element of truth in it, but since he neglected to specify how the newspapers had misrepresented him, his claim was less than convincing. Beyond that, he expressed his views on unions including the necessity for them to organize to "secure justice from organized Capital," to upgrade "the condition of workingmen," and to secure "just and adequate wages." "I am much more afraid that the great corporations, combinations and trusts will do the country deep harm than I am that the labor organizations will harm it," said Wilson with an emphasis that his supporters in the press applauded.[93] His comments in this instance represent a departure from his previous views on the subject, but his suggestions about labor in his recommendations for the proposed Democratic platform substantiate his sincerity in making them, as did his later statements and actions.[94] Encouraged by reports he received about his open letter, Wilson felt it had "made a good impression."[95]

Progressive Democrats, however, would not be converted by a single public letter. When the convention convened on September 15, their delegates opposed Wilson's nomination while Old Guard Democrats supported it. Led by the Smith organization, the latter managed to nominate Wilson by a narrow margin on the first ballot. Then the convention received the announcement that Wilson was en route to address the gathering in person. Joseph Tumulty, one of the disappointed progressive Democratic delegates, later wrote, "The deft hand behind this clever move was that of Colonel Harvey. This announcement literally sets the Convention on fire. Bedlam breaks loose. The only sullen and indifferent ones in the hall are those of us who met defeat a few hours before. For us, at least, the mystery [of] who was Woodrow Wilson and what were his ideas and intentions is about to be solved." Then and later, Tumulty had reason to be thankful that he remained to hear Wilson. He was instantly converted to Wilson as he spoke about being unfettered by commitments and promises, about the new emerging era of unselfish democracy, about the reawakening of sober public opinion, and about making the Democratic Party the instrument of reform, including the regulation of business and the control of corporations. Just as important was the tone of the speech, which like style in writing, is a reflection of character. "The future is not for parties 'playing politics,' but for measures conceived in the largest spirit, pushed by parties whose leaders are statesmen, not demagogues, who love not their offices, but their duty and their opportunity for service," Wilson said. "We are witnessing a renaissance of public spirit, a reawakening of sober public opinion, a revival of the power of the people, the beginning of an age of thoughtful reconstruction. . . ." When the speech ended Tumulty, who would later become Wilson's private secretary, recalled, "Men stood about me with tears streaming from their eyes. Realizing that they had just stood in the presence of greatness, it seemed as if they had been lifted out of the selfish miasma of politics . . . [and] to the cause of liberating their state from the bondage of special interests."[96]

Like the delegates in attendance, Democratic newspapers, in particular, welcomed the speech with enthusiastic responses. Wilson had entered the political stage, and the press and individual journalists had opened the way for him. Among the journalists who were instrumental in bringing him to this point, George Harvey held the preeminent position and to him Wilson wrote:

> I do not know just how to express to you my sense of obligation for the unselfish work you have been doing in my behalf. I have admired very deeply your disinterested part and your true friendship in the whole matter, and want to say how thoroughly I have admired it all. I do not deserve to be so ideally served in the matter of my public career; but, if I cannot justify it, I can at least be sincerely grateful for it, and give in return my deep admiration.[97]

Harvey, of course, was not alone among the journalists who had encouraged Wilson to make this move, nor was the press solely responsible for it. For eight years, however, his involvement with the press had grown, and its largely favorable and often laudatory reaction to his acts and words had been indispensable in the building of the public reputation he now held. It was, of course, only a harbinger of the role the press would henceforth play in his life.

Chapter 4
Wilson's Gubernatorial Campaign and the Press

The political terrain of New Jersey was a landscape unknown to Wilson. In no state of the union did lenient corporate laws attract more "trusts" than in New Jersey, and in no state did boss-controlled political machines, often in alliance with large corporate interests, wield greater power. There were, to be sure, progressives in both parties who had protested the machine–special interest combination since the turn of the century. Most of these progressives, and the best organized ones, were in the Republican party. Known as the "New Idea" men, they were suspicious of Wilson, whose nomination the Democratic bosses had sponsored and secured. That fact also continued to trouble many Democratic progressives. Moreover, the mainline Republican party had dominated state politics since the 1890s. These were hard realities, and the university president would need help in dealing with them.

He would also need help in presenting himself to the press and the public. As one authority on New Jersey's history observed, "Voters never take to a highbrow, nor admire a theorist, nor do they turn out at the polls to vote for a man whose face and life is unknown to them."[1] Even some of his erstwhile promoters worried that he was too much identified with concerns apart from or beyond those of the state and too little associated with matters the average Jerseyman deemed important. Wilson would need favorable press publicity to overcome these difficulties. However, New Jersey Republican newspapers outnumbered Democratic ones 92 to 52. When the state's 86 independent newspapers are added to the equation, the problematic nature of the support Wilson could expect from the state's newspapers can be appreciated. In fact, the mainstream newspapers in most of the state's major cities were either independent or Republican.[2] Then there were the large metropolitan dailies of New York and Philadelphia to consider. The *New York Tribune*, for instance, made a habit of targeting New Jersey commuters with news and opinion about their state, and the *Philadelphia Record* claimed a circulation of about forty thousand in South Jersey.[3] Just as Wilson could expect support from the orthodox Democratic newspapers in New Jersey so he could expect similar support from some of the major papers in New York City (e.g., the *Evening Post*, the *Times*, and the *World*). Nevertheless, Republican standards like the *Tribune* and the *Press* maintained a formidable presence there and had an influence across the Hudson. As for Philadelphia, Republican newspapers dominated the press in that city.

I

As the campaign opened, Wilson had to feel encouraged by the way the press received his nomination. Democratic newspapers across the state applauded it. This was also the response of two of the states' most influential progressive newspapers, the Republican *Jersey Journal* of Jersey City and the independent *Newark Evening News*, the largest papers in their respective cities championing New Idea insurgency. The *Jersey Journal*'s editor complimented the Democratic party on "the excellence of its judgment" and pledged his support of Wilson.[4] He would be "the candidate of thousands of Jerseymen who had never been allied with the Democracy," predicted the *Newark Evening News* while the *Trenton True American* proclaimed "A NEW ERA IS DAWNING."[5]

That sentiment also permeated Wilson's mail from New Jersey journalists. The managing editor of the *Paterson Guardian* told him that his election would "mean the dawn of a new day for Democracy in New Jersey."[6] The editor and publisher of the *Passaic Daily Herald* wrote to Wilson that "scores of Republicans" were flocking to his office to report that they planned to vote for him. His newspaper encouraged that movement in laudatory terms. "It now behooves all the people who love their state . . .," ran its postconvention editorial, "to throw aside all minor differences and save the state and the nation from the despoiling hands of Special Privilege, and, regardless of party, march a united, invincible host for Liberty, Justice, and Peace, uner [*sic*] the stainless banner of Woodrow Wilson."[7] In fact, the idea that Wilson would have pulling power among Republicans and independents was a primary reason his spirited supporters in the press cheered his candidacy, and there was reason for their enthusiasm. Even Thomas B. Delker, the editor and publisher of the *Hammerton South Jersey Star*, who held that he was a confirmed independent but who normally supported Republican candidates wrote to Wilson, "Unless . . . the Republican party . . . puts up a better man and a better platform, you may count on me [*sic*] doing hard work for you in this County and effective work in others."[8]

A most interesting aspect of Wilson's nomination was the way in which it resonated beyond the Garden State. Most of New York's Democratic and independent newspapers announced his nomination as an indication of great things to come for New Jersey and the nation. The *New York Times* found it difficult to contain its enthusiasm for the nomination while Oswald Garrison Villard's *Evening Post* proclaimed it "one of those electrifying events which make politics seem worthwhile."[9] Already in August, Villard pledged his influential newspaper to do battle for Wilson.[10] So did Joseph Pulitzer. Endorse Wilson as the Democratic candidate for governor of New Jersey, he told his editor Frank Cobb. "Force his nomination. Great thing for [the] party, not only in New Jersey but all over the country."[11] The *World*'s editor followed that advice and assumed a prominent position among the New York newspapermen anxious to applaud the nomination.[12] Even the reactionary *New York Sun* editorialized that Wilson held the "high ideals" and "sense of public duty" needed to attract New Jersey's independent voters.[13] Moreover, by no means was enthusiasm for his nomination limited to the press of the northeast. Southern newspapers were especially vocal in expressing their pride and interest in Wilson's good fortune.[14]

Prominent national weekly and monthly journals were no less interested in his nomination. George Harvey's *Harper's Weekly*, of course, could be expected to applaud the nominee, and it did by labeling him "The Foremost American Democrat" and offered as evidence for that claim reference to a number of the nation's leading large city newspapers that supported the nomination.[15] The *American Review of Reviews*, edited by Albert Shaw, Wilson's old Johns Hopkins classmate and friend, editorialized along similar lines. Wilson was not only "an orator of great charm and distinction" but also "one of our foremost authorities upon all questions pertaining to the science of politics and government," it observed, while predicting his election by a "considerable majority."[16] As a personal friend, Shaw might be expected to write in this vein, but even the pro-Roosevelt *Outlook* editorialized along similar lines. "Patriotic Republicans as well as patriotic Democrats ought to welcome the nomination of Dr. Wilson . . .," it noted. "He is not the kind of a man that the old-time 'bosses' like to select."[17]

The hundreds of congratulatory messages for Wilson made it clear that journalists of various political persuasions took heart in Wilson's nomination. For example, Edward Bok, the provocative long-time editor of the mass circulating Philadelphia based *Ladies Home Journal*, wrote to him: "Republican as I am, may I congratulate you, and particularly the people of New Jersey? I wish I lived in your state. May you be elected with a majority that shall speak."[18] Charles Grasty, now president and general manager of the *Baltimore Sunpapers*, telegraphed Wilson asking to be advised of any way the *Sun* could help him in the coming campaign, and from Louisville Henry Watterson exclaimed: "Hurrah for Wilson. Am going to do my best." Frank P. Glass, Wilson's old Princeton classmate, now a part-owner of the *Montgomery Advertiser* and publisher of the *Birmingham News* wrote to him: "Are not the seas of university management boisterous enough that you must seek the storms of politics? At any rate there is one newspaperman in Alabama, with a hand at the helm of two strong dailies, who will not forget his fondness for 'Tommie' Wilson in the old days at Princeton."[19] Another of Wilson's student friends, George S. Johns, now in charge of the editorial page of the *St. Louis Post-Dispatch*, echoed the view of many other journalists when he wrote, "Carry New Jersey and you will be in the running for the Presidential race."[20]

Encouraging as all of these and many other statements were, it would be wrong to assume, as some journalists did, that Wilson would be certain to win the election. When the Republicans nominated Vivian M. Lewis, it became obvious that Wilson would have to work hard to win the election. Lewis, a moderate progressive with 20 years' experience in public life, might be able to hold the New Idea insurgents for the Republicans. Wilson could not win without them. The *New York Times* allowed enthusiasm for Wilson to prevail over reason when it announced that Lewis was a weak candidate nominated to give Wilson "the least possible trouble" and predicted that Lewis's campaign would be only "perfunctory," one that would "in no wise endanger the triumph of Woodrow Wilson."[21] The *Times* missed the mark with that prediction. The Princeton president was untried as a campaigner for elective office, and, indeed, let his inexperience show by anticipating an uninvolved and inexpensive campaign.[22] His Democratic managers knew otherwise.

They might be able to hold their democratic voters for Wilson, but what about the progressive vote? Many progressive leaders, including the *Trenton Evening Times*' editor James Kerney, continued to suspect the legitimacy of Wilson's nomination and his professions of independence. Even if he meant what he said, could he, a political novice without practical experience in the trenches of everyday political combat, prevail against the pressures of big business interests and machine politics that had long dominated the state? Did the scholar turned politician know enough about state and local politics to be effective? Would he be able to argue the details of policy and did he have the fighting spirit needed to prevail? As the *Daily State Gazette* of Trenton put it, he had hitherto paid little attention to New Jersey's political affairs, and his "executive ability" had "yet to be proven."[23]

No, Wilson would not glide to victory. He would have to earn it. Indeed, after the convention, he held a strategy planning meeting with bosses James Smith, Jr. and James Nugent and various local Democratic leaders. James Kerney also attended that meeting and recollected that it was then that Wilson understood that "the Democracy of New Jersey had not been clamoring for him in any such unanimous way as had been represented to him at the New York meetings."[24] Considering the press interest in his candidacy for several months before the September convention, that line of discussion may have been disingenuous, perhaps a ploy to hold Wilson in line and to remind him of his dependence on his political managers. Nevertheless, he understood how essential the Democratic State Committee was to waging a successful campaign. James Nugent, the chairman of the committee and also James Smith's chief lieutenant in Newark, took charge of campaign arrangements and, as Wilson told an interviewer who asked if he would make a speaking tour, "I shall place myself in the hands of the Democratic State Committee. I shall do whatever that committee thinks best and wise."[25]

II

Several things gave impetus and shape to the role the press played in Wilson's campaign. First of all, the Democratic organization took immediate steps to pull the Democratic newspapers in line behind the candidate. Even before the official opening of the campaign in Jersey City on September 28, Nugent was busy assuring the allegiance of those newspapers at the Democratic party state headquarters in Newark. "You are invited . . . for the purpose of perfecting the organization of Democratic editors," he said in greeting them. Before moving on to outline the background and aspirations of the party in the campaign, he reminded the editors that "the reciprocal relations between the press and our party organization should be strengthened. The present age is essentially an age of publicity." He showered generous praise on the editors for their "great services" and advised them about the issues the party would advance in the campaign and about the publicity it hoped to receive from them. He had boilerplates of ready-to-use printed matter prepared with accompanying proofsheets. The plates included a variety of items (e.g., the party platform, articles about Wilson from newspapers both in and out of state, and reports on Lewis's voting record) for the editors to receive free of charge.[26]

Nugent's effort to motivate Democratic editors was only the start of his campaign management. Under his tutelage, the Democratic State Committee mapped out plans for a vigorous campaign and provided the needed organization and funds to facilitate it.[27] Nugent not only accompanied Wilson as an advisor on his speaking trips, but he also helped to mobilize additional publicity on the candidate's behalf. Moreover, it was Nugent who arranged to have Joseph Tumulty join the traveling campaign entourage. Wilson was impressed by the young enthusiastic Jersey City progressive Democrat from the start, and thus began a relationship that would be indispensable to Wilson in his press relations for the next ten years. Undoubtedly, the candidate benefited from Nugent's understanding of state politics in many ways, and from his connections with the state's Democratic press. From the start of the campaign, he also received counsel from another quarter, one that personalized his association with the press.

He accepted guidance from influential publicists. It was natural, of course, for Wilson to receive advice on political tactics and publicity matters from George Harvey. Now he urged Wilson to have someone collect his speeches and make a composite statement of his ideas from them. That document would have maximum impact if used in a timely way, and Harvey wanted to publicize it about a week before the end of the campaign. He had contacted Melville Stone, general manager of the Associated Press, who agreed to publish it in all of the newspapers subscribing to his news service.[28] "I shall act upon it at once," Wilson responded. "It is an excellent idea and does seem worth while."[29] At Wilson's suggestion, Harvey stayed in touch with him during the ensuing weeks about the progress of the campaign. However, while the editor continued to encourage Wilson during the campaign and to report to him about his prospects of victory, his correspondence with him indicates that he offered little additional advice on specific issues and tactics at this time.[30] It is clear, however, that candidate Wilson helped himself by his prompt and cordial replies to inquiries from various editors and publishers. His correspondence during the campaign indicates how careful he was to present himself as one anxious to maximize the opportunity presented by the communiqués to develop constructive relations with them.[31] They, in turn, were not shy in offering him their counsel.

The journalist who was most energetic in offering advice to Wilson early in the campaign was the *True American*'s Henry Eckert Alexander. He threw himself and his newspaper behind Wilson with an enthusiasm undimmed since he first began to promote the Princeton president for the governorship nearly a year ago. Unlike the Harvey–Wilson correspondence during these months, Alexander's letters to Wilson are full of suggestions about which issue to champion and when and why. The editor alerted him about politicians he could trust and those to engage warily. He warned of political traps to avoid and told the candidate, "Personally you have never seen the baser side of politics. You will find that plausible men will come to you and seek expressions from you in order to use them against you."[32]

Alexander helped to inform Wilson about the preferences and moods of the average Jerseyman, and in several important junctures he led the candidate in significant ways. For example, when the *New York Press* charged that Wilson had said that "No man not a college graduate should hold elective or appointed office," it was Alexander who advised him on a proper response to that charge, and it was he who guaranteed Wilson space for a full rebuttal by having him interviewed for *True American*.[33] When Wilson's Republican gubernatorial opponent announced that he would govern only by constitutional methods, that he would not interfere with the legislature except when appropriate, Alexander alerted Wilson to the opportunity that statement afforded. He urged Wilson to tell the people that he would not remain inactive. To the contrary, he would remove his coat, "roll up his sleeves," employ all the powers the people had voted him, and all the strength God gave him to employ in defense of their rights. He should tell the people that he would appeal to them to help him in such an effort. Alexander prodded candidate Wilson to declare that he would be a fighting governor willing to use all his power against any obstinate legislator or political boss who impaired the public's interests. "*The people of the whole state*," he predicted, "*will be electrified by such a declaration*."[34]

Wilson took Alexander's advice and on the following day, October 3, delivered a rousing speech at Trenton. "If you elect me," Wilson asserted, "you will elect a Governor who in the opinion of Mr. Lewis [his opponent] will be an unconstitutional Governor." Then, after disclaiming all intention to employ any immoral pressure on the legislature, he declared, "Every honorable method or urging upon the legislators of this State things to do in the interests of the people of the State is assuredly constitutional, and will be resorted to by myself, if I am elected Governor." Even more to the point, he announced that he did not "regard anything that concerns the public interests as confidential" and said, "I give notice now that I am going to take every important subject of debate in the Legislature out on the stump and discuss it with the people." The legislators, he added, could also go to the public, and it would be for the people to decide whose position they preferred. It was a "perfectly even game" and also a "perfectly 'constitutional' " process, Wilson concluded.[35] Even his progressive critics applauded this declaration.

Nothing however, enhanced Wilson's press support more than his speaking appearances. The Democratic State Committee arranged for him to speak in every county and more than once in several of them. Whether or not he could reach the rank and file audience of "the Democracy" remained an open question. Before his acceptance speech at the Trenton convention, he had spoken mainly before intellectual and well-informed audiences and selected civic groups. Now, despite an unreassuring opening campaign speech on September 28, he soon proved that he could reach a popular audience. In fact, he enjoyed it. The campaign allowed him to leave the burdens of the Princeton presidency behind and to test his ideas before "the Democracy." The thought of beginning the public career he had dreamed of pursuing excited him, and almost from the start, his managers realized that their candidate was an extraordinary campaigner, a gifted political orator—one of the best the country has known.

At home on the platform, Wilson used his rhetorical skills to great advantage. He modified his speaking style to engage a varied public. By developing a simple and direct oratorical manner and yet without speaking down to his audiences, he took them into his confidence and appealed to their progressive spirit.[36] Wilson spoke in a serious way about democratic principles and current political issues, and he introduced humor, and sometimes a folksy story, into his message when illustrating a point. Moreover, here and there in his speeches, he displayed that eloquence of language which would later become one of his hallmarks in history. Such rhetoric was spontaneous with him, for he spoke with the aid of only a few rough notes. Audiences responded to his words and to his presence. They interrupted his speeches with outbursts of applause and timely laughter. He spoke to overflowing crowds in auditoriums, theaters, and court houses across the state and responded to demands for impromptu talks in many less formal settings. Crowds cheered him everywhere, even in Republican strongholds, as reports in the press indicated.[37] Considering those speeches together, it is possible to see a unifying theme emerging. It was a moderate progressive democratic one against the excesses of big business and the legislative influence of special privilege, against political bossism and legislative standpattism. Most of all, Wilson promised, if elected, to make government public. "There is no air so wholesome as the air of publicity, and the only promise I am going to make, . . . is that I will talk about government to you as long as I am able. . . . We want the contact of public affairs with public opinion. That is what we are after in this state, and that is what we are going to get."[38]

There was a refreshing aspect to his speeches that veteran campaigners appreciated. As one reporter traveling with him, one who had covered a score of campaigns, explained, "He is the most remarkable speaker I ever heard. Here we have been with him and heard all his speeches for six weeks, and yet every mother's son of us is just as anxious to hear him every time as though we had never heard him before. He is always interesting. No two speeches are alike. He sometimes makes notes, but he never refers to them during his speech."[39] Beyond his success with the spoken word, Wilson provided an abundance of what the reporters called "good stuff" for their dispatches. Unlike other politicians of the day who dressed for their stage appearances wearing frock coats and high shirt collars, Wilson appeared in a brown suit, usually baggy at the knees, and wore an ordinary shirt collar, with a four-in-hand tie. As the fall weather grew chilly, he appeared in a short black overcoat and a felt hat. He displayed none of the aloofness and haughtiness that his critics tried to fix on him. His ordinary appearance and unpretentious manner as well as his oft-expressed confidence in the innate honesty of the people and his frank answers to their questions, impressed the reporters. They discovered that the university president had many more "common" groundings than they supposed, and they found him inspiring.[40]

Reporters accompanying Wilson during the campaign were drawn not only to his ability as a speaker but also to the man. He made himself accessible to them. As the three cars carrying Wilson, Nugent, Tumulty, and a group of reporters and stenographers hurried across the state on rough, dusty, and sometimes impassable roads, candidate Wilson remained patient and congenial. He was gracious about campaign inconveniences and impromptu demands made upon him.[41] He loved telling a good story as well as listening to one, and he had an impressive reservoir of limericks to underscore a point. As for the idea that the political bosses would control him, he deemed this one appropriate:

> There was a young lady of Niger
> Who smilingly rode on a tiger.
> They returned from the ride
> with the lady inside
> and the smile on the face of the tiger.[42]

Moreover, Wilson let his regard for the reporters traveling with him be known. He often bought them together to ask their opinion on a point. If he agreed with them, he acted accordingly, and they developed an appreciation of the man. As one of them put it, "He likes to sit at the dinner table after a hard day's work and tell stories. His stories glisten with humor, and it is all pleasant and wholesome. . . . He is pleasant and companionable."[43] Wilson's modest ways, the consistency of his manner on and off the platform, his sincerity in making pledges, and his refusal to speak abusively of his opponent, impressed the reporters. One of them went so far as to say, "We have learned to love this man, whose character is the kind that lasts and not the shining sun put on for campaign purposes."[44] No single reason, of course, explains the positive, even flattering, image of Wilson that characterized the reports these journalists wrote about him, but the friendly relations he established with them and their growing personal perceptions of him, no doubt accounted for it in part.

The pro-Wilson editors left nothing to chance. He fulfilled their hopes for a reform candidate as he did their desire for an effective campaigner. They published flattering interviews with him that portrayed his human qualities and afforded him the opportunity to rebut criticism while extolling his ideas about needed reforms. In their newspapers, they presented him as a college president with the vision of a statesman and the tact of a diplomat who stood above the self-interest too often characteristic of politics. This "historian and publicist" was hardly the "schoolmaster in politics" as his opponents tried to stereotype him. In the expressed opinion of the pro-Wilson editors he was determined to promote the public good of the people of the state and had the knowledge of government necessary to do it. He was a new and better type of politician.[45] In some cases, these editors did more than cover and comment his campaign—they boosted it. This tendency appeared not only in the attention they gave him in their newspapers but also in the superlative comments they used to accompany references to him. His words were "impressive" and "stirring"; his audiences, "record breaking" and uncommonly "enthusiastic."

Figure 1 *Philadelphia Record*, October 10, 1910. Portrays Wilson's ascendancy over politicians during his 1910 gubernatorial campaign.

Newspaper reports of Lewis's campaign lacked that spark. Even in a Republican newspaper like the *Philadelphia Inquirer*, which gave Lewis greater coverage than Wilson during the campaign and believed he "ought to win out," found it difficult to publish news of Lewis with the arousing quality associated with that of Wilson. Side by side special campaign reports appearing in its columns toward the end of the campaign underscore the point. While one report described Lewis as being "warmly received" everywhere he went in Essex County, a Democratic stronghold, another report on Wilson's appearance in nearby Passaic highlighted the fact that he spoke to the largest audience ever assembled there to hear a political speaker.[46] Lewis's image in the press was that of an able and well-qualified candidate while Wilson's had an extraordinary quality about it.[47]

III

It should not be assumed, however, that Wilson escaped significant opposition in the press. First of all, Progressive newspapers like the *Hoboken Hudson Observer* and the *Trenton Evening Times*, which had fought his nomination, continued to express doubts about him after the campaign began. Claiming that it was the essential question of the campaign, the *Evening Times* wanted to know, "How much of Woodrow Wilson is Bourbon, how much progressive?"[48] It is not surprising, therefore, that as he began to appeal more and more to progressives, whether Democratic or Republican or independent, that his commitment to progressivism would be challenged. In one of his early campaign speeches, he had mentioned that he would "welcome any politician in the State to a debate upon the platform upon a public question."[49] It was only an offhand comment, but George L. Record, the most prominent New Idea leader, seized upon it.

Record, an impressive figure in New Jersey politics, was a leading progressive and a fine orator. In 1910, he not only wrote a column for the Republican *Jersey Journal* of Jersey City, but he also was a progressive Republican candidate for Congress. Reformers like Record believed that Wilson hedged his promises for reforms in generalities, and they were also still uneasy about his association with the Old Guard controllers of the Democratic party. Consequently, Record accepted Wilson's challenge to debate in public. Wilson's political managers feared a trap and advised him to avoid the challenge. At first he was inclined to accept their advice. He and Nugent decided to take up the gauntlet only if the Republican State Committee and the Republican gubernatorial candidate designated Record their spokesman. Record scoffed at that response and announced in his *Jersey Journal* column that "The great Dr. Wilson, who is to lift the politics of New Jersey to a new and higher plane, at first test has gone down to the Jim Nugent plane and commences to dodge and pettifog."[50]

Wilson knew he faced a campaign crisis. George Harvey was less than reassuring when he told Wilson that "Record's seeking the limelight . . . [was] trifling." To provide a buffer for his candidate, the editor suggested a covert plan of action. He would send his lieutenant, William Ingles, to the Library of Congress to make transcripts of Record's past comments in the *Jersey Journal* about the Republican bosses, the state legislature, and other political matters. To examine the files in the *Journal*'s office would be too obvious. Harvey believed there could be found "an abundance of material with which to convict the blatherskite out of his own mouth" and told Wilson that the object was to lead the lamb "unsuspecting to the slaughter."[51] Wilson, however, rejected the plan on the grounds that he was not opposed to stating his own views and that Record's "turgid assertions" were already well known. The candidate had decided on another course and had already contacted

Record about it. Informing Harvey of his action, he added that he had been told that "it would make a very bad impression in Hudson County if I seemed to try to dodge his onset, because of course I am trying for the votes of the New Idea Republicans, with whom he has high standing."[52]

Indeed, Wilson's progressive advisers believed the challenge could not be allowed to rest. It would appear that he was in retreat and, as a consequence, would lose the very progressive support he was beginning to attract. In particular, the publishers of the *Jersey Journal*, Joseph and Walter Dear, warned him of this outcome, and they made Wilson promise he would make a more assuring reply to Record's challenge.[53] He did so with a public letter to Record saying that although his prearranged speaking program made it impossible to arrange for the two to meet in debate, they might debate by means of letters, which could be made public. Record accepted Wilson's counter challenge, knowing that it gave him the chance to confront Wilson with the most delicate and detailed questions about Democratic bosses and big moneyed interest, questions that could lead Wilson to alienate important people and interests in his own party when he answered them.

Once again some of Wilson's advisors balked at this idea, but he refused their advice. Before replying, however, he sent for James Kerney of the *Trenton Evening Times* whom he had met during his post-nomination meeting with Smith and Nugent. Kerney had tried to prevent Wilson's nomination because of his connection to conservative politicians and financial interests. He also argued that Wilson was unconvincing in an explanation of his position in regard to labor and that he was vague on the issues. Kerney feared that Wilson, if elected, would be "managed by the Democratic machine" that nominated him, a point he reiterated in the *Trenton Evening Times* the day previous to this meeting.[54] The two men discussed campaign issues for over an hour. Wilson wanted to know what the effect would be if, in his reply to Record, he denounced the boss system, including the Democratic bosses. Kerney assured him that the effect would be great. It would guarantee the support of the state's independent newspapers and win the election for him.[55]

Record had submitted 19 pointed questions for Wilson to answer, and when he did so the day following his meeting with Kerney, he took the editor's advice. His answers were published in the major New Jersey's newspapers.[56] They won over Kerney and many other progressives. Wilson's answers were a masterful example of a forthright and convincing campaign declaration. They went straight to the core of each of

Record's questions. Yes, he favored a Public Utilities Commission having "full power to fix just and reasonable rates to be charged by all public service corporations." Yes, he supported the popular election of U.S. Senators. Yes, he favored passage of a "drastic corrupt practices act" prohibiting excessive election practices and financial contributions. Yes, he believed that industries should assume the expenses of employees injured in the proper conduct of their work. Most of all, he agreed that the boss system existed in the state. It was "notorious," "bipartisan," and yes, it constituted "the most dangerous condition in the public life of our State and nation today." How could it be abolished? By the reforms posed and affirmed in these exchanges, by the election of committed reform candidates, and by "pitiless publicity," Wilson said.[57] Wilson had gambled and won. Far from placing him in an embarrassing corner, his statement was the biggest publicity triumph of the campaign. Congratulatory letters from New Idea men and others poured into his headquarters. Walter Dear predicted that Wilson's "straight forwardness and unequivocal attitude [in his response to Record]" had won him "thousands of friends and votes."[58]

As progressive journals now aligned themselves behind Wilson, press opposition remained in other quarters. First, orthodox Republican newspapers, while often admitting the eloquence of his speeches, tried to affix various labels on him, all with derogatory intent. Accordingly, Wilson was an "ingenious academician," a "schoolmaster," a "scholastic recluse," a "dodger," and a "boss toy."[59] Regarding the last of those labels, the *Woodbury Constitution*, a stalwart Republican newspaper, stated that Wilson was a "good dog" whose sad fate it was to be associated with "bad dogs." The idea that Wilson was the candidate of the Democratic bosses was a charge that newspapers of this persuasion kept alive until the end of the campaign. The *Constitution* explained it in this way.

> It seems almost beyond the range of possibility that any intelligent voter could believe that Dr. Wilson would accept the nomination at the hands of a little coterie of Democratic bosses; be their boon companion throughout the fatiguing campaign, . . . and then, in event of his election, turn against them, and with a wave of righteous indignation command them to "depart from me, ye cursed, etc." Voters, this is not the way political matters are conducted now, ever have been, or ever will be—after election.[60]

While Wilson denied he was under the influence of anyone, it did him no good to have the *Newark Star*, owned by James Smith Jr., omit those declarations from reports of the candidate's speech, and to be caught at

Figure 2 *Paterson Daily Press*, October 3, 1910. Portrays Wilson's association with Democratic political bosses as he campaigned for the governorship of New Jersey in 1910.

it.[61] Meanwhile, Hearst's *New York American* brushed Wilson's denials aside and portrayed his nomination as the result of boss controlled politics and proclaimed him the "Candidate of Wall Street."[62]

Press criticism of Wilson assumed various forms. If it could be personal, it could also be high-minded. At their best, opposition editors argued that although Wilson was a fine candidate with progressive intentions, Lewis was equally fine and sincere, plus he had years of efficient public service behind him and was familiar with the business of the state. As to the argument that Wilson was better than his party, they admitted that point. They countered, however, that the Republican party was better than the Democratic party and had been implementing a progressive program to prove it. Why, then, vote for the untested Wilson?[63]

Sometimes opposition editors displayed little regard for the truth in their efforts to embarrass him. For instance, in order to underscore the point that he had never participated in Democratic party activities in New Jersey, the *Trenton State Gazette* stated he had only been a resident of the state for "a little more than ten years" when, in fact, he had lived there for 20 years. In order to prove Wilson's economic views "silly," and absurd, the *Woodbury Constitution* claimed that he "simply displays his ignorance of practical business affairs when he asserts there is no relation between trade and Tariff."[64] That was a clear misrepresentation of the candidate's oft-expressed views on the tariff, which ran through many of his campaign addresses. He was not against a tariff in principle, only against the high protectionist policy as reflected in the Payne–Aldrich Tariff Act of 1909 and the high-handed means that Speaker Joseph Cannon had used to force the measure through Congress.[65]

It was, however, difficult to dismiss some of the charges the opposition press made. He was, after all, a scholar with no previous political experience, and the political bosses had promoted him. At one point, a friendly and often quoted newspaper, the *Long Branch Record*, attempted to summarize and answer the charges, at least those deemed worthy of an answer, against him. It was true, it reasoned, that he was a scholar and would have to stand guilty as charged on that count, but fortunately, it was "not a hanging crime." It was also true that he lacked political experience, but "feeding at the public crib is not prescribed by law as a necessary qualification for any office." To counter the idea that he was a boss led tool of Wall Street, the *Record* offered "the story of his life and public utterances as proof of the contrary." Finally, to answer the charge that he opposed labor unions, it cited his pro-labor statements in recent speeches and his pledge to fight for effective employer's liability legislation.[66] Even such a sprightly defense did not dislodge fears of Wilson's connections with the political bosses, and concern about his past statements on organized labor. Hostile opposition newspapers like the *Woodbury Constitution* called his present efforts to win the labor vote "feeble" and a "dismal failure." "Had Dr. Wilson imagined for one moment that he would ever be selected as the Democratic candidate for Governor, it is safe to say that he would have left unsaid some of his past utterances in relation to organized labor," charged the *Constitution*. "Too late now, Professor, the labor element is not in love with any see-saw argument."[67] A number of labor leaders, who were unwilling to dismiss Wilson's past statements about unions, shared this view.

As the resolutions the New Jersey State Federation of Labor passed against Wilson's candidacy for the Democratic nomination on August 17

Figure 3 *Asbury Park Journal*, October 18, 1910. Reviews the charges brought against Wilson in his 1910 gubernatorial campaign.

had shown, his alleged abrasive ideas about unions remained an irritant for some union spokesmen. His open letter to the *American Labor Standard*, in which he claimed he had been misrepresented and had declared his positive support of labor unions, helped but failed to quell that irritation. Union spokesmen were particularly disturbed by comments about organized labor he had made in his public addresses like his baccalaureate address to Princeton's graduating class the previous year when he had claimed that some unions impaired production by limiting hours of work permitted to the level of the "least skillful" workers.[68] Although it made reference to "some" unions, the comment rankled union leaders who now sought to exploit it. Literally speaking, Wilson's reference to that practice was correct. Even one of the union leaders asking him to clarify his statements admitted that "a small minority of unions engaged in it." However, he also said that Wilson made it appear as if it were characteristic of unionism in general. Many other unionists made that same assumption.[69] They overlooked his qualifying "some," which was a slim defense in the broad contours of the political arena, and they believed an anti-union pattern could be detected in his thought. In an earlier address, in 1905, Wilson had stated that "labor unions reward the shiftless and incompetent at the expense of the able and industrious," a comment he had based on flimsy evidence.[70] The New Jersey Republican organization as well as Republican and labor newspapers knew such statements made him vulnerable, and they broadcasted and embellished them throughout the campaign.

Some labor publications were adamant in denouncing Wilson. One such journal, the *Labor World*, was published jointly in New York City and Jersey City. Even before the campaign opened, it reprinted the references to organized labor that Wilson had made the previous year in his baccalaureate address, and after reviewing his initial speech in the campaign it labeled him "A THEORETICAL, HIGHFALUTIN, HIGH-BROW," "A SOUTHERN ARISTOCRAT" at home among "THE ARISTOCRATS AND OVERLORDS." Worse yet, in that speech, Wilson gave a playful example of individual responsibility by saying that if he took a gun and shot someone whom he would "dearly love to shoot—and I could name several" that he, not the weapon, would be seized for that action. The *Labor World* responded by taking him at his word. New Jersey should not elect a man "who has the shooting idea in his heart" for it was "only fear that has kept him from shooting people." Indeed, "if he were elected Governor, he could call out the troops and have them shoot for him, indiscriminately." Moreover, since Wilson believed that good men should be elected to office, be they Republican or Democrat, the *Labor World* charged that he was no Democrat at all, for "it has always been that even a bad Democrat was better than a good Republican to elect to office."[71] As the campaign progressed, the *Labor World* praised the record of Vivian Lewis and tried to stereotype Wilson as an impractical "bookworm" without a grasp of real conditions and as the "arch-enemy of trade unionism and . . . [the] willing mouthpiece of vested rights." "BURY THIS MAN," it urged.[72]

Another means used to spread Wilson's prior statements about organized labor was the publication and dissemination of circular literature. These pamphlets and notices were bitter and unforgiving in tone. They sought to create dramatic effect by highlighting his questionable comments about unions. One cited references he made to workers as "servants" saying he intended "to give the word 'SERVANT' a menial construction." Anyone familiar with Wilson's use of the words "servant" and "service" in his speeches for years would have dispelled this interpretation, but this circular deemed such a reference as an expression worthy of an assembly of slaveholders in the antebellum South. It went on to declare that "IT IS HIS OPINION THAT MOST OF US IN THIS CLASS ARE SHIRKERS, THAT WE ARE LAYING DOWN ON OUR JOBS; . . ."[73]

The source of this campaign literature remains uncertain, but it probably originated with the Republican State Committee. Labor leaders, labor organizations, and Republican newspapers all received it. Toward the end of the campaign several labor leaders denounced this type of publicity and, at least in one case, specified that the Republicans had been circulating it in pamphlet form.[74] Moreover, the editor of the Republican *Cape May Herald* informed Wilson that the literature he received from the Republican State Committee was of such a "defamatory character that it has gone into the printer's 'hell box,' the place for refuse."[75] Finally, other demeaning literature about Wilson alleging that he was anti-Catholic and antiimmigration as well as antilabor appeared during the campaign and was believed to have been circulated by the Republican State Committee. The appearance of an advertisement in the "New Jersey Special" of the *New York Jewish Daily News* claiming that Wilson was the enemy of Jewish immigration and paid for by the Republican State Committee tends to give credence to that belief.[76] In no case, however, were the accusations of greater potential harm to his campaign than in the charge that he was antiorganized labor.

As serious as these charges and subsequent press commentary based on them were, they failed to convey the whole story of how the editors of labor newspapers treated Wilson during the campaign. Some supported him, not the least was Edgar Williamson, publisher of the *American Labor Standard*, of Orange, New Jersey, who had earlier published his open letter on labor. During the campaign, he met and corresponded with Wilson saying, "my heart has warmed to you . . . and I now know you to be the very opposite of what your enemys [*sic*] paint you to be." Williamson also said that union members had reason to support him as he declared "how ridiculous it is for the state Republican

Committee to pose as the *only union pure* friends of labor" after all the things they had failed to do for workingmen. "We poor misguided union men are hoodwinked by these crafty [Republican] politicians," Williamson said as he warned Wilson to beware of the "dirty tactics" resorted to by his opponents. Finally, the editor urged the candidate to sharpen his appeal for the labor vote, for based on his everyday association with laborers, he could report that many were "on the fence" and could "turn either way" at the election.[77] The next day in a speech at Salem and four days later in another at Elizabethport, Wilson made perhaps his strongest pro-organized labor statements of the campaign.[78]

Williamson claimed that his newspaper had a circulation of 100,000 so his support was significant.[79] Another such supporter was William Delahunty, who published the *Industrial News* in New York City. He promised Wilson to "leave no stone unturned" in his effort to "reach the great army of wealth producers in a way that will speak for itself when the votes are counted."[80] Proving himself as good as his word, his newspaper was able to editorialize after the election, "We supported him enthusiastically for the nomination and loyally in the election. We are the only paper in the country that predicted for him a majority of over forty thousand votes more than a week before his election."[81]

Although it is impossible to estimate what percentage of labor newspapers supported Wilson, it is clear they were divided about his candidacy. There is, however, circumstantial evidence of different sorts that underscores the support he did receive in the labor press. For example, on October 3, the *New York Times* reported that the Federation of Labor Leaders were "regretting the hasty action of the Federation's State Convention in its formal protests against Dr. Wilson's candidacy before he was put in nomination."[82] Also, as the end of the campaign approached, several New Jersey labor leaders made public statements on Wilson's behalf and, in some cases, attacked Lewis's record on labor legislation. Wilson, moreover, received enthusiastic welcomes when he appeared before audiences of workingmen.[83] On one occasion they demonstrated their enthusiasm in an unusual manner. The incident occurred on November 5 at Port Reading. As Wilson's entourage approached the railroad yards where dozens of Reading Railroad locomotives were parked, the engineers tied down their engines' whistles in unison. Other railroad men stood in the rain with their red lamps to block the road. Rain or no rain, they wished to greet the candidate. Afterward, arriving at the hall where he was scheduled to speak, he found the railroad men's red, white, and blue lanterns lighted to welcome him, and inside, the hall was decorated with bunting strips of the same colors. The railroad men raised "voluminous" cheers when Wilson appeared.[84] Meanwhile the legislative committee of the Brotherhood of Locomotive Engineers, the Order of Railway Conductors, and the Brotherhood of Railway Trainmen in New Jersey issued an open letter supporting Wilson to their 45,100 members in the state.[85] On the other hand, the New Jersey State Federation of Labor refused to reverse the resolution it passed in August in opposition to Wilson.[86] The labor press, therefore, reflected the division of New Jersey labor itself, but judging from the results of the election, it can be questioned how accurately the above resolutions represented the opinion of the rank and file of laborers.

IV

Nevertheless, by early November the tide of mainstream press opinion was running strong in Wilson's favor and on November 8 he won a resounding victory. He not only won by a plurality of 49,056, but he also led the Democrats in their gaining control of the state Assembly. The extent of his victory can be measured by the fact that Republican William Howard Taft had carried New Jersey by over eighty thousand votes in his bid for the presidency in 1908.[87] Wilson's backers were jubilant and the journalists friendly to him stood in the front rank of those cheering supporters. Some Republican publicists even charged that a "newspaper conspiracy" existed whose sole purpose was to win the election for Wilson. There was, in fact, no doubt that what was coming to be known as a pro-Wilson "editorial chorus" had emerged by the end of the campaign. Composed of Democratic, progressive Republican, and independent newspapers, its editors prophesied great things to come for Wilson and for New Jersey.[88]

The "editorial chorus" clearly emerged after Wilson's open letter to Record, and it became emphatic with his victory on November 8. Among the flood of congratulatory letters that then descended upon him were many from journalists who were elated by the quality of his campaign as well as by the victory itself. None was more important than the one he received from the most influential Democratic publisher in the country. "I congratulate you and your state and our republic upon your splendid victory," wrote Joseph Pulitzer, "and I must thank you warmly for the intellectual delight your great speeches have given me. Speeches truly democratic not because they serve the democratic party but because they strengthen democrats [*sic*] institutions against libels and lawlessness."[89]

Figure 4 *Newark Star*, January 23, 1911. Portrays Wilson's reliance on the progressive Republican, George Record, and the compliance of what his opponents called the "newspaper chorus."

The labor press, of course, shared Pulitzer's enthusiasm only in part, and the same could be said of the African American newspapers, then growing in political significance in the northeast.[90] Most of them struggled to stay in print, and most were small weeklies with abundant clipped content from the mainstream press and other black newspapers.[91] It cannot be expected, of course, to find the black press speaking with one voice particularly at a time when its leaders were so divided about the proper road to take to gain greater justice and opportunity. On the one side, there were those leaders who supported Booker T. Washington and his ideas of greater education and economic advancement for African

Americans along with accommodation to white society; on the other side there were the more militant leaders, like W. E. B. DuBois, who rejected Washington's ideas and demanded full equality. Black newspapers reflected this division. Some of them urged their readers to consider abandoning their loyalty to the Republican party, which they claimed was no longer the party of Lincoln, and to support at least some Democratic candidates. Consequently, the nomination of Wilson perked their interest.

Nevertheless, the response of African American newspapermen and newspapers to Wilson's nomination and campaign was only sporadic. The most important expressions came from beyond New Jersey.[92] He found an unexpected ally in William Monroe Trotter, cofounder and then editor and publisher of the *Boston Guardian*. He was a magna cum laude graduate of Harvard, the first black student elected to Phi Beta Kappa at the college, and a militant journalist whose spirited weekly was circulated across the country and often quoted in other black newspapers. Along with other prominent African American spokesmen, he was a leader of the National Independent Political League, a black organization that supported Wilson for governor of New Jersey. During the campaign he had promised he would be the governor of all of the states' people, and Trotter took this to mean that he would "treat all citizens alike." That was probably a misreading of Wilson's intention.[93] Nevertheless, when the league's secretary received Wilson's response to his initial communiqué, which suggested that he might receive its support, he termed that response "very gratifying."[94]

The area's black press questioned that sentiment. Consider the reaction of the *New York Age*, arguably the most important black newspaper in the country, to Wilson's campaign.

> Mr. Woodrow Wilson is making for himself a high name as a political campaigner; and New Jersey hears many fine words from the lips of the Cavalier turned Yankee. The Democrats are as happy as three crows in a watermelon patch. . . . The colored men of New Jersey may or may not be thinking of supporting Wilson. . . . If they are thinking . . . [of supporting him] perhaps it would be well for them to inquire into Mr. Woodrow Wilson's record at Atlanta, in Virginia, and on many public occasions when he took a shot at the Negro. . . . Also and particularly, has the color-line that disgraces Princeton tightened or slackened under Wilson? If there is no reason to vote for him [Lewis was "able" and "courageous,"] there may be many reasons to vote against him.[95]

Although the *Age*'s references to Wilson's taking shots "at the Negro" were unclear, the message the editorial conveyed was vivid enough. It identified him as a Southerner, and that alone would alienate some black voters from him. It also called attention to the exclusionist admission policy at Princeton, which Wilson continued during his presidency.

Beyond receiving their support or opposition, there was another, sad to be sure, aspect of his having the backing of black newspapers or groups. It surfaced in his correspondence. Editors like Joseph Dorsey of the black *Baltimore Crusader* might wish to back Wilson. However, whether or not such support was a political asset was a question at the time. As the secretary of the National Independent Political League put it, "I hope that our action [endorsing Wilson] will not lose you any white support." Regardless, Wilson appreciated such support.[96] "I particularly appreciate your generous confidence in my friendship for my African fellow countrymen," he appended (probably for his secretary to include in his response) to a letter of congratulations upon his election from the head of the United Colored Democracy of Manhattan and the Bronx.[97] However problematic or effective the black press may have been in Wilson's gubernatorial campaign, its surfacing interested him. Like that of the labor press, it was also an omen of the wider press attention that would characterize his political future.

There was no question, however, that the mainstream press of New Jersey and surrounding areas was a major asset in Wilson's gubernatorial victory, and it is also beyond question that he welcomed its opinion. Shortly after the election the governor-elect met with several New Jersey journalists, including James Kerney, at his home, and he startled his guests by saying that the *New York Evening Post* was the only newspaper he had time to read, that he read no New Jersey newspapers.[98] Historians have often cited that comment as evidence of Wilson's indifference to the state press. But such indifference was not the case during the campaign. Even before he was nominated, he wrote to Harvey, "Thank you very much for your note of Saturday. I take the *TRUE AMERICAN* and had seen the editorial you were kind enough to enclose."[99] Consider, too, the hundreds of press clippings found in Wilson's personal papers. Were they clipped for utilitarian purpose or only for posterity? As evidence, they are only suggestive, not conclusive. More convincing of his sensitivity to the state's press was his correspondence with editors and publishers of New Jersey newspapers. In their letters to him these journalists often enclosed their own articles or sometimes those from other area newspapers. Nor was it unusual for them to comment on the current of public opinion on various campaign matters. Their correspondence with him also indicates that he was prompt and courteous in his responses to them. In those responses, he might even invite their suggestions, in his words, "as they arise" throughout the campaign.[100]

Finally, he also drew on the opinion of the state's newspapers through his association with some of its leading practitioners. His relationship with Henry Ekert Alexander, James Kerney, Joseph and Walter Dear, and others underscores how he welcomed and acted upon their advice. So long as they did not vary from pursuing their own political ideals and retained their own freedom of expression and advocacy, they felt within the boundaries of journalistic ethics when they boosted and counseled candidates for office. In Wilson's case, they found an inspiring candidate. As has been seen, this was also true of the reporters covering him, and unlike some of his earlier and later frustrations with reporters, he appears to have been comfortable and even friendly with them during the campaign. There was, indeed, every reason to believe that he had built up an abundance of goodwill among New Jersey journalists and that, in the months ahead, he could expect a continuation of compatible relations with them and the support of a friendly press.

Chapter 5
Governor Wilson and the Press, 1910–11

Neither Wilson's plunge into politics nor the press's interest in it slackened after his election. The period from his November victory extending through the spring of the following year marks a distinct and action-filled time in his political evolution. During the campaign, he had repeated his belief in "government by public opinion," and in using the "air of publicity" to purify politics.[1] The press had an obvious role to play in this promised mobilization of public opinion, for as Wilson put it, when newspapers were "public instruments," in touch with and serving the public, they were "capable of great good."[2] He hoped, of course, that a press so committed would support him during his tenure as governor. As it turned out, a political crisis occurred even before Wilson's inauguration, one that stirred intense feelings in the press of the area. Following its resolution, as the state legislature debated the main planks of his reform program, he proved to be the engaged governor that his supporters had prophesied. It was also at this time that he developed the style of press relations that would characterize his governorship. Finally, a movement began, with journalists in the forefront, to advance the governor as a candidate for the presidency.

I

The crisis Wilson faced in the wake of his election centered on James Smith, Jr. Before the euphoria of victory settled down, he informed the governor-elect that he wished to return to the U.S. Senate. Prior to this announcement, Wilson had assurances that Smith would not be a candidate for election to this office. The former senator reiterated that decision at various times until after the election. His change of mind placed Wilson in a precarious position. Judged by his own standards, he was a formidable Irish American leader. With his genial demeanor and imposing presence, he did not fit the stereotype of an old-fashioned political boss, but as has been seen, the wealth and influence he commanded made him a powerful figure in New Jersey politics. Wilson owed his election to Smith, as much as he did to anyone. However, if he failed to stop Smith's bid for the Senate, it would appear that his repeated campaign declaration that he was free of any pledge or any kind of deal was a mere political subterfuge. The November elections complicated the matter even more. They produced an unexpected Democratic majority vote for the state legislature, which would name the next U.S. Senator in January. Also in the November elections, James Martine received the Democratic majority for the senatorial position, but according to the prevailing New Jersey law, that primary vote was not binding on the state legislature.

Smith, therefore, began his own campaign for the position in the weeks following the election. Moving in his customary way, he won the support of Robert Davis, the Democratic boss of Hudson County, and tried to persuade the Democratic legislators-elect to pledge themselves to his candidacy. Martine, a Bryan Democrat and well-liked state politician known as "Farmer Jim," had run for many state offices without ever being elected. The fact that he had neither Smith's influence nor his ability, made the latter's candidacy more plausible. Nevertheless, if the legislature sent Smith to the Senate, it would make a sham of Wilson's fight against the bosses.

The problem could not be evaded. As soon as Smith's intentions became known, progressives from across the state pressured Wilson to stand firm against it. To them it was a classic issue pitting, in the words of the *Hoboken Observer*, "the forces of democracy" against "the beneficiaries of special privilege." By such reasoning, Boss Smith and his supporters were "cohorts of greed and graft in the dark" who had behind them all the "subterranean agencies" and "powers of darkness" in the state.[3] Wilson's campaign performance had helped to dispel fears that the inexperienced "professor" would be duped by mischievous and self-serving political bosses. Nevertheless, whether or not he would be able to act upon his declarations against the boss system and establish his freedom from it remained a question. Progressives of all kinds (politicians, professional people, and ordinary citizens) sensing the consequences of Wilson's response to Smith's challenge took it upon themselves to write to the governor-elect urging him to stand by his campaign promises.[4] Progressive journalists, with their hope for a new era in New Jersey politics buoyed by the election, were prominent among these petitioners.

William W. St. John, founder of the *Elizabeth Evening Times* and organizer of the Trenton News Bureau, was the first major journalist urging Wilson to confront the issue by countering Smith. At this time he wrote a syndicated political letter from Trenton. A veteran progressive, he believed that Wilson was also a "genuine" progressive. He had, moreover, been instrumental in persuading Martine to enter the primary. On the eve of Wilson's election, St. John laid out the facts before Wilson in an explicit letter. The Democrats would win the legislature the next day; the matter of the senatorship should not be a problem; Democratic voters had already confirmed the candidacy of Martine by means of the primary. "As perhaps you may already know, such influential newspapers as the Newark Evening News, the Jersey City Journal, the Hoboken Observer and the Trenton Times, not to say anything of many other smaller papers, are committed to the principle of accepting the result of the direct primary voting on the Senatorship." Then he urged Wilson to make a public statement to that effect.[5] He reinforced this line of argument when he spent the afternoon of the next day with Wilson at his Princeton residence.

Other journalists soon offered Wilson their advice on this matter, in some cases responding to his request for their opinions. For instance, James Kerney began one of his letters to Wilson on the subject, "Answering yours of the 3rd inst., I think my personal attitude on the senatorial situation is best expressed in the position of the Times," a clipping he enclosed with his reply.[6] In another instance, the editor of the *Bergen County Democrat* of Hackensack answered that he was "pleased to advise that my views regarding the selection of Mr. Martine as U.S. Senator are entirely in accord with those expressed by you."[7] Some editors warned the governor-elect of the consequence of Smith's quest for the senatorship. His winning "despite any promises of Nugent and Davis, would give their style of politics such an impetus that it would not be possible to get any reform legislation this winter," cautioned James Kerney.[8] Wilson also consulted Joseph A. Dear of the *Jersey Journal* about how to proceed in this matter. Dear urged Wilson either to make a public appeal to the legislature or to issue a "public letter to the voters."[9]

The most emphatic advice came from one of Wilson's original promoters for office, Henry Watterson, who urged him to take up the gauntlet that Smith had thrown down. Appeal to the people, the famous Kentuckian urged. "Smith is a wolf and the rest are of the same species. Publicity, publicity, and again publicity, is the killing dose to such predatories." Wilson should take the field, make "aggressive war," proclaim "the moral issue," and reassert the personality that won him the election, the editor urged with his characteristic rhetorical flare. "Win this fight in the open—so that all men may see and know—and the rest will follow; complete possession of the local machinery and a place of vantage in the national field."[10] It is doubtful that Watterson's friend George Harvey would have agreed with those sentiments, but New Jersey's progressive newspapers did. They urged the author of the slogan "Publicity, pitiless publicity" to put that formula into action.[11] Was New Jersey's "Democracy AN HONEST PARTY or is it merely A POLITICAL FRAUD?" asked the *Trenton Times*. The answer was Wilson's to give.[12]

His first impulse was to avoid deciding in favor of either Smith or Martine. Instead, he believed that the preferential ballot designating Martine as the Democratic candidate was inconclusive, and he preferred to have the Democrats send someone of exceptional qualifications to Washington. He had in mind John R. Hardin, an outstanding lawyer whom he had known since student days at Princeton. Such a tactic soon proved unworkable as the press made the Smith–Martine matter urgent news, and as progressives continued to press Wilson to announce in favor of Martine. Two of these progressives, Martin P. Devlin and Joseph Tumulty, shared in that effort, and later Wilson claimed that it was Devlin who had most influenced him on the issue. The governor-elect, however, enjoyed the company of both of these Irishmen. Needing someone with intimate knowledge of New Jersey politics as his private secretary, Wilson turned to Tumulty who had delivered speeches on his behalf during the campaign. Considering Tumulty "one of the ablest" young Democrats in his state, Wilson designated him for the position, an appointment that pleased New Jersey progressives. The pressure these men and others exerted on Wilson produced results. He plunged into the Smith–Martine affair in a way that made him a champion of New Jersey progressivism, proving himself, in the words of the *Philadelphia North American* "a first rate fighting man."[13]

It would be hard to fault that observation. Once committed to the fray, he acted in the manner of a combatant. First, he met with Smith to persuade him to withdraw his name. When that failed, he wrote an explicit letter to Harvey for him to share with Smith. Respectful toward Smith though it was, the letter failed to produce results. Next, Wilson tried to dissuade Robert. Davis, the Democratic chieftain of Jersey City, only to find Davis was committed to Smith. After another futile meeting with Smith, he gave a public statement to the newspapers in which he delineated, closely following St. John's original line of argument, reasons why the election of Martine was the principled course to take. Then he took the battle into Smith's own bailiwick by inviting the Essex County legislators-elect to meet with him. By the end of December, Wilson had presented his case to most of the Democratic legislators-elect. He then released a review of the controversy and its progress to the newspapers. Finally, in the first week of the new year, he delivered a rousing speech on the subject in Jersey City, followed a week later by a second one in Newark. All the while, journalists in and beyond the state maintained a steady production of editorials supporting him and many sent personal letters of appreciation and encouragement as well. Wilson was so deluged with letters of this kind from journalists and other progressive-minded people that he had to resort to a brief form letter to thank them for their generous support.

Still Boss Smith refused to acquiesce in the publicity battle over his nomination. He employed not only all his political influence but also every journalistic weapon his Newark newspapers commanded. Those two newspapers, the morning and evening *Star*, attacked Wilson with headlines, news reports, and political cartoons. Only a month before, the once pro-Wilson *Star* proclaimed that he represented a "popular revolution" and "truth and sincerity" in his campaign. Now it found him out of touch with public sentiment, inept in his dealings with Essex County politicians, and a dupe of Republican party leaders, especially George Record, whom the *Star* labeled the "Apostle of Discord." The *Star* also claimed that Wilson was working in secret with a "chorus of four state papers none of them Democratic" in order to create an "overwhelming popular sentiment for Martine."[14]

The *Star*'s personnel were also known to cast journalistic ethics aside in advancing Smith's chances. One friendly editor told Wilson:

> A representative of the Star called at my office this afternoon and requested me to "dope out" a good half column or so about the "growing preponderance" of Smith sentiment in this locality, and the great revulsion of feeling caused by Governor Wilson's adoption of George L. Record as a political advisor. To my objection that I knew of but two men in this entire section who could be construed as in any way favorable to Smith his reply was, "It doesn't make any difference about the *truth* of it; we want a good local Smith story, and you can write it, and will be well paid for it. It's a mere matter of business, and your personal preference doesn't make any difference to us."[15]

Of course, such disreputable practices were not unique at that time, but like the rest of Smith's efforts to win by wielding his influence, this desperate tactic was to no avail. Almost without exception, Democratic, independent, and progressive newspapers in the state remained steadfast behind Wilson.[16] A week after Wilson's inauguration as Governor of New Jersey on January 17, the legislature dealt with the issue of electing a U.S. Senator. Smith received three votes. Martine received 47, placing him far ahead of Smith and well in front of his closest Republican rival. The once powerful Newark Democratic boss had been trounced by the legislators, by the press, and by the court of public opinion. As for Martine, having won the right to represent his state in the U.S. Senate, he did so without distinction.

The fight with Smith was a landmark in Wilson's growth as a political leader. Progressives, regardless of party affiliation, deemed it not only a glorious victory, but also a confirmation of Wilson's own commitment to progressivism and his emergence as a statesman. Indeed, the excitement about his victory over the bosses reverberated across the country. Newspapers near and far had followed his fight with Boss Smith, leading the *Jersey Journal* to editorialize, "As an advertisement Woodrow Wilson is one of the greatest assets New Jersey could possess. He has fixed the attention of the whole country upon this state. He represents the type of statesmanship which recalls early days when men labored or died for their country. He has brains, character, eloquence, originality, tact and courage."[17] James Kerney, now a leading editor of the pro-Wilson "chorus," believed the fight with Smith was the "real contest" that landed Wilson in the White House two years later.[18] For the present, it created momentum for his reform program as governor.

The major reforms Wilson achieved in New Jersey occurred early in his governorship—by the end of the legislative session of 1911 on April 23. After that he divided his time between the governorship and campaigning for the presidency. At the start of the session, the fate of progressive legislation in the state lay with him, and his ability to guide it along heightened the national attention already focused on him. Passage of a reform program could not be guaranteed. Smith and Nugent were now alienated from him, and the Republicans still controlled the state Senate. Wilson had written and campaigned on a platform that had four main planks: the extension of direct primaries, control of public utilities, workingmen's compensation legislation, and corrupt practices legislation. They struck at the base of boss rule, trimmed corporate excesses, and expanded popular participation in government.

In championing the legislation, Wilson proved himself a fast learner of New Jersey politics. He engineered the legislative and popular

Figure 5 Trenton Evening Times, April 25, 1911. Portrays New Jersey's satisfaction with Governor Wilson's program.

support for the measures, using a variety of political tactics. Reaching out to progressives in both parties, he established constructive relations with the opposition party in the Assembly and even had his old adversary, the Republican politician and publicist George Record, use his detailed knowledge of the issues involved to prepare the preliminary drafts of the reform bills. Wilson also welcomed the advice of other insurgents, from Martin Devlin and William St. John—and, of course, from his private secretary, Joseph Tumulty—during the months when the bills were being debated. He included editors of the four major independent newspapers in the state in a bipartisan conference about the reforms at the start of the session. In February he made the case for the bills in addresses before an assembly of the state's editors and several state boards of trade. Smith's *Newark Star* railed against Wilson, accusing him of being a dictatorial governor pushed by an "editorial chorus" and charged that he was an ingrate willing to damage the Democratic party, and even willing to accept advice from the Republican progressive, George Record.[19] Meanwhile, Democratic party chairman Nugent did all he could to hold his party in line against the reforms. In March, Wilson summoned Nugent to his office for a showdown regarding their differences, particularly over the extension of direct primaries. Allowing their tempers to flare, Nugent accused Wilson of using patronage to coerce legislators, and Wilson curtly dismissed him from the office. It became clear, indeed, that Wilson was a fighting governor when news of the confrontation was leaked and featured in newspapers across and beyond the state. Also in March, Wilson took the unprecedented step of appealing before a Democratic caucus to argue the details of the legislation.

By the end of April, the major reforms the governor sought were on the statute books. Progressive editors were delighted with his performance and so was Edgar Williamson. He was spreading good news about Wilson, as indicated by an article in his *Labor Standard* by a writer he called "one of the ablest men in the American Federation of Labor." Entitled "DR. WILSON MAKING GOOD AS GOVERNOR," it matched organized labor's original questions about him against his record and concluded, "Today a large number of thinking men in the movement of labor look upon him as a friend and man upon whom the people can rely, something rare or practically unknown in the political world."[20] Support for that sentiment was in evidence at the annual convention of the State Federation of Labor held on August 21 in Camden. There, in the presence of representatives of 108 labor organizations, President Cornelius Ford of Hoboken rose to say:

> Knowing that men of labor will give credit where credit is due, I take this opportunity of repeating at this convention that labor has never had a better friend in regard to legislation during the past session of the New Jersey Legislature than Governor Wilson.
>
> Every measure introduced for and by labor received not only encouragement from the chief executive of the state, but all bills passed in the interest of wage earners received the Governor's signature.[21]

It was, however, Wilson's one-time challenger who caught the tenor of elation being expressed by the main body of reform-minded journalists. Writing in his *Jersey Journal* column, George Record said, "This is a remarkable record of achievement which a few months ago seemed as remote and impossible as could possibly be imagined." He credited the achievement to the long struggle that, in large part, progressive

Republicans had made on its behalf and "in part to the truly wonderful leadership of Governor Wilson. Without him nothing of substantial importance would have been passed."[22]

Record was right on both counts. The progressive impulse was, by no means, a new phenomenon in New Jersey, and the Republican majority in the state's Senate and the progressive Republican minority in its Assembly had supported Wilson's program. Had the latter joined with the Democratic opposition in the Governor's own party, his program of reform would have gone down in defeat. Wilson made it a bipartisan effort and provided the leadership necessary for its successful conclusion. Even the venerable Republican *New York Tribune* said that "it would be unjust and churlish not to give the highest credit to governor Wilson" for this achievement.[23] Only the most adamant conservative newspapers withheld their acclaim for this legislative achievement.[24]

II

As part of the leadership style that was proving successful for him, the governor nurtured friendly relations with the press. He engaged in correspondence with newspaper editors and publishers, welcomed their advice, and tried to answer their queries. No doubt they appreciated his many letters thanking them for support, ones that James Kerney termed "handsome letters of appreciation" that Tumulty urged him to write.[25] A cordial and attentive host, Wilson also granted private audiences to them upon request, and took their advice on various matters. When debate about his proposed reforms began in the legislature, he appeared before the New Jersey Editorial Association to outline, in precise language, the measures that embodied his platform pledges.[26]

The governor was no less accommodating for reporters and correspondents. He maintained an open door policy at Trenton as part of his promise to take the public into his confidence. "Everybody is accustomed to seeing the Governor whenever they want to," wrote one reporter. "No Governor within the present generation has devoted so much of his time to the business of the State and to meeting those who come 'to see the Governor' as has Mr. Wilson."[27] Well into his tenure as governor, reporters, too, could benefit from that privilege. Wilson also received the correspondents as a group in his office for their daily "seance" at least once a day while the legislature was in session. Sometimes he met them during the day; other times, late in the evening.[28] Equally beneficial to the reporters was the room designated for their use. Located across the hall from the governor's office, it allowed them to observe the coming and going of visitors.[29]

Late in January, Wilson seized the opportunity to appear before Washington correspondents at the National Press Club for their annual "Hobby Night." The journalists invited six prominent figures to speak for ten minutes about their hobbies. When it was Wilson's turn to talk, he spoke impromptu and continued a theme introduced by the previous speaker, the popular British Ambassador James Bryce, who had remarked about British and American newspapermen. Reaching the main point of his comments, Wilson stated, "My hobby, if I have any, is the hobby of publicity," linking his thoughts to newspapers and to the responsibility they had in the type of publicity he favored.

> There is a very clear reason, in my mind, why so few newspaper men have universally influential views. It is because our newspaper men are connected with newspapers that are known *not* to be disengaged from private interests. If you can once establish the reputation that you are speaking, . . . from the view point of the common interest then your views will be influential, and in proportion as they are disinterested they will be influential.[30]

That comment was consistent with other public statements he had made about newspapers in recent years and also with his own oft-repeated belief in the virtue of serving the public good.

While referring to the press in this manner hardly implied a new departure in his political philosophy, it was an important public statement to make. It positioned him, once again, in step with the progressive impulse and its emphasis on open politics as a remedy for the sins of special interests. The newsmen, moreover, knew of what he spoke, for critics both without and within their ranks were also attacking those newspapers that placed private above public interests. As one critic wrote, "A journal whose news columns are prostituted to the interest of a faction or a 'Boss' does not deserve the name of a newspaper. The same is true of a journal subsidized by private interest of any kind to tamper with the news."[31] Will Irwin, the best known press critic of the day, also singled out private interests as one of the corrupting influences of the press. He told Senator Robert La Follette that a peculiar kind of newspaper had grown up in the past few years.

> It is known, roughly, among newspaper men as the "kept sheet." It is owned by a man of great wealth and many interests and kept not so much to make money as to further his other interests. In that class are the Milwaukee Free Press and to a certain degree the Sentinel . . . and

> the Cincinnati Times-Star. It is notorious that Charles P. Taft does not calculate to make much money out of the Times-Star. He gets his coin out of it in other ways, through its service to his larger interests.[32]

Press critics were not alone in raising this charge.

In fact, none other than William Randolph Hearst also recognized how private, outside interests shaped the policy of some newspapers. To an associate he explained:

> When a financier buys stocks or bonds in a newspaper, it is usually in the effort to control the policy of the newspaper in some way, or to put the newspaper under certain obligations to him. A newspaper that can be so controlled is generally a worthless sheet, to begin with, and if it is not absolutely worthless, the control of its policy in the interest of any financial clique speedily makes it absolutely worthless.[33]

Hearst cited the *New York Sun* and the *Chicago Interocean* as two newspapers in the process of failing because of this type of financial interference. It was, of course, only necessary for Wilson to think of Boss Smith's newspapers in Newark to find an example closer to home.

At the bottom of this line of press criticism was the idea that newspapers should be independent of private interests just as they should be independent of political parties. The argument that the press was, in the main, a vehicle for public information and that it should advance society's goals had been growing for decades. Progressive era reformers held that the mainstream press should be honest in promoting the common welfare, that it was a quasi-public institution.[34] As for the role of reporters, in the opinion of a newspaper like the *Trenton True American*, they, legislative reporters in particular, were "public servants" who worked for newspapers but were conscious of their "duty to the people" of the state.[35] That Wilson shared such beliefs positioned him more and more on the progressive side of politics, and it helps to explain why Washington journalists were anxious to observe him in person.

Their interest in this governor had been running high. Now they had their first chance to meet him, and they were not disappointed. He impressed the two hundred or so newspapermen gathered that evening not only with his speech but also with the way he engaged them afterward, providing direct answers to all their questions. "WILSON CAPTURES WASHINGTON FOLK: Pleases and Amazes by Frankness in Answering Questions," one newspaper headlined its report of the evening.[36] "Wilson Well Received at Capital: Makes Great Impression on Washington Newspaper Men," ran another.[37] One journalist wrote to him, "Your . . . talk before the Press Club is the talk of the town, and I am not exaggerating when I say it was the chief topic of conversation in the press galleries today, which are the daily rendezvous of 180 correspondents."[38] Since his election victory, the Washington correspondents had perceived Wilson as a possible candidate for president in 1912, and his performance before them on "Hobby Night" confirmed that perception. Some contended that it might even be forced by public sentiment.[39]

Meanwhile, back in New Jersey, Wilson continued to nurture friendly relations with journalists. Sometimes he shared with them the lighter side of his personality usually confined to his private life. One such time occurred at the Legislative Correspondents Club's annual banquet in March. Styled after the annual celebration of the Gridiron Club in Washington, the banquet was one of the biggest events held in the state. U.S. Senators and congressmen, state senators and assemblymen, and, of course, the governor were all in attendance for an evening of banter and humor. Usually none of the guests were expected to speak, but the toastmaster broke that custom by introducing Wilson to address the group. When he stood up a burst of amusing barbs and a comic imitation of the Princeton cheer greeted him. According to a news report, he rose to the occasion with a smile and "as fast as the digs and dashes were thrown at him he handed them back goodnaturedly." Finally permitted to speak, he gave a short humorous address in keeping with the spirit of the evening.[40]

Despite his generally friendly relations with reporters, his old frustration with them sometimes reappeared. Indeed, on one occasion he rebuked a Trenton newspaper correspondent. Wilson felt that since assuming office he had been subjected to misrepresentation in press reports. When a report appeared about his confrontation with Nugent stating that the governor had "threatened to use fisticuffs" on the Democratic State Committee chairman, he could no longer restrain his irritation. Determined that this sensationalized distortion could not be allowed to stand, he sought out the responsible reporter, Charles A. Kelly, and sharply reproved him not to write about him again in that manner. His action in this instance was not unique. Others had found it necessary to respond to similar cases of false news reporting. Wilson's predecessor, Governor John Franklin Fort, had to denounce a reporter for publishing false information about him. Other news stories, either sensational or fictitious, originating in Trenton and mostly traceable to Kelly, had led the secretary of the city's Chamber of Commerce to confront the errant reporter in the belief that such stories damaged the city's reputation. In Wilson's case, local newspapers presented the misrepresentations as a case of "newspaper faking" traceable to the demands "yellow" journals made on their reporters. While contending that most reporters were honest in their newsgathering, the *Trenton Times* believed the governor's action would encourage the "greatly needed reform" of those who were devious in their work.[41] Regardless, incidents of this sort could rekindle his old displeasures with reporters, but for the most part, Wilson was patient in his dealings with them.[42] Until late in his governorship, he remained accessible to reporters and enjoyed lighthearted moments with them. Typical of those friendly times, as Kerney recalled, "the Trenton newspaper correspondents frequently strolled along the river bank with Wilson, and he delighted them with his yarns."[43]

Friendly editors and publishers in New Jersey were also pleased with the way Wilson tried to accommodate them, as evidenced by their numerous letters to him.[44] Yet, at times, either his insensitivity to or ignorance of the practical matter of releasing news could frustrate them. In several cases, they felt his announcement of important news placed their newspapers at a disadvantage. Joseph A. Dear, whose *Jersey Journal* was supporting Wilson, complained to him about a news story that had appeared in the *Hoboken Observer* regarding the then governor-elect's planned visit to Jersey City. "That you should arrange for such a visit and leave us entirely out of the reckoning, thus enabling the Observer to print the story, and us to be beaten on it, is not at all to our liking," he began, and then continued with this defense of his criticism:

> We are asking for no favors, yet you must realize that some of the most effective assistance you received from any newspaper during your campaign was rendered by the Jersey Journal. Furthermore, you cannot be ignorant of the fact that the Observer did all it possibly could to prevent your nomination. Under these circumstances, we might at least look for sufficient consideration from you to prevent us from being beaten by a story like this in our own county.
>
> I know the running of a newspaper is not your business, . . . still, I do not think that we should have been placed in a position of such disadvantage.[45]

A few weeks later Edward W. Scudder, editor of the *Newark Evening News* and one of Wilson's former students at Princeton, raised a different complaint. He said it related "to a matter of quite serious importance to us" and to Wilson in his present position. Scudder was writing during the Smith–Martine controversy, at a point when word was spreading that Wilson was about to issue another statement defining his position. Would it be possible for him to release it for the afternoon rather than the morning papers? There were only five prominent morning newspapers in the state. Most of New Jersey's large newspapers were afternoon publications. Indeed, the *Evening News* alone had a circulation about equal to the combined circulation of the five prominent morning newspapers. By releasing statements to the morning newspapers, Wilson was placing the large afternoon journals in the same position as out-of-state publications. "It does seem to me," Scudder argued, "that a New Jersey Governor ought to give the largest part of the New Jersey press an equal show with the out-of-state papers."[46] Complaints of this sort ceased after Tumulty assumed his position as Wilson's secretary. Then the chief concern centered on the newspapers and news services receiving advance copies of the governor's speeches, an ongoing problem for them since Wilson continued, with only occasional exception, to speak from rough notes.[47] These complaints and suggestions, of course, came from journalists friendly to him, to his reform program, and even to his chances of becoming the Democratic presidential nominee in 1912.

III

It is interesting to see how active early-twentieth-century journalists could be in promoting candidates for office. Vestiges of the partisan journalism of the previous century were still present even as more and more newspapers declared their political independence. The line separating their private and professional endeavors was less well demarcated than it would become later in the century. Editors and publishers like George Harvey and Henry Ekert Alexander, and many others too, sensed no conflict of interest between their political activism and the positions they held as journalists. They encouraged Wilson to seek high office and then advised him in private as he pursued that goal, supporting him in print in a manner that was far from even handed. Their brand of support was never more apparent than it was after he became governor as they began to promote him for the presidency.

Of course, the idea that Wilson could be a presidential candidate in 1912 was hardly a new revelation in the spring of 1911. Harvey had plotted it for years, and Wilson enthusiasts speculated about it from the time of his success in the gubernatorial contest. Joseph Pulitzer, for one, recognized Wilson's presidential potential and, upon his election, took steps to "present Dr. Wilson's Presidential possibilities to the press and to the country."[48] He initiated plans to have Wilson's campaign speeches produced and distributed in pamphlet form, and he directed his papers to support the governor's efforts in New Jersey. "As to the Presidency," he told his editors, "build up Wilson on every suitable occasion showing the greatest possible sympathy for and appreciation of his remarkable talents and character."[49] Pulitzer had speculated about Wilson as a possible presidential candidate since 1907, but felt some reserve should be shown in discussing him. To George Harvey, he confided, "I admire him greatly, but there are others. It is too soon. We must see what he does."[50] Pulitzer, moreover, wanted to retain his journalistic independence. "With the greatest admiration for Wilson and [the] hope that he may be President, I would not hesitate to say what I think," he told the editor of his *World*. In the early stages of the Smith–Martine controversy, for instance, Pulitzer doubted that Smith was corrupt and that Martine was fit for office. Should his doubts prove correct, he advised his editor to "criticize Wilson instantly. . . . Yes that is what I call independence."[51]

Wilson's performance at Trenton soon reassured Pulitzer's hopes for the governor's presidential chances. At one point, the great publisher reflected to his editor that it was "difficult to separate reputation from ability." He believed that both reputation and ability depended on opportunity.[52] More and more, he recognized that Wilson could, with his political ability proven and his reputation enhanced, achieve the nation's highest office. Both in private conversation and through his newspapers, Pulitzer worked to help Wilson take advantage of that opportunity, but more than the support of even the most influential Democratic publisher in the country would be required for Wilson to become president.

Where could that support be found? Wilson had already alienated Democratic machine politicians in New Jersey and beyond, and, with his attacks on "special interests," he had caused unease among financiers, including those who had supported him earlier. While the governor's works and actions caused chagrin among defenders of the status quo, they appeared to confirm his progressive credentials. However, Senator Robert LaFollette of Wisconsin was the leader for many progressives; William Jennings Bryan, for others. Nor could Wilson, at this point, match the deep-rooted national popularity of former president Theodore Roosevelt should he decide to run again in 1912. There was, however, a Wilson-for-President movement emerging composed of his old and new friends and supporters, reform-minded progressive political figures across the country, and, in many cases, influential journalists joined its ranks. Moreover, journalists even directed the movement in various instances, and throughout were crucial to its success. At first the movement lacked cohesion and had a reluctant candidate to champion, but it gained a rudimentary organization in the spring of 1911 as Wilson became a more willing candidate.

The movement eased forward by several means. From the start, for instance, Wilson-for-President Clubs sprang up in the East and South. Princeton alumni, Wilson's former students, and progressives whom Wilson impressed took the lead in organizing the clubs, and their numbers continued to grow up to the months preceding the election. This type of spontaneous enthusiasm for Wilson surfaced, especially in the South, soon after he began his governorship. In February 1911, George D. Armistead of the *San Antonio Daily Express* wrote to Wilson urging him to visit Texas and attend the State Fair in Dallas the next fall. To that prodding he added: "By that time there will be Wilson for President Clubs scattered all over the state. . . . One year hence I expect all the world to look on your nomination as something inevitable."[53]

These spontaneous efforts on his behalf were indicative of Wilson's popularity and potential as a presidential candidate, but they represented only one element of the movement to propel him to the White House. His term as governor had just begun when a number of journalists began to advance the possibility of his nomination in 1912; none with greater determination than the irrepressible Colonel Harvey.[54] He was jubilant after Wilson's gubernatorial victory in New Jersey, and in an editorial entitled "To Be Continued," he reviewed the role *Harper's Weekly* had played in promoting his political rise. "We now fully anticipate the nomination of Woodrow Wilson for President of the United States by the Democratic national convention of 1912," he concluded.[55] Although Wilson's break with former Senator Smith distressed the editor, who was still close to the senator, he put the best construction possible on it in an effort to retain party harmony. Harvey explained in his *Weekly* that it had been a struggle between an old and a new order, and that Smith, though a strong partisan, was "a good sportsman." As for Wilson, he displayed courage in appealing to public opinion, an action that captured the public's imagination and won him "universal commendation." He was the "Knight Errant of the New Democracy," and his nomination to oppose William H. Taft's reelection bid was now assured.[56] Despite Wilson's increasingly progressive stance, the editor was beginning the next phase of his drive to make him president, as subsequent articles in the *Weekly* and a longer, more analytical editorial, "The Political Predestination of Woodrow Wilson," in his *North American Review*, would show.[57] In private Wilson commented, "Colonel

Harvey has again become eloquent, and ingenious, on the subject of my being the Democratic nominee for the president."[58]

Harvey published his most ambitious endorsement of Wilson's nomination at this stage of his campaign five months later, in April. In another long article in the *North American Review*, he tried to describe the deepest problems facing the nation. It was a generous, broad-minded analysis arguing that "co-operation, a drawing together in frank and unselfish tolerance of one another's opinions, is positively essential to the settlement of every great question." Reflecting that "great occasions find great men," Harvey then directed his pen toward Wilson whom he presented as a son of the South, but a national figure, who bore comparison to Thomas Jefferson and James Madison as a champion of the people and as a proponent of national harmony.[59] Eloquent, clear, and forceful, here was Harvey at his best. Upon reading it, Wilson commented, "Colonel Harvey has broken loose again. . . . He pays me a really beautiful tribute. I wish that it were deserved. I should like to be the true original of such a portrait."[60]

Harvey and other eastern editors and publishers were not the only journalists taking an interest in Wilson's presidential possibilities. Southern editors also led in the expansion of his "editorial chorus," and they hurried to inform him of their enthusiasm through personal correspondence. "Georgians and The Georgian are intensely interested in your campaign for the governorship of New Jersey, and I am not sure but that your campaign is being watched with more eagerness than even those in our neighboring states," wrote the managing editor of the *Atlanta Georgian* in a typical communiqué.[61] There was nothing tentative in the interest these southern journalists were taking in Wilson. "We don't even know that you would like to be president," George D. Armistead of the *San Antonio Daily Express* wrote to Wilson. "We are going to elect you anyway. All we ask of you is to keep the course that you seem to have marked out."[62] Equally direct was this word from Charles J. Harkrader of the *Bristol* (Va.–Tenn.) *Herald Courier* who, writing shortly after Wilson's election, told him, "You are unquestionably the choice of the democracy of the south [*sic*] for president in 1912 and I believe that with you at the head of our ticket the result will be a repetition of what happened on Nov. 8. . . . The south [*sic*] believes in you; believes in your honesty and sincerity of purpose and in your ideas of public service." It is worth noting, however, that some southern journalists like Harkrader, still considered Wilson a conservative, albeit a "wise" one.[63] Progressive southern journalists had a different view of him.

Along with progressive politicians throughout the region, these journalists were among Wilson's most enthusiastic promoters. To explain his pulling power among these southern progressives who were anything but a cohesive group here as elsewhere, several things should be kept in mind. First, southern progressivism was a movement that occurred in the post-disfranchisement South and was, in the words of C. Vann Woodward, "for whites only."[64] Wilson's southern roots were reassuring on this point. Second, the movement had both conservative and populist roots and appealed to whites whom the contemporary historian of the new South, Edward L. Ayers, describes as "neither reactionary diehards nor Populist radicals."[65] In the main it was an urban, middle-class movement in favor of curtailing industrial and commercial plutocracy, of ending corrupt machine politics for a return of representative government to the people, and of fostering economic reforms—particularly a lower tariff.[66] Wilson championed these ideas, too.

Of all the southern progressive journalists, Josephus Daniels deserves particular notice as a Wilson enthusiast. Through editing various newspapers in his native state of North Carolina, he had practiced journalism since 1889 before acquiring the *Raleigh News and Observer* in 1894. Under his editorship until 1913, the *News and Observer* (the "Old Reliable" or the "Nuisance and Disturber," as it was variously known) became the "Democratic Bible" of North Carolina, and in the process, Daniels became the dominant political editor of the state, a Jeffersonian Democrat, emphatic in his belief that "all Special Privilege is robbery of the many for the enrichment of the few."[67] His democratic roots were broader than those of Henry Watterson, and if his writing lacked the rhetorical flare of his Kentucky friend, it manifested a lucidity needed to give forceful expression to the range of reforms he championed. Starting with Grover Cleveland's second administration, Daniels also had an active career as a public servant, but it was journalism that claimed his first allegiance.[68]

Like many other progressive southern editors, Daniels, a relentless Democratic partisan, had supported William Jennings Bryan in his three presidential campaigns. However, he would support Wilson in 1912, and later become his Secretary of Navy. He first met Wilson in 1909, though Walter Hines Page had broached the idea with him as early as 1886 that Wilson might someday be president.[69] In 1909, in Raleigh on his way to deliver an address at the University of North Carolina, Wilson took the opportunity to visit the *News and Observer*'s editorial office. There he expressed his thanks to Daniels, a trustee of the university, for the invitation to speak, and thus began their long friendship. Before leaving North Carolina, Wilson had made a profound impression on Daniels.[70] Two years later, in March 1911, he began his editorial campaign in support of Wilson for president. George Harvey had visited Daniels shortly before that to advance Wilson's prospects, but it can be questioned whether the editor, who was already calling the governor "a modern Andrew Jackson," needed Harvey's encouragement.[71]

Once begun, the Wilson-for-President movement gained momentum across the South. Democratic liberals and progressives throughout that section, previous supporters of William Jennings Bryan, were turning to Wilson. Aware of this emerging movement, the governor made two trips to the South to speak in Atlanta in March and a month later in Norfolk. In Atlanta he spoke before the Southern Commercial Conference and received a tremendous ovation—greater than that accorded to Theodore Roosevelt the previous evening. At accompanying dinners and receptions, Wilson met and impressed a host of southern leaders gathered at the conference. "It had been a long time since there has been a more popular speaker in Atlanta than the Governor of New Jersey," the *Savannah Press* editorialized. "He is looked upon as a very reasonable presidential possibility. If he makes good in the governorship nothing can keep him from being a leading candidate."[72] Before the governor left Atlanta, he had won the editors of the *Atlanta Journal* and the *Atlanta Georgian* to his cause, and they began to champion his nomination in their editorial columns.[73] It was also during this visit that he gained the support of Georgia's reform governor Hoke Smith, who endorsed Wilson's candidacy a few weeks later. The Atlanta trip marked the start of his prenomination campaign, but he was more direct about his intentions with his comments at Norfolk.

He had a particular reason for returning to his native state. As he explained to a close friend: "I wanted to say something at this particular time in the South . . . because there seems to be gathering in the South a really big body of sentiment . . . in favor of my nomination for the presidency. The South is a very conservative region—just now probably the most . . . conservative section of the country—and I am *not* conservative. I am a radical. I wanted a chance to tell my friends in the South just what I thought, . . . before they went further and committed themselves to me as a 'favorite son.' "[74]

It is surprising to hear Wilson speak of himself as a radical. Neither his reforms in New Jersey nor his own political temperament (he even preferred the label "liberal" to that of "progressive") justified his "radical" identity. Moreover, he claimed it at a time when the radical political fringe was clamorous in denouncing American business enterprise and government. Nor was this the last time in 1911 he would refer to himself as a radical. Throughout this year, he continued to make his political position known to the public, and he sprinkled his rhetoric with frequent, and often differing, references to it. In Atlanta, for instance, he announced, "The older I get the more radical I get along certain lines. Radical in the literal sense of the word, and I long more and more to get at the root of the whole matter." In this case, he was appealing to the diversity of the South and expressing his disbelief that the area was, as sometimes claimed, "conservative to the point of being reactionary." Before long he spoke of radicalism again in a speech, this time in an effort to define it in his own way. He was denouncing class warfare in this instance, hardly a radical gesture as many of that persuasion understood the term, and explained, "I tell you, the so-called radicalism of our times is nothing less than an effort to release the energies of our times. This great American people is in love with what is equitable, pure and of good repute." In another speech he aligned himself with progressives by saying, "It is customary to speak of this new classification as a division between progressives and reactionaries, but after all it is the old division between liberals and tories [*sic*]." He went on to equate the liberal program with the Democratic program and elaborated on that idea by cautioning, "it [the liberal idea] does not represent a revolutionary temper. . . . Its purpose is not to upset things but to set them right." Finally, in a somewhat later public statement, he proclaimed himself a conservative not a radical. "I'm a conservative yet, but conservatism demands different things in different circumstances. If those of us who are conservative get a move on it is not because we are radical but because we are going to preserve the institutions of the country and not destroy them."[75] Vestiges of his old admiration for Edmund Burke could still be detected in his thought.

What, then, did he mean by referring to himself as a radical? It is true that his varying references to the political labels he used to describe his position could confuse matters for reporters and for press coverage of him in general. It is, moreover, no less true that he blurred political realities when he made public statements like, "The only essential difference in American politics today is the difference between Progressives and Reactionaries."[76] Yet in that dichotomy lay the basic truth of his preferred political identity. He was aligning himself with the forces favoring reform within the framework of the two major national political parties as opposed to those forces wishing to maintain the status quo. Depending on the meaning implied for a particular label, the reform forces could be described as liberal or progressive, or even as conservative or radical. To refer to them as radical exaggerated the point, but it drew a clear distinction between the reform forces and those of the status quo. Having moved ever more into the progressives' camp since 1908 and having achieved a progressive reputation in New Jersey politics, he had no wish to be identified with defenders of the status quo, with the standpatters as they were known in the political vernacular of the time. He wanted to distance himself from them, and he would have been less than honest if he had failed to do so among southerners, many of whom were at odds with the progressive politics he was embracing.

The speech he delivered in Norfolk, while not radical, emphasized that distance as it underscored the governor's identity with the progressive cause. Wilson seized the moment to denounce machine politics, the covert practices of public corporations, and standpatters in politics and business as he acclaimed the virtues of publicity in civic matters. His declaration may have cautioned southern conservatives in the audience and beyond, but his forthright words before "men whose word is power in politics and men high in financial and corporate institutions" pleased the *Norfolk Virginia-Pilot*. In its report of his address, that newspaper called him "the most commanding figure on the American political horizon" and one who was "wildly greeted as the giant apostle of modern and progressive Democracy upon whom the nation will call to again entrench in power in Washington the party of Jefferson, . . ."[77] The governor's performance in Norfolk won more converts to his cause, and more would join the movement as it spread across the South.

Thousands of educators, students, and clergymen joined with progressive Democrats in general to swell the Wilson tide in the South. Throughout the section, journalists led the gathering current. There is abundant evidence to support Arthur S. Link's reflection that if he "had to single out the group of men that made the greatest contribution to the Wilson movement in the South, he would almost inevitably name the southern editors. . . . Their work in presenting the man to the people and in engendering enthusiasm and support for his cause was the foundation stone of Wilson's campaign in the South."[78] To be effective, however, a presidential movement must have an organization capable of promoting a candidate before the entire nation and be able to raise the funds needed for waging a campaign.

Several southerners living in New York took the lead in initiating this organization early in 1911. Among them, Wilson's friend and an eminent publicist, Walter Hines Page, would now play a major role in the governor's political future. Page was a North Carolinian who, after a short stint in journalism in his native state, moved north to edit first the

Forum, and then the *Atlantic Monthly*. In 1899, along with Frank Doubleday, he founded Doubleday, Page, & Company, which was soon placed among the country's successful publishing houses. The following year he inaugurated his own magazine, the *World's Work*, a public affairs magazine that gained distinction in the field and gave him a national editorial platform. By temperament Page was a moderate reformer interested in numerous causes, the revitalization of the South in particular, and a broad-minded southerner whom his recent biographer labeled "an intersectional ambassador."[79]

Page had long been interested in Wilson's political promise. Since their first meeting in 1882, the two men had often corresponded and enjoyed meeting together. Wilson contributed to the *Forum* and to the *Atlantic Monthly* while Page was editor. Already in 1907, the editor mentioned Wilson in *World's Work* as a possible presidential candidate; in 1910 he urged Wilson to seek the New Jersey governorship as a step toward the presidency and thereafter publicized his successes in that position.[80] Early in 1911, Wilson agreed to have one of Page's top staff writers, William Bayard Hale, observe him at work for an entire week as background for an article. The editor believed it would balance pieces about the governor appearing in conservative magazines like the *Saturday Evening Post* and *Harper's Weekly*.[81] Wilson, moreover, sought Page's advice on various matters, and had been discussing with him the idea of starting a "little campaign publicity."[82]

Meanwhile, some of Wilson's friends formed an organization to promote the governor's nomination for the presidency. Early in February, James C. Sprigg, an Essex County progressive, Walter McCorkle, a Virginia born southerner living in New York, and several other southerners residing in the city approached him. McCorkle, who appears to have led in making the proposal, was president of the Southern Society of New York, an important fraternal and patriotic organization in the country. Among its members were men prominent in national as well as New York affairs and several, other than McCorkle, who would play instrumental roles in the Wilson movement. Founded in 1886, the Southern Society, with its over one thousand active numbers, perpetuated the noblest traditions of the old South, the South that produced George Washington and the Declaration of Independence, and it professed a strong interest in the progress and prosperity of the entire nation.[83] To men like McCorkle, Wilson appeared as a potential national leader with roots in the South but with a political vision that far transcended that section.

Wilson, however, had doubts about the proposal McCorkle and his friends suggested. He knew that Sprigg was not known as a practical man, and beyond that, he was uneasy about a plan of this "ambitious kind." He advised the group to contact Page for some "hard headed advice."[84] Page complied and told Wilson that he had "some very definite notions" about such an organization. They were, he explained, "very simple and very old-fashioned notions, but they are based upon a life-long study of the fickle thing that we call public opinion."[85] This exchange of messages led to a meeting at the Aldine Club in New York on February 24 when Page, McCorkle, and William F. McCombs, one of Wilson's former honor students at Princeton involved in the affairs of the Southern Society, gathered to formulate their plans. There they refined their ideas and arranged to publicize Wilson in the press, to contact senators and congressmen, to take steps to raise money on his behalf, and to have him make a western speaking tour.[86]

Afterward the three men took steps to implement their plans and met with Wilson to report on their actions. As he explained it, "There is a group of generous men there [in New York] who are going to collect a fund and effect an organization to promote my chances for the presidency. They wanted to see me to arrange for a western trip in May, when they want me to go all the way to the Pacific coast and make a series of addresses." These "generous men" also explained their other plans to Wilson, but the western trip was at the center of their proposals. "I feel an almost unconquerable shyness about it," Wilson said, but he added "I dare say I shall grow brazen enough, however, before it is all over."[87] The job of making arrangements for the tour fell on Page's shoulders. Notwithstanding Wilson's reservations regarding the trip, it was crucial to any hopes he had to win the Democratic nomination, and journalists had a central role to play in it.

Chapter 6

The Wilson Presidential Movement: Publicity and Opposition

For the remainder of 1911 and on into January of the following year, the pendulum of Wilson's political future swung to and fro. His nomination seemed unstoppable at first. The western tour that his "generous" friends planned was a huge success, and it provided the momentum needed to make the Wilson movement national. In time, however, opposition to his nomination emerged and produced several journalistic efforts to derail his prospects. But little of that opposition appeared as he departed on his western tour at the beginning of May.

I

McCorkle, McCombs, and Page knew that the proposed western tour was a crucial test for any prospect of Wilson's reaching the White House. They alone provided $3,000 to cover the expenses for the trip and took steps to find additional means to finance their other plans for the governor. It was Page who became the prime mover of the trio. To accompany Wilson on the tour, Page found Frank Parker Stockbridge to serve as publicity manager, and the editor oversaw his preparations for the trip. Together they discussed speeches for Wilson to deliver en route, and laid plans for their advanced distribution to reporters. Wilson, however, frustrated that idea by insisting he speak mostly in his customary extemporaneous manner. Undeterred, Page made arrangements for Stockbridge to circulate proofs of a William Bayard Hale article, "Woodrow Wilson: Possible President," that was scheduled to appear in his *World's Work* in May. Just as important, the editor embarked on a campaign to persuade the financier Henry Morganthau to become a financial contributor to Wilson's candidacy.[1] His success in that endeavor was a huge boost to Wilson's chances of winning the Democratic nomination a year hence.

Stockbridge proved himself an able performer in his role. He had wide experience as both a newspaper and magazine journalist, and in 1901 founded the *American Home Magazine*. Since 1908, he had been the political editor of the *Cincinnati Times-Star*, but he had genuine enthusiasm for the western venture and told Page that he was willing to give it "his whole time."[2] Stockbridge brought the practical expertise of a newspaperman to the publicity arrangements for the tour only to discover that he was dealing with a recalcitrant governor. At first Wilson agreed to provide the outlines of his speeches prior to the trip. Stockbridge explained to him that this would allow him the necessary lead time to have them typed and sent to the press associations, which in turn could mail them to their constituent newspapers. But with only days remaining before departing, Wilson had yet to write a single word. Stockbridge prevailed upon him for the outlines of his first two speeches for the tour, but still Wilson resisted. "The Governor thinks he can work out their [the speeches'] basic ideas on the train and dictate them to stenographers along the line. . . . He is not yet fully educated up to the value of publicity," Stockbridge complained to Page. Then he added, "Colonel Roosevelt . . . never overlooks a bet when it comes to publicity" as he urged the editor "to get this idea into his [Wilson's] head by every means at your command." So it fell to Stockbridge to arrange for a "relay of stenographers clear across the continent" and have the dictated comments distributed to the press associations while en route.[3]

That was not all. Before starting the tour, Wilson placed limits on Stockbridge's publicity efforts. "I am not to be put forward as a candidate for the Presidency," he explained. He questioned the propriety of seeking the presidency. As in the case of making himself available as a gubernatorial candidate in New Jersey, he felt one should be called to high office. "No man is big enough to seek" the presidency, he informed Stockbridge. "I should not refuse it if it were offered to me, but only if the offer came from the people themselves; no man is big enough to refuse that." Consequently, he told Stockbridge to hold his pronouncements to answering inquiries for information and when answering such questions to tell the "whole truth," for there was nothing "to be concealed or glossed over." Stockbridge later reflected that restricting his comments to matters of information and to relating Wilson's positions on public policy meant "a departure from many previously accepted publicity and campaign methods and the devising of new ones."[4]

When he first met Stockbridge, Wilson commented in jest, "So you are the gentleman who is going to make me famous."[5] That was, in fact, Stockbridge's intention, and despite the restrictions Wilson insisted on, he laid the groundwork to elevate the image of the governor throughout the West. By contacting his fellow journalists and friends in other fields in the cities designated as major stops on the tour, he rounded out Wilson's initial itinerary by arranging for various organizations in those locales to invite him to address their members. As news of the tour became known, spontaneous speaking invitations from groups across the West saturated his mail. In some cases, editors and publishers responded to the news with personal letters of invitation for Wilson to speak in their communities and published complimentary articles about him in their newspapers before the tour began. Stockbridge contacted newspapers in the cities that Wilson planned to visit advising them of his arrival and departure times. He scheduled press receptions for him and suggested the best time for interviews. He invited newspapermen covering states that the governor did not intend to visit to join him at an appropriate point on the train or at a station. Finally, to reach the great number of people living beyond the major cities in the West, Stockbridge prepared boilerplate columns of information about Wilson for the American Press Association to distribute to hundreds of weekly newspapers throughout the area.[6] The preparations thus completed, he stood ready to serve, in his words, as Wilson's "combined courier, press agent and companion" in the month ahead.[7]

Wilson and two newspapermen left on May 3 for a seven state speaking tour in the West. Escaping the grind at Trenton and anticipating the chance to take to the platform put Wilson in high spirits. In a lighthearted comment to a friend, he quipped, "Stockbridge, the wide awake newspaper man who is traveling with me as my manager, and McKee Barclay, representing the *Baltimore Sun*, a capital cartoonist and good fellow, and your humble servant," composed the party as the "tour" began "most auspiciously."[8]

Beginning with stops in St. Louis and Kansas City, they moved on to Denver and then to the West Coast. Wilson's entourage visited Los Angeles, Portland, and Seattle before circling back by way of Minneapolis and St. Paul to end in Lincoln. At each stop, speeches and meetings filled the governor's schedule, and he seemed to enjoy it. He did not, however, appreciate the twice daily sessions that Stockbridge arranged for reporters. Although he accepted these sessions and tried to be accommodating, he failed, as Stockbridge said, to "become quite reconciled to interviewers; what he had to say he said in his addresses and the personal and often unintelligent questions asked by local reporters caused him a good deal of annoyance, which, however, he managed to conceal in their presence." After suffering through these

Figure 6 *Baltimore Sun*, May 3, 1911. Portrays the *Sun*'s premier cartoonist, McKee Barclay, leaving to accompany Governor Wilson on his Western tour in May 1911. The tour marked Wilson's first major move to win the presidency, and Barclay was one of the two journalists who joined him on the trip.

interviews in Kansas City, Wilson asked if he had to endure them again. "Everywhere we stop," Stockbridge replied. Later he reflected that Wilson learned to conduct the interviews "with outward grace, but with much inward protest."[9]

The tour was a triumph when judged by any standard. Large and enthusiastic crowds greeted Wilson everywhere, and pages of newspaper reports in the western states announced his arrival and acclaimed his public performances while friendly eastern editors echoed his successes in articles and editorials.[10] The governor performed adroitly with only rare exceptions. One embarrassing moment occurred in Denver. Responding to an interviewer's question about his presidential aspirations, he replied, "Really, I have not thought about the Presidency." It was an incredulous statement for him to make, and his wife Ellen, who followed the newspaper coverage of the tour, warned him not to repeat it. The statement gave "the cynics an opening which they seize with glee. The '*Sun*' of course had an outrageous little editorial about it," she told her husband.[11]

It was also in Denver that Wilson fulfilled a prior commitment to address a Presbyterian congregation on the subject of the Bible and progress. Arriving there he discovered a mass meeting in a large auditorium planned for his presentation. Instead of making informal comments to a small gathering, he would be delivering a major speech to a capacity audience of over twelve thousand people on short notice. His crowded, prearranged schedule allowed him only one hour to prepare for it. The speech in which he linked progressive democracy with Christianity was an immense success. "I have never in my life seen such a profound impression made upon an audience," the veteran journalist Stockbridge wrote to Page. "Personally, I have never been so deeply impressed with an address on a religious subject as I was by this. It gave me new light on the Bible with which I had been familiar since childhood."[12]

That speech, in fact, exemplified the success Wilson was enjoying. "Everybody is talking about Woodrow Wilson," William Rockwell Nelson, the owner and editor of the *Kansas City Star* wrote to his friend Henry Watterson. "If Wilson were running right now he couldn't be beaten."[13] As the tour progressed, Stockbridge reported that the newspapers had been friendly "all along the line" and that "the publicity we have obtained has exceeded all my expectations." Then he reflected, "One of the things demonstrated beyond cavil is that Gov. Wilson has been uppermost in the minds of a great section of the American people as a Presidential choice for 1912, [and] another . . . is that his personal contact with people immeasurably strengthens their previous good impression of him."[14] Even Wilson sensed an extraordinary quality about the reception he received from the public and the press in the West. "I am having a sort of triumph out here," he wrote to a friend, "wherever I go they seem to like me—men of all kinds and classes. . . . It is almost amazing to have scores of persons . . . speak to me, in a sort of matter of course way, as the next President of the United States."[15] The news reports, indeed, assumed that he was a strong presidential possibility.[16] Wilson was so impressed by the reception he was receiving that he commented in private, "It daunts me to see their admiration and trust. I shall have to be a much better man than I really am now to deserve even a part of the confidence they now have in me."[17] Did deserving that confidence include placing aside previous equivocations about wanting to be president? Toward the end of the tour, he admitted to McKee Barclay that it did.[18]

"Woodrow Wilson: Possible President" was the thought behind the enthusiastic press coverage he received in each state he visited. It was also the title of William Bayard Hale's article appearing in the May issue of the Page's *World's Work* at the conclusion of the western tour. Based on his week-long observation of the governor in February, Hale took 14 pages to describe Wilson as "a new type of man in our public life" and a "looming figure in the world to-day." In support of this claim, Hale reviewed Wilson's entrance into politics, his particular preparation for it as a scholar, his intervention in the Smith–Martine affair, and his methods of effective progressive leadership as governor. "No man in our time," Hale wrote, "has carried the discussion of public questions to so high a level of thought." He presented Wilson as good-natured with a lively sense of humor and, most of all, as a practical politician committed to enacting his pledged reforms including reform of the mechanism of government. Hale stressed the term "practical politician," and pointed out that it was Wilson's interest in discovering and explaining how institutions actually worked that informed his major studies on government. The prevailing image of the governor in the article was that of an effective man of action interested in plain facts rather than "beautiful theories." One of the *World's Work*'s distinctive features, a pioneering one for twentieth-century news magazines, was its generous use of photographs. This article featured 14 photographs of Wilson including one depicting him as New Jersey's vigorous, progressive governor. With a full page cover picture of the governor and an editorial designating him as the fittest presidential choice for progressive Democrats, this issue of the magazine could be called "Wilson's."[19] That fact became even more obvious with the ambivalent treatment the magazine afforded Judson Harmon, the Ohio governor, whom many considered a strong presidential contender, in its next issue.[20] Indeed, when Hale interviewed Harmon for his article, he wrote to his wife, "Spent the afternoon with the Governor [Harmon] who is *not* the equal of Wilson."[21]

Page was not Wilson's only champion wishing to promote him. James Kerney and, of course, George Harvey were busy spreading news of him in the weekly press, and Josephus Daniels took the lead in publicizing him in the South.[22] Before returning home after his western tour, Wilson ventured south for several prearranged speaking obligations in North and South Carolina. Josephus Daniels had made the governor's performance in the West front page news in his *Raleigh News and Observer*, but that was a mere prelude to the coverage accorded him now. His newspaper tracked Wilson's every move in the state with pages of news and publicity. "GOV. WOODROW WILSON CAPTURES NORTH CAROLINA," read its headline on the front page devoted exclusively to him on the day he departed, and retrospective articles followed for a few more days. The state's progressives were delighted.[23]

From Raleigh he went to Columbia, where he had spent his teenage years, to deliver several more addresses. The most important one, given before the South Carolina Press association, was a fighting attack on the concentration of money power in politics and on the "hidden alliances" it engenders. Wilson targeted southern progressives in the audience as he concluded:

> I would rather . . . consult the ordinary man of business in a small way who is in the great struggle for existence with regard to the real situation in America than to discuss it with any captain of industry. . . . The man who knows the strength of the current is the man who is trying to swim against it.
>
> Have we lost the vision of America? Have we forgotten that America was intended for the service of mankind? Have we so lost that vision that we suppose that America was intended for the creation of wealth only? We shall cease to be America when we prefer our material resources to our spiritual impulses, and I tell you what is to be recovered in the immediate future of America is that original spirit of her affairs shown in those days of the Revolution, when men turned their back upon their interests and set their feet in the path of duty.[24]

Nor did he forget he was speaking to an assembly of journalists. He asked them, as editors, to act as statesmen, elucidating news in a manner conducive to the constructive public discourse needed to "erect a new politics for a new age."[25] Afterward he met the editors and later state politicians and educational leaders, and left having won most of them to his cause.[26] He had, however, one more stop to make before returning home.

To move the campaign to its next stage, Page arranged a meeting in Washington of the men involved with it thus far, including a few others. There, McCombs, McCorkle, Stockbridge, and Tumulty joined Wilson at the Willard Hotel on June 4. They urged him to form a campaign organization and appoint a manager for it, but he balked at the idea. The governor believed "that everything ought to come as a spontaneous movement of public opinion." That attitude frustrated Page, who believed Wilson could be either right or "dead wrong" and thought it fell to his friends to persuade him he was "dead wrong." The editor feared that public opinion could not be trusted and understood that it did not always control convention delegates. "The truth is," he explained to a friend, "I went to Washington simply to put this idea into him, and I told him with all frankness that my opinion was that we ought to have a manager at once. . . ."[27] Wilson seemed to grasp the point, but a few days later his old feeling about the proposition returned.

The Washington conference concluded his 10,000-mile journey across the West and on into the South. For the rest of the day, however, he remained in Washington until 7 P.M. to receive throngs of Democrats. Although the day had been long and the hour late, when he arrived back in Trenton he took the time to meet with the newsmen who awaited him. He "went at once," the *True American* reported, "to the Hotel Sterling, where he talked to the ten or dozen newspaper men who were on hand to greet him." The next morning the *True American* announced in a bold face front page notice, "GOOD MORNING GOVERNOR WILSON. ALL NEW JERSEY WELCOMES YOU HOME AGAIN."[28]

II

Following Wilson's trip around the country the momentum pushing his candidacy was at full force. Wilson Clubs were multiplying near and far. Of course, any Democratic candidate professing progressive principles would have to have at least a favorable nod from William Jennings Bryan, the three-time Democratic nominee for president, who still commanded a fervent following among Democrats at the grass-roots level. Based on their previous views of one another, Wilson and Bryan were different types of Democrats. Wilson, while admitting the charm of the man, had labeled Bryan's political beliefs "foolish and dangerous."[29] Bryan, the "Great Commoner," had been suspicious of the Wall Street support for Wilson in his recent election and of the way that conservative publications like *Harper's Weekly* and the *New York Sun* had endorsed his cause. However, as Wilson proved himself a progressive governor and even, at Bryan's suggestion, urged the New Jersey legislature to adopt an income tax amendment, the two men drew closer together. In March, when Bryan was in Princeton to speak at the Theological Seminary, Wilson hurried home from Atlanta to host a dinner for him at the Princeton Inn. Afterward Wilson wrote in private that having seen him "close at hand" he now found the "Great Commoner" abounding in "sincerity and conviction and a truly captivating man."[30] Shortly, thereafter, the two men appeared together at a Democratic rally in Burlington, New Jersey and generously complimented one another in their platform remarks. Wilson made Lincoln, Nebraska the last stop on his western tour, in order to visit Bryan's home. Although Bryan was in New York at the time and could welcome the governor only by telegram, his wife and brother were present to offer him a gracious reception. Few politicians in the country could miss the implication of that visit. Several days later, Bryan was a guest at George Harvey's home in Deal, New Jersey where the two were reported to have had an extended and pleasant conversation about the possible candidates for the Democratic nomination.[31] That was also a favorite topic of many newspapers.

At the time of the western tour, Stockbridge observed that Wilson and Governor Judson Harmon of Ohio were the only real candidates in the Democratic field and that enthusiasm for Wilson was mounting.[32] The attention Wilson received from journalists throughout the summer and fall of 1911 proved Stockbridge correct. "Every progressive vote in the state [Maryland] is for you—not a single exception," wrote McKee Barclay.[33] To a fellow Kentucky editor, Henry Watterson confided, "I shall do my best for Woodrow Wilson because I believe him as clearly to be the intellectual leader of Democracy as Mr. Tilden was thirty-six years ago."[34] Wilson appreciated Watterson's support and told him, "It is always a genuine pleasure to read your editorials. They are so straightforward and have such extraordinary vigor that they always quicken the blood and put tonic into a man."[35] Some of Wilson's other original supporters in the press were also promoting his candidacy. L. T. Russell, editor and owner of the *Elizabeth Evening Times* and a frank and critical voice of public figures whether he sympathized with or opposed them, considered Wilson "his ideal in a public official." He told the governor that as a matter of public interest he intended to take part in "all affairs where you and your administration are concerned." He even engaged a business manager for his newspaper to have more time to devote to editorials and to staying in touch with politics.[36]

Among the many newspapermen supporting Wilson, few could match the effort of F. L. Seely, editor and publisher of the *Atlanta Georgian*, who had become an early convert to Wilson's cause. After visiting the governor during the summer, he wrote to explain a project he had undertaken "to place him properly before the people." He was sending copies of the *Georgian* containing editorial commentary about the growth of sentiment favoring Wilson's nomination as the Democratic candidate for the presidency, gleaned from newspapers across the country, to 800 Democratic dailies. To "guide a lot of friendly publishers in the South," he was also sending them reprints of the articles he gathered. Seely invited the newspapers receiving the material to use it in any way they wished, and he assured them that all this publicity was being done "at our own expense and our own volition."[37]

When it came to boosting Wilson's candidacy, Page and Harvey were not to be outdone. Page promoted the Governor every week in his *World's Work*. In August he conducted a poll among 1500 subscribers to his journal about their choice for president in 1912, representing every state in the union, and published the results in a prominent *World's Work* article. The top seven choices were:[38]

Woodrow Wilson	519
Wm. H. Taft	402
Theodore Roosevelt	274
Judson A. Harmon	96
Robt. M. LaFollette	91
Champ Clark	45
W. J. Bryan	34

Then, in October he began publishing a six-part biography of Wilson by William Bayard Hale in *World's Work*.[39] Harvey kept Wilson before the public with constant editorial references to him and by running full page ads for his *A History of the American People* in *Harper's Weekly*. In August he published a long interview with him by Charles Johnson.[40] Toward the end of the year, he launched his major journalistic offensive for Wilson in the *Weekly*. On November 11, 1911, he began running the banner "For President: WOODROW WILSON" on the masthead of the *Weekly*'s editorial page followed by a two-page article that had all the markings of a nominating speech. Describing the governor as "thoroughly equipped" for the presidency, as a man "dedicated to public service" who was "constructive and effective," and as a person free from political obligations except those due to the people as a whole and his own conscience, Harvey pronounced Wilson electable. For the next three weeks he published articles surveying press support for Wilson in every section of the country. He capped the offensive on December 9 with the full text of a recent speech, "For Government by the People," that Wilson delivered in Madison, Wisconsin.[41]

However much Page and Stockbridge wished Wilson to allow them more leeway in publicizing him, material could be found in abundance. George W. Miller, a correspondent for the *Detroit News*, proved the point when he explained to Wilson how he had gone about gathering information for a six-part series.

> In them, first by means of the interview and then by extracts from your speeches, things told me by your friends, the legislative records at Trenton, some investigations I made at Princeton, Newark, the New York Wilson headquarters and so on, I believe I am going to give the people of Michigan a pretty clear, fair and unbiased understanding of the kind of governor New Jersey has at this time. Incidentally I have become so steeped in Wilsonia that I believe I could deliver a good lecture on your honorable self, although I am by not any means a Chautauqua expert.[42]

To manage the accumulating material and to answer the mass of correspondence he was receiving for copies of his speeches and information, Wilson agreed to have Stockbridge open a clearing house operation. He was not to act as a press agent, nor was he to originate publicity material. The governor, still disliking the idea of "promoting" himself as a candidate, had a type of information bureau in mind, however difficult the distinction between that and a publicity bureau may be. McCombs had the task of raising the money for it. When Stockbridge reached the end of his capacity working in this manner, Wilson said the time would then be appropriate to change the organization. Consequently, Stockbridge opened a small office eventually located at 42 Broadway in New York, from which he answered correspondence, fulfilled requests for copies of Wilson's speeches, and circulated news about him.[43] The campaign, regardless of whatever Wilson chose to label it, was entering a second stage.

Stockbridge stretched the limits of his office as Wilson defined them and did more than simply answer letters and fulfill requests. His office subscribed to every newspaper clipping service in the country and, based on the information gathered in that manner, issued a "clip sheet" to friendly newspapers. At the request of its editor and owner, Stockbridge took over three pages of the *Trenton True American*'s Saturday edition each week and filled them with information about the governor from other newspapers. His staff then compiled a list of newspaper editors and everyone they could designate who was or had been active in Democratic politics. With the financial assistance of Wilson's old college classmate Cleveland Dodge and several of his friends, they mailed that issue of the *True American* to about forty thousand people a week by the fall of the year. By that time, too, Stockbridge's staff grew from 1 assistant to 30.[44] It was, moreover, at this time that Walter Measday, a feature and political writer for the *New York World*, was appointed to accompany Wilson on his speaking tours as his "personal representative with the press."[45]

As for McCombs, Wilson may not have wished to consider him a campaign manager, but McCombs acted as though he had a de facto claim to that position. He raised money for the campaign, wrote dozens of letters every day on Wilson's behalf, garnered information from many personal contacts about public sentiment relevant to the movement, met with some of the most important newspaper editors in the country to advance the governor's cause, and introduced him to various men who could provide him with needed support.[46] In October, Wilson finally named McCombs his official campaign manager with the authority to establish Wilson organizations at the state level.[47]

Several men destined to play large roles in his political future now joined the campaign. The first was a Tennessean, William Gibbs McAdoo, the chief promoter of building the twin tunnels under the Hudson, completed in 1909. He first met Wilson by chance on a Princeton bound train to see his son, a student at the university, in 1909. Like Wilson, McAdoo's background was Scotch–Irish, southern, and Presbyterian, and he had enormous energy and organizational ability. As president of the New York Southern Society, McAdoo invited Wilson to speak to the group in December 1910, and then introduced him as a "future President of the United States." In the summer of 1911, he made a contribution to the McCombs organization and volunteered to join in its work.[48] With all of his resourcefulness and drive, McAdoo had much to offer the organization. He assisted McCombs and joined him in weekly campaign strategy meetings with Oswald Garrison Villard, the editor of the *New York Evening Post*, who was urging Wilson's candidacy.

The second important figure to enter the movement was another southerner, Colonel Edward Mandell House, a quiet and sophisticated Texan. House had pursued politics as a student of public affairs and opinion since the Hayes–Tilden election of 1876, had managed political campaigns in Texas, and had a capacity to establish friendships with important people. The mechanics of government and human relationships intrigued him, and though he sought no position himself, he enjoyed influencing the process from within. Realizing that 1912 might well be the time for the Democrats to regain the presidency, he was anxious to find the right candidate to support. He met Wilson for the first time in November 1911, and from the beginning they formed an intimate friendship that would perk the curiosity of historians. As an assembler and reporter of information and opinion, House would acquire a unique position as a counselor to Wilson. For the moment, however, he filled the role of occasional advisor to him and McCombs and devoted his main effort to the Wilson organization in Texas.[49]

Yet another southerner, the North Carolinian Thomas Pence, joined the Wilson campaign late in the fall of 1911. Pence is not well known in history, yet he played a major role in Wilson's campaign. As a correspondent for Daniels's *Raleigh News and Observer* in Washington, he demonstrated a genius for cultivating intimate contacts with people of consequence in the capital. He had a first name association with most senators and congressmen. They in turn knew him as "Tom." Pence was a progressive southerner and had been working informally since the first of the year to promote Wilson's candidacy.[50] In December he joined the campaign as head of the Washington branch of the governor's New York bureau. The Woodrow Wilson Publicity Bureau, as Pence named the Washington office, inaugurated an aggressive promotion of the candidate. In contrast to the New York office, which still operated by answering requests and recycling news about Wilson in the press, Pence's operation originated and distributed material. He furnished original news items and stories of Wilson to about eight hundred daily newspapers and to weeklies by the thousands, as his office soon became the effective center and he the chief spokesman for Wilson publicity.[51] There was, however, more to Pence than his promotional ability. His grasp of Washington politics and widespread political associations made him indispensable. Daniels said that Pence "had an uncanny gift for political diplomacy and . . . spent it generously." Before long he became "Tom" to Wilson—one of the few men whom Wilson accorded the distinction of being called by their first names.[52]

As formidable as Wilson's publicity operation had become, it was only one of the sources giving momentum to his nomination. Many business and professional men and politicians across the country were rallying to his banner. The work of what Wilson called "the spontaneous efforts" of his friends must also be taken into account.[53] His old college classmate Cleveland Dodge alone contributed more that $50,000 to Wilson's preconvention campaign and raised $35,000 more for him among the Governor's Princeton friends.[54] Dodge, moreover, made a generous contribution to a $35,000 loan to Henry Ekert Alexander, which he needed to keep his *True American* afloat.[55] Then there were the efforts of the Wilson Clubs and Leagues and, of course, Wilson's own ability to sway large numbers of people by his words and deeds. In the six months following his return from his western tour, he delivered 20 addresses in New Jersey and in seven other states. Speaking on his favorite political topics, he ventured all the way to Texas and Wisconsin. Nor can his instate campaign efforts be overlooked. He made almost 60 more speeches supporting Wilson Democrats in New Jersey in the fall primaries and elections. During those same six months, he granted no less than six lengthy, formal interviews for publication in major newspapers and national journals. Although more restrained in tone than the interviews that appeared during his gubernatorial campaign, these articles were in keeping with the contemporary journalistic standards for formal political interviews. They offered complimentary personal descriptions of him and provided a forum for him to expound his views about political leadership, the role of public opinion in politics, and his stand on major national issues.[56] It would appear, therefore, that the swelling movement for Wilson's candidacy was advancing unhampered by serious problems. That, however, was not the case.

III

As the movement gathered momentum, opposition to it also emerged. It came in part from the appearance of other aspirants for the Democratic nomination. At first only Governor Judson Harmon of Ohio was competing with Wilson for the nomination, but by the end of 1911 two other men became candidates for that honor—Congressman Oscar W. Underwood of Alabama, the chairman of the House Ways and Means Committee and popular tariff reform leader, and James Beauchamp (Champ) Clark of Missouri, the Speaker of the House and loyal apostle of William Jennings Bryan. More than the backing for Governor Harmon's nomination, the movements on behalf of Underwood and Clark were escalating and could threaten Wilson's southern as well as his progressive support. There were, however, other reasons for the mounting opposition to him that now occurred.

It stemmed, in part, from his endorsement of various progressive measures intended to advance the idea of direct democracy. Early during his western tour, for example, he irritated many traditional southern Democrats by announcing in favor of the initiative, the referendum, and the recall—measures he had opposed as scholar and teacher. Nor did his later refinement of his position on these measures quell the unease that people opposing them began to feel. Old-line southern Democrats were unreassured by his explaining that the initiative and referendum were not blanket remedies to be applied everywhere, that they were only a means to be taken, if justified, by states and communities to meet their "peculiar needs and emergencies." In states where genuine representative government existed, such measures would remain unnecessary. Nor did his belief that the judiciary should be exempt from the recall allay fears. Along with his endorsement of other progressive measures like the short ballot and the direct primary, his modified support for these measures identified him in the mind of conservatives as a dangerous radical. After all, the Populist movement had advocated both the initiative and referendum already in 1892, and as the Election of 1912 approached, extreme opponents of these political innovations viewed them as a form of socialism. If southern conservatives were disturbed by Wilson's advocacy, however qualified, of these progressive measures, northern conservatives were no less disturbed by his attacks on the nation's great financial interests. The governor referred to them as the "money trust," "the money monopoly," and as a system of "concentrated capital." In a sense, his criticism of the "money trust" can be seen as a continuation of his battle against people representing unyielding privilege at Princeton. It can be traced back to the criticism of banking he expressed in his 1908 address, "The Banker and the Nation," and to the attacks on special interests that he made during his gubernatorial campaign.[57] Now he not only criticized the "money trust," speaking in defense of "the small banker, the small merchant, and the small manufacturer" but even declared that it was a monopoly in the hands of a few men that "must be destroyed."[58]

The governor's positioning himself on the above issues caused some of his previous supporters in the press to distance themselves from him and for others to question his direction. His acceptance of the initiative and referendum encouraged the charge not only that he was experimenting in theory with the instruments of government but also that he had deserted his previous conservatism to embrace, as one correspondent put it, "the most radical proposals born of demagoguery."[59] Conservative southern newspapers were explicit in their agreement with that charge. "Dr. Wilson admits having always heretofore pronounced these things mere bosh, but intimates that he has seen a new light. It would seem that the clear-mindedness of the scholar has become confused by the aspirations of the public man who hopes to be elected President next year," declared the *Charlotte Observer*. Among the many other southern newspapers agreeing with that accusation were those like the *New Orleans Picayune*, which went even farther by labeling him as a "Democrat of the most radical type" who favored doctrines "adopted from the socialists" with the intent "to create a situation in which the people eagerly follow any leader who can first captivate their fancy and subsequently mold the masses to his will." The *Picayune* reflected that this was the formula that degenerated the Roman republic and centuries later produced Napoleon Bonaparte.[60]

The conservative southern newspapers were not the only ones to complain about Wilson as he became a more emphatic progressive.

That bulwark of reactionary opinion, the *New York Sun*, had become disillusioned with him months before as he championed reform legislation in New Jersey. Although it had once supported him for governor, it lost faith in him during his western tour, and became the vanguard of anti-Wilson sentiment. By July it was labeling him "the leading apostle of Change by means of the Open Mouth." The *Sun* lost no opportunity during the next six months to belittle the governor's deeds or to portray him as a political opportunist who considered himself "the Indispensable Man in Trenton." "As for principles," the *Sun* editorialized, "the Indispensable has movable, new principles. See how coyly he moves now toward, now away from, the initiative and referendum. There is one and only one immortal political principle: Get office."[61] Meanwhile, at the national level *Leslie's Weekly* magazine, which spread its unabashed conservative political content along with its entertaining features among readers numbering in the hundreds of thousands, announced in July that Wilson was losing ground as a presidential aspirant because of his radicalism. By October it merely observed that he had a chance for the nomination at one time but had "sacrificed it when he went over bodily to the Bryan camp."[62]

Continued opposition from publications like the *Sun* and *Leslie's* could now be expected. More harmful to Wilson was the criticism from important newspapers known for their more moderate positions, whether conservative or progressive. Newspapers like the *New York Times* and the *Springfield Republican* found it impossible to condone his attack on the "money trust." Was he becoming Bryanized, they wondered? When the governor in an interview dismissed the preliminary report of Senator Nelson W. Aldrich's National Monetary Commission as worthless while admitting at the same time that he had yet to find time to give "sufficient study" to currency reform, the *New York Times* "deeply" regretted his making those statements. The hard truth was that the *Times* even thought them "deplorable" and stated, "It is . . . discouraging to get from him so trivial and so shallow an opinion upon a great question or to get any opinion at all so long as he confesses his lack of qualifying preparation to express an opinion worth giving."[63] Criticism of this sort could have serious consequences for the Wilson movement.

People close to Wilson, including some of his friends in the press knew and acted upon that realization. To counter the accusations about Wilson's radicalism, McCombs initiated a series of meetings with Louis Wiley, the business manager of the *New York Times*, late in August. After the first of these meetings, McCombs informed Wilson, "I think Mr. Wiley has accepted the 'faith' and from his assurances I believe the

'Times' will be all right."[64] At a second meeting with Wiley, accompanied this time by the *Times*'s managing editor Carr Van Anda, McCombs learned of another reason for the coolness of the *Times* toward Wilson. Van Anda was irked because the governor had written to him several months before complaining about the *Times*'s New Jersey correspondent but had failed to reply to the editor's request for particulars.[65] Although McCombs managed to sooth over that irritation, there remained Wilson's published statement about the Aldrich Commission. Consequently, McCombs met yet again with Wiley. While they were dining, one of Wiley's friends paused at their table and Wiley casually asked him: "What do you think of Woodrow Wilson?" His friend answered that he believed the governor was "a radical" whose views were "subject to change for political reasons." And, how did he form that impression? From the New York newspapers, came the response. That was a fortuitous comment, and McCombs used it to justify a question of his own. Was it not "the bounden duty of the great journalists to make a thorough study and analysis" of Wilson's views, he asked Wiley, who agreed that it was.[66] McCombs had reason to feel that he was successful in his reassurances about Wilson to the controlling figures at the *Times*, for Wiley, then president of the Daily Newspaper Club of America, subsequently interjected complimentary remarks about Wilson in a speech he made before that association.[67] Nevertheless, the *Times* prided itself on its independence, and its support for the governor remained an open question.

Another journalist who perceived the damage that Wilson's criticism of the "money trust" could render his chances for the nominations was William Garrot Brown, an editorial writer for *Harper's Weekly*. He so feared that the governor could destroy confidence in his leadership if he persisted in that line of criticism that he addressed a long letter to him, written in the spirit of "aggressive good-will." After going to exhaustive lengths to prove how carefully he had inquired into the work of Aldrich's Commission, he begged Wilson to resist further comment on monetary reform until he could made a thorough study of it. Brown even told Wilson, "Your reported speeches [on the question] seem to me not only dangerous but unfair and unworthy of you." He implored him to master the question and deal with it "as bravely and candidly as you did with the machine-rule in New Jersey . . . ."[68] Wilson answered Brown that he had gone off "half cocked about the Aldrich matter," and that he planned to say nothing more about it before giving it his "sincere study." He believed, moreover, that it would be advisable to withhold advancing any definite scheme about it until such time that the Democrats had a stronger possession in Congress.[69] Wilson's reply was more than Brown "dared hope for," and he agreed that delay was the best policy in this case.[70] Still, Brown's forthright cautioning of Wilson was indicative of the apprehension that many editors were expressing about his views on the monetary question and, at the urging of McCombs and Colonel House, he now redirected his attention on fiscal matters to the tariff. This shift of focus helped to lessen his opponents' criticism of him, but they also had issues of a different sort to raise against him.

During the summer, Wilson campaigned for additional progressive legislation, particularly for the adoption of the commission form of municipal government and later campaigned again for candidates who opposed machine Democrats in the September primary elections. It was all part of his leadership style and also part of his struggle to wrest control of party affairs from the political bosses and their machines. The bosses, however, still had fight left in them, as could be seen in their manipulation of the bill for adoption of a commission form of government. Early in April, Wilson began to champion that bill, but after returning from a speaking engagement in Indianapolis, he learned that the machine politicians had seriously compromised the measure by means of amendment. The amended measure passed, and it remained for the municipalities to accept or reject it, but despite the governor's whirlwind campaign supporting it, most of the state's major cities rejected it.[71] Anti-Wilson newspapers like the *New York Sun* followed the municipal voting on the act and rejoiced when voters in the various cities turned down this "favorite policy of the Hon. Woodrow Wilson" and displayed their "sanity" by refusing to "accept at second hand the manias of the Hon. William Jennings Bryan."[72]

Meanwhile, anti-Wilson newspapers in his own state, like the *Trenton State Gazette*, challenged the governor from another angle. He was building a political machine of his own, they claimed. Old school Democrats, at the very least, were wary of his relationship with the party organization, and their feelings on the matter ran deep. This was evidenced by James Nugent's intemperate action on the night of July 25 while spending the evening among personal and political friends at a café in Neptune Heights. Well into the evening, and no doubt well into his drinks, with a party of New Jersey National Guard officers seated at a nearby table, the State Democratic Chairman rose and offered a toast. "I propose a toast to the Governor of New Jersey, the commander-in-chief of the Militia, an ingrate and a liar. I mean Woodrow Wilson. I repeat, he's an ingrate and a liar. Do I drink alone?" According to reports he did drink alone. Even his friends tabled their glasses while the nearby National Guardsmen emptied theirs on the floor.[73] Nugent, old-time political boss that he was, after helping Wilson to become governor, had spent months thereafter fighting his reform legislation, as the governor proved to be beyond his control. However frustrated he now felt as he saw his own power crumbling, his outburst cost him his party chairmanship. The incident became a newspaper sensation. With sentiment running against him and despite strong-arm tactics he employed in an attempt to hold power, the Democratic State Committee met two weeks later and voted him out of office.[74] Nevertheless, distrust of the governor persisted among the organization men, and anti-Wilson editors reported any evidence, however tentative, that might imply the chagrin of the party workers toward him.

The major opportunity to fight Wilson came with the November legislative election. Crossing the state to boost Democratic candidates, he waged a vigorous campaign putting his administration on the line and asked voters to return progressive candidates. But when the results became known, Republicans had gained control of the assembly and widened their lead in the Senate. Pro-Wilson, progressive editors rushed to his defense, charging that the Smith–Nugent machine in Essex County had robbed the Democrats of control of the lower house by putting up an entire slate of anti-Wilson Democrats. The people had the choice of voting for Democrats who opposed the governor's progressive administration, of voting for Republicans, or of not voting at all. In the end, many chose the last option, thus allowing the Republicans to win. Even the conservative *New York Sun* conceded that point.[75] The rationale was more than postelection apologetics, for the Democrats had outvoted the Republicans statewide. Only two years before the Republicans had a large (41,502) statewide voting majority in the legislative election and now the Democrats had a majority of 3,100 down from its 14,470 voting majority in 1910, but a clear edge. Wilson could take considerable credit for that gain, and, determined to find victory in defeat, the *True American* declared in its bold headline, "Figures Show Wilson Has Made New Jersey A Democratic State."[76]

The salient fact, however, was that Wilson had campaigned hard only to find that the Democrats lost their majority in the state assembly. Surprisingly, some of the leading Republican newspapers in the country, considered the above circumstances and gave Wilson the benefit of the doubt in their editorials.[77] That was also the response of many of the national periodicals. But in New Jersey, Boss Smith's *Newark Star* gloated over the outcome of the election. What was the "why and wherefore" to explain how the Democrats, victorious in last year's election, had managed to be defeated a mere year later, it asked. In its opinion, the answer was not "far to seek." Pointing to Wilson, the *Star* offered this explanation.

> A year ago the Democratic organization was a unit. . . . How this splendid organization was shattered need not be told. The shadow of Presidential ambition fell across its path. . . . The result is witnessed in an election in which the Democracy . . . met defeat and humiliation. Gov. Wilson, who on the eve of the election assured Democrats that all would be well, can contemplate the results, for which he cannot disavow responsibility.[78]

The leading Republican newspaper at the capital, the *Daily State Gazette*, echoed a similar opinion. Its postelection front page headline read, "PEOPLE SAID 'NO' TO GOV. WILSON'S PLEA FOR VOTES" and its accompanying editorial, "Tired of His Policies."[79] Harsh as these accounts were from press opponents in his own state, an indictment bearing greater potential damage to his presidential hopes came from neighboring New York City.

There his advisors had courted the good opinion of the *New York Times*, and at this point Wilson could ill afford to have that newspaper against him. For years the *Times* had been fair in its treatment of Wilson, and despite recent differences with him, it had often championed his cause. The *Times* had pulling power; other newspapers frequently quoted its opinion. Moreover, under publisher Adolph Ochs its prestige had risen as it acquired the reputation of being a newspaper of record. He positioned the *Times* as an independent Democratic newspaper with an emphasis on the word independent. It never, for instance, trusted William Jennings Bryan in his three efforts to win the presidency, and, as a result, it had supported Republican candidates twice in the last three presidential elections. It defended sound money and steady policies that would keep the Democratic party from embracing radical nostrums. At this time, it still believed Wilson had moved too far to the left, and it held him responsible for the Democratic reversals in New Jersey. The politicians had rejected him, it editorialized, and he disappointed the people. Why? Because he chose "to join with dangerous elements in the political life of the nation and to indulge in what seemed to some of his former admirers perilously like demagoguery." Moreover, when it came to the question of currency, he had "shown either inconceivable ignorance or unaccountable perversity." Believing that he had allied himself with a popular cause, the *Times* concluded that he had been deluded. "His failure to secure the support in his own state which he so earnestly asked for may open his eyes to the extent and nature of his delusion, and of the disaster which yesterday befell his Presidential ambition."[80] Perhaps his failure in this instance should not be considered a "portent" for next year's presidential election, the *Times* allowed in a second editorial on the subject, but in its judgment, his responsibility for the defeat and his misdirected championing of a progressive agenda were serious blows to his chances for the Democratic nomination.[81] McComb's efforts to mollify the *Times*'s directors about Wilson's alleged radicalism had proved unsuccessful, as shown by its position toward him at this point. The goodwill the *Times* had offered him early in his governorship was slipping away.

IV

The governor's fate in the fall elections allowed his opponents to exploit what they deemed a setback for the Wilson movement. By the time of the Democrats' Jackson Day Dinner early in January, marking the formal beginning of the preconvention campaign, his adversaries had launched two attacks on him, orchestrating revelations about his past in the hope of tarnishing his character. In both cases, the *New York Sun* made the disclosure. As indicative of the type of journalism the *Sun* practiced in the early twentieth century, its attempt at the time of Wilson's election as president of Princeton to show by means of innuendo that he was involved in a plot to force the resignation of his predecessor might be recalled.[82] Under the editorship of Edward P. Mitchell, the *Sun* had a fondness for personalizing political news and for publishing sensational exposés. Although his friends might refer to him as a man "free from the slightest partisan bias," just the opposite was the case.[83] He was a spokesman for Wall Street and big business, and, now perceiving Wilson as a threat to those interests, he set out to do irreparable harm to his chances for the nomination. Consequently, by means of journalistic exposé, he initiated two attacks on the governor, both intended to make him an unacceptable Democratic candidate.

On December 5, the *Sun* sounded the alarm for an action Wilson had taken the previous year. After resigning from Princeton, he had applied to the Carnegie Foundation for the Advancement of Teaching for a pension. Created in 1905, the pensions were intended for persons who had reached the age of 65 with at least 15 years of service as a professor and to those with 25 years of distinguished service as a professor. Wilson thought he qualified for the latter, but after his application for the pension the Trustees of the Foundation eliminated the 25 year pensions and, therefore, rejected Wilson's request. Now the *Sun* publicized the request and headlined its report:

WOODROW WILSON SOUGHT A PENSION
Carnegie Foundation Considered and Denied His Request
NEVER HAD ANOTHER LIKE IT
And Really, You Know, With His Youth and
His Prospects It Didn't Seem—

The article went on to explain that he was only 53 at the time of the request, that he was "moving toward" an office worth $10,000 a year, and that his *History* was then being widely advertised. Noting that Wilson had been on the Board of Trustees of the Foundation but had resigned before applying for a pension, it suggested that a shadow of opportunism covered his action. The *Sun* concluded that Wilson's claim for a pension was "purely financial"—suggesting that it was also dishonorable. Nowhere did it explore the provision regarding 25 years of distinguished service as qualification for a pension. The article, therefore, created a false impression by failing to explain that there were two categories for eligibility; and third, by failing to explore the rationale for that provision. Furthermore, it claimed that one of the trustees said that the underlying reason for the application had to do with the "public discussion" surrounding Wilson's entrance into politics. The trustee alleged that there was a feeling that "It would have been . . . an asset to have the endorsement" of the Carnegie Foundation behind him and the pension would be "financially for the good of a campaign fund."[84] The slant of the article, its sarcastic tone, its implications, and its quoting a trustee about a "public discussion" that never occurred make its partisan bias inescapable.

The exposé had been long in the making. A *Sun* reporter began digging for details about Wilson's request for a pension almost a year before the story appeared. He approached the president of the Carnegie Foundation for the Advancement of Teaching about it, only to find that he refused to divulge any information on the case. "I suspect he was trying to work up a story in the interest of those who are fighting you," the president informed Wilson.[85] That was also Wilson's opinion about it a year later when the story broke.[86] He dismissed it with a single public statement explaining his action.[87] Nevertheless, the anti-Wilson editors jumped at the chance to use the *Sun*'s revelation to belittle the governor. How could he apply for such a pension, the *Pensacola Evening News* asked. "What want-wolf howls at his door? What work has he done?"[88]

In his own capital city, the *Daily State Gazette* used the revelation as another means to chip away at his reputation. He had made a good salary as Princeton's president. Why had he failed to save enough money to provide for his family, it asked. He had proved himself a poor businessman. Could he, therefore, be trusted to manage the public interests? Besides, noting that he had taught his students the fallacy of the initiative, referendum, and recall for 20 years but now believed he had misled them about those measures, the *State Gazette* concluded, "False teaching doesn't merit a life-time pension."[89]

The disclosure gave southern conservative editors, in particular, occasion to denounce Wilson. James Calvin Hemphill, among the best known southern journalists whose family had been eminent in southern life since Revolutionary times, was a case in point. Back in 1906, while editor of the *Charleston News & Courier*, Hemphill had been one of the original promoters of Wilson as a possible presidential candidate.[90] Thereafter, he continued to approve of Wilson, perceiving him to be a states' rights conservative and a fellow Presbyterian, something Hemphill valued as much as the southern democratic principles he believed Wilson to possess. However, he turned against the governor in response to the *Sun*'s revelation. Now, as editor of the *Charlotte Observer*, he declared, "The Carnegie Foundation was created for indigent teachers and not for indigent politicians," and in private he began to punctuate his correspondence with references to Wilson as "the pension grabbing Governor of New Jersey."[91]

The best defense pro-Wilson newspapers could offer was to remain silent about it. Only a few like the *New York World*, placing aside its previous concerns about his views on the "money trust," came to his defense. Aside from his original statement about it, Wilson remained silent about it too. The matter had been closed a year ago. But in private, he said that people who wished to discredit him were finding means to do so "personally if not politically. . . . They are very trying."[92]

The *New York Sun* would soon try his patience again. On January 7, on the eve of the Jackson Day dinner in Washington, that principal annual celebration of the Democratic faithful, it published a second revelation about Wilson under the headline "WILSON LETTER ATTACKING BRYAN: Cannot We Devise Some Way of Getting Rid of Bryan for All Time?" The article offered a rough summary of the letter, the full text of which it printed on the following day. Wilson had written it back in 1907 to Adrian Joline, who was the president of the Missouri, Kansas, & Texas Railroad and a trustee of Princeton University. After making a hard-hitting attack on Bryan in a speech to the M K & T's directors, he sent Wilson a copy of it. The two men were on friendly terms at the time, although three years later Wilson would oppose Joline's reelection to the Board of Trustees. In thanking him for the speech, Wilson said he agreed with it and added, "Would that we could do something at once dignified and effective to knock Mr. Bryan once and for all into a cocked hat."[93] In 1911 the *Sun* acquired a copy of the letter and subsequently published it at an opportune time. With the Democrats gathering in Washington and given the fact that Wilson would have to have Bryan's support to win the nomination six months hence, the "cocked hat" disclosure just before the Jackson Day Dinner sought to discredit Wilson among progressives and to drive a wedge between him and Bryan. Both were scheduled to speak at the dinner.

At first the revelation seemed to have a chance of achieving its intended purpose. For different reasons, the publication of the letter irritated both Bryan and Wilson. Bryan learned of it while in Raleigh visiting Josephus Daniels, and it was there that he made his initial response to it to a *New York Sun* reporter, who had managed to reach him for a comment. Hardly in a complimentary mood toward Wilson, he remarked, "You may just say that if Mr. Wilson wanted to knock me into a cocked hat, he and the *Sun* are on the same platform."[94] However, the Great Commoner and Daniels traveled together to Washington, and by the time they reached the capital, the editor had mollified Bryan's feelings about the disclosure.[95] Besides, Bryan was not one to hold a grudge, and by no means did he wish to have progressives divided as they approached the nominating convention.

Wilson made his initial public comment about the letter to Washington journalists as a guest of honor at the National Press Club. "A man should feel embarrassed neither at having a previously written letter published nor by deciding to change his mind," he told them. "The people who do not change their minds are very impossible people."[96] Then, after making some complimentary remarks about journalists in general, he had this to add. "I do not mind getting licked in an open fight. . . . If they [other men] will lay their whole case before the people and the people decide against me, why, that's sport. What I object to is private council frame-ups, ..."[97]

That was as far as he would go in alluding to the disclosure. But before he left the Press Club, William K. Devereux, a Democrat from Asbury Park active in party affairs and a man known to have a sense of humor, made his way into the line of people waiting to greet the governor. There he managed to defuse, for the moment, the serious implications of the Joline letter. Coming abreast of Wilson, Devereux assumed a serious demeanor and said, "Governor Wilson, I inform you that I have in my possession a letter written by you to General George Washington in 1776 just before the battle of Trenton, in which you criticized the Ocean Grove Campmeeting Association [the Methodist organization that owned Ocean Grove, N. J.] because it objects to that resort being made a borough." Without pause, Wilson retorted, "I am aware of the existence of that letter. Be a perfect gentleman and give it to the press." "That shall be done," Devereux replied, "and I shall have it published in full on the sporting page of The Ladies Home Journal."[98] Unfortunately, although the Joline letter could be the subject of such playful repartee, its damaging implications could not be wished away.

Nevertheless, for the moment, the disclosure of the Joline letter appeared to have gone awry. Both men were conciliatory when they met at the banquet, and their speeches relieved the tension in the audience evident at the beginning of the evening. Wilson was in top form when he spoke. He concluded his remarks by referring to the "irrepressible ideal" the Democrats shared that allowed them to look back and say: "Yes; from time to time we differ with each other . . ., but, after all, we followed the same vision, after all we worked slowly stumbling through dark and doubtful passages onward to a common purpose and common ideal." Then, turning toward Bryan, he added, "Let us apologize to each other that we ever suspected or antagonized one another; let us join hands . . . around the great circle of community counsel and of interest which will show us at the last to have been indeed the friends of our country and the friends of mankind."[99] The applause of the audience prevented him from completing the last sentence as he intended it. No matter, while the cheering resounded around them, Bryan put his hand on Wilson's shoulder and said, "That was splendid, splendid." "Bryan was moved as I never saw him before or afterwards," recalled Josephus Daniels, who also recollected that the Great Commoner referred to Wilson's words the next day as "the greatest speech in American political history."[100]

In the end, the Joline letter incident strengthened Wilson's relationship with Bryan and drew the governor's progressive supporters closer to him. Nevertheless, he confided to a friend, "Publicity is beginning to beat upon me,—not my own kind of publicity, the publicity of public affairs, but the kind the sensational newspapers insist upon, the publicity of private affairs . . . ." He predicted the effort to discredit him would continue "by fair means or foul," and subsequent press attacks would prove that prediction correct.[101]

Chapter 7
The Press and Wilson's Preconvention Campaign

In January 1912, as the preconvention campaign for the nomination formally opened following the Jackson Day Dinner, only a seer could have predicted the troubles that awaited Wilson. The Democratic nominating convention, to be held in July in Baltimore, was six months distant, and by the time it convened, he would become the target of press attacks that deserve a place among the most vicious in American history. For the moment, however, he had reason to feel confident about the press coverage accorded him. Despite the Carnegie pension and Joline letter revelations, which anti-Wilson editors would continue to flout, his press relations and support appeared strong.

Wilson, held an enviable position in the press among the aspirants for the Democratic nomination, and there were encouraging signs that he would retain it for the next six months. As presidential campaigning reached a new threshold of activity, his managers continued in their vigorous promotion of his candidacy, his stalwart supporters in the press remained firm in their advocacy of his nomination, and he acquired the support of one of the great press lords of the time. These fortuitous circumstances, however, were misleading, for before long, press opposition to his candidacy would rise to unprecedented levels. Worse yet, at the start of the preconvention campaigning, Wilson became the target of another attempt to discredit him on personal grounds.

I

In the aftermath of the Jackson Day Dinner, a revelation about Wilson filled newspaper columns from coast to coast. It was the work of three journalists—George Harvey, Henry Watterson, and John Calvin Hemphill. Harvey, of course, had been the first major promoter of Wilson for the presidency, and back in 1906, he had attracted Watterson to the idea. Watterson, or "Marse Henry," as he was often known, was a vivid personality whose editorials gave his *Louisville Courier-Journal* the national reputation it enjoyed. He had a legion of friends in politics, business, and the arts, and many journalists in the South and beyond followed his lead on the issues of the day. Hemphill was typical of the southern editors drawn to him. As a presidential aspirant, Wilson valued Watterson, but, as one of his fellow Kentucky publishers put it, he was "as changeable as a chameleon."[1] The governor would soon learn the truth of that assertion.

The incident that the three editors now foisted upon the public had occurred at New York's Manhattan Club the previous month. There on December 7, Harvey and Watterson met with Wilson to discuss campaign financing. Watterson and, after him, Harvey, had already approached their mutual friend, the financier Thomas Fortune Ryan who agreed to contribute to the campaign. Harvey then spread word among key figures in Washington that Ryan was willing to aid Wilson; however, at the Manhattan Club meeting, Wilson balked at the idea of taking money from Ryan. After all he had said about vested interests, if news about contributions by someone like Ryan leaked out, it would be disastrous to his campaign. No hint can be found in the record to suggest that the meeting was anything but congenial, but upon leaving, Harvey asked a "frank question" of Wilson,—was *Harper's* support "embarrassing" him? The governor responded that friends mentioned it was "not doing any good in the West." Harvey replied that he would "have to put on the soft pedal." In a friendly manner, the men then departed and soon thereafter Harvey removed Wilson's name from *Harper's* editorial masthead.[2]

Wilson was unaware that anything out of the ordinary had transpired.[3] However, upon hearing of the exchange, his brother-in-law Stockton Axson warned him that he may have offended Harvey. Wilson then wrote to Harvey lamenting how unthinking he had been responding to the question of his support as a "matter of fact" without acknowledging Harvey's "generous support" and his "hope that it would be continued." He asked Harvey to, "Forgive me, and forget my manners!" Harvey wrote back in a similar spirit that "no purely personal issue could arise between you and me." The matter had ended, he said, and "whatever little hurt I may have felt as a consequence of the unexpected peremptoriness of your attitude toward me is, of course, wholly eliminated by your gracious words."[4] Two more letters followed in which Wilson professed his friendship and appreciation for Harvey's help while Harvey assured Wilson that there was "no particle of resentment left in him" and that he had "not said one word to anybody of criticism of you." The editor mentioned that he would have to make a brief statement to his readers to explain why Wilson's name had been removed from the *Weekly*'s editorial masthead, which he did on January 20.[5] With that the episode ended, or did it?

A number of Wilson's friends believed that incident was a plot to brand him an ingrate and thus publicize the idea that he had a disqualifying character flaw.[6] There remains an extensive paper trail running through the correspondence of the three editors that tends to confirm that interpretation. A few weeks after the Manhattan Club meeting, Watterson wrote of that meeting that Wilson was an "ingrate; austere, unyielding, if not tyrannous; insensible to personal obligation. Then and there I turned away from Wilson."[7] At that point, Watterson had just returned from a trip through several southern states during which he had discussed the episode with various editors, most of all with Hemphill of the *Charlotte Observer.* During these weeks, the three editors corresponded about publicizing the incident in order, as Hemphill said, "to put Mr. Wilson in a hole."[8] When to go public, remained a question. Harvey wanted to act sooner rather than later and sent an emissary to persuade Watterson of the wisdom of that course, but Watterson and Hemphill advised waiting, no doubt in order to allow rumors to mount.

Beginning on January 5, rumors of a Wilson–Harvey "break" became public when Hemphill published a dispatch written by Watterson. It suggested that stories of the "break" were circulating and offered a synopsis of the alleged episode.[9] "I think I have fired a shot this morning that will be heard around the country," Hemphill wrote to President Taft, to whom he had already communicated his intention to break some news in the *Observer* about Wilson's "cold blooded selfishness. . . . the worst I have ever heard of."[10] Wilson issued a statement saying there had been no break, but the big metropolitan dailies jumped on the story and sought more information about it. As it turned out, Harvey and Watterson released that information on January 17, when the former issued his brief statement explaining the removal of Wilson's name from his *Weekly*'s editorial masthead, and the latter gave out a long explanation of the episode. Harvey announced that he had acted in response to Wilson's statement that the *Weekly*'s support was "affecting his candidacy injuriously."[11] Watterson took a more verbose approach as he reviewed the circumstances of the incident in a statement for the Associated Press and emphasized the "shock" he felt upon hearing Wilson, "without the least show of compunction," allow Colonel Harvey

Governor Wilson to George Harvey (as he kicks over the scaffolding of Harper's publications)—Goodby, George! I can get along without you now!

Figure 7 *New York Tribune*, January 17, 1912. Portrays Wilson's alleged discarding of George Harvey, who had been instrumental in advancing his candidacy for president.

"to consider himself discharged." Marse Henry concluded, as he had previously explained in private to his friends, that Wilson had no sense of "common cause," nor of "political obligations," nor of the fact that "except for Colonel Harvey, he would not be running at all."[12] In short, Wilson stood condemned of ingratitude.

News of the "break" and speculation surrounding it captured headlines and editorial attention across the country. The anti-Wilson newspapers rejoiced in the opportunity to denounce him. The most strident among them declared that public opinion had convicted the governor of "nothing less than coldblooded ingratitude tinged with falsehood—he is a dead duck, floating out on a swift ebb tide; probably his name will not be mentioned when . . . [the Democrats] gather in Baltimore next summer."[13] In North Carolina, Hemphill did all he could to inflame opinion against the governor. "This is not the first time in the politics of this country when politicians have dropped their pilots when they thought themselves safely in port. There is an old proverb which reads, 'Gratitude is the least of virtues, ingratitude the worst of vices,'" he wrote in a column, part of a series of his editorials on the subject.[14] That was mild compared with the wrath against Wilson that he spread through his private correspondence. "If Woodrow Wilson is not crooked, I would not be able to tell a crooked man when I see him" he charged while reflecting, "the worst of it is that he is a Presbyterian."[15] Reaction to the revelation rumbled through the press until the end of the month, but it was put to rest when Villard published, with their permission, the letters Wilson and Harvey exchanged about the meeting in his *New York Evening Post*.[16]

Who was responsible for manipulating the incident and what effect did it have? It appears that Hemphill and Watterson were accomplices rather than instigators. Hemphill, who did not attend the meeting itself, repeatedly asked Watterson for information about it. As for Watterson, in the end he felt left in an embarrassing position by the consensual publication of Harvey's letters forgiving Wilson. They left him vulnerable "to every manner of misrepresentation and abuse. . . . [They] did . . . leave me the bag to hold," he mused.[17] All during 1911, Harvey had seen his influence with Wilson wane as new managers came into his campaign, and the distance between them widen as the governor became more progressive in word and action. "I am still wondering," Watterson wrote to Hemphill, "how George Harvey came to write those letters to Woodrow Wilson. His hatred of Wilson is positively intense. He told me . . . that it long antedated the incident in my apartment at the Manhattan Club. For an entire year Wilson had been treating him shabbily."[18] Watterson believed he would play the role of supporting Harvey in the unfolding intrigue, but in his letters to Wilson, Harvey excused himself of any responsibility for what transpired. He did the same in his statement to the press about dropping Wilson's name from the *Weekly*'s editorial masthead by neglecting to mention that he had prompted Wilson with the question and the request for a frank answer.

Harvey's cleverness notwithstanding, it is possible to have some sympathy for him as his influence with Wilson receded. Nevertheless, he appears to have instigated the fray.[19] He was, moreover, as has been seen, no stranger to proposing the entrapment of an opponent.[20]

In the end, the episode did have an effect among journalists, but it was not always that which the intriguers anticipated. Anti-Wilson editors now had more ammunition to use in attacking him, and many of the newspapers which were previously lukewarm toward his candidacy, now turned away from him. However, progressive editors were pleased to see Wilson distance himself from the conservative Wall Street interests with which Harvey had close ties. Hemphill, in fact, discovered that the progressive spirit in North Carolina was stronger than he supposed. Many of the *Charlotte Observer*'s readers disagreed with the adamancy he displayed in denouncing Wilson. As one of those readers wrote to him, "Wilson was acting in thorough accord with his Democratic principles, . . . Give the Devil his dues Mr. Hemphill. You do not admire . . . prejudice in others and others do not like the same in you."[21] Even Hemphill's publisher urged him to stop "lambasting" Wilson and to be more "fairminded."[22] Indeed, their disagreement over this matter led Hemphill to resign his editorial position.[23] Meanwhile, Wilson's advisors took steps to minimize the effects of the disclosure. McAdoo urged Wilson to publicize his exchange of letters with Harvey, and Pence launched a counteroffensive in the press suggesting that the reason for the "break" lay in the Governor's refusal to accept aid from the Wall Street financier Thomas Fortune Ryan.[24] As in the two previous attempts to blemish Wilson's character, this "affair" cost him support among journalists, and opposing editors would publish references to it for the remainder of the year. No matter, as the fanfare over the incident ebbed, *Outlook* magazine conducted a poll of the press and found that Wilson remained the candidate who most appealed to voters "irrespective of party."[25] The pro-Wilson editors and his managers had done their work. Wilson was still the favorite and the most publicized Democratic candidate, and in Progressive era politics such publicity was worth having.

II

Publicizing presidential candidates reached a new level in the 1896 Bryan and McKinley campaigns when both parties mass produced and distributed unprecedented amounts of campaign literature. Henceforth, until the radio became available to supplement personal appearances of the candidates in the 1920s, the mass circulation of all types of printed materials was a hallmark of every presidential election campaign. The day of the old press agent had passed. Now people spoke of the "art of publicity" and candidates established publicity bureaus as early as possible in the preconvention period.[26] These bureaus, like the one Tom Pence headed for Wilson, flooded the states with literature extolling their candidates as the contests for the election selection of delegates neared.[27] It should not be supposed, however, that this publicity activity ruled out candidates' stumping on their own behalf. Just the opposite was often the case. In 1896, William Jennings Bryan toured the country by train, covering no less than 18,000 miles, campaigning like no other presidential nominee before him, and four years later, Theodore Roosevelt traveled no less than 21,000 miles as President McKinley's running mate.

Presidential election tactics were modernizing. Moreover, the entire process of publicizing and stumping in 1912 would be of longer duration than in previous campaigns. As a consequence of the new presidential primary laws appearing across the country, candidates would now begin their quest for public support earlier. Though they varied in kind, 24 states had some type of primary in place in 1912.[28] The ramifications of these laws as well as that of the greater role reformers of the era assigned to public opinion was obvious. "Publicity, because of the direct primary law in many sections of this year's campaign, is becoming more and more an indispensable adjunct to political campaigns . . .," observed the trade journal *Fourth Estate*.[29] Quite true, but the press also had its own information and opinion about the candidates to circulate, and the fact that it had grown in size as well as in independence from political parties made its influence on campaigns more problematic than the candidates may have wished. Never before had so many newspapers and magazines reached so many people. The number of English language daily newspapers in the country reached 2,200 in 1910 and to that figure 14,000 weekly newspapers could be added. In fact, between 1870 and 1900 the number of daily newspapers in the United States quadrupled. By contrast, the country's soaring population had not quite doubled during the same period. The increase in number and circulation of magazines at the turn of the century was no less striking.[30] Moreover, if the day of the political party press had passed and if space for regular political news had been reduced to make way for the greater variety of news, which, in turn, drove up circulation, interest in politics remained. The press was an integral part of every political movement of the time, and no one relished wielding political influence more than the press lords who had forged chains of newspapers that, in several cases, reached across the country.

Amid these interacting forces of campaign publicity and political journalism, with their common interest in a candidate's public performance, Wilson had an edge over his Democratic rivals, for none of the other Democratic candidates could match his performance on the platform. The publicity value of his campaign speeches was threefold. While fulfilling their basic purpose of rousing the public to his support, as ovation after ovation proved, they also attracted press attention and, in many instances, provided Pence's publicity bureau with material to reproduce and disseminate in pamphlet form. Between January and April, Wilson made 15 speaking trips and spoke in 16 different states, sometimes several times, from New Hampshire to Florida and as far west as Kansas. One of his speaking engagements was especially noteworthy.

On February 2 he spoke in Philadelphia at the annual dinner of the Periodical Publishers' Association of America, a gathering of the country's leading editors, writers, and publishers that had acquired national status. The other major speaker at the dinner was Senator Robert LaFollette, the former Wisconsin governor and progressive leader who denounced the evils of his day with an intensity that defined his political manner. An air of excitement prevailed among the publicists at the dinner as they waited to hear these two progressive champions. Wilson spoke first. After giving a series of speeches in Virginia the previous day, he had little time to prepare for this one. Nevertheless, he was in top form and delivered a brilliant if short speech, progressive in spirit, and well tailored to fit the audience.

By contrast, LaFollette's speech was a disaster. After months of campaigning, he was exhausted and no doubt anxious about his daughter who lay seriously ill in a nearby hospital. His speech became an incoherent tirade against moneyed interests' control of the press, and it lasted over two hours before an audience that had already been sitting for more than four hours. His inconsideration for and antagonism toward his audience, led people to desert the room by the score. LaFollette's speech had dire consequences for him. Republican progressives, fearing his performance implied nervous exhaustion, turned to Theodore Roosevelt to bear their standard, and on February 24, the former president "threw his hat into the ring."[31] Roosevelt's appeal was more national than LaFollette's, and it made a serious split in Republican ranks more probable. That, in turn, enhanced Democratic prospects for victory in November and attached greater urgency to their quest for delegate support at this time.

Wilson's position now appeared unassailable. He was the frontrunning candidate, and he had retained extensive press support. That support became greater yet when E. W. [Edward Willis] Scripps took an interest in him. Scripps, was a legend among journalists, an individualist par excellence, and a crusty figure with a cantankerous personality, who lived in seclusion on his California ranch and shunned publicity. A compulsive reader since youth, he had a powerful mind and an autocrat's conviction about his own opinions. He was an uncompromising people's champion, and a press lord who intended his newspapers for the masses. In reaching them, he felt that sensationalism was "absolutely necessary to a newspaper." It produced curiosity and concern while being entertaining.[32] Vivid headlines, brief news items, short but lucid editorials, and a variety of human interest features characterized his newspapers, and he insisted they be independent, interesting, and inexpensive. Newspapers with a polished appearance, he held, were the enemies of real journalism—"men make newspapers and money does not."[33] No one would accuse Scripps's newspapers of having a polished appearance, nor would anyone doubt their passionate advocacy of the progressive democracy. If Scripps insisted that the production costs of his newspapers be minimized, he also insisted that editors rather than business managers have control over their content—a fact manifested in the many reform causes they championed.[34] In 1912, his publishing empire consisted of 32 newspapers, mainly small city publications located across the West and in the South; the Newspaper Enterprise Association, a national newspaper feature service; and the United Press Association. He called this vast conglomerate "the concern," and although retired, his influence over it remained dominant, as evidenced by his round-robin correspondence with his editors.

Support from "the concern" was important to Wilson. It would help offset difficulties he was experiencing with the labor press, and it would enhance his chances in the Midwest and West where his opponents were popular. However, Scripps and his editors had ambivalent feelings about supporting Wilson. They wanted a true progressive to occupy the White House, and Senator LaFollette appeared to have the best progressive credentials among the candidates of either party. On January 1, Scripps convened a meeting of his editors at which they decided that LaFollette was their first choice for the presidency, Wilson their second choice, and Roosevelt their third—though they had serious doubts about Roosevelt in any case.[35] Although Wilson appealed to Scripps and his associates more than any other Democratic candidate, his brand of progressivism fell short of that which Scripps avowed. Restraint tempered Wilson's progressivism. As he explained it:

> In every one of my speeches in which I have put forth what seemed [a] radical doctrine, I have accompanied the radical exposition with a statement of absolute necessity that . . . we should recognize our task not as one of hostility to any interest but as one of accommodation and readjustment so that we seek the interest of all.[36]

Scripps, on the other hand, had little use for restraint. "As a journalist," he told a fellow progressive,

> it has been my life long custom to plead the cause of the poor, and working class, be they right or wrong. It is my duty to uphold them when they are right, . . . [and] to prove that the weak, the ignorant, the poor, the hard-worked and consequently badly instructed working-men, are not so much to blame for their lack of judgment and even morals, as is society as a whole.[37]

His editors shared that attitude, and it helps to explain the hesitation they had about supporting Wilson.

Hesitant or not, the Scripps editors came out for Wilson. At first, they found it easy to admire Wilson's action in the Harvey incident.[38] Then, after the feared "breakdown" of LaFollette in Philadelphia, they backed away from him and sharpened their advocacy of Wilson. H. N. Rickey, editor in chief of the Scripps newspapers in Ohio, said it was his intent "to hammer our friend Harmon and do everything possible to encourage the candidacy of Woodrow Wilson."[39] The comment was typical of many others the Scripps editors reported in their correspondence in the following months. Nevertheless, despite this and many other indications of support for him among journalists, it was at this time that damaging opposition to his candidacy escalated in the press.

III

The contest for the nomination tightened, of course, as the preconvention campaigns of Champ Clark and Oscar W. Underwood, now his major opponents, escalated. As it did, criticism of Wilson in the mainstream press became more searching. Some newspapers found him too conservative; others too progressive. He was too idealistic, too untried in national politics, too aloof. He held dangerous views about tariff reduction. His speeches were too general; his positions too vague.

Even newspapers whose support he might expect still questioned what he meant, for instance, when he attacked the "money monopoly."[40]

Wilson's most adamant opponents in the press used additional arguments in their criticism of him. Some of these critics, usually citing his current endorsement of the initiative, the referendum, and the recall, however qualified, after previously opposing those measures of direct democracy, claimed he was vacillating. Others questioned the source of his campaign funds, for without the support of the established Democratic organization, Wilson's managers had to find the money to develop their own organizations in the states and to supply them with abundant campaign literature. A favorite criticism of him dealt with the amount of time he spent on his various speaking tours. Even friendly newspapers sometimes voiced their regret about the amount of time the governor spent campaigning, but his opponents in the press relished publicizing his travels. "Wandering Woodrow," they dubbed him as they suggested he should be known as the "railroad candidate" because of the amount of time he spent campaigning away from home.[41] Most of all, they stressed the idea that, because of his frequent absences, he was neglecting his duty—one that the people of New Jersey paid him $10,000 a year to fulfill. At least Wilson's machine-backed predecessors had "attended faithfully" to their duties, the argument ran, and should he by "hook or crook" become president, no doubt "he would be just as neglectful of his duties there as he has been as governor of the state of New Jersey."[42] Moreover, it would have been a strange campaign, indeed, if the old charges against him in his gubernatorial campaign, about his being unfriendly to organized labor and too friendly with political bosses, had not reemerged in this contest, which, of course, they did. Nor would the more caustic anti-Wilson editors allow his seeking of a Carnegie Foundation pension, his "cocked hat" comment about Bryan, and his "break" with Harvey to pass into oblivion. Nevertheless, these criticisms alone fail to explain the extreme negative tone and scathing personal attacks on Wilson that came to characterize so much of the preconvention hostility to his nomination.

These attacks came from several quarters. Before the furor over the alleged Wilson–Harvey break had receded, several of his old Princeton friends with connections to various national political leaders warned him of another "country-wide attack" that would soon be made on him. "It consists," they cautioned, "of a collection of extracts from your United States History, excoriating especially the Italians and Slavs. These matters have been carefully compiled and are in the possession of your opponents."[43] Their warning proved accurate, for there were compromising passages in his *History of the American People*, enough to be harmful to anyone seeking high political office. For instance, of the immigrants (Magyars as well as Slavs and Italians) who arrived in this country toward the end of the century, Wilson wrote: "Now there came multitudes of men of the lowest class from the south of Italy and men of the meaner sort out of Hungary and Poland, men out of ranks where there was neither skill nor energy nor any initiative of quick intelligence; . . . as if the countries of the south of Europe were disburdening themselves of the more sordid and hapless elements of their population, ..." He even compared these new immigrants to the Chinese who had emigrated to the Pacific coast states, whom he described as skillful, intelligent people with a "hardy power of labor." In the latter case, the fears and demands of those men whom they threatened to "displace," led to the Chinese exclusion legislation.[44] Equally damaging were some of the other passages in his *History*. Not only had he been unsympathetic in his remarks about labor unions and strikes but he had referred to the "errors of opinion" and "radical heresies" of the Farmers' Alliances, the late-nineteenth-century agrarian reform movement. His reference to the program of the People's (Populist) party of the 1890s, one of the antecedents of progressivism a few years later, was little better. Of the party's program he wrote that it "smacked of the extremist purposes of experiment in the field of legislation."[45]

Such comments were sufficient to embarrass any Progressive era presidential candidate. Wilson's *History*, in fact, reflected the conservative views he held when writing it. His impulse then was to defend existing institutions and most of the tenets of a free and competitive economic philosophy, to reject advanced solutions to economic grievances in favor of gradual change in the general public interest. There were, of course, commendable aspects to his *History*, but it was far from his best literary effort. As historians, then and later, pointed out, it was imbalanced, often superficial, and showed signs of hasty construction. One of his Princeton colleagues later called it "a gilt-edged potboiler."[46] Wilson finished it ten years prior to the 1912 campaign at a time when abundant resistance to the politics of protest and concern about unrestricted immigration existed. Despite some notable exceptions, he had been more guarded in his views about labor in subsequent years and deserved high marks for his position toward labor as governor. But his critics did not search his writings to grant him the benefit of such considerations. They sought and found passages that would embarrass him before labor and immigrant communities whose support he hoped to have.

One Wilson opponent who mined his *History* for political profit was a former Populist leader in Massachusetts, George Fred Williams, now a Clark manager in that state. Wilson's application for a Carnegie pension had offended him earlier. "I cannot understand how a real Democrat could touch such money. It is steeped in the human blood of Carnegie's workers, shot down by his hired Pinkertons, while struggling for a decent wage out of the hundreds of millions which their labor was rolling into the Carnegie coffers," he stated for publication.[47] After reading Wilson's *History*, Williams wrote a public letter to Richard F. Pettigrew, the former Populist senator from South Dakota, in which he declared that it was "Toryism of the blackest type," and then he quoted the compromising passages such as those relating to labor, immigration, the Farmer's Alliances, and the Populist party.[48] The charges put Wilson on the defensive, for try as he might to explain them, the fact remained that he had written those passages. Of course, it could be questioned why Williams published the letter and why now. The *New York Times* offered this answer. "Now that Henry Watterson has left the field, George Fred Williams . . . has taken a hand in 'baiting' Gov. Woodrow Wilson."[49] Williams may have "taken a hand" in denouncing Wilson, but the person who took the lead in the endeavor was the formidable, if unorthodox, publisher William Randolph Hearst.

Since Hearst wielded the influence he did and since he now became Wilson's preeminent adversary in the press, he merits particular attention. Having entered the newspaper publishing ranks when he took over the *San Francisco Examiner*, one of his father's properties, in 1887, Hearst became a dynamic journalistic entrepreneur in the fashion of Pulitzer. The senior Hearst, a U.S. Senator, had made a fortune in mining. With that money behind him, his son turned the *Examiner* into a leading West Coast newspaper before invading New York City in 1895 by purchasing the *Morning Journal*. There, as in San Francisco, no production expense was too great for his newspaper; no desired news story, too costly; no enterprising journalist, too highly priced to hire—or to lure away from a competitor. There was never reason to question the talent of the staffs he assembled to man his various publishing enterprises. Once established in New York, he launched one of the most brutal newspaper wars in the history of American journalism as he engaged Pulitzer's *World* in a battle for leadership in mass circulation. Hearst expanded the methods of the New Journalism and made them gaudier than ever. As the contest for circulation advantage continued, the term "yellow journalism" emerged to describe the tactics the two publishers employed. The competition reached its zenith at the time of the Spanish–American War, after which Pulitzer toned down the sensationalism of his *World* while Hearst continued to embrace "yellow" tactics. In fact, aside from the press of the South that resisted the trend, "yellow" newspapers could be found in cities from coast to coast at the turn of the century.[50] It was the journalistic tactics associated with it that caused its many critics to deem it disreputable. To them it embraced a contemptuous mixture of murders and scandals, of sensationalism and exaggeration (even falsification) of news, and of obsession with circulation and excessive self-promotion.

Hearst had his defenders, chief among them was Arthur Brisbane, his leading editor. He described Hearst as "the most useful man in the country" whose only object was "to be of use." Brisbane said his employer was a maligned and misunderstood man and argued that "where other men have succeeded in spite of poverty—which . . . happens every day—Mr. Hearst has succeeded in spite of wealth, which is very rare and happens not once in a hundred times."[51] Indeed, an air of mystery lingered about Hearst. In his personal demeanor, his charm, wit, and compassion was obvious. Yet his aggressive nature led him to unleash attacks on public figures he opposed and to conduct spirited press campaigns on behalf of ordinary people with whom he sympathized. "Hearst was to me a puzzle," one of his editors reflected. "Conducting the most brazen and blatant newspapers, he was personally almost shy."[52] Hearst placed his stamp on the newspapers he published and filled them with his opinions. He wrote and signed many editorials that appeared, sometimes on the front page, in those newspapers and allowed his own thoughts on sundry topics to be quoted as news. By mid 1912, he published newspapers in San Francisco, New York, Atlanta, Boston, Chicago, and Los Angeles plus several national magazines. He also had political ambitions. Starting in 1902, he twice won election to the U.S. Congress, once almost won the mayoralty race in New York City, and once came close to being elected governor of New York. In 1904, he challenged Alton B. Parker for the Democratic presidential nomination, and four years later he bolted the party in favor of Thomas Hisgen, his handpicked presidential candidate for the Independence party, which he controlled.[53] In 1912, Hearst rejoined the Democratic party hoping to emerge as a dark horse nomination, but for the present, he promoted Champ Clark.

It is hardly surprising that Hearst would choose to support Clark rather than Wilson. He became friendly with Clark while serving his terms in Congress and considered the Speaker of the House a well qualified and "true" Democrat. He believed, on the other hand, that Wilson was a theorist who shifted his ground to advance himself.[54] Hearst, as a college student who preferred pranks to studies, was expelled from Harvard during his junior year; Wilson, who valued studies as preparation for service, had spent years distinguishing himself as a scholar and university president. Hearst had "a monumental anti-British bias"; Wilson a great appreciation of things British.[55] Hearst was noisy, rough, and self-aggrandizing in his political campaigns; Wilson, restrained, even reluctant. Hearst preferred the term "striking" to describe his style of journalism; Wilson considered it disreputable.[56] If these differences were insufficient to alienate the two men from one another, Wilson had snubbed Hearst by declining to meet with him in 1911. Wilson wanted nothing to do with Hearst, and told a friend, "God knows I want the Democratic nomination . . . , but if I am to grovel at Hearst's feet, I will never have it."[57] The rebuke notwithstanding, Hearst had already made public his opinion of the governor when he stated in an interview, "There is an uneasy feeling that if . . . [Wilson] were installed in the White House[,] the principles he advocates today he might . . . repudiate tomorrow."[58]

The campaign that Hearst now launched against Wilson boded ill for the governor. It signified the effort Hearst was making to lead the forces determined to block his nomination, and it would be a brutal, prolonged, and personalized assault. It was, in fact, a comprehensive, nationwide press offensive that lasted through the spring and one that played an important role in dethroning Wilson as the front-runner for the nomination. Hearst moved on several fronts. He began by sending his lieutenant, John Temple Graves, to Washington to raise compromising questions about Wilson. Graves, already alienated toward Wilson because of the rebuff when trying to arrange a meeting between Hearst and the governor, now moved to stereotype Wilson as an ingrate. Then Hearst purchased the *Atlanta Georgian* and sent Graves south to edit it. That maneuver struck a double blow against Wilson. The *Georgian*, a pro-Wilson paper sent by its publisher to hundreds of other Democratic dailies across the country, now became a voice of hostility to Wilson in the South as Graves used it to crucify "the professor" for, what in his judgment were, his many antidemocratic sins.

Hearst's editors used Wilson's *History* as a basis for their criticism. They kept Wilson's abrasive comments about immigrants and labor in that study before the public in newspapers stretching across the country from January to May. Hearst took a personal hand in embarrassing the governor in his newspapers. He also consulted Wilson's *History* and concluded that it was not the work of a true Democrat. Hearst considered Wilson's statements about immigrants shameful and his praising of Alexander Hamilton, the Federalist, while criticizing Thomas Jefferson and Andrew Jackson, founders of the Democratic party, inexcusable. Wilson had also written complimentary passages about Jefferson and had acknowledged the sometimes arrogant ways of the Federalists, but those passages were of no interest to Hearst. Wilson was no Democrat, not even a Republican—he was a Federalist! So concluded the publisher as he labeled Wilson an opportunist lacking all conviction. "To my mind," Hearst wrote, "he is a perfect jackrabbit of politics, perched upon his little hillock of expediency, with ears erect and nostrils distended, keenly alert to every scent or sound and ready to run and double in any direction on the slightest intimation of danger." As if this were insufficient argument to make his point, Hearst embellished his statement with references to Wilson as "Judas" and as someone who, if elected, would be "a positive danger to his party and to the country."[59] As strong a denunciation as this was, worse was yet to come.

In 1911 Hearst purchased the *World To-Day*, soon renaming it *Hearst's Magazine*. In this periodical, he had Alfred Henry Lewis, one of his premier writers, attempt to deliver the coup de grace to Wilson's hope for the nomination. Lewis, a well-known, picturesque writer of western stories, had been with Hearst since 1894. While his trenchant writing style and his scorn for the established order won him a place among the early-twentieth-century muckrakers, his cynical, fatalistic attitude toward life made it difficult for him to appreciate a man like Wilson. Had that been his goal in writing about the governor, he would have been out of his depth, but Hearst did not assign him the task of writing about Wilson for that purpose. He wanted a scathing and ranging attack, and that Lewis could write.[60]

Lewis produced a ten-page diatribe against Wilson for *Hearst's Magazine*. Appearing in the May issue, the article scoured "Dr. Wilson's" entire life searching for items to present with a derogatory twist. Accordingly, as a young boy he imbued "Presbyterian piety" from his forebears. Before departing from college "neither distinguished nor extinguished," he began reading *Gentleman's Magazine*, an English publication that was not only "aristocratical" but "supercilious." While still in college he published an article in the *International Review* proclaiming the British Parliament superior to the American Congress and went about the Princeton woods reciting speeches of Edmund Burke. It was also while in college that young Wilson entered his "mocking bird period," became a Glee Clubber, and was "remembered for the masterful way in which he was wont to impale a certain high note, near the end of the 'Star Spangled Banner,' upon his piercing tones. It was something folks journeyed miles to hear."[61]

According to Lewis, as Wilson grew in years, so he grew in his "attitude of pure superiority." His writings proved he was a Federalist who distrusted "the People." "Were a bank next door to an orphanage and both caught on fire," Lewis explained to illustrate the baseness of the Federalists, "the Federalist would save the bank while the Democrat turned the hose on the orphans." Wilson, moreover, had denigrated southern European immigrants in his *History* and, as his reversal on the issue of the initiative, the referendum, and the recall revealed, he was a political "chameleon." Lewis proclaimed Wilson "cold blooded," "narrow," and "egotistical," and, worse yet, made egotistical by "his trade of teacher—a trade in which one reads many books and meets few men." It was also egotism that led him "to beg for a Carnegie pension." Lewis concluded by placing Wilson in comparative perspective. "As an American, he is not the Bunker Hill kind. He is the English kind, the *Gentleman's Magazine* kind, the Hamilton-Federalist kind."[62]

It can, of course, be argued that all politics are personal, but this article was a classic example of character assassination. Only three references to the issues on which Wilson was campaigning can be found in it, and they were cited in an attempt to dishonor him, to show he lacked principle. Lewis declared that Wilson now condemned the boss system but had been an "apologist" of it for years, and that after 20 years of teaching his students of the perils of the initiative, the referendum, and the recall, he now found them to be workable safeguards of democracy. To call into question Wilson's ability to fight for lowering the tariff, Lewis theorized that had he received a Carnegie pension it would have made it difficult for him to separate himself from the "arch-protectionist" Carnegie since he would have been in his debt.

Rather than discuss the issues, the article emphasized Wilson's unfitness for office and argued that he lacked integrity, dependability, and strength of either character or conviction. Lewis also crafted the wording of the article in a way to suggest the unworthiness of Wilson's appeal to various constituencies whose votes he needed. What Democratic worker would vote for someone who had sought "Carnegie gold," bearing "the unclean mark of the beast?" How many Baptists and Methodists who filled the Democratic ranks in the South would be impressed by Wilson's "Presbyterian piety?" How could anyone who read the *Gentleman's Magazine* (it was mentioned eight times in the article) or who admired the British Parliament and the speeches of the famous British conservative, Edmund Burke, be anything but an effete

Anglophile that real Democrats and true Americans would find alien to their cause.[63]

Hearst's campaign against Wilson did not go unchallenged. Governor Wilson had proved himself a friend of labor, and in the first legislative session during his term no less than 16 laws favoring labor had been passed as New Jersey had taken its place in the forefront of the states willing to legislate for the protection of workers.[64] Consequently, when Hearst and others charged that Wilson was unworthy of labor's support, the executive committee of the New Jersey State Federation of Labor adopted a resolution approving of his administration and asserting, "Organized labor would be derelict in its duty if it allowed to pass this opportunity to show appreciation for services rendered the workers of New Jersey." The *Trenton True American* published the declaration, which the Wilson organization printed and distributed in pamphlet form across the country.[65]

Nor were the pro-Wilson editors silent about the Hearst attacks. Norman Hapgood, the liberal editor of *Collier's Weekly* and the most vocal among them, led in defending Wilson against the Hearst juggernaut. He parried the charge based on Wilson's comments about the lowest classes in Italy, Hungary, and Poland emigrating to this country by pointing out that equally derogatory comments could be found in current *New York Evening Journal* editorials, references to "an ignorant man" being "more or less an animal." In Wilson's case, however, he continued to widen his understanding of such national issues and "to face new truths."[66] In the Scripps's empire W. H. Porterfield, the editor in chief of his California newspapers, was the most outspoken about Hearst. "We are going to it up and down the line for Woodrow Wilson," he told E. W. Scripps, "but my chief reason for desiring the success of the Wilson ticket, is to defeat Hearst's professed attempt to deliver the California delegation to Clark."[67]

At one point Wilson added his own voice to the criticism of Hearst. He was campaigning in Illinois, a state with a large number of delegates to be won in its primary and a state in which the Clark and Hearst forces were strong and his own organization weak, when he made a personal response to the Hearst attacks. "William R. Hearst has 'decided' I am not to be nominated," he said at one campaign stop. "What an exhibition of audacity. What a contempt he must feel for the judgment and integrity of the American people." Later, he used a similar tactic before another audience when he explained, "I find myself a good deal embarrassed because I have just heard that Mr. Hearst has decided I am not to be nominated, but that somebody else is. I regret I did not find it out sooner; I would have been spared a long journey. What a commentary it is upon our affairs when one man should suppose he can frame the affairs of the nation. . . . What an exhibition of contempt he must feel for the judgment and independence of the American people." In Springfield he put to rest what he termed Hearst's "deliberate falsehoods," and he went even farther in Peoria by referring to the publisher as a "character assassin." It was to no avail, for on April 9 Clark won a resounding victory in the Illinois primary by a vote of 218,483 to 75,527.[68] Wilson may have been right in what he said, but he made a wise decision when he chose to make this line and tone of response to the press baron the exception rather than the rule in his campaign addresses.

The Hearst campaign against Wilson produced results. Immigrants by the thousands read his newspapers in New York, Boston, and Chicago, and they found in them not only the anti-Wilson writings of his editors but also abundant statements protesting the governor's publicized views about them from their own ethnic leaders. In the Hearst newspapers, the editors of the foreign language press found an ally. The *Nation*, one of Wilson's strong supporters, tried to fend off these protests as "efforts to play upon the time-worn trumpet of race hostility."[69] Considering that Wilson had been active in the movement against immigration restriction in 1906 and was a director of the National Liberal Immigration League, which fought anti-immigration legislation, the *Nation* had a point. However, Hearst's promotion of ethnic concern, even anger, about Wilson was significant. With only rare exception, the editors of foreign language newspapers were against Wilson. He failed to carry states in which there were Hearst newspapers plus a large European immigrant population.[70] In fact, Wilson lost California, Georgia, Illinois, Massachusetts, and New York—all the states in which Hearst newspapers were located.[71]

Just as the Hearst press had led for months in the effort to derail Wilson's nomination, so it had led even longer the promotion of Speaker Clark for that prize. Hearst began his Clark publicity late in 1911, when he had Alfred Henry Lewis write a laudatory article about the Speaker in *Cosmopolitan Magazine*. The "Honorable Champ," as Lewis called him, epitomized the West, but standing "by his game and his guns," he would not overlook the East.[72] Other Hearst writers fell in line praising Clark's attractive and progressive qualities.[73] Many newspapers, particularly across the upper South and West, agreed with that opinion. The strength of Clark's candidacy cannot be denied. After serving a term in the Missouri legislature, he won election to Congress in 1892, where he would remain except for two years (1894–96) until 1920. Clark was an able parliamentarian and in 1908 his Democratic colleagues named him their minority leader. Three years later, he became Speaker of the House of Representatives when the Democrats gained control of that body for the first time since 1894. Most progressive legislation received his support and during the heyday of William Jennings Bryan's popularity, he had been a follower of the Great Commoner. Consequently, he had a strong claim on western Democrats and agrarian radicals. As a veteran congressman and Democratic leader, he also enjoyed the support of many of the party faithful as well as most of the big city Democratic machines. Years before he had served briefly as president of Marshall College, West Virginia's first normal school, but he projected the image of an old-fashioned country politician. "I sprang from the loins of the common people, God Bless them! and I am one of them," he told one campaign interviewer.[74] Clark's strength among Democrats became obvious as he won delegates from state after state, many whose support Wilson had hoped to have, and far outdistanced Wilson in delegate strength as the convention approached.

As the campaign continued through the spring, there were indications that Wilson's supporters in the press had become less outspoken on his behalf than he would have wished. Already in March, Scripps's son John, editorial chief of eight Scripps newspapers, wrote to his father, "I feel that Harmon has a better chance than Wilson. . . . We are doing what we can for Wilson—how well we are doing it I don't know. Anyhow he's pretty much of an icicle to cuddle up to these frosty nights." He elaborated further a few days later when he wrote, "I don't like the idea of sitting on the fence, but in this case it is hard to support anybody. Here in Ohio the Wilson boom, even, is in the hands of corporation Democrats. . . . ."[75] Gilson Gardner, Scripps's Washington correspondent for the widely circulating N. E. A., was advocating Roosevelt in the Scripps papers, and E. W. Scripps saw nothing wrong with that since Roosevelt was then the most talked about person in the country. In addition, he believed that Gardner's departure from "the concern's" policy of supporting Wilson was good journalism. It indicated a commitment to fairness and an effort to "keep our papers as clean from our prejudice and bias as we possibly can."[76] Newspaperman that he was, Scripps also realized the value in giving Roosevelt fair play in print. "We are bound to be sensible journalists," he explained to one of his editors, "and hence caterers to the public demand for news. . . . There can be no doubt . . . that one line about Roosevelt will be more interesting than a column about Wilson, and that a trifling event in the Roosevelt movement will awaken more public interest than the biggest kind of an eruption in the Wilson field."[77]

Undoubtedly, the phenomenon that journalists referred to then as the "Roosevelt circus" or "Roosevelt mania" did attract interest away from Wilson. Roosevelt knew how to create news. Yet that fact fails to explain the ebbing of Wilson's fortunes in the Democratic and independent press. Some conservative editors, of course, had second thoughts about him as he became more progressive. Other editors, especially in the West, preferred Clark to Wilson. There was also speculation at the time that none of the Democratic candidates would have the required number of pledged delegates to guarantee his nomination at the opening of the Baltimore convention, and some Democratic newspapers found that idea acceptable. This circumstance, which would allow the Democrats to nominate the person best able to cope with the outcome of the Republican convention meeting a week before the Democrats gathered, was an advantage that should "not be destroyed by snap-shot decisions in advance of the event," the *New York World* announced.[78]

However explained, the weakening of Wilson's press support frustrated his managers. He needed all the backing he could find to counter Clark's advantage. After Wilson won a crucial victory, in Wisconsin on April 2, the result of an all out effort in that state, McAdoo added this comment to his vote of congratulations, "I see, as usual, that the New York papers have not featured it as it deserves."[79] The *New York Times*, despite its slogan, "All the News That's Fit to Print," had to select the news it printed, and during the spring campaign of 1912, it slighted Wilson in making that selection. From March on into June, its front page and news columns were filled with reports about Roosevelt and Taft that often were accompanied by a lengthy editorial. News of Wilson was relegated to inside pages, and failed to gain editorial notice. Not until the end of May did it afford Wilson any prominence in its pages.[80] Meanwhile, his campaign was stumbling in an area in which he expected to have deep-rooted press support—in the South.

IV

Among southern editors, Wilson had found much of his early backing. Progressive editors like Clarence Poe, whose *Progressive Farmer* enjoyed one of the largest circulations among weeklies in the region, remained steadfast behind the governor. Editors of like persuasion considered Underwood similar to Alton B. Parker, the conservative Democratic candidate of 1904, and a disaster to the hopes for a Democratic victory in November. As Poe put it, "I regard Woodrow Wilson as the real hope of the progressive element of the country, a man whose profound mind and high character would keep him from being unsafe, but who would stand for healthy and genuine reforms in national life such as he has so effectively supported and accomplished as Governor of New Jersey."[81] Many southern editors, however, had a different view of the Democratic candidates and of Democratic chances of winning the presidency.

When Oscar W. Underwood announced his candidacy for the Democratic nomination in February 1912, Wilson began to lose his hold on the press in the region. His liberalism disturbed southern conservatives. They found Underwood, more than Wilson, a true son of the South. Underwood had resided there most of his life and had practiced law in Birmingham since 1884. Elected to Congress in 1895, he gained stature as an able tactician. First as a party whip, then as chairman of the Ways and Means Committee, and, after 1910, as majority floor leader of the House, he proved himself a skilled congressional director of his party. Southern conservative editors portrayed him not only as a man of proven leadership and of integrity but also as one who believed in sound tariff revision and disavowed the initiative, the referendum, and the recall, those progressive measures that they so distrusted. The widespread expectation that Roosevelt would win the Republican nomination also worked in Underwood's behalf. Believing that it would be unwise to try to compete with the former president in terms of popularity, many Democrats thought their best hope for success lay in nominating someone identified with an issue. Underwood's championing tariff revision made him their logical choice. "To name a radical like Woodrow Wilson to oppose such a pronounced radical as Mr. Roosevelt," warned the *Atlanta Constitution*'s Washington correspondent, "would be like expecting the moon to outshine the sun. His doom in the west would be sealed in advance."[82] Originally the Underwood movement aimed to promote him as a "favorite son" candidate in Alabama, but after February it became a regional movement.

The conservative press in the South formed the vanguard of the movement. Prominent newspapers in the southeast, beginning with those in his own state, came out for him in February 1912 when he formally announced his candidacy. Wilson's managers in Alabama felt it would be counterproductive to campaign there as the *Birmingham Age-Herald*, the *Birmingham News*, the *Mobile Register*, and the *Montgomery Times*, newspapers once favorable to Wilson, all announced for Underwood. Despite the efforts of his old Princeton classmate and Alabama newspaper publisher Frank P. Glass, the best that could be done for him was to secure his position as a preferred second choice should Underwood's nomination fail.[83] During the spring months, the Underwood movement gained momentum across the southeast as Wilson's slipped, and a number of powerful Democratic state organizations and important newspapers beyond Alabama like the *Atlanta Constitution*, the *Florida Times-Union* and the *Memphis Commercial Appeal* hastened its advance.[84]

Underwood's managers, led by Senator John H. Bankhead, employed several publicity tactics to publicize his cause. They advertised his southernness with slogans like "The South for a Southerner" and played up his leadership in tariff reform, an issue dear to the South.[85] Another one of their publicity efforts occasioned a response from the Wilson camp. Bankhead mass-produced endorsements and other materials praising Underwood and offered them to newspapers, especially small country weekly newspapers, throughout the southeast. Newspapers choosing to run these two- and four-page supplements would receive full advertising rates from 10 to 15 dollars depending on the extent of their circulation. It was an expensive project. The supplements appeared for weeks in every issue of some 200 or 300 small newspapers. As a means of introducing Underwood to thousands of farmers and to show how his tariff revision plans would profit them, it was a master stroke, but, it invited criticism on two counts. First, from the perspective of the Wilson campaign, they appeared unethical. Although Bankhead denied the charge, the supplements suggested that newspapers carrying them endorsed Underwood. They seemed to make a dramatic statement for many rural weeklies following a practice of largely avoiding national political issues.[86] Second, since the Underwood managers proclaimed that theirs would be an inexpensive campaign, one operating only in Alabama and neighboring states, where did they find the money for these costly advertisements? Wilson's Washington office charged that the money had come from Thomas Fortune Ryan, the same New York financier who was alleged to have been backing Wilson some months before. Bankhead denied this charge and claimed that Underwood Clubs in Alabama had raised the money.

Pro-Underwood editors also rushed to his defense. The *Montgomery Advertiser*, for instance, referred to Wilson's managers as "certain paragons of left-over virtue" and wanted to know where Wilson had found the money for *his* campaign. It pointed out that pro-Wilson literature had flooded every newspaper office throughout the country for months. That was not the worst of it. The Wilson material was "fancy literature, well-written, well printed, . . . and sent out from headquarters located on that distinguished thoroughfare of the plutocrats, Brodway [*sic*] and very near to Wall street [*sic*] New York." It was the most "thorough newspaper publicity campaign ever conducted on this continent," the *Advertiser* claimed. By contrast, it contended that the Underwood forces had declined to run such an expensive campaign.[87] Nevertheless, time would show that Ryan did, indeed, finance a large portion of Underwood's campaign.[88]

Underwood's candidacy gave Hearst yet another opportunity to block Wilson. It was his original intention to support Clark by purchasing the *Atlanta Georgian*; however, once Underwood's campaign gained momentum Clark's chances in Georgia grew remote. Consequently, John Temple Graves, whom Hearst had assigned to the *Georgian*, negotiated an arrangement with two of Underwood's newspaper friends, Clark Howell, editor of the *Atlanta Constitution*, and Edward W. Barrett, editor of the *Birmingham Age-Herald*. Accordingly, the *Georgian* would support Underwood who, in turn, would skip the Tennessee contest for the nomination. Both Underwood and Bankhead denied having any knowledge of the agreement when, as a result of Underwood's entry into the Tennessee contest, Graves charged them with bad faith.[89] Nevertheless, Underwood made a point to thank Hearst for his help and Hearst replied that he was "exceedingly glad that the attitude of the Georgian met with your approval. . . ."[90]

In Florida and Georgia, two states Wilson hoped to carry, criticism of him sometimes assumed a bitter edge. At first the anti-Wilson press exploited his application for a Carnegie retirement grant, but the criticism soon broadened. One persistent opposing newspaper, the *Pensacola Evening News*, published a letter from one of the governor's enemies in New Jersey stating that he had not voted in 1908. Wilson's written denials failed to put that rumor to rest. Even after the *News* received an affidavit from the voting board of Wilson's New Jersey ward as proof that he had voted in 1908, other newspapers invented and spread the charge that he had rarely, perhaps never, voted Democratic.[91] As the campaign progressed, the state's conservative press became more upset by Wilson's progressivism. Papers like the *Tampa Morning Tribune*, and the *Tallahassee Semi-Weekly True Democrat* claimed that Wilson "smelled" of socialism, that he was anti-Semitic, anti-Catholic, anti-Jefferson, and anti-Jackson. As for his espousal of the initiative, the referendum, and the recall, they were dangerous, unconstitutional measures and a "retrogression toward Greek mobocracy." Conservative and rural Floridian editors of this persuasion saw Wilson as an unsafe candidate who had deserted the South. Underwood, by contrast, was sure, safe, and southern.[92] On April 30, he captured support throughout rural Florida and won the primary.

Perhaps Wilson would fare better in Georgia. According to McAdoo that state was essential, and he told Wilson, "We must not lose it."[93] Georgia, in fact, occupied a crucial position in his bid for southern support, and Wilson felt it would endorse him. He had spent most of his youth there, and his father had served for 13 years as the pastor of Augusta's First Presbyterian Church. His wife was Georgia born and raised, and should Wilson gain the presidency, Georgia could take pride in having one of its own as first lady. When he visited Atlanta in March of the previous year to address the Southern Commercial Congress, editors and public leaders present gave him a tremendous ovation and talked of his becoming the next president. Soon after he departed the state, Hoke Smith, the former reform governor of Georgia and now U.S. Senator, who controlled a large faction of the state's Democratic party, declared for Wilson, and Pleasant A. Stovall, a boyhood friend of Wilson and now editor of the *Savannah Evening Press*, began a Wilson boom in the state. Other Georgia newspapers, most important of all the *Atlanta Journal*, championed his cause. A poll taken of the members of the Georgia legislature in the summer of 1911 showed that he was by far their favorite candidate.[94]

Yet, ominous signs loomed. Underwood's managers poured money into his campaign in the state, sensing that he could make victory there the stepping stone to even greater campaign conquests in the South. Conservative Georgian Democrats gravitated toward Underwood, and the entire political organization of Governor Joseph M. Brown, the predominant one in the state, enjoined the effort to defeat Wilson at the grass-roots level. Moreover, despite the press support Wilson received, a full 80 percent of the state's newspapers were against him in the end. Among them were not only important metropolitan newspapers like the *Atlanta Constitution* and Hearst's *Atlanta Georgian*, but also the vast majority of the country weekly press. However, Wilson's bitterest opponent in Georgia's press was the old Populist leader Tom Watson. He remained as fiery in print as he was on the stump, and he despised Wilson.[95]

As politician, orator, and editor, Watson was a power in Georgia with a large following throughout the South. He was an agitator whose denunciations could arouse the emotions of the rural poor. Blunt and combative, Watson's journalistic style was a mixture of accusation, ridicule, and abuse presented with unrivaled flamboyance. The core of all of the newspapers and magazines he published and edited, dating back to 1891, could be found in his long, spirited editorials.[96] He had made his feelings known about Wilson already in 1905. The editor found Wilson's treatment of the South in his *History* offensive and considered his claim that trusts would be "moralized" rather than abolished as utter nonsense. He advised Wilson:

> Go back to thy gerund-grinding, Woodrow—thou insufferable impractical prig. Among the dead Greeks and the extinct Romans thy labors may, haply be useful; but when thou comest among the practical men of today seeking to master actual conditions and to take part in the great battle of thought, motive and purpose which rages around us thou art but 'a babby, and a gal babby at that.[97]

By 1912 Watson's prejudices had grown to pathological proportions, and in his implacable editorials he voiced a vile hatred of blacks, Catholics, foreigners, Jews, and now of Woodrow Wilson.

Watson leveled vicious attacks on Wilson in his weekly newspaper, the *Jeffersonian*, as the state preferential primary neared. He presented the governor as someone who heaped insults on the South in his *History* and as one who held contempt for laborers and farmers. Wilson, he claimed, had deserted his post as governor and traveled afar campaigning for the nomination, and he had even appointed a Jesuit (a reference to Joseph Tumulty who was Catholic) as his private secretary. But those charges were mild compared with his further accusations. The governor, he charged, was "two-faced," a "cad," an "arrant liar," a falsifier of history, an "abject coward wherever Rome was concerned," a "typical Down-East Yankee," and a tool of Wall Street financed by Thomas F. Ryan.[98] Watson wrote that Wilson would even address blacks in the same manner as he addressed "distinguished white men." Worse yet, in an article, "The Nigger and the Governor of New Jersey," he accused Wilson of befriending Booker T. Washington, the eminent black educator, by sending him a message of "consolation and confidence" when he was alleged to have been caught "peeping through the keyhole of a white woman's bedroom" in New York.[99] Would a Southerner much less a Georgian, have sent a condolence? As for Hoke Smith's support for Wilson, Watson claimed that he was only a political opportunist who wished to elect "Woodrow Booker Washington Wilson" in order to "retire from public life by way of a cabinet appointment."[100]

Despite the crudity of this type of journalism, it succeeded in damaging Wilson's chances for the nomination. Watson's name-calling and unsavory rhetoric helped his publications to grow in popularity. Only a few years before, they were operating at a loss. Now they made "handsome"

A Gold Brick

Figure 8 *Watson's Magazine* (Thomson, Ga.), June 1912. Portrays the opinion of Tom Watson, Wilson's most implacable opponent in the press, of the trustworthiness of candidate Wilson.

profits.[101] He claimed a circulation of 45,000 for his *Jeffersonian* weekly, and even allowing for possible exaggeration, the figure shows that the weekly had considerable outreach, even beyond the region. It could be purchased at newsstands in Washington, D.C., and in Texas Champ Clark's forces reproduced and circulated 15,000 copies of "The Nigger and the Governor of New Jersey" in pamphlet form, despite Wilson's denial that he had sent the letter in question.[102]

Georgia's preferential primary took place on May 1, and on that day its conservative press trumpeted the news of Wilson's previous day's defeat in Florida. "**BURIED!** WILSON BOOM LAID TO REST IN FLORIDA," headlined the *Atlanta Constitution.* "Wilson, twisting, evading, dodging, catches at every economic rainbow that bears promise of a few votes," it charged. Moreover, a victory for Underwood would reestablish the South's national political prestige—it would be a victory for "political manhood." In extolling Georgians to vote, the *Constitution* warned that a vote against Underwood would "admit craven fear of a dead fetish, death of self-respect, and injustice to generations yet to be born."[103] Such was the crisis atmosphere that anti-Wilson editors of even the respectable newspapers tried to create as Georgians went to the polls. They were jubilant when the returns came in announcing Underwood's victory. Wilson, however, carried most of the large cities in the state—every one in which he campaigned. He carried his boyhood home city, Augusta, his wife's home city, Rome, and could claim a solid victory over Underwood in Atlanta. Even the *Constitution*, with its voice now subdued, admitted that it was a tribute to Wilson, to "his grip on people and his essential charm, that where he was best known he should have made the most formidable showing." It was the rural counties that defeated Wilson.[104]

Factional party politics at the state level also contributed to Wilson's defeat, but, in the main, Underwood beat him in the rural counties. That is where Tom Watson's strength lay, and Underwood recognized the fact. "I write to express to you my sincere appreciation of your support for my cause, and to thank you for the strenuous work that you have done in the campaign," read a statement from the Alabamian that appeared in the *Jeffersonian* after the election.[105] His campaign manager in Georgia, as well as many of the state's officials and journalists, credited Watson for Underwood's victory.[106] James R. Gray, the editor of the *Atlanta Journal* held that Watson's editorials had lost the Georgia delegation for Wilson.[107] His editorial in the *Journal* about Watson's influence was explicit. The Underwood forces in Georgia, it declared, were "gloating over a campaign that was won through the slanderous aid of the Democratic party's most despicable traitor and foe. If they think it was their prowess which defeated Woodrow Wilson in the Georgia primary, they are sorely mistaken. It was a vulgar falsehood spawned and disseminated by Thomas E. Watson that did the work."[108]

Could the tide rising against Wilson be stemmed? Underwood's momentum continued in the southeast as he won contests in Mississippi,

Louisiana, and Virginia, and gained the majority of Tennessee's delegates. Early in May, Marse Henry announced that Wilson's "BUBBLE HAS BURST," that his "campaign of hot air and printers ink" had petered out. He advised people now to refer to him as, "THE LATE WOODROW WILSON."[109]

V

Meanwhile, in the northeast and West, state after state fell to Champ Clark, swelling the size of his preconvention delegate strength. E. W. Scripps observed that it was "evident that Wilson will not be nominated."[110] Wilson even had a fight on his hands in New Jersey where his old adversaries, James Smith, Jr. and James Nugent were at work mobilizing an anti-Wilson movement. However, as the Wilson movement plummeted toward its nadir early in May, the pro-Wilson editors began to see the real possibility of Clark's winning the nomination. That disturbed them, for they did not consider the Speaker a fit candidate to lead the Democrats to victory in the fall. Consequently, they became more aggressive in criticizing him and more urgent in their promotion of Wilson.

Norman Hapgood explained why it was necessary to check the draft to Clark in his editorial, "Why Woodrow Wilson?" in *Collier's*, whose circulation was reaching the 500,000 mark. Either Harmon or Underwood would split the Democrat party and neither would be able to win the West, he explained. Clark would "be battered to pieces in four months of bombardment." If the nomination fell to Bryan, the old story would be repeated. His popularity notwithstanding, he would fail to prevail in the East. Only Wilson could pull votes away from Roosevelt, gain the confidence of the growing numbers of independent voters in the country, and have a real chance of winning the backing of the "majority of the great magazines and great independent dailies" of the nation.[111]

Other pro-Wilson editors became even sharper in their criticism of Clark. They feared that "the interests" would influence him too much and that many intemperate comments he had made over the years would return to haunt him in the election campaign. Despite his amiability, the *New York Globe* claimed he was "as loose of mind as he has been of mouth."[112] Considering his comments about annexing Canada and Cuba, abolishing the Civil Service System as well as the diplomatic corps, and his reference to Grover Cleveland, the last

Democratic president, as a Benedict Arnold and a Judas, the concern of these newspapers can be understood.[113] The *New York World* summarized their feeling by stating, "Champ Clark's nomination would be Democratic suicide."[114]

A revitalization of the Wilson movement was occurring. On May 15, Wilson's forces in South Carolina managed to hold that state for him and to sidetrack Underwood's march through the southeast. More good news followed as Wilson scored victories in Texas, Utah, South Dakota, and Minnesota, and won most of North Carolina's delegates. But could he carry his own state? To lose New Jersey would be disastrous. There his inveterate press opponents were belittling his "talking corps" in the press and predicting that "the clouds" were "lowering on the Wilson propaganda, not only in this state but elsewhere."[115] Moreover, Wilson deemed it "unbecoming" to make a state-wide canvas for votes in his own state where he felt the people knew him. He only made several campaign speeches and published one long public letter in which he pleaded for the people to send a progressive slate of delegates to the Baltimore convention. That was enough.

On May 28 the people of New Jersey rewarded him with a victory of landslide proportion that spurred onward support for him elsewhere. The next day, McAdoo told Wilson, "My friends on the 'World' tell me that something interesting will appear Thursday morning, the 30th, and that it ought to be pleasing to us."[116] McAdoo was, indeed, the bearer of good news, for the *New York World* seized the opportunity afforded by these victories to declare in favor of Wilson the next day with the single most important editorial of the campaign. "We have not hesitated to warn him when we thought he was going astray, and shall not hesitate to do so in the future," Frank Cobb began the editorial. Then he cited the ways in which Wilson had proved himself by his political courage and by his soundness on tariff reform, corporation control, plutocratic influence, judicial independence, and on the "principles of constitutional government." Cobb concluded with this reassuring sentiment.

> Gov. Wilson has had more public experience than Grover Cleveland had when he was elected President. He is better known to the rank and file of the party than Samuel J. Tilden was when he was nominated for President. *The World* believes that he would be a progressive constitutional President whom the American people could trust and for whom they would never have cause to apologize.[117]

A few days later, Cobb wrote to Wilson, "It will gratify you, I think, to know that no other editorial printed in The World in many years met with such public response as the one advocating your nomination for President."[118]

Amid the upswing apparent in Wilson's campaign, a salient fact remained. Clark had accumulated 436 pledged delegates by the end of the prenomination campaign. That was short of the 545 majority vote needed for the nomination, but it was far ahead of Wilson's 248. The delegate strength of Underwood, Harmon, and various favorite son candidates trailed far behind Wilson's total, but the way was open for deals to be struck that would give Clark the nomination. Wilson had enough pledged votes to keep Clark from a first ballot victory. Beyond that, only a fighting chance.

Midway through the campaign, the *New York Globe* commented that it was "doubtful whether American political history, full as it is of reckless slander, furnishes an instance of character-assassination more contemptible than that of which Woodrow Wilson has been victim."[119] The severest attacks on his candidacy lend credence to that observation, not simply because they manifested bias, exaggeration, misrepresentation, and sometimes pure invention in their appeal to emotions, but because they tried to destroy the reputation of an honorable man. These personalized attacks represented the worst features of journalism of that time. Wilson, had long been concerned about reckless journalism, and he found in the instances of the bitterest press attacks against him in the preconvention campaign, confirmation of those concerns.

There were also, of course, many journalists who continued to support Wilson throughout the campaign, and but for them his position at the end of the campaign would have been even more precarious. If some of them wavered at times or offered support, as in the case of the Scripps editors, sometimes less than desired, the fact remains that their backing was indispensable to Wilson. They effectively promoted him in the early months of the campaign, defended him against what one journalist termed "the many canards . . . published in attempt to injure" him, and helped to reinvigorate Wilson's political fortunes in May.[120] Moreover, the image they advanced of him in June as an unusually skilled governor, as a reformer, as party unifier, and as a leader with the qualities needed to be a statesman in a new political age, was an effective one to nurture in the final days before the convention. Among the pro-Wilson journalists was a core of believers who were unrelenting in defending and forwarding his cause. Josephus Daniels personified the group. Years later when reflecting on his participation in political campaigns covering no less than 50 years, he said the preconvention fight for Wilson in 1912 was the most difficult one of all.[121] In it he made an extraordinary effort on Wilson's behalf, both in print and, as was the custom of many journalists of the time, as an active campaigner. "You are certainly a friend worth having," Wilson told him at the end of the campaign.[122] The comment was typical of those Wilson made to his most loyal supporters in the press, and in doing so he was recognizing an undeniable fact of the contest then ending.

Chapter 8

Wilson and the Press at the Democratic Convention and Afterward

The weeks preceding, encompassing and following the Democratic convention were among the most exciting in American political history. After a riotous preconvention struggle for delegates, President Taft's supporters managed to organize the Republican convention in June in Chicago and to have him renominated on the first ballot. However, supporters of former President Roosevelt considered that result fraudulent. Nor was Roosevelt content to abide by the convention's decision. He announced that he would accept the nomination of a new party should his supporters decide to form one and offer him its nomination. His delegates responded by gathering in Chicago's Orchestra Hall to found a new Progressive party, and they agreed to hold their own national nominating convention early in August. True to their word, they returned to Chicago the first week in August and nominated Roosevelt to head their ticket. With the Republican party split, the way appeared open for the Democrats to sweep to victory in November, if they could nominate a strong candidate. There were, however, several unpredictable factors to consider. Roosevelt's campaigning prowess and his large and devoted following could never be discounted. Nor could the fact be dismissed that the Progressive or Bull Moose party, as it was soon nicknamed, was well financed. Nevertheless, when the Democrats convened in Baltimore following the Republican convention in Chicago, it was the split in the Republican ranks that excited them. To whom would they turn to take advantage of the Republican party split and to counter the popular support that Roosevelt might marshal behind him in the fall campaign?

I

Stalwart Wilson supporters in the press left little to chance in promoting him in the weeks before the convention opened. Undeterred by the odds against his nomination, they employed various strategies in their efforts to place him foremost among the candidates in the public mind and in that of the delegates gathering in Baltimore. The *New York World* led the surge to increase the tempo of enthusiasm for Wilson. Day after day throughout June, it published articles about his record as reform governor of New Jersey, about how he had defeated the political bosses and grafters and succeeded in having progressive legislation passed where others before him had failed. It promoted his accomplishments on behalf of labor, and in particular, it lauded Wilson's fight for the passage of an Employers' Liability and Workingmen's Compensation Act, calling it "the best law of the kind now in force." In one article, "Every Promise Wilson Made the People He Has Performed," it listed the 12 planks of the platform on which he was elected and explained how he had fulfilled each one.[1] To its "People's Forum," the space it gave to letters from readers on the editorial page, the *World* added a special feature entitled "FOR PRESIDENT—WOODROW WILSON," and ran it for over a week. Letters in praise of Wilson from people and paragraphs of editorial opinion favoring him from other newspapers, many in response to the *World's* May 30 editorial, filled these columns. They came mainly from the East and South and represented parties of various political persuasions.[2] Afterward the pro-Wilson letters continued to appear in the "People's Forum" columns.

Another major newspaper backing Wilson, the *Baltimore Sun*, employed a different strategy. Its president and general manager Charles H. Grasty had admired Wilson for years, and the *Sun* had been one of the first newspapers to advance Wilson's nomination. Now Grasty and his staff devised a plan to promote Wilson at the convention. They sent copies of the *Sun* to all the convention delegates for four weeks prior to its opening. During this time, according to Grasty, it "gave all candidates a fair show." On June 4, for instance, it reprinted Frank Cobb's editorial endorsing Wilson in the *New York World*, and on the next day, an editorial by Henry Watterson in which he criticized Wilson as untrustworthy and strongly argued for Champ Clark. The idea was, in Grasty's words, to keep "the minds of the delegates open to our 'poison.'"[3] If they acquired the habit of relying on the *Sun*, the newspaper would be in a position to maximize its influence during the convention.

Thomas B. Delker, the editor and publisher of the *Hammonton South Jersey Star*, targeted other newspapers as well as delegates in promoting Wilson. He sent a number of copies of his "boost numbers" to the chairman of each state delegation and 2000 copies to Wilson's convention headquarters. He also reproduced an article from the *Philadelphia Record* and sent it to newspapers in Baltimore, Boston, Chicago, New York, and Washington for use during convention week. After Wilson thanked him for that effort, he sent an additional 1,500 "boost numbers" to the "firing line" in Baltimore.[4]

Wilson's own publicity bureau was also preparing for the Baltimore convention. Tom Pence made certain the conventioneers had copious material about the governor. More than a week before the convention opened, he reproduced the *New York World*'s editorial, a particularly effective article from the *Elizabeth Evening Times*, and other pertinent newspaper items and sent the packet to each delegate. In the sample mailing he sent to Wilson, Pence added his comment: "I am also enclosing herewith editorial expressions from the leading independent newspapers, located in every section of the country, backing up the position taken by the New York World in favor of your nomination at Baltimore. I am sending a lot of matter of this type to the delegates."[5] Meanwhile, Wilson's campaign managers were able to use their final preconvention endorsements as a source of encouragement for the delegates pledged to the governor. As evidence of the growing conviction in favor of Wilson's nomination, the managers referred the delegates to "the splendid support which his candidacy is receiving on the eve of the convention from the independent press of the country, without which no Democratic nominee can win, . . ."[6]

Nevertheless, no amount of activity among the pro-Wilson editors could dispel the hard fact that Clark had a substantial majority of pledged delegates. Not since 1844 had the Democratic candidate with the majority of votes failed to win the nomination, and the Wilson forces would have an uphill fight at the convention. Yet their spirits were high. As the convention opened on June 25 in Baltimore's Fifth Regiment Armory, the grey stone, fortress-like facade of that building belied the atmosphere inside. Scenes of hard-to-control demonstrations and boisterous battles over procedure characterized the gathering from the start. Not even the stifling summer heat of the city, which sent many delegates scurrying to nearby bars for refreshment, could dim the excitement of the ensuing sessions. In years to come old convention goers would look back on this gathering as the most dramatic one of all.

Lasting eight days, the convention became the scene of fluctuating expectations for victory on behalf of the leading candidates as ballot after ballot failed to produce a winner. William Jennings Bryan was responsible for some of the fluctuation of political fortunes. Determined to have a progressive nominated, the Great Commoner refused to support any of the conservative nominees. He would back Clark or Wilson, both of whom could lay claim to progressive support. Bryan withheld his endorsement from either candidate, but he was chairman of the Nebraska delegation which was pledged to Clark. However, he soon became convinced that Clark's forces were acting in collusion with those of Tammany Hall, the bane of the progressive's reform hopes. Charles F. Murphy, the Tammany Hall boss was there in person to direct the 90 votes of the New York delegation, and with the arrival of August Belmont and Thomas F. Ryan, both powerful financial barons, Bryan's conviction grew that the progressive cause was imperiled. He persuaded the convention to adopt an anti-Wall Street resolution pledging delegates to reject any candidate who was obligated to J. P. Morgan, Thomas F. Ryan, or August Belmont. Then on the fourteenth ballot, Bryan shifted his vote and those of the Nebraska delegation to Wilson. Although pledged to Clark, he said the state they represented was progressive and would oppose candidates committed to Tammany hall and Wall Street.

Bryan's action, as symbolic as it was, did not determine the outcome of the convention. On the tenth ballot Boss Murphy shifted New York's 90 votes from Harmon to Clark, an action intended to launch a landslide movement for Clark, but it stalled short of gaining the two-thirds vote needed for victory. Wilson's delegates remained firm as did those of Underwood. The hundred or so votes pledged to the Alabamian would have provided Clark the required two-thirds vote; consequently, it was the Underwood forces that now held the balance of power in balloting. However, early in the balloting Wilson's convention managers met with the leaders of the Underwood delegations and agreed, should Wilson bow out, to use all their influence to have his delegates shift to Underwood. The Underwood leaders, in turn, agreed to remain firm behind their man. The agreement held, and when it finally became clear that Clark could not win and as the votes for Wilson continued to mount, Underwood released his delegates on the forty-sixth ballot. Wilson had been their second choice all along and now their shift to the governor created an irresistible tide that carried him to victory. There were, of course, other shifts to Wilson that occurred along the way, those led by Thomas Taggart, the Democratic boss of Indiana, and Roger

Sullivan, the head of the Illinois Democratic machine, in particular. Taggart's move led to the convention's naming Governor Thomas R. Marshall of Indiana as Wilson's running mate. Nevertheless, in the end nothing was of greater consequence in Wilson's victory than the agreement made many ballots before between his forces and those of Underwood.

The pro-Wilson press also played an important role during the convention. From the start, it portrayed the procedures in Baltimore as a struggle between progressive and reactionary forces. That dichotomy worked to Wilson's favor, especially as Clark's name came to be associated with Tammany Hall and also, perhaps, with the financial barons. As the *Charlotte Daily Observer* put it, "Missourian Losing Strength, Result of His Coalition With Tammany Murphy and Thomas F. Ryan of Wall Street."[7] The pro-Wilson newspapers did all in their power to build enthusiasm behind his candidacy. For example, the *Chicago Daily News* headlined its main news article after the balloting began "WILSON STAR RISING IN DEMOCRATIC SKY AFTER FIRST BALLOT" despite the fact that as a result of that ballot Clark received 440 and one-half votes to Wilson's 324.[8] Most delegates, moreover, assumed that New York's 90 votes would soon be added to Clark's column. Other newspapers like the *New York Times* stressed the theme that Wilson should be nominated because, more than the other candidates, he could unify the party, and he would be the candidate the Republicans would most "dread."[9]

The *Baltimore Sun*, however, was the most read newspaper at the convention. As the balloting progressed it printed and rushed extras to the convention hall within minutes of important breaking news. In an effort to report the proceedings in unrivaled detail, it sometimes devoted six or eight pages to convention news. The *Sun*'s newsboys found that hawking various editions of the *Sun* for five cents when their actual price was one, two, or three cents was no deterrent to their booming sales.[10] The *Sun* announced the arrival of both William Jennings Bryan and Thomas F. Ryan in Baltimore with large three-column front-page pictures of each marking the first time pictures had appeared on its front page. In the case of Ryan, when he tried to slip into the city undetected, a *Sun* reporter discovered him and managed to bypass his guards to talk with him. The *Sun*'s subsequent article, appearing under the large front-page picture of him was headlined "Thomas F. Ryan, Money King, Here To Direct Big Fight" and it began "For the first time one of the great money kings of America has appealed in person at a national convention to carry on the fight for the money interests."[11] The *Sun*, however, declined to announce in favor of Wilson, although it did so by implication, until July 1. On that day it ran a long, two-column editorial typeset in larger-than-usual print. Headlined "**Name the Strongest Candidate!**" it offered a comprehensively detailed and persuasive endorsement of Wilson.[12] Upon reading it, Wilson wrote to Charles Grasty, the Sunpapers' president, "I need not tell you how deeply I am gratified by the editorial. It is as extraordinary as it is reassuring to receive such support as I am receiving from newspapers of the country and newspaper editors in whose integrity we all believe."[13]

Wilson had more reason than he knew to be gratified by Grasty's efforts on his behalf. Early in the convention, when Bryan was dejected about the conservative direction he feared the deliberations were taking, Grasty visited him in his hotel room. The *Sun* would soon make its support of the governor "more pronounced," Grasty told Bryan as he urged the Great Commoner to do the same. A few days later, on Sunday, June 30, when the exhausted delegates were in recess for a day, Bryan telephoned Grasty. Would he care to drive him and Mrs. Bryan out into the Maryland countryside? Soon the three were enjoying a ride through Green Spring Valley north of the city. Returning by Falls Road, a cooling drive in the heat of summer, Grasty invited the Bryans for a potluck supper at his home, an offer the Bryans readily accepted. The potluck turned out to be a handsome spread. Grasty later recalled that Bryan, living up to his reputation, "plied an active knife and fork, especially when dealing with the ham." Following supper the men fell into a lengthy conversation about the convention, about Wilson's candidacy in particular. Bryan still expressed doubts about Wilson, but again Grasty reassured him that "on the question of Wall Street taint Wilson was letter perfect." Bryan was not the only one Grasty tried to persuade with his pro-Wilson arguments. He also sought out Senator Clarence W. Watson of West Virginia, an original opponent of Wilson whose influence extended to the delegations of Virginia and Kentucky.[14] Did personal intervention of this sort effect the outcome of balloting? It is impossible to say with certainty, but in this case both Bryan and Watson were behind Wilson by the end of the convention. Afterward, Wilson's campaign manager wrote to Grasty about the enthusiastic support the *Sun* had provided for Wilson. "Its work cannot be overestimated," he said.[15]

While his managers labored to gain him victory at the convention, Wilson stayed abreast of their endeavors from the governor's summer home, known as the "Little White House," at Sea Girt, New Jersey. He stayed in touch by telephone and telegraph with news from the convention, but to reporters covering him and hoping for some newsworthy comment about the reports from Baltimore, he had little of substance to say.[16] The convention may have been a "desperate struggle" and "one of the greatest battles which the Democratic party . . . [had] ever witnessed," as the *Baltimore Sun* claimed, but the governor refused to offer predictions about the outcome or to reveal his feelings about the various turns of fortune to the reporters.[17]

Wilson, however, remained on good terms with the reporters stationed at Sea Girt to cover him. He joked with his wife and daughters in their presence, bantered with the newsmen as he fended off their questions about his opinions on the convention, and told them humorous stories or recited an appropriate limerick that fit the moment. Sometimes he invited the reporters to visit him in the "Little White House." At other times, he joined them at their press tent. At one point, he watched and then umpired a baseball game the reporters had organized among themselves. He was in a lighthearted mood at the time, and after three runs had been scored on three errors, he chided the reporters saying, "I never saw such uniform incompetents. You are worse than the worst reactionaries." When a burly reporter was called out after making a long slide into third base, Wilson said it reminded him of a comment he had heard about Roosevelt to the effect that he was "trying to steal third." After the reporters tried in vain to have the governor elaborate on the comment, the game continued as did his reproaching the journalists for their poor playing. But was it not true, one of them pointed out referring to a Wilson campaign biography, that in college the governor had been "a fine baseman and fielder, but was too lazy to run bases?" Laughingly, Wilson admitted the truth of that statement, as they all retired from the field.[18]

During these days, Wilson's own thoughts about the shifting tides at the convention remained hidden to the reporters. He remained calm even as they hoped for some emotion from him. When news that he had passed Clark in the balloting reached Sea Girt, an excited reporter with 20 some others close behind, broke into the governor's family circle gathered on the veranda of the summer home. "Governor," pleaded the leader of the group, "won't you please let us see you excited just for one minute. We have written about the quiet pastoral scene here till we simply can't do it any longer." Smiling Wilson replied that they could report that "Wilson received the news that Champ Clark had dropped to second place in a riot of silence."[19] The governor's calm continued to the end. It seemed to spread to the reporters. When news of his impending nomination came, instead of doing a "serpentine dance to the home" as they had planned, they went "hats in hand and in sober silence." Wilson greeted them smiling, but it was his wife who broke the solemnity of the moment. She allowed her comments to roam over the feelings she and her husband had experienced throughout the last week and "confided things that the colony of reporters stationed . . . [there] had not guessed." At one point, she confessed, they had given up hope of victory. Feeling that Clark's lead could not be overcome, they had begun to prepare for a trip to Mount Rydal in England, a place they both loved. When her husband learned of impending victory, he told her, "Well, dear, I guess we won't go to Mount Rydal this summer after all." Although talking to reporters in this manner was a new experience for her, she managed to give them some of the kind of human interest detail they hoped to have for their stories.[20]

Later that day, Wilson walked over to the press tent and announced that he had something to say. His demeanor was serious. "You must have wondered," he began, "why I did not show more emotion as the news came from the convention. . . ." Then he explained that he had feared giving the impression of being too self-confident as the votes mounted in his favor. "The fact is," he said, "the emotion has been too deep to come to the surface as the vote has grown, and as it has seemed more and more likely that I might be nominated I have grown more and more solemn." He confessed in conclusion, "I do not see how any man could feel elation as such responsibilities loomed nearer and nearer to him, or how he could feel any shallow personal pride."[21] Returning to the summer residence, he received news confirming his nomination.

His days of grace were ending. Within two hours, throngs of people descended on Sea Girt, cheers filled the air, and a brass band arrived playing "Old Nassau," the Princeton song. The next day was consumed by his greeting friends and enthusiastic supporters and later by a dinner with his family, Dean Harry Fine and his wife from Princeton, and William Elliott Gonzales, editor of the *Columbia State* of Columbia, South Carolina, a newspaper Wilson considered "one of the most able papers" that reached him in his mail. After dinner, the governor received his class in "Progressive Democracy," as he called the reporters who had been with him all week.[22] However, with the arrival of a swarm of other reporters to Sea Girt, the distance that his press companions of the last week had allowed him would no longer be respected.

Once nominated, Wilson became the biggest news story in the country, and the reporters who now descended on Sea Girt were there to make the most of it. They were unrelenting and everywhere, and they showed no restraint about asking him any question, however trivial it might be, whenever they wished. His daughter Eleanor later wrote, "We had become accustomed to reporters, but now the human interest variety descended upon us in full force. Father had told us to be good sports and try to be as pleasant as possible, but even he sometimes withdrew into silence, after being subjected to hours of silly personal questions."[23] Since his daughters did not give interviews, the men and women of the press simply invented them. One day they described the three daughters as "highbrows"; on another, as "frivolous and gay."[24] Nor did the governor's wife escape the onslaught. As soon as she appeared outside her own quarters, photographers besieged her with orders to look this way, turn around, as they assumed preemptive rights. The family came to feel imprisoned in their upstairs rooms. After two days of this harassment, Wilson met with the correspondents as a group.

Anticipating an agreeable conference, he appeared happy to see them as he leaned against his desk surrounded by his inquisitors. He soon became disillusioned as they asked for some "hot stuff," and for some "dope" about what he had been doing that day. The entire tone of their questions was offensive to him. He had expected a discussion of his candidacy along lines of what he liked to call "the laying of minds along side of each other." Although he tried to remain congenial, it was clear to those present who knew him that the brassiness of some of the reporters, their petty questions, and their poor preparation to discuss serious political matters disturbed him.[25] Of these postnomination encounters with journalists, Eleanor reflected:

> Father was very courteous and patient when he . . . was questioned, but he resented almost fiercely the attempts to pry into family affairs and tried to protect us as much as he could. I have always believed that the first rumors of his "aloofness" and "unfriendliness" were the result of his annoyance at this first onslaught upon us. The newspaper people could not understand the sensitive shyness and delicacy which were an essential part of his character.[26]

In fact, there were a number of precedents for the annoyance with reporters that he now experienced, but it remained to be seen whether they or his more pleasant encounters with them would define his ensuing relations with the newsmen.

Nevertheless, Wilson had reason to feel at least a qualified satisfaction regarding how the mainstream press received his nomination. Pro-Wilson newspapers across the country called him an ideal nominee, portraying him as an honest, decent, enlightened, intelligent, dignified, open-minded, and erudite candidate whose record as governor proved his political ability and courage. The *New York World* contended that he had "re-Americanized" the country by his "re-establishment of the faith of the American people in their own institutions."[27] Democratic papers like the *Atlanta Constitution* and *Montgomery Advertiser*, which had preferred either Underwood or Clark as the nominee, now pledged themselves to Wilson. The *Advertiser* expressed its newfound advocacy by saying that differences with him among Democrats were now "fed to the wind" and "Harmonious Democracy" stood ready to follow his lead.[28] Even the Hearst papers placed their backing of Clark behind them and offered their reluctant support, while Colonel Watterson's *Louisville Courier-Journal* editorialized "being a daily newspaper and unable to take to the woods, [it] would perforce be obligated to support his satanic majesty."[29] Some pro-Roosevelt papers like the *Philadelphia North American* applauded Wilson's nomination as a victory for "popular rights" while continuing to endorse Roosevelt should he accept the nomination of the new party.[30] Other more orthodox Republican newspapers, as might be expected, struck a caustic, unforgiving tone in their response to his nomination. He remained, in their opinion, inexperienced, a theorist made "pedantic" by his years at Princeton, and a nominee too willing to abandon his former well-founded principles and sponsors.[31] Many of these opposing newspapers, including his old nemesis, the *New York Sun*, expressed their relief that he had replaced William Jennings Bryan as the principal figure in the Democratic party. Regardless, the potential strength of newspapers opposing his election could not be underestimated.

Reassurance, however, could be found in the personal messages that he received from hundreds of journalists. They came among the barrage of congratulatory wishes that people from across the country sent to him after his nomination. In the case of journalists, some came from old friends in the field like Hamilton Holt, Frank P. Glass, and George S. Johns; others, from journalists whose admiration he had won in the course of his speaking engagements and casual or professional encounters over the last ten years; others yet, from newsmen who were attracted to his cause but unknown to him personally. Some like W. H. Bagley of the *Raleigh News and Observer* punctuated their congratulations with a jocular note. "I believe now I am ready to forgive you all of the suffering I went through as a youth when studying 'The State,'" he wrote.[32] The editor of *Century Magazine* found it difficult to restrain not only his enthusiasm for Wilson but also for other things the convention achieved. "Think of it!" he exclaimed: "I. The unspeakable Hearst foiled, II. The redoubtable Murphy rolled in the dust of the party's contempt,

III. Ryan and his dirty money scorned, IV. Roosevelt and the third-term madness, well-nigh but out of business, and V. Bryan's aspirations for the nomination, which would have been disastrous—squelched. Sound the loud Timbrel!"[33] James Gray of the *Atlanta Journal* and Herman Suter of the *Nashville Tennessean* announced that they had already launched a "popular campaign" to raise money for the Democratic National Committee.[34]

The journalists, moreover, were anxious to offer the governor their advice on a variety of matters. Suggestions for his campaign, information on the currents of opinion in various states, and, of course, requests for interviews or campaign materials can all be found in abundance in their letters. An interesting one came from William Bayard Hale, the author of Wilson's campaign biography serialized in *World's Work*. Writing to an intermediary rather than to the governor himself, he underscored a particular service he thought the campaign would need. What Wilson needed, Hale explained, was a "confidential assistant," perhaps himself, perhaps someone else, to help manage the throngs of visitors wishing an audience, the immense amount of mail he was receiving, and the matter of the press. "The reporters need to be taken better care of. They are not getting half of what there is in every day's developments, (That is nobody's fault, mind you!) and they are now out of sorts—from causes which only a newspaper man could understand," Hale argued. Furthermore, "the press needs not only to be well taken care of, but watched. Someone ought regularly and rigorously to read the leading papers, and see that nothing that Mr. Wilson ought to know gets past him."[35] Hale had a good argument, and although he remained on friendly terms with Wilson and would serve him later, he was not chosen as an advisor at this time.

II

Following the convention, Wilson assembled his team for the campaign. He named William McCombs to chair the Democratic National Committee and to direct his campaign. Since McCombs was near to nervous exhaustion as a result of his heading the Wilson forces at the convention and since neither the governor nor the progressives in the party trusted him, the latter believing him too conservative, this decision put Wilson to the test. For political purposes, however, he had no choice but to continue with McCombs, since he had been his campaign manager during the long preconvention campaign. William McAdoo, whom Wilson would have preferred as chairman, ended up as vice chairman in charge of campaign headquarters in New York City. Josephus Daniels became the director of publicity for the campaign and assisting him were the indispensable Tom Pence, Robert Woolley, a former journalist close to McAdoo and a man with an aptitude for publicity, and Joseph Wilson, the governor's brother and experienced newspaperman. Walter Measday continued to serve as Wilson's traveling secretary in charge of press relations and on-the-spot publicity during the governor's speaking tours. The team had its work defined as troublesome preconvention issues promised to reemerge, and by the presence of the flamboyant Roosevelt in the race. Personality and public perception of the candidates would rival discussion of the issues in the coming months. Consequently, good press relations were a prerequisite for the hope of victory in November.

There were limits to what Wilson's staff could do in nurturing those relations. Much depended on how successful he would be in dealing with those areas of the press, other than the orthodox Republican press, in which doubts about him existed. How would he fare in his personal relations with the representatives of the special interest press or with the press barons? Just as important, would he be able to establish the necessary rapport with reporters covering him to encourage favorable treatment in their reports? Some of the reporters who congregated at Sea Girt after the convention had already tried his patience. But there is evidence to indicate that he was making headway with the reporters. James J. Doyle, a journalist who spent three weeks in August covering Wilson at Sea Girt, upon leaving wrote to the governor to make amends for his "former prejudice" about him. "To be frank," he said,

> I went to Sea Girt prejudiced against you. I returned convinced that the information I had, and upon which my prejudices were formed, was all wrong. You had been represented as a man who had little of the milk of human kindness; that you had little in common with your fellow man, . . . I had been told that you were a theorist without any practical knowledge of affairs and . . . [without] sympathetic consideration of the common people.

After three weeks of contact with Wilson, Doyle admitted that he now saw him "as the direct opposite" of his preconceived ideas about him. He discovered that Wilson was courteous, well informed about public questions, and sincere in his determination to improve the "welfare of the people." When he returned to New York City, Doyle set out to correct the erroneous ideas about Wilson in the mind of "many persons" who shared his pre-Sea Girt impression of him.[36] The governor could use that type of image correction from a well-placed New York newspaperman. Unfortunately, Doyle would have to promote Wilson informally, for he was associated with the *New York Press*, an entrenched Republican newspaper.

It is clear that Wilson was trying to be more accommodating to reporters. After conferring with McCombs in New York City about his campaign plans, he appeared before the reporters with a written statement about their discussion for the newsmen to use and then elaborated on it for their benefit.[37] An advance statement for the newsmen! The record suggests that he was attempting to do all he could for them to the limit his personality allowed. For all of his love of privacy, Wilson had to adjust to the personal discomforts his candidacy entailed. Nowhere was this more apparent than in his relationship with reporters during the summer months. Sixteen of them, his "sixteen keepers" as he called them, accompanied him everywhere.

He found it difficult to reconcile himself to this circumstance. "The reporters," he complained,

> are required by their papers upon pain of dismissal, to know where I am, who is with me, and what I am doing at *all times*. They must move as I move, go where I go. If there is anything they are not told, they will spy, must spy it out. I must be under observation without intermission. All eyes are watchful of my slightest action. I have lost all freedom of all privacy. It is all but intolerable.[38]

Yet tolerate he did with one exception. He found it necessary to request the recall of Isaac K. Russell, the *Times*'s man among the "sixteen keepers," and he did so as gently as possible. Wilson told the newspaper's business manager that Russell was "a *very* honorable, likable, ingenious fellow, of whom, we are all very fond, and I would not for the world do him a disservice." Yet he felt the reporter lacked "a political sense" that allowed him to see things as they actually were. By adding a "human value" to his stories, Wilson believed he put "the humans of whom he is writing in a very false light." Wilson asked that Russell be "withdrawn without any humiliation or detriment to himself" and replaced by someone "of a less complex mind" who could see things "as they are."[39]

This incident provides an indication of the effort he was making to maintain friendly press relations. Knowing how irritated he could be when he felt he was misrepresented in the press, the tact—even the concern for the reporter—he displayed on this occasion should not go unnoticed. Moreover, it merits mentioning that Theodore Roosevelt, whose skill in dealing with reporters has often been acknowledged, also closed the charmed circle of journalists who covered him at his home in Sagamore Hill during the 1912 campaign to a reporter who displeased him.[40] At any rate, Wilson grew more accustomed to his "keepers," and not for the first time, enjoyed the company of individual journalists. Writing about an evening he spent in New York City late in August, he recounted, "I got to town last evening about 7:30 (accompanied by my keepers) and, after a bite at the station went to the theater to see *The Merry Countess* with [Charles Raymond] Macauley, the World's cartoonist, an interesting fellow."[41] All considered, Wilson was making a genuine effort to encourage good press relations.

However, to maximize his relations with the press in the coming campaign, he needed to do more than to be accommodating to reporters. There were editors and publishers to take into account. The problem was not with those who supported him and whose ranks had expanded after the convention. Throughout the summer, Wilson continued his customary cordial and appreciative dealings with them by means of both correspondence and personal meetings at Sea Girt. However, the editors and publishers of some of the special interest newspapers posed a different sort of challenge.

The black press represents a case in point. Many black newspapers agreed with the postconvention declaration of the *New York Age* when it stated, "It is perfectly clear to us that the Negro in the United States cannot support Woodrow Wilson without proving a traitor to himself and to his race."[42] Nevertheless, Wilson soon had opportunities to soften some of the doubts about him held by editors and publishers of the special interest press. His first chance came when he met with several delegations of African Americans. The more important meeting was with the Reverend John Milton Waldron, organizer of the National Independent Political League, and the journalist William Monroe Trotter, whose *Guardian* was the official organ of the league.[43] At first, the results of this meeting seemed positive when Trotter wrote to the governor thanking him for the "considerate hearing." The editor then told Wilson how he was reporting the meeting in his newspaper by explaining, "I am saying that you told us that you were not in sympathy with race and color prejudice, or with discrimination, disenfranchisement or lynching because of race or color, that you respect the constitution in its entirety including the amendments and will carry out the law not only to its letter and spirit, but also in the spirit of the Christian religion, endeavoring to be a Christian gentleman to all, according even-handed justice and equal rights to all regardless of race, color or nativity."[44] If taken literally, the editor's interpretation of the meeting probably exceeded what Wilson thought he had conveyed in his discussion with the delegation, but he made no response to this letter.

However, when he learned of the account of the meeting that Waldron was publishing, he termed it amazing. Waldron claimed that Wilson had promised he would veto any legislation "inimical to colored people," that he had made assurances about patronage, and that he desired "the colored vote and . . . was willing to do anything that was right and legal to secure that vote."[45] Wilson denied he had made these promises and asked Oswald Garrison Villard, the militant liberal editor of the *New York Evening Post*, to advise him about publishing a statement to correct Waldron's report.[46] The editor responded by passing the request on to Dr. W. E. B. DuBois, the African American intellectual who edited the NAACP's *The Crisis*. The resulting statement was chiefly the work of DuBois and, although it must be judged moderate by his standards, Wilson found it in advance of his own thoughts and declined to use it.[47] Consequently, he lost the opportunity to refute in print, as Waldron put it, "the falsehoods which are being so indiscriminately circulated against him by most of the colored newspapers."[48] In news reports of his meetings with various other black delegations, he only managed to convey his sympathy for African Americans and for their aspirations and to assure them that as president he would be fair and just in dealing with them. African American leaders and editors had hoped for more.

With only rare exception, the prevailing sentiment of Wilson in the immigrant press was as negative as that of the black press. The harsh comments he had written about the "new immigrants" in his *History* still circulated, and now suspicions of his views on immigrants received an alarming new boost. The president of the American Association of Foreign Language Newspapers issued a statement for the entire foreign language press that ended with this pronouncement, "No man who has an iron heart like Woodrow Wilson, and who slanders his fellowmen, because they are poor and many of them without friends when they come to this country seeking honest work and wishing to become good citizens, is fit to be President of the United States."[49] To make matters worse, the influence of foreign-language newspapers, when measured by number and circulation, was reaching its peak. There were over one thousand of these newspapers published in the country, and most appeared in cities in which the Democrats hoped to find support for their candidate.

How could Wilson engage and change this widespread press hostility toward him? As he had done during the preconvention campaign he began by writing dozens of letters to editors and various other leaders of immigrant groups.[50] Still he needed to do more. He considered inviting a group of prominent publishers of foreign-language newspapers to Sea Girt for consultation, but before he could implement that idea, 30 editors of the foreign-language press contacted his campaign managers with a request for a meeting with him. "All here feel that it is a matter of importance," Josephus Daniels told Wilson in forwarding the request to him.[51] Unknowingly, Daniels understated its importance, for when Wilson met with editors on September 4, he spoke not to 30 but to about a hundred editors, and he met them not at Sea Girt but at the National Arts Club in New York City.

The opportunity was an unusual one and Wilson tried to make the most of it. In regard to immigration, he drew the distinction between "voluntary" and "assisted" immigration. He approved of the former, which people seeking a new home and career composed, and disapproved of the latter, composed of people "induced by steamship companies or others to come in order to pay the passage money." Whether or not the editors would accept that distinction is problematic, but they would have no difficulty in appreciating the rest of his comments. "I am not the American and you are not the foreigners," Wilson declared as he pronounced it unjust to categorize Americans as foreign or native born. All were one in their belief in the American ideal. Then in closing he raised a "respectful protest" that the members of the audience called themselves "foreign editors." "Your newspapers and magazines," he explained, "are published in languages which are not the general language of America, which is modified English, but at this stage of the melting-pot process every language in which you print a paper is largely used in the United States, and is used for the conveyance of American ideas. Now, I would just as leave Americanize a language as Americanize an individual, and I welcome the process by which you are Americanizing other foreign languages as the rest of us have Americanized English, . . ."[52] Whether or not Wilson persuaded the editors with these well-intended remarks remained an open question, but he had made his case and had done so with his characteristic cordiality.

Regardless of what he may or may not have achieved with the foreign-language newspaper editors, his greatest success came when he met with the country's foremost labor leader. On July 9, Samuel Gompers, the president of the American Federation of Labor, and several other officers of that union, had an hour-long meeting with Wilson at Trenton. Gompers also edited the *American Federationist*, the most important single labor publication in the country, one whose leads many editors of local union newspapers followed. In 1908, Gompers had supported William Jennings Bryan for president, in his own words "through the columns of the American Federationist of which I am editor, and . . . on the platform throughout the country."[53] However, he had his doubts about Wilson, and he had hoped that his friend Champ Clark would win the Democratic nomination in 1912.[54] His meeting with Wilson on July 9, therefore, was crucial. It was Gompers first meeting with the governor, and it was a great success. "In that meeting," Gompers later reflected, "I felt my prejudices disappearing before the sincerity and obvious humanitarianism of the man. . . . I left Trenton feeling very much relieved."[55] That meeting, in fact, produced a lasting political alliance.

Another special interest group, the suffragists, had an expanding press at this time, with the *Woman's Journal* its vanguard. Although it maintained a nonpartisan position toward the election, it was a factor in the political culture of the era. By 1912 women had the right to vote in six western states and a vote on woman suffrage would occur in five additional states in the forthcoming fall elections. The struggle to enfranchise women was, in fact, one of the liveliest issues in the national debate over great public questions, and the press was a main forum for that debate. In part, as conducted in the press, it occurred in the clash between suffragist and antisuffragist newspapers. For example, the *Woman's Journal* found its antithesis in antisuffragist newspapers like the *Remonstrance* and the *Woman's Protest*, and the conflict of interest present in the news and sentiment that filled the content of such publications sparked attention to the debate in the mainstream press.

Beyond that, the once inexperienced Press Committee of the National American Woman Suffrage Association, the country's leading suffrage group, had become a major publishing operation by 1912, circulating regular news releases to newspapers and press organizations.[56] Indeed, the *Woman's Protest* complained, "It is a serious charge against the newspapers that they are chiefly responsible for the growth of the [suffrage] movement."[57] Although that charge would be difficult to prove, the fact remained that the general circulation press had taken an interest in the woman suffrage movement, as it would of any movement of its magnitude. As one suffragist wrote, "The lectures on suffrage, . . . the articles about suffrage, . . . are actually uncountable. It's lovely! . . ."[58] This well-publicized movement, with all of its vibrant activities, made the issue of woman suffrage part of the fabric of politics in 1912. It was, therefore, only natural that candidates professing a progressive preference would be pushed to state where they stood on this issue.

During the preconvention campaign, Wilson had remained noncommittal about equal rights for women. "It is not a national question but a state question" he told Governor Eugene Foss of Massachusetts, adding the reflection that his own mind on the subject was "in an uncertain balance."[59] That position failed to satisfy many progressive publicists who, like the editor of the *Wisconsin State Journal*, believed that the issue was a national one and queried Wilson: "Do you believe in granting to women equal suffrage with men?" Then he added, "I am not interested in an evasive answer . . . [either] you are for or against it."[60] Oswald Garrison Villard tried to impress the seriousness of the issue upon Wilson. Still the governor held to his belief that it was a matter for the states. "I am awfully sorry it is so and told him so frankly," Villard related to a woman suffrage leader in Boston who had contacted him about Wilson's stand on the issue. "I labored with him a year ago, but it was of no avail. I respect him for his consistency and honesty however sorry I am to differ from him."[61] No doubt Wilson's position on woman suffrage disappointed other progressive editors too, but his position would remain unchanged throughout the election campaign.

III

There were, however, yet other matters regarding the press that concerned Wilson. Imperative among them was the support he would or would not receive from the press lords. One of them, Frank Munsey, could be expected to oppose him. Munsey, a Roosevelt enthusiast, was an important figure in journalism. He was a self-made man and an aggressive materialist who equated progress with money and riches. Munsey began building his empire by publishing entertaining magazines, and in 1891 he acquired his first newspaper, the *New York Star*. By 1912 he owned newspapers in Baltimore, Boston, Philadelphia, and Washington.[62] To his credit, he advocated a new school of journalism composed of reporters who were widely educated and able to tell a story with brevity and clarity. He was also a stickler for accuracy in the news columns of his dailies. On one occasion, when Henry Watterson complained about being misrepresented in Munsey's *Washington Times*, he told Watterson, "Items like this from The Times are appearing all over the country every day, and [are] appearing in my papers every day in spite of my best efforts towards sincerity. . . ." Munsey said that this kind of reporting made him "sick of journalism . . . and sick of owning newspapers." "This loose kind of journalism has reached a point where

I, both as a citizen and a journalist, have no faith whatever in anything I see in a newspaper," he told Watterson.[63]

As laudable as his emphasis on honesty and accuracy in journalism was, he had other convictions that made him feared among newspapermen. An entrepreneur who believed in newspaper consolidation, he contended that "the combination of many newspapers under a single ownership" should be the hallmark of the coming "better journalism."[64] His belief in eliminating waste in newspaper production along with his lack of sentimental attachment to any newspaper led him in the course of several decades to purchase, sell, consolidate, and destroy newspapers at will. Consequently, while he considered himself a newspaper entrepreneur, many newspapermen despised him.

Munsey was devoted to Roosevelt and backed him with purse and in print. In the summer of 1912, he spent one million dollars to purchase the *New York Press* in order to have a major newspaper in that city to use in promoting Roosevelt's candidacy. Wilson, of course, knew that Munsey's choice for the White House was Roosevelt, but he had no way of knowing how complete the opposition to him was in the Munsey organization. Robert Davis, Munsey's confidant and longtime editor of his magazines, in the wake of the Democratic convention told the publisher:

> It is my opinion that Woodrow Wilson, the human anti-climax, will make a bad break or two before the election, step on his frock-coat, and break a leg right in front of the Congressional library. If he ever lands in the White House, this country has got its hands full. He is quarrelsome, dictatorial, and, like all pedagogues, imbued with the idea that his one function in life is to teach. He will turn Congress into a schoolhouse and select a Cabinet very much like the faculty of a fresh-water college.[65]

Davis, knowing of course that he was writing to a sympathetic Munsey, continued to denounce and belittle Wilson, while magnifying Roosevelt and his presidential prospects, throughout the summer. He claimed that Wilson was an autocrat, unwilling to confer with his "field-marshals," and insensitive to others, even to congressmen in his own party. "He will discover . . . that there is no caste in politics, and that . . . [he] is no more important before election than the sargeant-at-arms of the Twenty-Seventh Assembly Democratic Club back of Capital Square," Davis confided to Munsey. He even reported that "Wilson's captains are sore as a boil over his lordly attitude towards the rank and file, and chaos confronts him."[66] Aside from the disdain apparent in these comments, the judgment manifest in them helps to explain why the Munsey organization overstated Roosevelt's chances of victory until the end.

Although Wilson could expect no quarter from the Munsey press, he could expect fair treatment from it. Compared with Hearst's newspapers, Munsey's were models of respectability. They were conventional metropolitan dailies. The sensational techniques that defined the format of Hearst's newspapers had no place in Munsey's. Matter-of-fact news columns and editorials respectable to the point of dullness characterized Munsey's dailies. He had strong political views and gave them prominence in his own editorials, which sometimes appeared as featured front-page articles in his newspapers, but he was no muckraker, nor did he traffic in character assassination. As the treatment his newspapers accorded Wilson during his preconvention campaign proved, he insisted that political adversaries be treated with respect.[67]

How might Wilson fare with the other press lords, Scripps and Hearst? The word he received from the Scripps organization was encouraging. Milton A. McRae told him that his son-in-law, John P. Scripps, the editor in chief of the *Cleveland Press* and the other Scripps–McRae newspapers in Ohio planned to offer him his vigorous support.[68] The record also shows that Scripps's newspapers in California and elsewhere planned to take a similar stand.[69] But would this support remain intact? The Scripps newspapers had wavered in their support of Wilson during the preconvention campaign, and some of their key people continued to favor Roosevelt.[70] After the Progressives nominated the former president, E. W. Scripps, whose influence still permeated "the concern," began writing to his editors urging them to support the entire Progressive party, including Roosevelt. Scripps still believed that Wilson stood for a great deal "of what we stand for" but his party "was even more detestable than . . . Taft's party." After reviewing the acceptance speeches of Wilson and Roosevelt, he felt that Wilson's was flat whereas Roosevelt's "hit the nail on the head." "Some of us detest Roosevelt personally," he told his son, but his "professed principles and the platform he stands on, are our principles and our platform, and the rank and file of his party is largely the rank and file of our own party."[71] The support of the Scripps newspapers for Wilson was more problematic than he realized.

Hearst, of course, was as unpredictable as he was ambitious. He had been Clark's foremost advocate in the press, but many journalists believed he wanted the nomination for himself. The pro-Wilson editors had scant respect for Hearst, though some acknowledged his influence, but he sank even lower in their esteem when he cooperated with the Tammany Hall forces at the convention. That well-reported alliance intensified hostility toward him that remained deep and found its way into print after the convention. One Wilson loyalist, a foreign-language newspaper editor in his camp, believed Hearst had played an unprincipled and despicable role at the convention in his effort to encourage anti-Wilson sentiment, and in his postconvention editorial he vented his anger at the publisher. He wrote that Hearst was "a dwarf morally and intellectually" and was nothing but a self-serving "political and journalistic trickster."[72] Such was the depth that feeling about Hearst could reach.

Now the rumor was spreading among journalists that Hearst was ready to endorse Roosevelt.[73] Although Roosevelt found Hearst detestable, the threat of his supporting the former president was real and Wilson knew it. One of his friends even reported that Governor Foss of Massachusetts had told him, "I know that Gov. Wilson's managers are frightened to death for fear they will lose the Hearst support."[74] That support was paper thin, but before long, there was an indication from his organization that he wished to strengthen it. "The ticket deserves the heartiest support of the Hearst papers and should get it," an associate of the Hearst newspapers in Chicago wrote to Wilson.[75] No matter, Hearst's attacks on the governor during the preconvention campaign had won his enmity (Wilson had called him a "character assassin"), and now he refused to welcome the support of the press lord.[76]

As the maneuvering before the start of the fall campaign came to an end, Wilson's position in regard to the press lords was far from satisfactory. His press relations appeared stronger in other respects. He was on good terms with the reporters assigned to cover him, he had made headway with the special interest press, and democratic editors who had supported other candidates in the preconvention campaign were uniting behind him. The prevailing feeling in the country was that the split in the Republican party gave Wilson the advantage. However, Roosevelt's presence in the contest made it impossible to predict the election's outcome at this point. His media skills were unquestionable, and he began not only with the Munsey newspapers behind him but also other leading metropolitan dailies with pulling power beyond their own locales—newspapers like the *Chicago Tribune* and the *Kansas City Star*. Would he be able to attract progressive Democratic editors into his campaign? Beyond the Roosevelt factor and the opposition found in the special interest press, there were the conventional Republican newspapers to consider. They could be hard hitting in their criticism of Wilson, and they included some of the nation's most influential dailies such as the *Boston Evening Transcript*, the *New York Tribune*, the *St. Louis Globe-Democrat*, and the *San Francisco Chronicle*. Consequently the pro-Wilson editors had their work ready-made in the months ahead.

Chapter 9
Wilson's Election Campaign of 1912 and the Press

Despite the widespread assumption at the outset that Wilson would win, the election of 1912 was a fascinating contest rich in significance. The reasons for this go beyond the Roosevelt–Taft break and the subsequent three-way race for the presidency. A Democratic victory would mean that, after losing four consecutive presidential elections, the party of Jefferson and Jackson would regain the White House and probably have substantial majorities in both the House and the Senate for the first time, with only slight exception, since the Civil War.[1] It would also mark the reentry of the South into the main current of national politics, and with the exit of so many progressives from Republican ranks, it would have long range ramifications on the character of the Republican party. The election, moreover, occurred at the high tide of progressivism in presidential election politics, and now that Wilson had undergone, as historian Robert H. Wiebe said, "the intellectual migration of his generation," he, as well as Roosevelt, could lay claim to the progressive vote.[2]

There were, of course, differences between Wilson and Roosevelt, his foremost opponent, about how progressivism should be interpreted and implemented. Roosevelt called his progressive program the New Nationalism. Rooted in the Square Deal program he championed as president and further defined in his subsequent speeches, the New Nationalism called for increased activity of the federal government in American business and life. Roosevelt accepted the large size of business corporations as a fact of modern society, but he believed that the public, acting through the agency of the federal government, should exert control over them. Tariff revision by means of an impartial commission of experts was central to his program, but sometimes during the campaign he gave a protectionist twist to his views on the tariff. "We stand for a protective tariff, but we wish to see the benefits of the protective tariff to get into the pay envelope of the wage worker," he said on one occasion.[3] On the other hand, Wilson's program, which came to be known as the New Freedom, shied away from the type of big government regulation favored by Roosevelt, but not from big government itself. He contended that if the government undertook to regulate monopolies, as Roosevelt suggested, the monopolies would end up regulating the government.[4] In the belief that unregulated competition created monopolies, he preferred to regulate the competition by means of "remedial legislation" rather than by regulatory agencies. He wanted to use competition to destroy monopoly and to allow free enterprise to flourish.[5] Wilson was more insistent on tariff revision than Roosevelt, though he too could be indefinite when discussing it. Aside from these differences and with the exception of woman suffrage, which the Progressive party platform endorsed, Wilson and Roosevelt held many views in common about specific progressive reforms.[6]

Roosevelt, however, doubted the depth of Wilson's progressivism and questioned the governor's qualifications for the presidency. The former president reasoned that as a college professor and college president Wilson had advocated "with skill, intelligence and good breeding the outworn doctrines which were responsible for four-fifths of the political troubles of the United States." But after entering politics, he turned "an absolute somersault" discarding at least half of his doctrines while clinging to the other half. Worse yet, Roosevelt held that Wilson had "no real and deep-seated comprehension of the things that I regard as most vital." Convictions such as these led Roosevelt to consider Wilson an insincere progressive, one closer, in political terms, to Taft than to himself.[7] Given the increased press interest in a candidate's personal qualities, views such as these, which were neither unique nor new, would surface in the coming election.

The elevation of the personality factor in presidential campaigning had become a hallmark of the Progressive era. Societal changes and the presence of charismatic figures like William Jennings Bryan and Theodore Roosevelt on the political stage help to explain this phenomenon as do the growth of popular journalism and changes in political reporting. The appearance of modern campaign publicity focusing on candidates as well as on issues, must also be taken into account. By 1912, journalism trade journals were promoting "the art of publicity" in politics, and the *Fourth Estate* even predicted "publicity would play an important part in the coming election, and the victor will be the man who makes the best use of it."[8] The press, of course, was central to publicizing any presidential aspirant, not only as an outlet for the distribution of campaign publicity materials but also for its own opinion, which all campaign managers hoped to garner for their candidate. Indeed, the influence the press wielded never appeared more important than it did in this age of mass circulating newspapers and national popular magazines, of news services and newspaper syndicates, and now, thanks to film and sound technology, of yet newer forums for political news. Small wonder that progressive era politicians considered the press a "power" in politics.

Even Will Irwin opened his classic 1911 series of articles, "The American Newspaper," with the idea that "the 'power of the press' was greater than ever before."[9] Although it is more accurate to speak of the "influence" of the press than of its "power," both journalists and public figures considered it a political force. But how was this force employed? The most respected newspapers in the country adhered to the belief that their purpose was "to instruct, persuade, convince, stimulate, [and] guide" the public.[10] Others believed that there should be an entertaining or even a sensational quality added to political news. Moreover, the human interest factor now enmeshed in political reporting led some reporters with questionable scruples to disregard a person's feelings and desire for privacy in their pursuit of the story they wanted.[11] They assumed the right to frame their stories as they wished. At the very least, presidential candidates could expect criticism, some caustic, of themselves and their programs during their campaigns. Considering the emphasis on publicity, the ever widening reach of the press, the tendency of some newspapers to sensationalize content whenever possible and of others to indulge in character assassination, fortunate was a candidate who, like Wilson, had the benefit of a vigorous and far-reaching friendly press to counterbalance the varieties of criticism that greeted him during the campaign. Fortunate, too, was a candidate who, like Wilson, had an effective and ethical publicity department in his campaign organization.

I

The presidential campaign of 1912 soon narrowed down to a two-way contest between Roosevelt and Wilson. However central their different ideas about progressivism, particularly about the tariff and the role of the government in connection with the trusts, may have been, when viewed from the perspective of the press, it is clear that the personal factor was also an issue for each candidate. Neither could distance himself from it. Orthodox Republican newspapers condemned Roosevelt for wrecking the Republican party by his encouraging and then leading a third party drawn largely from its ranks. In some cases their condemnation of him reached extraordinary levels. The *San Francisco Chronicle* went so far as to call him a "self-willed specious, arbitrary and dangerous man" who was "devious . . . politically immoral, [and] consumed with ambition."[12] As for Wilson, the worst of the old preconvention campaign charges against him resurfaced to provide political ammunition for his present critics to use.

Wilson's publicity directors made rebuttals of these charges a large part of their campaign literature. Borrowing comments from his speeches and citing his record as governor, they produced and circulated items such as *Gov. Wilson a Friend of Immigration*, and *Wilson and Labor*. The most ambitious publication was a hefty pamphlet, *The Enemies of Woodrow Wilson: A Democratic Exposé of Misstatements and Misrepresentations*, that reviewed and dismissed all of Wilson's alleged offenses against immigrants, labor, and the democratic spirit. In particular, it emphasized the falsity of the denunciations that William Randolph Hearst and George Fred Williams had published about Wilson during the preconvention campaign.[13] As the volume of this literature grew, it became one of the primary means the Wilson organization used to shape press opinion in his favor. Josephus Daniels, who headed the campaign's publicity department, formed an operation intended, as he later explained, to "reach every newspaper in the country"[14] Newspapers could receive these materials in a variety of ways, not the least of which was through the expanding network of Wilson and Marshall Clubs that crisscrossed the country. One of the purposes of these and the older Wilson Clubs and leagues was to "furnish matter for local newspapers."[15]

The publicity directors of the Democratic campaign targeted the press in other ways too. After Wilson delivered his acceptance speech on August 7, they gathered comments on it from 50 prominent Democrats to send to "every Democratic and independent paper in the country."[16] To all newspapers that would use them, they provided political cartoons free of charge, and they advertised their candidate and party in newspapers, especially in labor and farm publications and in "big weeklies and Sunday supplements."[17] Wilson shared the directors belief that the smaller newspapers of the country were as important to reach as the larger ones. In a campaign speech to the Democratic Press Association of Missouri, he stated, "I feel that . . . particularly the country newspapers . . . are responsible for the exact slant which opinion is to take with regard to public matters."[18] Throughout the fall months, the publicity directors produced a steady flow of Wilson's speeches in "tabloid form," new pamphlets and items of lesser length to newspapers large and small.[19] They sent out a "daily letter" and "plate matter" as warranted.[20] Nor did they neglect the national periodicals.

Their efforts extended far beyond working through the print medium. The directors organized an extensive speakers' bureau as well as a number of activities such as rallies and special days to honor their candidate. In all cases, the personnel involved had to promote, and in some cases to defend, Wilson, and in addition they had to match or outdo Roosevelt's people who were also publicizing their candidate. At times, as in the case of the new media now available for political campaigns, the governor's managers had to prod him into action.

People considered Thomas Edison's phonograph or talking machine a novelty when it first appeared in 1877. Edison thought of it as a communication device suitable, in particular, for business people.[21] Before long media entrepreneurs discovered that it also had political potential. It would expand the reach of the spoken word and would conserve the physical strength that candidates exerted stomping to win votes. *Talking Machine World* even boasted that by using the phonograph candidates would be able to escape making "rash or intemperate remarks" and would be freed from having their speeches interrupted by "rude persons" asking "annoying questions" or making embarrassing "quips."[22] Be that as it may, phonograph recordings did hold certain advantages for candidates and, consequently, presidential hopefuls began using them in the election of 1908.[23] Four years later, Roosevelt, Taft, and Wilson each made a series of recordings in their presidential contest. Neither Roosevelt nor Wilson had made previous records, and in Wilson's case it was not a pleasant experience.[24]

Altogether Wilson made six campaign recordings. Starting with the acceptance speech he delivered on August 7 to a large gathering of Democrats assembled on the lawn at Sea Girt, they addressed the basic issues of the campaign. Wilson spoke well for the records. With his carefully modulated tones and precise selection and pairing of words, he conveyed the impression of being a voice of reason and reform. There was nothing trite or demeaning in his words. They contained no colloquialisms, no talking down to his audience. He discussed ideas, raised questions, and challenged his listeners to think.[25] The governor's managers planned to send out the records along with motion pictures in order to have him both seen and heard in theaters. Meanwhile, newspapers and the phonograph trade journals advertised the recordings, along with those of the other candidates, and predicted that they "should find a tremendous market where properly introduced by dealers."[26]

Making the recordings had all the markings of a campaign success, but Wilson was an unwilling contributor to whatever success the recordings achieved. He did not believe in "canned speeches" and thought his statements and ideas could be conveyed by the newspapers. Nevertheless, Josephus Daniels undertook to persuade him to record. It was a means by which he could reach the entire country, Daniels argued. Still Wilson protested. Finally Daniels enlisted the governor's wife to urge him to make the recordings. With that he relented, but later Daniels recalled what an unpleasant experience it was for Wilson. "He went at it as if he were going to the stake. . . . He spoke into the machine and made the records and when he came out he said he felt as though he had been offered up. I doubt if he ever heard one of these records. He acted as if Mrs. Wilson and I were his worst enemies and persecutors."[27]

Nor did Wilson like to pose for campaign pictures. They were too artificial, he said.[28] Most public men would have been more considerate of the photographers, but Wilson's personality rebelled against political posturing. In one respect this was unfortunate, for pictorial journalism was making rapid advances at that time. After the first successful projection of a motion picture in this country in 1896, the popularity of the new medium appeared irresistible. Three years after the first nickelodeon or nickel theater opened in Pittsburgh in 1905 about four thousand motion picture theaters had sprung up across the country. Their burgeoning numbers seemed to know no limit. At a time when upper balcony seats in a vaudeville theater cost 25 cents, the nickelodeons were a bargain, and they could be found right in one's own neighborhood. By 1912 the theaters were becoming more luxurious and entrepreneurs celebrated their openings as gala events.[29]

News films were a popular form of this new medium. They were separate films of newsworthy events (frequently ceremonies or natural disasters), but the camera also caught famous people. Grover Cleveland was the first president to appear on film. He was filmed while attending President McKinley's inauguration in 1897. Thereafter McKinley's successors in the White House followed his lead and had their own inaugurations filmed. Although the fictional film soon outdistanced actuality films, the latter had established a niche in early motion picture production, and in 1911 the first newsreel, the *Pathé Weekly*, appeared in the United States. Released on a regular schedule once a week, it offered new competition to illustrated periodicals, and the trade journal *Moving Picture World* predicted that it would "revolutionize pictorial journalism the world over."[30] By the time of the 1912 election, three more newsreel companies had been launched, thus underscoring the vitality of this new medium.[31] Candidates would be wise to take advantage of the advances in pictorial journalism if for no other reason than for the fact that workingmen in general, rich or poor, considered motion pictures their favorite entertainment beyond the home.[32]

However, in no area of the campaign was Wilson at a greater disadvantage compared with Roosevelt than when appearing before the motion picture camera. "I feel that Roosevelt's strength is altogether incalculable," he wrote to a friend. "He appeals to their imagination; I do not. He is a real, vivid person. . . . I am a vague, conjectural personality, more made up of opinions and academic prepossessions than of human traits and red corpuscles."[33] Roosevelt was, indeed, a "vivid" personality. No public figure in the country was more photographed than he, none more photogenic, none more newsworthy. He was the first president for whom there is an extensive motion picture record, and he knew how to embellish that record.

Roosevelt was an ideal subject for the cameramen to film.[34] One journalist reported, "T. R. always has one eye on the camera brigade and is unhappy if it is not on hand; he will postpone a gesture any time until the last photographer gets his . . . [camera] adjusted.[35] The *Moving Picture World* said he was "something more than a picture personality: he . . . [was] A PICTURE MAN."[36] This trade journal reported that when the film of his transcontinental campaign tour premiered on October 5 at Carnegie Hall, the audience "laughed with him in his humorous moments" on camera and "worked itself up into a fervor when he was plainly in earnest" amid shouts from the gallery exclaiming "Good boy Teddy, on your way to Washington."[37]

Wilson could not hope to compete with Roosevelt as a film personality. Nevertheless, from the time of his nomination, cameramen were able to capture him in both formal and informal situations.[38] When the monthly trade journal *Motography* announced that the campaign of 1912 would be "a national 'moving picture campaign,'" providing a "picturesque . . . struggle for the presidency," it reported that President Taft had already been filmed "in a variety of speech making gestures" and that plans were underway to capture Roosevelt "in his most strenuous fighting poses." But when it came to Wilson, *Motography* could only say that he had been "an involuntary actor in the 'photo-play,' having been trailed by a squad of moving picture men, who followed him from stump to stump."[39] As the campaign proceeded, they continued filming him "from stump to stump," captured him making speeches, and produced scenes from his campaign tours. Although Wilson did not generate the muscular public image that Roosevelt conveyed on film, the pictures of him were those of a confident campaigner at ease before the crowds he addressed, and cheerfully acknowledging their applause. The *New York Times* reported that "everywhere they [the Wilson films] have been shown the pictures have brought hardy applause from the audience."[40] Wilson actually came off well in the films, although he lacked Roosevelt's magnetic appeal and his ability to identify with audiences in a personal way.

The Democrats, however, would not be outdone when it came to another type of motion picture—the campaign promotional film. They contracted the Universal Film Manufacturing Company to prepare a one reel motion picture to publicize Wilson and several of the issues he defended, particularly those regarding the tariff. In its weekly trade magazine, Universal Films announced that while having "missionary value in securing support for the Democratic candidate" the film would also be "amusing and entertaining."[41] Based on a scenario written by the *New York World's* premier cartoonist, Charles Raymond Macauley, it fulfilled that promise. The film portrayed capitalist greed and worker exploitation and used exaggerated stereotypes to convey its message. Set in the luxurious office of a business tycoon with workers busy hanging large pictures of Roosevelt and Taft on its walls, it begins with a depiction of "The Old Way." The main character is an obese, pompous, demanding, and insensitive tycoon who parades around with "The Trusts" printed on the front of his shirt. When two workers enter the office in a humble manner to request a 5 percent pay raise, he rudely dismisses them for making such an outlandish suggestion. Next the tycoon greets "High Tariff Boss," who appears with the villainous features accorded scoundrels in silent films. The latter then requests "a million dollars to swing 100,000 votes," a request that delighted the tycoon. Opening his walk-in safe and revealing money strewn about as if it were coal, he orders two workers to shovel the required amount into the "Dough Bag," which "High Tariff Boss" presents. The film then switches to a worker walking past a poster labeled "PROTECTED INTERESTS" and featuring pictures of Roosevelt and Taft. The worker jeers at it. Then he walks past a larger poster of Wilson with an American eagle behind him. Slapping his chest, the worker says "That's for me."

The second part of the film, "The New Way," opens with a broadside advertisement

WANTED
100,000
EARNEST CITIZENS

TO
CONTRIBUTE EACH
ONE HONEST DOLLAR
TO ELECT A PRESIDENT
OF AND FOR
THE PEOPLE
No Trust Money Accepted

The broadside also explained that the contribution could be sent to the Wilson campaign headquarters. Upon seeing it, a worker is so pleased with the idea that he produces a dollar, addresses and mails an envelope containing it on the spot. In its simplicity and humorous exaggeration, the film underscored major issues in the campaign: the opulence of the plutocrats who ran the trusts at the expense of workers, the collusion between the trusts and corrupt political bosses, and the Democratic sympathy for laborers.[42]

II

Promoting oneself before the camera, like publicity itself, mattered, but it could only go so far. The contest weighed heavily upon how effective the two front-runners would be in handling their press relations and, in turn, on how effective the press favoring one or the other man would be in presenting its choice to the public. As any hope that Taft could win a second term receded in all but the most orthodox Republican newspapers, across the country the press intensified its attention on Roosevelt and Wilson. Notwithstanding the significance of the New Nationalism and New Freedom programs and of the differences between them, it was the candidates themselves that made this election one of the most engaging in American history.

Roosevelt, of course, was a seasoned campaigner. Like President Taft, he was well known throughout the country. His candidacy, moreover, had the support of some of the most influential newspapers in the country, and he was at ease with reporters. They loved his exuberant ways and the effort he made to accommodate them. Wilson, however, was a difficult candidate to cover. Unlike Roosevelt, he continued to refuse to give reporters advanced copies of his speeches. To do so would have benefited him and made the reporters' job easier, but it was contrary to his ways. Furthermore, the reporters needed human interest material to lighten their reports of his speeches. Wilson considered such stories trivial, which they could be; however, he never allowed their appearance to mar the courtesy and friendliness he displayed to the reporters accompanying him on his tours.[43]

In fact, the reporters found Wilson to be a good traveling companion, even a "jovial" one. The entourage traveled in two railroad cars, one for the governor and the other for the reporters, but they all dined together and Wilson frequented the reporters' car. Accepting no special consideration, he entered into the spirit of their banter. Wilson was "a good story-teller and not sensitive," one of his companions, Charles Willis Thompson, wrote to his wife, adding, "The Governor, I am surprised to find, cusses as much as Roosevelt, or even more, and nearly as much as Taft."[44] Some years later Thompson provided this description of Wilson:

> Where the idea came from that Wilson was a cold, self restrained man I never could understand. . . . He was full of hot blood, . . . loved a story and could tell one to admiration. His sense of humor was prehensile. He loved the ridiculous as well as the witty. And it was easier to make him 'mad' than any other public man I ever knew; nor could he control his rage easily. He was a swift and lively talker, enjoyed conversation greatly, took a vigorous part in it without ever trying to dominate it, and seemed in love with life in all its manifestations.[45]

Oliver P. Newman was another reporter who recorded his impressions of Wilson as a campaigner. He recalled Wilson's telling him that "it grieves me terribly to realize that there are a lot of people who think that, merely because I've been a college professor, I'm a stiff old ass who doesn't know anything." Newman was with Wilson on several of his campaign trips and following the election recounted some incidents that exemplified his human qualities. In Denver, for instance, after completing his public appearances, Wilson attended a reception for him at the press club. It was a convivial gathering with many journalists sitting legs crossed on the floor as the governor and the newsmen began exchanging stories. Newman reported that "as the evening progressed the stories got better and better and Wilson and his hosts got friendlier and mellower," as the newspapermen imbibed "various liquids" from time to time, always taking care to hand the governor a light soda or a lemonade. Finally, after consuming several such drinks, Wilson announced, "By birth I am an American, by paternal parentage I am Irish, but by thirst I am Scotch." The crowd responded by taking "the hint with a whoop."[46] With episodes like this, reporters came to like and appreciate the governor's unpretentious ways, his sense of humor, his genuineness, and his friendly demeanor toward them.

Important too was the fact that Wilson had become a skilled national campaigner. People and the press familiar with his past public performances on the platform knew how well he could present himself before a variety of audiences. "He is an uncommonly persuasive speaker," one newspaper, commented at the conclusion of the Baltimore Convention.[47] But what about the rank and file of people and newsmen, who had yet to see him in action? To their surprise, they found his affable manner and his ability to shift in the course of his speeches from serious discussion to humorous anecdotes impressive. Taken as a whole, his campaign speeches represent a tremendous achievement. They stand "among the greatest speeches of modern history," the editors of *The Papers of Woodrow Wilson* claimed.[48] That they resonated well with his audiences and his supporters in the press, is beyond question.

The widespread support of so many mainstream newspapers and journals was one of the reasons for Wilson's successful campaign. Roosevelt may have been the most picturesque presidential candidate since Andrew Jackson, but he frightened conservatives more than Wilson and people could tire of what was sometimes called his "political evangelism."[49] In comparison with Roosevelt, the pro-Wilson editors found their man to be an ideal candidate. They were impressed by the absence of partisan rancor in his speeches. The editors liked the nimbleness Wilson displayed in responding to charges that Roosevelt and other opponents made, and they appreciated his ability to keep the revision of the tariff the paramount issue of the campaign. That was an issue that could unify Democrats and direct attention away from some of the more progressive planks in the Progressive's platform, particularly the Progressives' declaration in favor of woman suffrage, that otherwise might have nudged away some of Wilson's progressive support. The pro-Wilson editors were also impressed by the gentlemanly manner Wilson displayed toward his rivals.[50]

With Wilson the editors had a candidate they could promote and one they were able to defend. Aside from proclaiming the soundness of his views on tariffs (even southern editors found them "conservative and sane"), trusts, and currency, they conveyed the idea that he was a new figure in national politics, and one with unique qualifications for the presidency. Capitalizing on the era's fondness for newness, they spoke of Wilson's plans for domestic reform as the "New Democracy," although it would later be known as the "New Freedom"—a term Wilson coined midway through the campaign. By revising the tariff, destroying monopoly, and reorganizing the currency and banking system, the editors explained, his program would revitalize both American democracy and the economy. They claimed he was a better "fundamental democrat" than Roosevelt, a better judge of men and better suited for

Figure 9 *Baltimore Sun*, October 9, 1912. Portrays the perception of Wilson publicized by the *Sun*, one of his most enthusiastic supporters in the press.

the presidency, and they argued that more than Roosevelt he would neither truckle to political bosses nor be injudicious in implementing his economic remedies. Furthermore, he was not only an authority on government but also, as he proved as governor, a practical man able to accomplish political reforms against stiff odds.[51]

Wilson also received support from the great chains of newspapers, but not as much as might be expected. Frank Munsey's newspapers were, of course, out of the question since he was Roosevelt's booster among the press lords. But what of Scripps and Hearst? As has been seen, the Scripps organization, or "the concern," was a multifarious collection of newspapers and news services. The editors of Scripps newspapers considered themselves true progressives and, although Wilson was their choice as long as the contest was between him and Taft, their outlook changed in August when the Progressives nominated Roosevelt and produced a more progressive platform than the Democrats had offered. For years the Scripps newspapers had advocated principles that the Bull Moose platform now endorsed. Consequently, some of the key figures in "the concern" began to see the candidates in a different perspective. Moreover, as one of Scripps editors put it, Wilson was proving himself a party leader who, when given the chance would "play the game of politics" and would even "likely get into bed with Belmont, Ryan and the others who finance and manage the Democracy."[52]

As Scripps's editors began to drift away from supporting Wilson, McAdoo grew uneasy. He was then acting chairman of the Democratic National Committee due to the illness of McCombs, and he tried to reassure the Scripps personnel about Wilson. McAdoo went to Cleveland to see Scripps's son John who was "the concern's" editorial director. E. W. Scripps's confidant J. C. Harper was also present at the meeting, and he left a detailed account of what transpired. McAdoo told the Scripps' men that Wilson stood for what the Scripps newspapers championed, and with the support of a Democratic Congress, he could accomplish more than Roosevelt. McAdoo also pointed out that, due to Wilson's leadership, the Democratic party in New Jersey had been transformed by the ascendancy of progressives in its ranks. That line of argument impressed Harper and John Scripps, and they admitted that Wilson was "more progressive than his party" while "the third party was more progressive than its leader." However, their reservations about Wilson remained. They told McAdoo that the "danger of a Democratic landslide" failed to bother them, and that they cared neither about consistency nor about being on "the winning side." The Scripps policy, they said, "had not yet been decided" and would be decided on the basis of how it could do "the most for the cause, irrespective of individuals."[53] McAdoo had hoped for a more definite commitment.

While it is true that Wilson was more moderate than the Scripps editors may have wished and seemed to become more moderate yet as the campaign moved forward, he retained his ability to impress journalists in personal meetings. The Scripps personnel proved no exception to the governor's persuasiveness. Two influential people in the Scripps organization, R. N. Rickey and Roy Howard, the president and general manager, respectively, of the Newspaper Enterprise Association (N. E. A.) and the United Press Association, visited Wilson in August and left being "wonderfully impressed." They reported to a colleague, that if he were elected, he would "probably raise the devil to a greater extent" than any occupant of the White House for the last half century because he would "carry out the policies he stands for, and he is more radical than the general public believes." Wilson told them "that actions spoke louder than words and that, if elected, his acts would be better than his proclamation of intent."[54] Another associate of "the concern," Milton McRae, a Republican, visited Wilson late in August and left with this impression of the governor. "I believe that character is the foundation of all success in any man, a politician not excepted, and Wilson's character is unsullied."[55] Nevertheless, some of the key figures in the Scripps organization like Negley Cochran, the editor of the *Toledo News-Bee,* still preferred Roosevelt, and E. W. Scripps insisted that nothing should prevent Gilson Gardner, the N. E. A. man in Washington and Roosevelt's friend, from continuing to advocate the former president.[56]

Thus a division of opinion prevailed within "the concern" toward Wilson. As a result, the best the Scripps newspapers could do for him was to hold news and opinion about him and Roosevelt in balance, but that balance sometimes tilted in favor of the latter.[57] The attempt on Roosevelt's life made shambles of this policy. After the would-be assassin shot him on October 14, the wounded former president insisted on making his scheduled speech, which he did before allowing his advisors to rush him to a hospital. That courageous act so impressed E. W. Scripps that he telephoned his son James to talk about how "the concern" should respond. Following that conversation, James Scripps telegraphed all the Scripps editors:

> ON HEARING OF ROOSEVELTS ATTEMPTED ASSASSINATION E W SCRIPPS STATED THAT ROOSEVELTS SPEECH AFTER HE WAS SHOT PROVES NOT ONLY HIS COURAGE AND SINCERITY BUT HIS TRUSTWORTHINESS. THAT A MAN CANNOT LIE FACING DEATH. . . . SINCE OUR LAST DOUBT HAS BEEN REMOVED A MUCH MORE FRIENDLY ATTITUDE TOWARDS ROOSEVELT IS ADVISED.[58]

The change in the Scripps newspapers was immediate. Harold Cochran, who was with the *Chicago Day Book*, reported on the day after receiving the above message that yesterday the staff has come "through strong with the T. R. dope. Today, after getting the N. E. A.'s good line of T. R. art, we came right back and tonight we have a right good looking Day Book."[59] For the remainder of the campaign, the Scripps newspapers used their news reports to show their preference for Roosevelt.[60] That left only the Hearst newspapers among the country's sprawling press chains, and Wilson had little reason to expect much support from them.

In fact, following the Baltimore convention, an abundance of pro-Roosevelt news and editorials appeared in the Hearst newspapers.[61] No one could say what position the press lord would take in the months ahead. Then, on September 13, Hearst published a front-page editorial over his own name disapproving of Wilson's views on the tariff. "W. R. Hearst on Free Trade/'I Believe in Protection'/Wilson's Views Criticised," read the headline under which he declared, "I do not approve of Mr. Wilson's policy of a tariff for revenue only, nor do I think that he improves his position when he declares in support of a gradual reduction of the tariff." Hearst concluded, "Mr. Wilson's dogmatic . . . declarations have all the positiveness of the pedagogues who has [*sic*] theories on everything and experience in nothing. His is the customary attitude of the college professor who knows nothing, having read it in books, where it was written down by other college professors with equally infallible knowledge based on universal inexperience."[62]

But Hearst could be as erratic as anyone in politics. Within days of writing that editorial, he sent this message from Paris, intended for Wilson's eyes and forwarded to him. "Wilson swinging into aggressive campaign. That is what is needed. We will now unlimber some Standard Oil guns that I think will make the breach through which he can march to easy victory. You may not have understood my silence. Frankly, I was disappointed that gentleman didn't seem to realize my support depended not upon what he thought of my speeches but upon what I thought of his."[63] His reference to his own silence hardly reflected his own published comments about Wilson, but he was correct in believing that the governor had begun to strike a sterner tone in his speeches. The way was open for better relations between the two men, and this time Wilson acknowledged the gesture Hearst made. In reference to Hearst's cablegram, John Temple Graves, who had moved from Atlanta to become editor in chief of Hearst's *New York American*, wrote to Wilson, "It [the cablegram] vindicates the view expressed to you that everything would come right in time from our camp. If we come late, I believe we will come with sufficient strength to make up for lost time. I am sure your message had much to do with it." As proof of the direction the Hearst press would now follow, Graves called attention to the current issues of the *New York American* and the *New York Journal* and also *Hearst's Magazine*, claiming that they had "dealt Roosevelt the heaviest blow he has so far received."[64]

Hearst did offer Wilson support, of sorts, in his newspapers as the campaign continued. He even modified his views on the tariff, but not quite along the lines of the Democratic platform. In another one of his front-page, signed editorials, he announced that the Democrats should adopt tariff reciprocity and preferential duties as their policy. In typical fashion, the editorial appeared under the bold headline, "HEARST MAKES REPLY TO TAFT; SUGGESTS THE TRUE POLICY FOR THE DEMOCRATIC PARTY." Upon reading this article, Woolley commented to Daniels that this was what they could expect from Hearst and said that he believed it would be unwise "to play up that gentleman's articles."[65] That was a wise course to take, for Hearst offered only questionable support for their candidate. He declined to publish a personal endorsement of Wilson, and that which he allowed his newspapers to make was feeble. The advocacy the *New York American* extended is a case in point. When other pro-Wilson newspapers were extolling the governor's extraordinary qualities, the *American* was satisfied to speak of him as "the hand and voice of the Grand Average." Its argument conveyed little enthusiasm but it did refer to Wilson's willingness to make public his private thought, as compared with Roosevelt who was more private and "cunning," and it did acknowledge him as "the intelligible commander" in the campaign.[66] The Hearst newspapers were less tepid in their final endorsements of Wilson in their election eve issues, but even at this point, their statements in his favor were either short or more about recommending the Democratic party than about electing him.[67]

III

However strong or ambivalent their support, the pro-Wilson editors had to counter a ranging press opposition to Wilson's candidacy. Along with Frank Munsey's east coast newspaper chain, it included some of the country's leading publications like the *Boston Transcript*, the *Chicago Tribune*, and the *Kansas City Star*. Moreover, a number of the nationally circulating periodicals preferred either Roosevelt or Taft over Wilson. *Munsey's Magazine*, the *Outlook*, and the *Saturday Evening Post* were for Roosevelt, and so too was the *American Review of Reviews*, which Albert Shaw, Wilson's old friend, edited. In the middle of October, Robert Collier forced his pro-Wilson editor, Norman Hapgood, to resign and took over the editorship of *Collier's* to convert it to a pro-Roosevelt magazine—a move Wilson said was "nothing less than a national calamity."[68] Meanwhile, the *Forum*, *Leslie's Weekly*, and the *Independent* favored Taft. Wilson could also expect opposition from many of the special interest newspapers although he had won the backing of some of their important editors.

Figure 10 *Lake County Times* (Hammond, IN.), September 11, 1912. Portrays the insurmountable obstacles to Wilson's presidential campaign.

The criticism raised against Wilson took several forms. First, it centered on the two major issues: the tariff and the trusts. The opposing mainstream newspapers argued that his call for tariff revision subverted the benefits the existing protective tariff had brought to the country. A protective tariff was as necessary as a bulwark against cheap foreign made goods as the dikes were "to keep the oceans out of Holland," the *Grand Rapids Herald* reasoned in expressing the widely held view.[69]

Misrepresentation often appeared in oppositional accounts of Wilson's tariff views. Instead of describing his position on the tariff as revisionist, which it was, some claimed he was a proponent of free trade. Such a line of argument led to the charge that Wilson was trying to trim his position since he had professed his belief in a free trade principle but now was changing his stand on tariffs by announcing that he merely favored a reconsideration of the rates. In the words of the *Milwaukee Sentinel*, it was "like the Irishman in the play who took a drink whenever he felt like it, but was 'a teetot'ler in principle.' "[70]

Opposing editors also marshaled a variety of arguments in their criticism of Wilson's attack on the trusts and their political influence. His plan to regulate them by means of competition, they said, lacked specificity and only skimmed the issue. Most of all, they were persistent in charging that he had done nothing to reform trusts and monopolies as governor of New Jersey, "the home of trusts." After promising much, he had failed to put his words into action. He had done, in the opinion of one newspaper critical of his record, "not one blessed thing!" to curtail the corrupt influences of the trusts and to end the "injurious restraint of trade and monopolistic enterprise" in his own state.[71] The point was literally true, and it could be made with telling effect. It overlooked, however, the fact that the Republican-controlled New Jersey Senate had refused, in their endeavor to thwart Wilson's progressive measures, to respond to his repeated urgings to make the corporation laws effective.

Much of the press criticism of Wilson centered on the candidate himself. Charges that he was an untried politician and an unworthy progressive abounded. Old preconvention charges against him now resurfaced in the press. "If Governor Wilson had never written a book," explained one of the chairman at the western headquarters of the Democratic National Committee, "we would have had a splendid easy time in this campaign. But the truth is, that it has been a campaign of misrepresentation and calumny from the start, and it has been incumbent upon some of us . . . to meet these things. As soon as one thing was killed some other thing was put in its place."[72] In fact, the mere mention of "forgive my manners" or a reference to knocking Bryan into a "cocked hat" sufficed to revive the old accusations of ingratitude and mendacity.[73] Nor were Wilson's references to laborers and immigrants in his *History* allowed to recede from view.

Perhaps the most scurrilous denunciation of Wilson made during the campaign came from one of his former students, Joseph W. Park. When the Woodrow Wilson College Men's League contacted him for a contribution, he answered saying he was unable to comply because he knew Wilson to be neither a democrat nor a progressive. Park based that statement on several comments Wilson had made to him while he was a student at Princeton. He recalled Wilson remarking, "I do not believe in democracy—the rule of the many. I believe in aristocracy the rule of

Figure 11 *Social-Democratic Herald* (Milwaukee), October 26, 1912. Portrays Wilson's attitude towards labor before and after he entered politics.

the few; but I wish an aristocracy of brains, not of wealth." Park also remembered Wilson's telling him that he "opposed . . . higher education for the common people," and saying, "Somebody must do the dirty work of the world, why shouldn't the children of the working classes be brought up to do the work their parents are now doing?" Supposedly, Wilson had made these statements to Park about 20 years before, in the early 1890s, but that failed to restrain the *Los Angeles Tribune* from publishing them now. Nor was it restrained in using Park's effort to prove Wilson's aristocratic preferences by making the absurd claim that "every reactionary journal [including, he said, the *New York Sun*] every organ of special privilege" was "either openly or secretly exerting every effort . . . [for] the election of Dr. Wilson." Although Wilson denied

Park's comments, the exposé continued, particularly in the pages of another western newspaper, the *Herald Republican* of Salt Lake City. It converted Park's recollections into a series of seven sensational editorial articles.[74] Nevertheless, such articles remained localized and failed to surface in the main currents of press criticism of Wilson. Although there is scant evidence to explain the truth and purpose of these charges, they could have caused severe damage to Wilson's candidacy. Why they failed to gain greater circulation remains unknown, but the fact that they entailed a range of unanswered questions may help to elucidate why they remained stillborn.[75] Of course, many opposition newspapers made much out of Wilson's alleged undemocratic preferences, usually citing his long association with privilege at Princeton to give credence to the charge.

Two other matters of a personal nature circulated about Wilson during the contest. Either one could have damaged his campaign had it become a topic that the newspapers deemed newsworthy. First there was the case of Mary Ellen Hulbert Peck, a woman Wilson met in 1907 while vacationing alone in Bermuda. This attractive, witty, and engaging woman had gone to Bermuda regularly since 1892, and while in residence there, she was known as a brilliant hostess to celebrities. When Wilson visited Bermuda, trying to preserve his health during the bitter graduate school fight at Princeton, he found the relaxing atmosphere of the island along with her literate conversation an escape. Their association developed after 1908 into a close friendship that lasted for about seven years. Its exact nature will never be known beyond doubt. At any rate, Wilson corresponded with her frequently, and his letters, prior to 1912 in particular, to his "Dearest Friend," were passionate enough to be indiscreet for any public figure who was married and had three daughters. They would be compromising if discovered, and Mary Peck was not one to make a secret of them. Then in September 1912, as Wilson's campaign was reaching full stride, he heard that one of his letters to Mary had been shown to a judge in Pittsfield, where Mary's husband lived, in connection with her divorce proceedings then underway.[76] Shocked to think that he might "in some way be implicated in the matter," Wilson wrote to Mary, "No matter how completely discredited later, [it would] just at this juncture ruin me utterly, and all connected with me. . . . The mere breath of such a thing would, of course, put an end to my candidacy and to my career. It is too deep an iniquity for words."[77]

Wilson was fortunate. With rumors persisting about him and Mrs. Peck, one of Roosevelt's political managers brought the matter to his attention. Despite his increasingly bitter rivalry with Wilson, the former president balked at using this type of information. He refused to resort to slander, and according to the journalist William Allen White, who knew him well, he added, "What's more, it wouldn't work. You can't cast a man as Romeo who looks and acts so much like the apothecary's clerk."[78] As for the newspapers, they declined to pursue the rumor, and it is only possible to speculate about their reasons for that decision. Perhaps without the actual letters in hand the risk of raising the charge was too great. Furthermore, the Hearst press, which did traffic in innuendo on occasion, became at least a nominal supporter of Wilson after the convention. Regardless, talk of Wilson and Mary Peck remained confined to the whispering chambers.

A second rumor that circulated about Wilson dealt with the suspicion that he was intolerant of Catholics. It was without foundation, and the fact that journalists like Tom Watson raised suspicions about Wilson being pro-Catholic in his *Jeffersonian* added an ironic twist to the charge of his intolerance.[79] He sensed the irony himself when he observed that while some ideas circulated about his being "hostile to Catholics" others were afloat implying that he was seeking to identify himself "politically with the great Catholic body." They were all "fabrications" he said and when placed together "would make very amusing reading."[80] Amusing or not, considering the large Catholic population in the northern cities where the Democrats hoped to find support, the talk of his prejudice against Catholics was serious. Recognizing the potential damage such talk could do, one member of the Democratic National Committee, New Jersey publicist J. C. Monaghan, wrote to all the editors of the Catholic press to reassure them about Wilson. He also wrote a campaign pamphlet, *Is Woodrow Wilson A Bigot?* for the Democratic National Committee's use.[81] James Kerney, of the *Trenton Evening Times*, also tried to stall the spread of false reports of his anti-Catholicism by reassuring correspondents that Wilson had "absolutely resisted all political pressure that was brought against the naming of Catholics to office."[82] Such efforts helped to marginalize the effects of the rumor.

IV

The special interest press included some of Wilson's harshest critics. These newspapers spoke with many voices and oft-times without reservation when expressing their opinion. Many African American editors, for example, remained unmoved by his pledge to be president of all

GETTING IT FROM BOTH SIDES

Figure 12 *New York Age,* October 24, 1912. Portrays the opinion of most African–American newspapers of both Wilson and Theodore Roosevelt.

people. They exhorted their readers to maintain their traditional loyalty to the Republican party and to reject the governor. As the *Chicago Defender* argued, Wilson was the "advanced guard of business depression" and although he "now attacked successful businessmen" he had during "his school-teaching career been a parasitic beneficiary of the philanthropic fruits of their business acumen."[83] African American editors also remained bitter about the failure of black students to gain admission to Princeton University while the doors of other northern colleges were open to them. For this grievance and for the failure of any African American to be appointed to a significant state office in New Jersey during Wilson's tenure as governor, they held him responsible. His southern origins and Democratic affiliation also troubled them. Had not the Democratic party subjugated and brutalized black citizens in the South? If Wilson won the election, would "southern democracy" be in control? Would the future of African American federal appointments be safe?[84] The fact that these editors found Roosevelt equally unacceptable made little difference.[85]

These editors were for Taft who befriended their people and Booker T. Washington, in particular, in many ways. Taft defended Washington when he was assaulted for an alleged indiscretion in New York City in

1911 and consulted him about general appointments for African Americans during his presidency. Washington, whom Taft said in a speech was "one of the greatest men of this and the last century, white or black," had even written a portion of the president's acceptance speech, that dealing with African Americans, for him.[86] Of equal consequence was Washington's influence with strategically placed black newspapers. He controlled the *New York Age*'s policies for some years, and even after Fred Moore took responsibility for it in 1911, he retained informal influence over that publication. "The fact that the New York Age was giving the President so loyal support, . . . was largely done through my friendship for you and your friendship for the President," its editor wrote to Washington in the spring of 1912.[87] Washington, moreover, tried to arrange subsidies for W. Calvin Chase's *Washington Bee*, a newspaper that made a habit of supporting his policies.[88] The influence of the Tuskegee educator, of course, extended far beyond any one publication, and a year before the campaign began he could tell President Taft that five-sixths of the 187 black newspapers in the country favored him.[89]

Nevertheless, some black editors assumed a contrary position, chief among them were William Monroe Trotter and W. E. B. DuBois. Both were leaders in the "anti-Bookerite" movement that had been growing since 1908 as a protest against Washington's policies of gradualism and his acceptance of segregation. Based on the vague promises Wilson made to him and his delegation when they visited him in July, Trotter backed Wilson in his *Guardian*. Meanwhile, the National Independent Political League, for which the editor served as secretary and the *Guardian* as its voice, published pamphlets and broadsides portraying the governor as a good, Christian man who had "never harmed our race" while reviewing the dissatisfactions African Americans had with Republicans in recent years.[90]

As the editor of the *Crisis*, the official organ of the recently formed National Association for the Advancement of Colored People, DuBois held a strategic position among African Americans.[91] The *Crisis* was a militant journal, and although DuBois aimed it mainly for "the talented tenth," much of its content was of interest to all African Americans.[92] Furthermore, it had a national circulation and the benefit of DuBois's editorials, which were without equal among African American periodicals. At first DuBois had hopes for the Progressive party, but after it rejected a proposed plank favoring the repeal of discriminatory laws that he had written for its platform committee to adopt, and after it denied convention seats to the majority of African

American delegates, he dismissed that idea. When his fellow "anti-Bookerite," Bishop Alexander Walters, visited the governor and received his assurance that he would be "absolutely fair" in assisting African Americans in "advancing the interest of their race in the United States," DuBois, somewhat uneasily, turned toward Wilson.[93] "The Negro is asked to take a leap in the dark without specific promises as to what protection he may expect after the Democrats are in power," he admitted. In defense of his position, he offered this rationale: "We sincerely believe that even in the face of promises disconcertingly vague and in the face of the solid caste-ridden South, it is better to elect Woodrow Wilson . . . and prove once for all if the Democratic party dares to be Democratic when it comes to black men."[94] Thus Wilson was able to make some inroad into the majoritarian African American press support for Taft. The assurances he gave to the African American editors who sided with him in the campaign helped somewhat, but in the main, he benefited from their disenchantment with the Republicans and with Roosevelt along with their revolt against Booker T. Washington and his policies.

Did Wilson fare better with the foreign-language and ethnic newspapers? Because of the great diversity of these often short-lived publications, it is impossible to generalize about them with certainty. Wilson frequently reiterated his explanation for the comments he made about immigrants from southern and eastern Europe in his *History* during the campaign, and he may have converted a few foreign-language newspapers to his cause. The *Progresso Italo-Americano* of New York, a prestigious Italian American newspaper, was unwavering in its support of Wilson. It moved beyond what he had written about immigrants in his *History* in the belief that he now favored a liberal immigration policy.[95] Also, late in August, a Newark newspaper correspondent, Antonio Petroni, led a delegation of Italians to see the governor and told him that his critics on immigration "had made a mountain out of a molehill" and that "intelligent Italians . . . [were] willing to allow the historian the latitude that the writing of impartial history requires."[96]

There is, however, reason to doubt how far this vein of opinion extended. "For once the entire Italian Press in America has taken a stand, in the disdainful silence with which it greeted the Democratic candidacy of Woodrow Wilson, for President of the United States," announced Chicago's *L'Italia* as the election approached. After rehashing the abrasive passages about immigrants from Wilson's *History*, it dismissed his more recent complimentary references to them as mere " 'elasticity' of political programs expounded on the eve of an election."

L'Italia felt that the only true gage of Wilson's opinion of Italians lay in what he had written, and it concluded its editorial by saying, "It is difficult for us to show a smiling face for one who wrote of our race as 'cursed rabble.' Wilson has classed the Italians as lower than the Chinese? Very well, let him go [to] the Chinese, for votes."[97]

Wilson stood a better chance of winning support among the foreign-language newspapers of nationalities from northern and western Europe. The Germans, for example, had the highest literacy rates, and the number of their publications almost equaled that of all other foreign-language newspapers and magazines combined.[98] They produced a number of newspapers of both Democratic and Republican persuasion in politics. The *Deutsche Correspondent* of Baltimore, for instance, the leading German newspaper in Maryland, resembled a mainstream urban American publication, and it represented a conservative point of view. In 1912, however, it rejected both Taft and Roosevelt in favor of Wilson, a position favored by other "middle-class" German language newspapers.[99] There is also evidence to suggest that Wilson made slight inroads into the traditionally Republican Swedish American press although Roosevelt gained more than Wilson from that defection.[100]

Nevertheless, the heterogeneity of the foreign-language press must be kept in mind. It comprised newspapers published in 33 different languages—some primarily religious, others nationalist, and others yet, cultural. Nor can the socialist identity of those ethnic publications with strong political views be discounted. The different brands of socialism they favored may have increased their heterogeneity but not their extreme leftist orientation and hostility to Wilson.[101]

The one ethnic community that had positioned itself largely within the Democratic party was the Irish. In the late nineteenth century, as mainly industrial workers in urban America, they filled municipal departments of government and its civic service ranks, and ran most of its political machines in the East and Midwest.[102] But could Wilson count on their support? His earlier writings about immigrants, even if directed toward other nationalities, rankled their sensitivities, as did his fondness of England. Moreover, when he spoke of being of Irish descent, it was the Scotch–Irish he had in mind, not the nationalist Irish. His persistent attack on machine politics also disturbed the Irish, who were so involved in and beholden to those big city organizations, and who often voted based on loyalty rather than on which candidate was best qualified for office. They questioned how Wilson could attack the political machines when he owed a great deal to the Jim Smith machine for his election as governor and to the Thomas Taggert machine in Indiana and the Roger Sullivan machine in Illinois for his presidential nomination. Finally, the stereotypical image of him as an idealistic professor rigid in his middle-class ways and unyielding in his views, which the editors opposing Wilson worked to keep in the public mind, was not the image of a man likely to receive a warm response from the Irish.[103]

By far the most influential Irish newspaper in this country was the *Irish World and American Industrial Liberator*. Its founder and editor, Patrick Ford, was an Irish nationalist and a formidable antagonist known for the power of his pen.[104] He favored Roosevelt in the election. Taft was unacceptable because of his efforts to secure a comprehensive arbitration treaty with Britain, and Ford feared Wilson would pursue a similar course. But the main fault he found with Wilson centered on his views on labor. He considered the governor's alleged free trade principles to be detrimental to labor in the belief that free trade could be equated with cheap labor. Furthermore, there were Wilson's old abrasive comments about organized labor to take into account. Ford deemed them, "an indictment of organized labor such as has never before been framed by a candidate for the great office of President." To vote for Wilson, he concluded, would be to announce "that organized labor may be maligned and abused with absolute impunity."[105]

Wilson, however, could expect more support from the organized labor press. His favorable labor record as governor of New Jersey gave substance to his claim that he was a friend of labor despite what critics said about some of his former statements in reference to unions. Those comments, it may be recalled, led the convention of the New Jersey Federation of Labor to pass a resolution in August 1910 condemning him for his attitude toward organized labor.[106] Although that resolution remained unrescinded, the Executive Board of that organization took a later action that, in effect, countermanded it. It passed a second resolution on February 14, 1912, commending him for his "unremitting and untiring efforts in assisting to bring about better conditions for the wage earners of New Jersey" and endorsing his administration.[107] Wilson's implacable adversary among New Jersey's union newspapers and the official organ of the Mercer County Central Labor Organization, the *Trades Union Advocate*, called the latter resolution "a farce" and claimed that Wilson had only signed the favorable bills into law because he was seeking nomination for the presidency.[108] But the 16 laws that the board's resolution specified as favorable to labor spoke for themselves. Furthermore, the board forwarded its resolution to the public press in New Jersey and to labor organizations across the country. Later the Democratic National Committee made the board's declaration the centerpiece of its campaign pamphlet, *Wilson and Labor*.[109]

An even more important labor endorsement came from "the Grand Old Man of the Labor Movement," Samuel Gompers. After meeting with the governor following the Baltimore convention, Gompers became one of the most effective proponents of Wilson's candidacy. Speaking as the president of the American Federation of Labor (A. F. L.) and through his powerful editorials in the *American Federationist*, his voice carried weight unequaled by any other labor leader in the country. Although the official position of the A. F. L. was not to endorse a particular candidate, Gomper's left no question about his and the A. F. L.'s preference. In his editorials he pointed out all that the Democratic party had done for labor since gaining control of the House of Representatives and reducing the number of Republicans in the Senate in 1910, and he stressed how receptive to labor's cause the Democratic convention had been in 1908 and again in the present year.[110] He went into great detail to explain how the A. F. L.'s Executive Council had submitted identical proposals addressing labor's concerns to both the Republican and Democratic conventions, and then elaborated the many ways the Democrats had offered favorable responses to those proposals in their platform while the Republicans had "studiously avoid [ed] all reference to these . . . essential demands of the workers. . . ." Gompers admitted that the Progressive party had also incorporated labor's demands in its platform, but his heart remained with the Democrats. In his final preelection editorial, he used a full page to highlight the 26 pro-labor measures that the Democratic House of Representatives had passed since 1910. "Let each toiler," Gompers concluded, "examine the acts and promises of individual candidates, [and] weigh the sincerity of party pledges in the light of what each party has done to make good those pledges." Then on election day, vote and "Stand faithfully by our friends."[111]

Naturally some unionists would take exception to Gompers' position in the presidential campaign, and some labor newspapers would prefer other candidates. The *Trades Union Advocate* of Trenton, for instance, refused to yield in its hostility to Wilson, and the *Utica Advocate*, the A. F. L. local paper in that city, preferred Taft to Wilson fearing his and his party's tariff views and doubting that the governor had the strength of character needed to be president.[112] Nevertheless, in the support he received from Gompers, the A. F. L., and the *American Federationist*, Wilson won one of the great prizes of the campaign.

Other special interest newspapers remained either nonpartisan or noncommittal during the campaign. Like the suffragist press, most of the religious newspapers declined to express a preference in regard to the candidates, and if they commented at all, they profiled the contenders and urged their readers to vote their choice. There were a few exceptions. The *New York Freeman's Journal and Catholic Register*, for instance, did carry a column of political analysis written by Robert Ellis Thompson, who also contributed a regular column for the *Irish World and American Industrial Liberator*. He detected serious flaws in Wilson. "I am convinced that Gov. Wilson is honest, although prejudiced and ill-informed," he wrote. It was Wilson's position in regard to the tariff issue that most disturbed Thompson, who said the governor was "violent and unqualified" on the subject and unfair to those people who held different views.[113] The *Catholic Universe* also included a column on politics. In this case it was opened to various writers, including an anonymous contributor, "A Life-Long Democrat" from Long Branch, New Jersey, who wrote a scathing denunciation of Wilson's record in his home state. Bearing signs of being written by one of his chagrined political opponents from the aftermath of his gubernatorial campaign, this account suggested that he was an opportunist rather than a reformer. Accordingly, the governor deserved credit for none of the reforms enacted by the legislature and had otherwise acted with ingratitude to advance his own personal interests in all that he did, yet the *Catholic Universe* gave it a prominent position on its editorial page as the election approached.[114]

On the other hand, a number of Catholic newspapers defended Wilson, and the other candidates too, against the attempt to inject religious prejudice into the campaign that editors like Tom Watson in his *Jeffersonian* were making. Although the general circulation press mainly closed its columns to such efforts, the charge that Wilson was under the influence of the Catholic church and favored Catholics in his official appointments circulated by means of widely distributed circulars and in newspapers like the *Jeffersonian* and the *Menace*, an anti-Catholic newspaper published in Aurora, Missouri. "Heresy-mongers" one Catholic news writer termed these malicious attacks in a typical comment about them while editors of numerous Catholic newspapers criticized Tom Watson, in particular, in emphatic language.[115] Some Protestant and nondenominational newspapers also commented on the campaign, and a few of these were enthusiastic about Wilson's candidacy, but even with the approach of election day, most of them remained neutral.[116]

V

As the election neared, there was a lull in the campaign following the attempted assassination of Roosevelt. Nevertheless, by the last week in October, the traditional preelection flurry of articles about the candidates and their families surfaced in the newspapers as long, end-of-the-campaign editorials appeared proclaiming the merits of one or the other of the candidates. There was, of course, little to be stated that was new. The question before the editors was about how persuasive they could be in their final appeals to the voters. Only in a few instances did questions remain about an important editor's position, and for Wilson, the most significant of these editors was Henry Watterson. Those questions vanished on November 2, when he published a strong editorial endorsing Wilson. "I have not a particle of personal grudge against him," he wrote to Josephus Daniels explaining his stand. "My quarrel was solely on account of his treatment of George Harvey. It may be that I exaggerated this; but . . . [Wilson] has impressed me as one not very sensible of the obligations of affection and friendship." Marse Henry's personal reservations about Wilson remained private, for in his editorial, he argued that the governor was "far and away the ablest leader who has appeared in our public life during the present generation."[117] Watterson's endorsement was good news, indeed, for Daniels and the other directors of the Democratic publicity organization, who were making every possible effort to keep the rank and file of Democratic newspapers in a solid line behind Wilson.

Wilson's publicity directors' final surge of activity was impressive. They declared November 2 "Wilson and Marshall Day" and asked their campaign workers to have a speech from Wilson read in every county and in every large center in all of the states. That was a unique idea in American politics. They also distributed a final round of promotional materials to the newspapers, including Wilson's "A Message to the American People," his final word on why he was seeking the presidency that he wrote in the form of an open letter to the "Voters of America." His publicity directors called it "a literary treasure," which it was, and "the most dignified, comprehensive appeal to voters ever issued by a presidential candidate in any campaign," which was a hard-to-prove rhetorical flourish. Moreover, since Wilson's speeches had been extemporaneous and, therefore, never published in full far from where they were delivered, the directors also sent the editors two pages of excerpts from the governor's campaign speeches, hoping that they would receive "as much publicity as possible."[118] According to a variety of polls that appeared toward the end of October and to the judgment of many astute politicians, Wilson's victory was assured. Taft had long before ceased active campaigning, and Roosevelt had started late and failed to appeal beyond his own progressive supporters. Nevertheless, Wilson's publicity directors wanted to avoid the "danger of over-confidence" and warned, "We Democrats must keep up the fight until the votes are in."[119]

Wilson, himself, insisted on fulfilling a speaking commitment in Paterson on election eve, an inconsequential engagement he could have skipped because of the after effects of a painful four inch long, deep cut on the top of his head he sustained two nights before when returning from a speech in Red Bank, his car struck a rut in the road. A newspaperman accompanying him on that final outing to Paterson mentioned to him afterward that he was surprised the governor had not passed up that meeting. "Tonight," Wilson replied, "I felt as if I wanted to keep driving right up to the last moment."[120] Thus, this memorable campaign ended with Wilson demonstrating that he was still the "fighting man" that the journalists had discovered him to be in the early months of his governorship.

The reporters were with him till the end. After casting his vote on election day, he had his picture taken surrounded by the newspapermen who had accompanied him throughout the campaign. Then he took them for a long walk out into the countryside around Princeton to points of special interest relating to the Revolutionary War. Along the way he stopped at various campus sites and shared his memories about each with the reporters. Afterward he strolled with a friend or two to revisit some of his favorite campus haunts, and then he retired to his Princeton home on Cleveland Lane. That evening only a few people, several friends and the group of reporters who had been with him during the past months, were invited inside the house to await the returns. After dinner Wilson spent a few hours with Ellen in her studio, and then joined the rest of his family along with friends and newsmen in the main room of the house. There Tumulty was busy manning the telephone, and in the nearby library the ticking of a telegraph key brought fresh news of the impending outcome. Amid this growing atmosphere of anticipation, Wilson remained calm. At about ten o'clock, the telegraph operator brought the news of Wilson's election to Ellen, who conveyed it to her husband. Meanwhile, as the college bell in Nassau Hall began to ring students gathered to celebrate. Joined by other well wishers, the throng marched with torches lit behind the college band to the Wilson home where they stood cheering and singing before the front porch. "Woodrow was deeply moved," his daughter recalled. "Standing on an old rocking chair which Tumulty had dragged out on the porch, he greeted them in a voice not as firm as usual." Characteristic of the man, he spoke not of victory but of his "solemn responsibility" as he faced the task ahead.[121]

The *New York Evening Post* called Wilson's election a "sobering triumph," and in a sense his comments to the Princeton faithful reflected that thought.[122] His words were reflective, and they befitted the campaign he had waged. At bottom Wilson made it an honorable and serious affair, one that excluded any vestige of demagoguery. In depicting his performance, the pro-Wilson editors seem to capture not only the essence of the man but also the tone of the campaign as he set it. Of equal importance, of course, was the intelligible support they offered him. In the contest, as waged in and through the press, they put forth his case persuasively and offered reasonable defenses to the oft-times caustic criticism the opposition editors leveled against him. They countered the efforts of those editors to profile him in dubious stereotypical ways. As important as anything else, with rare exception, they refused to break ranks and to rally behind Roosevelt, who called upon independent and progressive Democrats to follow him.

It is impossible, of course, to say to whom or to what part of the press Wilson was most indebted. Some of the editors of the special interest press, especially Samuel Gompers, rendered valuable service as did some of the editors of the Scripps newspapers. But in the end both the Scripps and the Hearst press offered only modest support. The backing of the southern Democratic newspapers was indispensable to his election. Although there were variations among them, they closed their ranks behind Wilson. Second to none in terms of influence was the wholehearted support that a number of metropolitan dailies rendered to his cause from start to finish of the campaign. They reached across the country. Conspicuous among them were the *Baltimore Sun*, the *Boston Globe*, the *Daily Oklahoman* (Oklahoma City), the *Dallas Morning News*, the *Newark Evening News*, the *New York Evening Post*, the *New York World*, the *Pittsburgh Post*, the *Raleigh News and Observer*, the *Rocky Mountain News*, the *Sacramento Union*, and the *St. Louis Post-Dispatch*.[123] There were, of course, many other metropolitan newspapers in Wilson's camp, and it would be risky to assign any order of priority to the contribution any one of them made to his election. Nor can the contributions that Wilson's publicity managers made through the media be overstated. Josephus Daniels and his lieutenants ably exploited both older and newer media in their successful promotion of Wilson.

In fact, the chief hallmark of Wilson's effective campaign, as the journalists and his publicity managers conducted it in the media, was its diversity. Along with those elements of the special interest press that supported him and those large metropolitan dailies anchored in his camp there were numerous small town and country Democratic newspapers to take into account. Wilson was correct to acknowledge their importance, for as the editor of one of these small Democratic newspapers put it, they had "at all times sounded the note of Democracy without wavering or flinching."[124] Of these editors Josephus Daniels once said that they had done more "than any other people" to assure Wilson's success.[125]

All considered, the media's involvement in Wilson's cause was a composite affair. It included publications large and small and those with a variety of political identities. Even some traditionally Republican newspapers crossed over to support the governor during the campaign.[126] Ranging from progressive journalists like Henry Ekert Alexander, Norman Hapgood and Ray Stannard Baker to those of a conservative temperament like George Harvey (his differences with Wilson now set aside) to old friends and associates like George S. Johns and Walter Hines Page and to the many newsmen attracted to him during the course of the campaign, they were a diverse lot. With all of their ideological and sectional differences, their diversity contrasted with the more monolithic press support accorded to either Roosevelt or Taft. To his credit, Wilson established the necessary friendly press relations and set the proper tone in his campaign speeches and appearances needed to create basic unity amid such diversity.

Chapter 10
On the Threshold of the White House

The months following Wilson's election victory provide a microcosm of his relations with the press. On the one hand, the compatibility he established with journalists in Trenton and nurtured during his campaigns continued, while on the other hand, old irritations with reporters reemerged—in some cases with surprising adamancy. Indications now appeared in his dealings with the press that suggested that the journalists might find him difficult to work with in the future. However, the president-elect had the benefit of having assigned the press a serious role in his thought about executive leadership in a democratic society and had gained many advantages in his practical experience with it and with journalists over the years. In determining his preparation for dealing with the press as president, these advantages would have to be measured against difficulties that had emerged in his dealings with journalists, with reporters in particular.

I

With some significant exceptions, Wilson remained on good terms with the correspondents, his "keepers," following his election. They felt comfortable enough to entrap him in a joke. Not long after the election, they invited him into Tumulty's office at the State House in Trenton to hear a recording of himself. The record began with a voice much like his own saying, "Do you want to gyrate with the gyrators or stand still with the stand stillers?" Cries of "No, no" followed. Realizing he had fallen into the hands of joking companions and was listening to a parody of an address he had delivered at the Brooklyn Academy of Music, Wilson responded with hearty laughter. The voice on the record continued, "Do you want a Democratic team with a captain . . . or do you want to play with [the] signals . . . [of] the last four years, . . ." Interrupting the record, the governor exclaimed, "I know that voice." Then a second voice could be heard on the record. It bore resemblance to Maud Malone, the militant suffragist who had interrupted Wilson's speech at the Academy of Music. "How about votes for women, Governor, . . ." the voice demanded amid cries of "Put the woman out." As the applause subsided, the mimicking of Wilson's voice continued, "Resuming where I left off, . . . I maintain that the woman's question is not pertinent onto the subject onto which I was discussing, . . . Do you want to set the Government free . . . ?" Cries of "Yes, yes" ensued. Then the voice concluded, "Well, I would rather triumph in a cause that I know someday will fail than to fail in a cause that I know some day will triumph." The governor clearly enjoyed the spoof.[1]

Wilson felt as comfortable with reporters as they did with him. He even told the photographers that he was "getting very meek" about having his picture taken.[2] Quite a change. Charles Swem, the governor's stenographer who accompanied him throughout his campaign, later reflected, "He was frank in his enjoyment of an intimate newspaper conference. He appreciated the keenness of the newspaper mind, . . . and his conferences with little groups of correspondents invariably called forth the best that was in his own mind. He had an unexplainable habit of indulging in the most intimate and open franknesses in his newspaper conferences." Swem recalled that he made "some of his frankest statements upon important and confidential matters before newspaper gatherings."[3] Nor, did he neglect the editors and publishers. He continued to accommodate them, and when a matter merited doing so, he would take into his confidence those editors whom he knew and whose advice he appreciated.[4]

Throughout his political ascendancy, Wilson had journalists among his trusted advisors and loyal supporters. Once he became an active candidate, many more rallied behind him. In some cases, no doubt, self-service or at least mutual benefit was involved. Some of his supporters in the press thought of him in terms of a winner, or as the candidate most able to unite the Democratic party, or as someone whose idealism inspired them. H. V. Kaltenborn, who would become the dean of radio news commentators, perceived Wilson as a candidate with a superb academic background, an authoritative knowledge of government, and a record of administrative ability, proven by his experience as university president and state governor. "This combination of practical and theoretical knowledge, not often found in those seeking public office, has always seemed to me to be ideal," he reflected some years later.[5] Wilson no less impressed the moderate muckraker Ray Stannard Baker, originally a LaFollette promoter. After interviewing the governor in 1912, Baker wrote in retrospect, that Wilson had "the finest mind in the field of statesmanship to be found in American public life."[6] Arthur Bullard, also writing some years later as a prominent international journalist, captured another aspect of what drew men like him to Wilson, by explaining:

> Every once in a while some "maverick" turns up, who talks with and to the people and does some straight thinking—puts his finger on "real issues"—and pretty soon he becomes President, to the disgust of the Old Guard. Wilson was one of these mavericks—he had not been branded. He found the Democratic party just as disorganized as it was in '24 [1924], but the people believed that he meant what he said and he said what the people believed—they trusted him to come through. I am not thinking, at the moment of the War President—that was on another plane—but of Wilson in 1910 and 1911.[7]

In some instances journalists were devoted to him. Charles H. Grasty, for example, then president and general manager of Baltimore's *Sunpapers*, wrote after the election, "If you should ever reach a point in standing bravely up to the high-minded course you have set for yourself where you were in need of a friend's help, in any way, mine will be yours for the knowing of the need."[8]

Nevertheless, for journalists to do their job, they had to be neither friend nor supporter of a public figure, but they had to have access to him. Public figures, of course, often resisted the probings of reporters. Even in an age in which the public's curiosity about them, about presidents in particular, was escalating, they claimed the rights of privacy allowed them to determine the access newsmen would have. Still, it was a time when the principle of publicity was growing along with the corresponding appetite for news of prominent people. Back at the start of the preconvention campaign Wilson had stated, "I am for the newspapers—which is merely another way of mentioning the fact that I am in public life. The public man who fights the daily press won't be a public man very long."[9] In many respects, he had tried to live up to his own words after entering politics, but that was not always the case. It can be recalled that Stockbridge had to force him to meet with reporters on his western trip in 1911. Moreover, dating back to his days as university president, he had been stingy about granting individual interviews.

II

During his months as president-elect, Wilson continued his mostly friendly relations with the reporters at Trenton. Accommodating them, however, became more taxing, and several incidents at this time indicated signs of strain. For instance, soon after the election, as reporters gathered in his office for their "seance," he greeted them in the best of humor suggesting they could ask him questions on any subject other than of his Cabinet selections. One reporter allowed the governor's qualification to pass unnoticed. Having just returned from a celebration with friends in New York City, and although not apparent in his presence, the effects of spirits consumed still lingered. With his mind "a universe away" he opened the session by asking Wilson who his attorney-general would be. The governor was irate. "Are you trying to insult me," Wilson charged. When the reporter, still unmindful of his indiscretion answered, "No, Governor, not at all. Only trying to get the news." Wilson snapped back, "You're taking the wrong way to get it." Still agitated, he managed to regain enough composure to continue. The hapless reporter was soon reassigned duties elsewhere.[10]

Other incidents followed as Wilson allowed his press relations to slip. He even managed to frustrate reporters while befriending them. After the election, he and his family vacationed in Bermuda and received reporters daily for congenial visits. The Wilsons, David Lawrence remembered, "accepted the correspondents as social visitors . . . rather than as professional callers. Many a visit which was begun with the object of getting news from the president-elect turned out in vain because of the charm and attractiveness of the drawing room where Mr. Wilson, his wife and daughters participated in a discussion of everything except news. It effectively prevented the scribes from conducting their usual cross-examination."[11] At best he felt his way along with the newspapermen and offered only general answers to their questions. Sometimes when alone with them he let his thoughts roam. Entranced by the beauty of his surroundings in Bermuda, he once mused, "This is an unreal country. It's a land of witchcraft, a fairy land, a land of make-believe." He told them that with matters of business, sometimes he had to shut out that beauty and mystery by closing the blinds and turning on inside lights. "Can we print that, Governor?" queried one correspondent. "Lord, no!" he responded explaining that while the people on the island would understand it, those "in a more prosaic land would simply think I had gone crazy." Charles Willis Thompson, who was one of the group, thereupon wrote to a friend, "another story gone wrong."[12]

The president-elect also had reason to feel frustrated about the search for news from the island. He went there seeking relaxation and he sought private time to think through his plans.[13] The correspondents, however, needed news, and they began to draw upon his merest comment. "It is extremely annoying to me," he wrote to McCombs, "to have these men constantly exciting comment in the United States over my casual remarks."[14] He was more than annoyed when news reports appeared the day after his daughter Eleanor had been seen dancing with a young Princeton man visiting the island. They claimed she was engaged to him. Wilson was furious. He asked the correspondents to deny the story, which they did—all but one who sent a second dispatch about Eleanor's romance to his newspaper. When Wilson demanded an explanation, the correspondent showed him a telegram from his home office that read, "Send more details about Eleanor Wilson's engagement. Ignore diplomatic denials." According to Eleanor, "Father told him that he might as well take the next ship home as he would never be given another interview."[15]

Wilson's fury erupted yet again. After returning from a bicycle ride with daughter Jessie, he found correspondents and photographers awaiting them. Knowing that after a long ride Jessie felt less presentable than young women of her time wished to appear when being photographed, he tried to shield her. He invited the cameramen to photograph him, "but," he added, "I request you not to photograph my daughter. . . ." A cameraman snapped a picture before he could finish. His face reddened in anger and his fists clenched, Wilson rushed at the man, charging, "You're no gentleman! I want to give you the worst thrashing you ever had in your life; and what's more, I'm perfectly able to do it."[16] That newsman also soon departed from Bermuda. Although the correspondents sympathized with Wilson in this instance, his relations with them appeared to be waning. During the trip home, David Lawrence told Eleanor that her father was making a "serious mistake" in failing to be more considerate of the press.[17]

Returning home, the reporters continued to press him about Cabinet selections. With many newspapers claiming that the Democratic party was only nominally united, that antagonistic factions controlled it, and while others hailed his election as a victory for conservatives, and yet others, as a triumph of progressivism, the delicacy of news about his Cabinet nominations can be appreciated. Consequently, feeling that the reporters were harassing him for news of his Cabinet appointments, he warned them, "I have been very much embarrassed by having newspapers print articles under a Trenton or Princeton date line, speculating as to who will or will not be in the Cabinet." Then he added, "Unless this practice ceases, I will be put to the necessity of publishing a card." No one knew what that statement meant. When asked to explain , he said, "I mean that I will publish a card in the newspapers saying that I am not responsible for anything published on this subject."[18]

Nevertheless, curiosity about his Cabinet choices continued. In February, while meeting with the reporters at the State House, one of the correspondents reminded him that there was still widespread interest in the country about his selections. Wilson fired back, "I am not here to amuse the newspapers. I am here to select a Cabinet for the people of the United States. If the newspapers think they can make me conduct myself in any other way they are wrong." The reporter countered that if he would announce his selections, it would no longer be necessary for him to deny erroneous reports about them. To that Wilson responded, "I cannot make myself over to please the newspapers. You will have to take me as you find me. I cannot assume a personality." Finally, with yet another reporter's attempt to have him announce his selections, Wilson angrily retorted, "I am doing what I believe to be best for the country and for myself. If the newspapers expect me to do anything else, I'll be damned if I will." Then he relaxed and said, "Pardon me for blowing up. These stories about Cabinet appointments are all false. I have told you men here in Trenton that I have made no selections for the Cabinet, and to keep on questioning me about it is to doubt my veracity."[19] Actually, by stating that he had "made no selections," he was being untruthful. Bryan, for one, had already accepted Wilson's offer to be secretary of state on December 23.[20] As Colonel House, who had become the governor's confidant, noted in his diary, "He has so many times grazed the truth in answering questions about his appointments."[21]

Indeed, Wilson's grazing the truth could be an embarrassment for reporters. An incident occurred toward the end of his governorship of New Jersey when the state senators had a dinner for his successor at the Hotel Astor in New York City. On the day of the dinner, the Trenton reporters accompanied him to New York, and on the train began to inquire about the dinner. Did Wilson plan to make a speech there? No, he replied, it would be a social affair. Would there be any speeches at the dinner? No, it would be a "purely informal" gathering, he said. Thus assured that the evening offered nothing of political importance, the reporters wrote a short advance story about the dinner, and then planned the rest of the day on their own. Departing from the train, the governor went to Colonel House's apartment supposedly on his way to the Astor. Seeing nothing unusual about that, the reporters scattered. Later, however, two of the reporters looked in on the affair at the Hotel Astor. Wilson was not there, nor was he expected. Hurrying to House's apartment, they learned that the governor was still there, that he intended to remain there for the night, and that important conferences were being held. The two reporters found out the nature of those conferences and filed stories about them to supersede their previous ones. The other reporters, however, had the dubious distinction of having submitted worthless new reports. In his conversation with the reporters, Wilson had told them the strict truth knowing that it was misleading.[22] Reporters expected public figures to be frank with them while understanding that some of the men they covered would lie. But as Charles Willis Thompson said in relating this incident, they had never met one who told "them the truth in such a way that they . . . [were] sure not to be deceived by him, but to deceive themselves."[23] They learned the necessity of having to scrutinize whatever he told them for misleading inferences in his words.

Nevertheless, the reporters were encouraged by several moves the president-elect did make. On February 5, he announced the appointment of Tumulty as his private secretary. Wilson had thought Tumulty was too provincial for the political environment of the capital, but he recognized the qualifications he did have for the position and made the appointment—it might be added, at the urging of Ellen, whose estimate of men and their views he trusted. Just as the reporters were discovering Ellen Wilson to be one of their favorite people, even one capable of pacifying differences that arose between them and her husband, so they knew that Tumulty was a person with a capacity to work well with the press.[24]

The correspondents were also growing curious about Colonel House when it became obvious that his friendship with the president-elect was growing. Wilson explained to them why he valued House. He said he appreciated his ability to penetrate to the core of matters, and his ability to be thoroughly objective. House would become famous in time as Wilson's special envoy who was, in the words of David Lawrence, "really analogous to the star reporter who is occasionally sent by his newspaper to make a general survey of a situation."[25] Along with fulfilling the roles of unofficial advisor and special envoy, House would serve Wilson as a liaison with the journalists. House was a man of means, of influence, and would become an interpreter of public opinion for Wilson. Even at this point, House was nurturing his relationships with journalists. His diary for these months recorded the visits that editors, publishers, and other publicists made to his New York apartment. It also recorded the subjects of his conversations with them, providing in the process not only his thoughts on political matters but also the interest he took in the workings of the press.[26] There were strong indications that he would be an effective intermediary for Wilson in his dealings with them.

III

There was no uncertainty, however, that Wilson would encounter a strong tide of criticism from the press in the years ahead. Speculation circulated, for example, that William Randolph Hearst wanted a Cabinet position, perhaps only to be able to reject it, and that he wished to confer with Wilson.[27] The governor and his advisors considered Hearst either an unethical opportunist or an enemy. Why should Wilson take him into his confidence? On the other hand, the press lord was a dangerous man to alienate. The problem even disturbed Ellen Wilson, who sought House's advice.[28] He opposed any meeting in the belief "that there was no way to satisfy Hearst, and if the Governor gave way to him in one thing he would want another until there would certainly be a point where he could go no further. A rupture would then come, and the conference would only have given Hearst an additional weapon with which to do harm."[29] Wilson, himself, saw no purpose in talking with Hearst.[30] His presidency, thus, would begin with the powerful press lord feeling, and not for the first time, that Wilson had slighted him.[31]

Unease about how his promised policies would affect the economy posed another problem for Wilson. During the campaign, Roosevelt had predicted that the Democratic proposals for tariff revisions "would plunge this country into the most widespread industrial depression we have yet seen; and this depression would continue for an indefinite period."[32] Variations of that theme resonated through Republican and Progressive newspapers and did not disappear after the election. There was even speculation that some financial manipulators might try to depress the stock market by making it appear that investors feared the incoming administration. Wilson met this talk head on in a speech to the Southern Society on December 17. He spoke of the "sinister predications" circulating about how his policies would disturb business. Then looking at the reporters seated below him, he announced there was such a thing as an "unnatural panic" caused by "certain gentlemen" who wished "to create the impression that the wrong thing is going to be done," and that machinery (e.g., the calling in of loans) existed to instigate such a panic. "I do not believe," he said, "there is a man living who dares to use that machinery. If there is, I promise him . . . a gibbit as high as Haman ['s] [a Persian courtier who was hanged for attempting to order the massacre of the Jews in Persia]. I don't mean a literal gibbet, but a figurative gibbet on which he will be punished as long as his quivering soul is capable of feeling a sense of shame." The *Sun* wasted no time in responding to this warning. It produced a cartoon depicting the president-elect as "Lord High Executioner Wilson" and ridiculed him in the caption that read "The New Gallows-Freedom"—in reference to his campaign promise of "the New Freedom" for the nation.[33] While resisting such ridicule, some more moderate newspapers had misgivings about Wilson's confrontational words, but more progressive newspapers, especially those of the Scripps organization, welcomed them.[34]

Still, newspapers like the *New York Journal of Commerce* were uneasy about his plan to initiate his promised economic reforms by calling Congress into extra session to deal with tariff revision. It claimed that there was an "insistent demand" to delay action on tariff legislation. On the other hand, the *New York World*, while admitting that Wilson was being pressured to follow the course the *Journal of Commerce* recommended, declared that such opposition to calling the extra session was "a counsel of infamy to which he can not and will not listen, . . ."[35] Thanks to assurances Colonel House gave to a gathering of the country's leading financiers, many of the fears of Wilson's economic "radicalism" were mitigated. Nevertheless, uncertainty about his economic reforms remained among conservative newspapers, and he knew their opposition would have to be overcome in the quest for public support for his reforms once his presidency began. These newspapers, as well as some of the leading pro-Roosevelt ones, continued to believe that the majority of the country still favored protection, and that argument was unlikely to disappear from future columns of his press critics.[36]

Nor had disparagement of him dissipated in various quarters of the special interest press. African American newspapers now feared the influence of Wilson's southern advisors.[37] Even the *Crisis* editorialized that Wilson would have to display determination to fulfill his campaign promises to African Americans, for he could be surrounded by a "Southern oligarchy," counselors who had little sympathy for them.[38] In fact, the president of the National Colored Democratic League alerted Wilson that, based on statements circulating in the press and on the comments of some of the Democratic leaders, speculation was spreading about the possibility of African Americans actually losing their present positions in Washington. Urging the president-elect to avoid that course of action, he told him, "Negro papers are on the qui vive to have you do something that would make trouble."[39] Elsewhere little had changed in the ethnic press. The *Irish World and American Industrial Liberator* predicted, "The incoming Democratic Administration will be merely an interlude as was the second Cleveland Administration."[40] Its sympathies were with the Progressive party to which, in its opinion, the future belonged. That was also the view of George Sylvester Viereck, the then editor of *Rundschau zweier Welten (Review of Two Worlds)*, who wrote to Roosevelt saying "In the past it was, 'We stand at Armageddon and we battle for the Lord' [the motto of the Progressives in 1912]. With Wilson and hard times coming it will be, 'We stand at Armageddon and we battle for our board.'"[41] Meanwhile, Socialist newspapers continued to portray Wilson as the dupe of capitalism.[42]

The governor's bitterest critics in the press saw no hope for his forthcoming presidency. Writing to one of his friends, the old populist firebrand Tom Watson warned: "You are going to [be] immensely disappointed in Wilson; you will see him truckling to the pope, just as Taft did; you will see him filling the most important offices with Roman Catholics; you will see him baffle the tariff reforms, just as Taft did; you will find him placing niggers in influential positions, just as Taft did; you will see him obeying Wall Street, just as Taft did."[43] The incoming administration could expect vitriolic criticism from Watson's *Jeffersonian* and from other publications of similar persuasion. In response to the rumor circulating around the country that claimed Wilson was going to appoint a Catholic as his postmaster general, the Methodist *Pentecostal Herald* of Louisville charged that the American people would rebel against such action. It would lead to the appointment of postmasters across the country, of men who would be "under the domination of the Roman Pontiff." In the belief that the Roman Catholic church was controlled by "unscrupulous" men in Rome who were anxious to dominate the "political life of this republic," the *Herald* declared that "the Protestant politician who lends himself to her [the Catholic church] in her nefarious work is a traitor of the deepest dye—a Judas Iscariot and Benedict Arnold united in one." A North Carolina merchant, fearing that Wilson might be contemplating such an appointment, sent him a copy of the *Herald*'s editorial.[44] There were, consequently, ample indications in specialized newspapers as well as in mainstream publications that criticism of various sorts and degrees would stir the public debate over the endeavors of his administration in the years ahead.

IV

As important as press criticism promised to be in Wilsonian presidential politics, there were mitigating factors to take into account. At the outset of his administration, he could count on widespread press support among Democratic and independent newspapers, and among them were those of Scripps, which now urged "every right thinking American, irrespective of politics" to serve himself and his country "by loyally supporting the new leaders. . . ."[45] Wilson also had the goodwill of many individual and influential journalists. Moreover, it should be admitted that during his two campaigns for office, he had demonstrated his ability to take personal criticism in his stride. Indeed, in the hard-hitting personalized attacks on him that appeared in the press, in the techniques yellow journalism used to besmirch his character, and in the efforts of some journalists to intrigue against him, he had experienced some of the worst features of Progressive era political journalism. They tended to confirm his disfavor of sensationalized journalism and even of many of the trends associated with the mass-circulating, commercial, popular press. His frequent annoyance at being misrepresented in the press only increased that feeling. If at times his complaints of being misquoted or of having his comments taken out of context were less than convincing, and if his refusal to provide advance copies of his speeches made reporting him difficult, the fact remains that, in voicing complaints about being misrepresented in print, he was echoing a common discontentment among public figures of the time. Considering all that appeared about him in the press, he had acquired a fairly strong armor against what he considered to be its abuses of him and his statements, and that too was an asset to have in discharging the responsibilities that now awaited him.

He had developed yet other assets that could enhance his future press relations and his ability to mobilize popular support for his programs. His commanding presence as a public speaker, one of the most effective in American history, was a political advantage to have, one that attracted press attention and one that he had employed effectively at every stage of his rise as a public figure. He learned through experience that bold political gestures, like his debate with George Record conducted through the medium of newspapers and his unprecedented appearance as governor before the New Jersey legislature's Democratic caucus, aroused public enthusiasm for his cause. It was, of course, the press that led in stirring reactions to those gestures. The deeper Wilson moved into politics the more his style of activist leadership became involved with the workings of political journalism. There were a number of indications that suggested he understood this involvement and took steps to nurture, and in some respects, to manage it. The public statements and open letters he published, the interviews he granted, his extensive communications with publicists, and his willingness to accept their counsel when appropriate were all indicative of the effort he was making to engage the press as a political medium. Moreover, the endeavors he made to establish friendly relations with the reporters who accompanied him boded well for his future press relations. Perhaps most of all, the way in which he accommodated reporters covering the governor's office in Trenton, both by providing them with facilities and by his meetings with them, signaled his interest in regularizing those relations as a chief executive.

Yet other indications suggesting that he intended to be actively engaged with the press as president can be found in his political writings and addresses. There was a continuum running through them that underscored, both by explicit and implicit reference, the significance he accorded the press as a factor of consequence in the nation's political culture. He once told a reporter in 1912 that the key to his political thought could be found in *Mere Literature and Other Essays*, a volume he published in 1896. It contained, he said, not only his ideas on the "political present" but also his "political philosophy for the future."[46] In fact, it is possible to find continuities in Wilson's thought about public opinion and political leadership, two topics bearing relation to the press in politics, beginning in his early writings and speeches and running through his political career to date. He began by discussing the interaction between a political leader and public opinion in his first book *Congressional Government* and returned to that theme in his last book *Constitutional Government*. In the former, published in 1885, he probed into the advantages an editor has over a political figure in shaping public opinion and how the political leader could only gain the advantage over the editor by means of "genius and leadership."[47] In *Constitutional Government*, published in 1908, he wrote that the president "can dominate his party by being the spokesman for the real sentiment and purpose of the country, by giving direction to opinion, by giving the country at once the information and the statements of policy which will enable it to form its judgments alike of parties and men."[48]

Echoes of those ideas reverberated throughout his public addresses and in various essays he penned during his early career. One of his successful addresses was "Leaders of Men." He delivered it four times between 1890 and 1898, each time broaching the need for an effective leader to perceive the deep, as contrasted to "the momentary and whimsical," currents of popular thought.[49] Years later, in "Hide-And-Seek Politics," an article he published in 1910, he turned his attention to the role of public opinion in the affairs of state. He spoke of a "government by public opinion," of how public opinion was "better informed" than ever before in this country, of how it was a force for the "betterment of the nation," and of how it was at present unable to fulfill its purpose.

Accordingly, he argued that it was machine-controlled politics that prevented public opinion from performing its intended role in political discourse.[50] The remedy, he believed, was to simplify the process of elections and procedures of the government and to have the press publicize in full the business of government.[51] As he did in his *Constitutional Government*, in "Hide-And-Seek Politics" he assigned public opinion a more active role in government, much in the same manner that he assigned presidential leadership a larger role in *Constitutional Government* than he did in *Congressional Government.* His thinking on these matters had evolved over the years. However, it is clear that the nature of political leadership, the role of public opinion in American democracy, and the need for publicity of the activities of government were integral parts of the fabric of his political thought over time. These topics, of course, involved the press as a means of implementation. They had since the beginning of the republic.

In fact, Wilson's interest in the press as a concomitant to elements he stressed in his political writings and speeches is clear. In his references to the press in *Congressional Government*, he portrayed it as a more consequential force than Congress in affecting public opinion. Years later in "The Modern Democratic State," which he worked on throughout the 1880s and 1890s, he equated the aggregate voice of the press with public opinion.[52] A decade or so later, in his *Constitutional Government*, he acknowledged the capacity of the modern press, with all of the technical advances in communication and transportation that it exploited, to create a common national consciousness.[53]

Looking back from the vantage point of 1913, it is clear that the role he attached to the press as a force in society was an ongoing dimension in his thought. Consider his early musings about a career in journalism, or recall what he hoped to achieve by his involvement in literary journalism. In his early comments about the press, he deplored the excesses of the New Journalism, and, in some of his public commentary while president of Princeton, he continued to do so. Yet he also encouraged students and journalists to consider journalism as a public service.[54] Later yet, speaking before an assembly of journalists in 1911, he referred to the editorship of a newspaper as a "kind of statesmanship"—albeit, "a minor kind of statesmanship." As he had in previous comments on the press, he again stressed the value of news. What he had in mind on this occasion was news presented comprehensively enough to allow readers to understand not only the issues of the day but also "the state of mind" from which they arise. Readers could then determine for themselves "whether the editor knows what he is talking about or not."[55]

All through these years, while he sometimes added his voice to those of others in criticizing sensational and unethical journalistic practices, he never wavered in his contention that the press could be a force for great good in society. That belief would serve him well in the years ahead.

Furthermore, he was fortunate in having worked closely with individual journalists as advisors and as managers for his campaign publicity. Without their help he would not now be standing on the threshold of the White House. Their association with him was typical of that which he enjoyed with many publicists, with editors in particular, and more than he could have known at the time, he was fortunate in his ability to attract the loyalty of many individual journalists to himself and to the causes he represented. That was a tribute to his character, to his commitment to expanding the public good, and to his public demeanor. Moreover, the fact that he had brought Joseph Tumulty and Colonel House into his official circle was a promising sign for the press relations of his administration. Both men had excellent rapport with newsmen.

Nevertheless, some of Wilson's recent actions gave the reporters cause to wonder about their future relations with him. His series of curt comments to them might be interpreted as disparaging indications of what awaited them in their endeavors to obtain news from him once he became president. Indeed, he admitted that he had a "naturally combative nature."[56] Was that the side of his personality now emerging in his exchanges with the reporters, and if it were, how would it affect his future press relations? His idea about what was newsworthy, particularly in regard to matters concerning his family, seemed bound to disappoint reporters who would be anxious to have news of some of his informal activities as well as his more formal ones. Early-twentieth-century Americans had an unabated appetite for news, but the news they appreciated and paid to receive was not only political news of presidents and policies, as important as that was, but also news informed by a now long-standing human interest tradition. In a democracy people want and need to know news that has political significance and news that relates to their well being. They also welcome news of general interest, and so long as it respects the dictates of good taste, they want news of the informal activities of their presidents. More than simple curiosity or the element of entertainment associated with the news content of the modern commercialized press drives this interest.

It relates to the ability of a modern president to achieve and hold popularity. Theodore Roosevelt, who so mastered the art of publicizing himself as president, in the words of historian Robert Dallek, was "our first celebrity president whose daily comings and goings, as well as those of his wife and six children, became the stuff of ongoing popular discussion."[57] In fact, given the advantages of the means of modern communication, the personality and character of a president, as revealed by knowledge of his activities beyond his official duties, is one of the variables in successful political leadership. It can help to build a reservoir of public trust for him. Washington newsmen had come to appreciate this fact. As Richard Oulahan, the premier of the Washington correspondents in Wilson's time put it, "Every line written of him in the press makes him more familiar to the public eye and that, broadly speaking, is the keynote to success on the political stage."[58] Looking ahead from the months when he was president-elect, how well he grasped this aspect of the presidency, as it was evolving in his time, remained uncertain.

Uncertain, too, was the matter of how he would conduct his press relations as president. Would he recognize that the press needed him as much as he needed the press? Political journalism had interests of its own, and to implement them at a time when reporting from the capital was becoming more president-centered, access to evolving news was necessary. The pacesetters of journalism in Wilson's time considered their enterprise to be near the center of politics. Like the president, they were also involved in shaping and interpreting public opinion and, indeed, in influencing policymaking. They were interested in background matter and in speculating about developing news—not just in reporting and interpreting the finished product. Wilson had a tremendous faith in rational debate in politics and believed that public opinion should be informed by means of reasonable dialogue accurately reported in the press. To what degree did he perceive the press to be a part of that reasonable dialogue? No one knew. However, the fact that, as governor, he had taken some steps to meet the needs of the press, might be taken as a hopeful sign.

Still, there was the personal factor to consider, and the president-elect had a complex personality. How would he conduct himself before the Washington correspondents? Following the lead of Adolph Ochs at the *New York Times*, the press bureaus of the major newspapers in the capital were increasing their staffs. The Washington press corps had grown, and its numbers could now be counted in the hundreds. Moreover, after a room was set aside for them in the White House renovation in 1902, reporters covering the White House acquired a type of official presence there. How would these newsmen in the capital fare with President Wilson?

It was true that ill-informed correspondents and wolfpacks of reporters, who descended on him during campaign trips and at other times, annoyed him, even as he fought to conceal his annoyance. Moreover, the strains that appeared in his relations with the Trenton reporters toward the end were of consequence. Did they imply that he would distance himself from the Washington correspondents? Although that possibility could not be discounted, the fact remained that he had been able to establish viable relations with newsmen, particularly those with whom he was in regular contact. Barring some exceptions, the cordiality he extended to them and the daily news conferences he held for them as governor could be taken as encouraging signs for his future relations with correspondents at Washington.

Nevertheless, reporters stationed in Washington and those covering the White House represented a larger and more diverse group of journalists than that which Wilson engaged in Trenton. Finding an effective way in which to deal with them would be one of his first tests as president. It was, however, only symbolic of other challenges he would encounter with the press in the years before him. At the core of his activist philosophy of presidential leadership as he entered the White House was the principle of publicity. That meant that the success or failure of his presidency would depend, in many respects, on his ability to form and maintain constructive relations with the press. It was a medium through which he could reach the nation, and through which, despite all the variables involved, the nation might speak to him.

Key to Abbreviations in Notes

Personal Names

ASL: Arthur S. Link
BTW: Booker T. Washington
DL: David Lawrence
EAW: Ellen Axson Wilson
EWM: Eleanor Wilson McAdoo
EMH: Edward M. House
EWS: E. W. Scripps
FPS: Frank Parker Stockbridge
GH: George Harvey
HEA: Henry Ekert Alexander
HW: Henry Watterson
JCH: John Calvin Hemphill
JD: Josephus Daniels
JK: James Kerney
JT: Joseph Tumulty
MAHP: Mary Allen Hulbert Peck
OGV: Oswald Garrison Villard
RB: Robert Bridges
RSB: Ray Stannard Baker
SA: Stockton Axson
WGM: William Gibbs McAdoo
WHP: Walter Hines Page
WW: Woodrow Wilson

Manuscripts, Collections, Libraries, and Archives

BTW Papers: Booker T. Washington Papers, Library of Congress.
DL Papers: David Lawrence Papers, Seeley G. Mudd Manuscript Library, Princeton University.
EMH Diary: Edward M. House Diary.
EMH Papers: Edward M. House Papers, Yale University.
EWS Papers: E. W. Scripps Papers, Ohio University.
HW Collection: Collection of Henry Watterson Papers, University of Louisville Archives, Microfilm Edition, Library of Congress.

HW Papers:	Henry Watterson Papers, Library of Congress.
JCH Papers:	James Calvin Hemphill Papers, Duke University.
JD Papers:	Josephus Daniels Papers, Library of Congress.
JT Papers:	Joseph Patrick Tumulty Papers, Library of Congress.
LDB Papers:	Louis Dembitz Brandeis Papers, Library of Congress.
MDLC:	Manuscript Division, Library of Congress.
OGV Papers:	Oswald Garrison Villard Papers, Harvard University.
RSB Papers:	Ray Stannard Baker Papers, Library of Congress.
SMMLP:	Seeley G. Mudd Manuscript Library, Princeton University.
WGM Papers:	William Gibbs McAdoo Papers, Library of Congress.
WHP Papers:	Walter Hines Page Papers, Harvard University.
WW Corresp., NJSA:	Woodrow Wilson Correspondence, New Jersey State Archives.
WWCP:	Woodrow Wilson Collection Papers, Seeley G. Mudd Manuscript Library, Princeton University.
WWP:	Woodrow Wilson Papers, Library of Congress.
WWPP:	Woodrow Wilson Papers Project, Seeley G. Mudd Manuscript Library, Princeton University.

Newspapers, Journals, and Published Papers

ARR:	*American Review of Reviews.*
BS:	*Baltimore Sun.*
HW:	*Harper's Weekly.*
LD:	*Literary Digest.*
NAR:	*North American Review.*
NYS:	*New York Sun.*
NYT:	*New York Times.*
PWW:	*The Papers of Woodrow Wilson, 69 volumes published by Princeton University Press.*
TTA:	*Trenton True American.*

Notes

Preface

1. "Presidential Echoes," Feb. 25, 1912, quoted in the *Owensboro Messenger*, clipping, reel 518, WWP.
2. RSB, *Woodrow Wilson: Life and Letters*, 8 vols (1927–39; reprint, Potomac edition, New York: Charles Scribner's Sons, 1946), 3: 368–9 and EWM, *The Woodrow Wilsons* (New York: Macmillan, 1937), 168.
3. James E. Pollard, *The Presidents and the Press* (New York: Macmillan, 1947), 631–5 and John Tebbel and Sarah Miles Watts, *The Press and the Presidency: From George Washington to Ronald Reagan*, 365–6. The best account of Wilson's early press relations is in George Juergens, *News From The White House: The Presidential–Press Relationship in the Progressive Era* (Chicago: University of Chicago Press, 1981), 126–40. Also, ASL makes extensive use of the press as a source and discusses Wilson's relations with various journalists in his comprehensive biography, *Wilson: The Road to the White House* (Princeton: Princeton University Press, 1947).

Chapter 1 Early Encounters with Journalism

1. WW to Ellen Axson, Feb. 24, 1885, in EWM, ed., *The Priceless Gift: The Love Letters of Woodrow Wilson and Ellen Axson Wilson* (New York: McGraw Hill, 1962), 118.
2. SA, *"Brother Woodrow:" A Memoir of Woodrow Wilson*, ASL et al, eds. (Princeton: Princeton University Press, 1993), 10.
3. Memorandum of a conversation with Mrs. Francis B. Sayre (i.e. Wilson's daughter Jessie), Dec. 1, 1925, reel 82, RSB Papers, MDLC. See also, Charles Swem, ms., "Humor and Storytelling," box 87, folder 10, Charles Swem Collection, Wilsonia materials, SMMLP. Hereinafter cited as Swem Collection.
4. Quoted in John M. Mulder, *Woodrow Wilson: The Years of Preparation* (Princeton: Princeton University Press, 1978), 270.
5. Quoted in ASL, *The Higher Realism of Woodrow Wilson and Other Essays* (Nashville: Vanderbilt University Press, 1971), 36–7.
6. Ibid., 24.
7. Ibid., and WW, "John Bright," Mar. 6, 1880, *PWW*, 1: 618.
8. WW to the editor of the *International Review*, Ca., Apr. 30, 1881, ibid., 2: 48.

9. Francis P. Weisenburger, "The Middle Western Antecedents of Woodrow Wilson," *Mississippi Valley Historical Review* 23 (Dec. 1936): 375–81.
10. William Allen White, *Woodrow Wilson: The Man, His Times, and His Task* (Boston: Houghton Mifflin, 1924), 7.
11. Weisenburger, "The Middle Western Antecedents of Woodrow Wilson," 385–7 and L. F. Andrews, "General Wm. Duane Wilson," clipping from the *Des Moines Register and Leader*, n.d., enclosed in Mrs. J. M. [Sayre?] to WW, July 4, 1909, reel 18, WWP.
12. White, *Wilson*, 12.
13. Interview, "A Conversation with the President of the United States," by Ida Tarbell [1916], folder "Collier's Article and Kansas City Star," Ida M. Tarbell Collection, Pelletier Library, Allegheny College, Meadville, Pa. See also, George C. Osborn, "The Influences of Joseph Ruggles Wilson on His Son Woodrow Wilson," *North Carolina Historical Review* 32 (1955): 519–43.
14. Quoted in Henry Wilkinson Bragdon, *Woodrow Wilson: The Academic Years* (Cambridge: The Belknap Press of Harvard University Press, 1967), 413, n. 2.
15. *PWW*, 1: 4 and 7, n. 8.
16. See, e.g., WW to RB Jan. 12, 1900, ibid., 11: 369; Aug. 22, 1880, ibid., 1: 673; and Jan. 23, 1887, ibid., 5: 433.
17. Burton J. Hendrick, *The Life and Letters of Walter H. Page* (Garden City, N. Y.: Doubleday, Page & Company, 1924–25), 1: 104–5.
18. Among the future scholars trained in the seminar were historians H. C. Adams, Jameson J. Franklin, Charles H. Haskins, Frederick Jackson Turner, and Charles M. Andrews.
19. WW to EAW, Oct. 26, 1884, *PWW*, 3: 376.
20. See, e.g., WW to Shaw, June 26, 1891, ibid., 7: 225. Another of Wilson's fellow graduate students at Johns Hopkins was Charles H. Shinn, who was managing editor of the *Overland Monthly* from 1884 to 1889, a West Coast literary magazine that his sister Milicent edited from 1883 to 1895. This connection, no doubt, led to Wilson publishing his essay, "Committee or Cabinet Government?" in the *Overland* in 1884.
21. GH to WW, Jan. 7, 1902 and WW to GH, Jan. 12, 1912, *PWW*, 12: 230 and 232–3.
22. Bragdon, *Woodrow Wilson*, 10.
23. Wilson's Shorthand Diary: "My Journal," Nov. 22, 1876, *PWW*, 1: 230.
24. WW to Charles Andrew Talcott, Oct. 11, 1880, ibid., 1: 683.
25. WW to RB, May 24, 1881, ibid., 2: 68.
26. EAW to WW, Feb. 11, 1900, ibid., 11: 402. See also WW to EAW, Feb. 20, 1885, ibid., 4: 271 and EAW to WW, July 31, 1894, in EWM, *Priceless Gift*, 191.
27. The articles "Work-Day Religion," "Christ's Army," "The Bible," "A Christian Statesman," "One Duty of a Son to his Parents," "The Positive in Religion," and "Christian Progress," appeared in the *North Carolina Presbyterian* between Aug. and Dec. 1876. See *PWW*, 1: 176–8, 180–1, 184–5, 188–9, 205–7, 211–12, and 234–5.

28. Quoted in Bragdon, *Woodrow Wilson*, 35 and 418, n. 40.
29. Ibid., 35.
30. Ibid., 36–41.
31. "Editor Wilson Runs 1879 'Princetonian,'" *Princetonian*, Feb. 27, 1927, 1–2 and 11.
32. WW to RB, Aug. 25, 1882, *PWW*, 2: 137.
33. WW to RB, Jan. 1, 1881, ibid., 10.
34. August Heckscher, *Woodrow Wilson* (New York: Charles Scribner's Sons, 1991), 44.
35. The biographical essays appeared in the *Virginia University Magazine*, Mar. and Apr., 1880, *PWW*, 1: 608–21 and 1: 624–42.
36. Ibid., 1: 666–70, 671, n. 1.
37. *WW* to RB, May 24, 1881, ibid., 2: 68.
38. Ibid., 2: 97–116.
39. Quoted in Mulder, *Woodrow Wilson*, 70.
40. "New Southern Industries," *PWW*, 2: 119–25 and "Convict Labor in Georgia," ibid., 310.
41. WW to RB Oct. 28, 1882, ibid., 148.
42. WW to RB, May 13, 1883, ibid., 358.
43. For the "age of journalism" see WW to Ellen Axson, July 28, 1884, ibid., 3: 263.
44. WW to Ellen Axson, Mar. 21, 1885, ibid., 4: 394.
45. WW to Ellen Axson, Oct. 30, 1883, in EWM, *Priceless Gift*, 34.
46. Bragdon, *Woodrow Wilson*, 107.
47. RB to WW, Feb. 15, 1884, *PWW*, 3: 24 and WW to RB, Feb. 20, 1884, ibid., 37.
48. WW to RB, May 31, 1884, ibid., 199.
49. Ford to WW, March 13, 1885, ibid., 4: 360.
50. "Congressional Government in Practice," *Bradstreet's* Feb. 28, 1885, ibid., 3: 288–93 and William F. Ford to WW, Mar. 13, 1885, ibid., 4: 360. Wilson also wrote a news article on Bryn Mawr College for the *New York Commercial Advertiser*, Apr. 29, 1885, ibid., 505–8.
51. Heckscher, *Woodrow Wilson*, 25, 32, 36, 42, and 50–2.
52. WW to Ellen Axson, Oct. 30, 1883, in EWM, *The Woodrow Wilsons*, 33.
53. Bragdon, *Woodrow Wilson*, 109.
54. *Indianapolis News*, Apr. 26, 1902, *PWW*, 12: 353.
55. Quoted in Bragdon, *Woodrow Wilson*, 198.
56. The articles he published in these monthly magazines were: "The Author Himself," *Atlantic Monthly*, Sept. 1891, 406–13; "Mere Literature," ibid., Dec. 1893, 820–8; "A Literary Politician," ibid., Nov. 1895, 668–80; "Mr. Cleveland As President," ibid., Mar. 1897, 289–300; "The Making of the Nation," ibid., July 1894, 1–14; "On Being Human," ibid., Sept. 1897, 320–29; "A Lawyer with a Style," ibid., Sept. 1898, 363–74; "A Wit and a Seer," ibid., Oct. 1898, 527–40; "The Reconstruction of the South," ibid., Jan. 1901, 1–15; "Democracy and Efficiency," ibid., Mar. 1901, 289–99; "On the Writing of History," *Century Magazine*, Sept. 1895, 789–93; "On An Author's Choice of Company," ibid., Mar. 1896, 775–9; "When a Man

Comes to Himself," ibid., June 1901, 268–73; "Mr. Goldwin Smith's 'Views' on Our Political History," *Forum*, Dec. 1893, 489–99; "A Calendar of Great Americans," ibid., Feb. 1894, 715–27; "The Proper Perspective of American History," ibid., July 1895, 554–99, and "Princeton in the Nation's Service," ibid., Dec. 1896, 447–61. Some of these articles also appeared in his books of collected essays, and occasionally he published in other journals.

57. "The Forum for Twenty-Five Years," *Forum*, Mar. 1911, 258.
58. Hendrick, *Life and Letters of Walter Hines Page*, 3: 2–11.
59. WW to WHP, Dec. 5, 1894, *PWW*, 9: 100–1.
60. "A Wit and a Seer," *Atlantic Monthly*, Oct. 1898, 540.
61. "Mere Literature," ibid., Dec. 1893, 820, 824–25, and 828. Among Wilson's other articles on style are "On Being Human," ibid., Sept. 1897, 320–9 and "On an Author's Choice of Company," *Century Magazine*, Mar. 1896, 775–9.
62. "On the Writing of History," ibid., Sept. 1895, 793.
63. "The Proper Perspective of American History," *Forum*, July 1895, 558–9
64. "A Calendar of Great Americans," ibid., Feb. 1894, 725.
65. "Democracy and Efficiency," *Atlantic Monthly*, Mar. 1901, 291, 296, and 298–9.
66. "The Making of the Nation," ibid., 14.
67. Norman St. John-Stevas, "Walter Bagehot: A Short Biography," in *The Collected Works of Walter Bagehot* (London: The Economist, 1965–68), 1: 77.
68. Rockwell D. Hunt to Bragdon, Aug. 6, 1957, Henry Wilkenson Bragdon Collection, MS254, JHU Copy, Special Collections, Milton S. Eisenhower Library, Johns Hopkins University.
69. "A Literary Politician," *Atlantic Monthly*, November 1895, 668–70, 674–5, 677, and 679.
70. Ibid., 679–80.
71. WW to Albert Shaw, June 26, 1891, *PWW*, 7: 225.
72. WW to RB, Jan. 14, 1881, ibid., 2: 11.
73. WW to RB, May 24, 1881, ibid., 69 and "A Literary Politician," 674.
74. *Congressional Government: A Study in Politics* (1885; reprint, New York: Meridian Books, 1956), 207–8.
75. Ibid., 209.
76. Editorial note, "Wilson's First Treatise on Democratic Government," *PWW*, 5: 58.
77. "The Modern Democratic State," ibid., 72–4 and 82.
78. Ibid., 73.
79. "On an Author's Choice of Company," *Century Magazine*, March 1896, 779.
80. Joseph R. Wilson, Jr. to Joseph Ruggles Wilson, Feb. 20, 1896, *PWW*, 9: 442.

Chapter 2 The President of Princeton and the Press, 1902–10

1. Bragdon, *Woodrow Wilson*, 269–75.
2. Early in 1902 a group of trustees asked Wilson, in consultation with several other designated people, to draw up plans for an executive committee that they planned to have direct the university. Bragdon, ibid., 276.

3. Wilson's public addresses and often the press reports of them can be found in *PWW*, vols 6–12. The reports were uniformly positive.
4. "Princeton for the Nation's Service," Oct. 25, 1902, ibid., 14: 177–8, 185.
5. EAW to Florence Stevens Hoyt, June 28, 1902, ibid., 12: 464.
6. *NYT*, June 11, 1902, 8.
7. WW to Edward Perkins Clark, June 16, 1902, *PWW*, 12: 427.
8. Clippings, reel 511, WWP and Bragdon: *Woodrow Wilson*, 460, n. 22. Articles about his election also appeared in various periodicals. The best one was Robert Bridges's "President Woodrow Wilson," *ARR*, July 1902, 36–9.
9. *Charlotte Daily Observer*, June 12, 1902 and *Atlanta Constitution*, June 11, 1902, 6.
10. *PWW*, 12: 440, n. 2.
11. WW to Edward Ingle, June 19, 1902, ibid., 12: 440.
12. RB to WW, July 17, 1902, ibid., 14: 21–2 and 22, n. 2.
13. "Princeton in the Nation's Service," in Richard Hofstadter and Wilson Smith, *American Higher Education: A Documentary History* (Chicago: University of Chicago Press, 1961), 2: 692.
14. WW to RB, July 17, 1902, *PWW*, 14: 21–2.
15. *NYS*, June 12, 1902, 1; June 13, 1902, 6, and June 14, 1912, 1. The *Sun*'s original report on the resignation-election (June 10, 1902, 1) was mainly a matter-of-fact one like that found in other New York newspapers.
16. No trace of friction or irregularity appeared in the faculty's official statement about Patton's resignation and Wilson's election. See "The Faculty of Princeton University. In Reference to the Resignation of Dr. Patton and the Election of President Wilson," June 3, 1902, reel 14, WWP, and *Princeton Alumni Weekly*, June 14, 1902, 625–8.
17. Ibid.
18. Theodore Roosevelt to WW, June 23, 1902, reel 14, WWP.
19. Theodore Roosevelt to C. H. Dodge, June 16, 1902, quoted in M. Taylor Pyne to WW, June 19, 1902, *PWW*, 12: 441.
20. Quoted in SA, "*Brother Woodrow*," 120.
21. "Princeton for the Nation's Service," *PWW*, 14: 170–85.
22. Theodore Roosevelt to WW, Dec. 6, 1902, reel 14, WWP.
23. Clippings for Oct. 25–26, reel 514, WWP.
24. "The Personal Factor in Education," *Youth's Companion*, Sept. 12, 1907, 423–4; "My Ideal of the True University," *Delineator*, Nov. 1909, 401; and "What is a College For?" *Scribner's Magazine*, Nov. 1909, 570–7.
25. For example, see *New York Herald*, June 11, 1905, *PWW*, 16: 113–19; *NYS*, Oct. 18, 1907, ibid., 17: 444–5; and *Philadelphia Press*, Oct. 17, 1908, ibid., 18: 465–6.
26. Edwin E. Slossom, "Princeton University," *Independent*, Mar. 4, 1909, 458.
27. Quoted in ASL, *Wilson*, 44.
28. Press Release, "The Princeton Course of Study Revised," June 14, 1904, reel 14, WWP.
29. "The Princeton Preceptorial System," *Independent*, Aug. 3, 1905, 239.
30. *Princeton Alumni Weekly*, June 12, 1907, 606.

31. Quoted in SA, "*Brother Woodrow*," 124.
32. *NYT*, Oct. 23, 1904, 6.
33. "The Preceptor Idea at Princeton," *Outlook*, June 24, 1905, 465. See also numerous press clippings, reels 154 and 511, WWP.
34. RB, "President Woodrow Wilson and College Earnestness," *World's Work*, Jan. 1908, 9792.
35. Louis Brownlow, "Wilson's Personal Relations," In *Lectures and Seminars at the University of Chicago in Celebration of the Centennial of Woodrow Wilson 1856–1956* (Chicago: University of Chicago & the Woodrow Wilson Foundation, 1956), 88. Copy, reel 537, WWP.
36. Quoted in Bragdon, *Woodrow Wilson*, 318.
37. When James McCosh, a revered former president of Princeton, abolished fraternities at the university some 40-odd years before, the reasons he gave were similar to Wilson's: "The fraternities were a divisive and anti-intellectual influence." Ibid., 321.
38. *New York Evening Post*, June 25, 1907, clippings, reel 511, WWP and *LD*, June 13, 1907, 60.
39. Clippings, June 25–27, 1907, reel 16, WWP.
40. *ARR*, Aug. 1907, clipping, ibid. Upon reading the *ARR* article, Hamilton Holt wrote to Wilson that he was "doing a great thing" and invited him to write an article on the subject for his *Independent*. Holt to WW, Aug. 1, 1907, *PWW*, 17: 333.
41. Johns to WW, with enclosure, July 3, 1907, reel 16, WWP.
42. Quoted in ASL, *Woodrow Wilson*, 47.
43. Bragdon, *Woodrow Wilson*, 323.
44. Ibid., 322.
45. See letters in the *Princeton Alumni Weekly*, Sept. 25, Oct. 2, Oct. 9, and Oct. 16, 1907.
46. Bragdon, *Woodrow Wilson*, 322–6.
47. Quoted in SA, "*Brother Woodrow*," 130.
48. Bragdon, *Woodrow Wilson*, 367.
49. ASL, *Wilson*, 72–3.
50. Clipping, *Boston Evening Transcript*, Feb. 12, 1910, reel 154, WWP. For a complete account of this complicated episode see Bragdon, *Woodrow Wilson* chapter 13 and ASL, *Road to the White House*, chapter 3.
51. Melancthon Williams Jacobs to Edward Wright Sheldon, Jan. 27, 1910, *PWW*, 20: 61–3.
52. Edward Wright Sheldon to Melancthon Williams Jacobs, Jan. 31, 1910, ibid., 68–9 and Bragdon, *Woodrow Wilson*, 370.
53. Brougham to WW, Jan. 31, 1910, reel 18, WWP. The editor later claimed that the *Times* already had its article issue "in print" and wished only to have Wilson's confirmation of the matters about which the *Times* had learned. Brougham to RSB, Aug. 21, 1924, quoted in RSB, *Wilson: Life and Letters*, 2: 328, n. 3. However, Brougham's 31 Jan. 1910 letter fails to confirm his later explanation. In the former he explicitly asked for "editorial guidance."
54. WW to Brougham, Feb. 1, 1910, reel 18, WWP.

55. Wilson's opponents, for instance, leaked information (some of it false) to the press, sprang a modification of the Procter offer on him unexpectedly at a crucial trustees' meeting, made deliberate efforts to humiliate him at trustees' meetings, organized a letter writing campaign against him, and in the case of Dean West, personally persuaded Isaac C. Wyman to leave his multi-million dollar fortune for a graduate school at Princeton with West himself as one of the two trustees of the bequest (Bragdon, *Woodrow Wilson*, 368–70 and 379–80).
56. *NYT*, Feb. 3, 1910, 8. Although Wilson's opponents thought he was behind this article, they could not prove it. It was ASL who many years later, discovered Wilson's role in its publication. See ASL, *Road to the White House*, 76.
57. *Princeton Alumni Weekly*, Feb. 16, 1910, 292 and 295.
58. *NYT*, Feb. 5, 1910, 8 and Feb. 6, 1910, 3.
59. Brougham to WW, Feb. 4, 1910, reel 19, WWP.
60. Clippings from dozens of newspapers applauding him for his perceived stand and victory can be found, reel 154, WWP.
61. A Friend of Princeton, "The Differences at Princeton," *Independent*, Mar. 17, 1910, 575.
62. According to the best source on the subject, there were ten pamphlets published of which seven were against Wilson. Bragdon, *Woodrow Wilson*, 482–3, n. 35.
63. The Board of Trustees consisted of 23 life members, five alumni members, the Governor of New Jersey, and the President of the University.
64. DL, *The True Story of Woodrow Wilson* (New York: George H. Doran Co., 1924), 30.
65. "Princeton Report Leaves Dispute Open," *NYT*, Feb. 9, 1910, 2.
66. *PWW*, Mar. 11–26, 1910, 20: 229–35, 272–6, 290–6.
67. Ibid., 296.
68. C. H. McCormick to E. M. Sheldon, Apr. 5, 1990, in ASL, *Wilson*, 79, n. 50.
69. For example, see Robert Fulton McMahon's letter to the editor, *NYS*, Mar. 22, 1910. He published a longer version of this letter in the *New York Evening Post*, Apr. 9, 1910, in which he revised and expanded in pamphlet form, *The Graduate College and the Quads* (n.d.) *PWW*, 20: 383, n. 6. Bragdon reported that a "groundswell of support began to appear in the letters and resolutions sent to the *Princeton Alumni Weekly*" at this time. *Woodrow Wilson*, 376.
70. Quoted in ibid., 375.
71. DL, *True Story*, 29.
72. Ibid., and *NYT*, Apr. 8, 1910, 1.
73. Quoted in Bragdon, *Woodrow Wilson*, 376.
74. SA, "*Brother Woodrow*," 157–8. Axson even reported one of his friends telling him that he had never seen Wilson so dejected as he was at Pittsburgh.
75. Wilson's recognition of a democratic purpose in his views on education can be detected well before the Pittsburgh speech. For example, see his speech at St. Paul's School, Concord, N. H., June 3, 1909, *PWW*, 19: 226.

76. "A News Report of the Pittsburgh Speech," *Princeton Alumni Weekly*, Apr. 20, 1910, ibid., 20: 373–6. News reports of the speech, which Wilson delivered extemporaneously, varied somewhat. He approved of this version.
77. Ibid., 20: 366 and *New York Tribune*, Apr. 18, 1910, 1.
78. Bragdon explained that a number of editorials suggested that Wilson made this a part of his effort to promote his candidacy for Governor of New Jersey (*Woodrow Wilson*, 378). Examples of newspapers that were kinder to Wilson were the *New York Evening Post*, Apr. 18, 1910, 8 and the *Philadelphia Press*, Apr. 20, 1910, 6.
79. James T. Williams Jr. (of the *Tucson Citizen*) to WW, Apr. 19, 1910, reel 19, WWP and David Graham Phillips to WW, Apr. 19, 1910, *PWW*, 20: 372.
80. Bragdon, *Woodrow Wilson*, 378.
81. Quoted in ibid.
82. Ibid., 379. The label "The Battle of Princeton" belongs to ASL. See chapter 3 in *Wilson*.
83. WW to Frank Thilly, Mar. 21, 1904, *PWW*, 15: 202.
84. WW to the editor, *NYT*, Nov. 24, 1907, ibid., 17: 521.
85. WW to the editor, *Daily Princetonian*, Oct. 17, 1908, *PWW*, 18: 466.
86. WW, address, "The Spirit of Learning," July 1, 1909, *PWW*, 19: 277–89 and *Springfield Republican*, July 3, 1910, quoted in ibid., 294, n. 1.
87. WW to the editor, *Springfield Republican*, July 8, 1909, quoted in ibid., 19: 293–4.
88. *Princeton Alumni Weekly*, June 9, 1909, ibid., 19: 238.
89. WW to the editor, *New York Evening Post*, Apr. 21, 1910, quoted in ibid., 20: 378–9 and the editorial response in ibid., 379, n. 2.
90. H. M. Eaton to WW, Apr. 23 and 27, 1910, reel 19, WWP. Wilson had only a slight basis for his claim of misinterpretation in this case, and a comparison of the *Press*'s report and the version of the speech approved by Wilson fails to support his claim that the dispatch was "entirely without foundation and fact." (*Philadelphia Press*, Apr. 18, 1910, 2 and "President Wilson's Address," *Princeton Alumni Weekly*, Apr. 20, 1910, 470–1.) The latter was the version of the speech that Wilson authorized, ibid., Apr. 27, 1910, 480.
91. Ellery Sedgwick, *The Happy Profession* (Boston: Little, Brown and Co., 1946), 179–80.

Chapter 3 Advent of a Public Statesman, 1906–10

1. Campaign address, Oct. 17, 1912, *PWW*, 25: 429.
2. RSB, *Wilson: Life and Letters*, 1: 104 and WW to EAW, Feb. 24, 1885, quoted in ASL, *Wilson*, 19.
3. Quoted in Kendrick A. Clements, *Woodrow Wilson: World Statesman* (Boston: Twayne Publishers, 1987), 23.
4. Quoted in ASL, *Wilson*, 34–5.
5. Richard Hofstadter, ed., "Introduction," *The Progressive Movement, 1900–1915* (Englewood Cliffs, N. J.: Prentice Hall, 1963), 5.

6. Ibid., 7.
7. JK, *Political Education of Woodrow Wilson* (New York: Century Co., 1926), 14.
8. Because some of Wilson's speeches are identified only by the name of the function at which he delivered them and for which there is no extant copy of the text, it is impossible to determine the exact number of noneducational speeches he made. But aside from after-dinner remarks, the record shows he gave at least 108 noneducational speeches between 1902 and 1910, and 94 of these can be identified as major speeches.
9. Mulder, *Woodrow Wilson*, title, chapter 9.
10. A list of Wilson's speeches for 1902–10 can be found in *PWW* 26: 296–305.
11. Quoted in RSB, *Wilson: Life and Letters*, 2: 196.
12. Ibid.
13. An old-Fashioned Democrat to the editor, *Indianapolis News*, May 1, 1902, *PWW* 12: 357. RSB identified the writer as Louis Howland, who was then on the staff of the *News* and later became its editor and believed that Charles R. Williams, a Princeton alumnus who was then editor of the paper, revised it for publication. RSB, *Life and Letters*, 3: 8, n. 1.
14. Clipping, *Boston Herald*, Mar. 14, 1906, reel 511, WWP.
15. The main source for publicizing Wilson as a possible candidate was *HW*, Mar. 10, 1906, Mar. 30, 31, 1906, 454, Apr. 21, 1906, 564, May 19, 1906, 716, and June 21, 1906, 782.
16. WW to Frank Arthur Vanderlip, n.d. 1908, reel 17, WWP.
17. Clipping, *Washington Star*, Dec. 11, 1908, reel 154, ibid.
18. Harvey was associated with the *Springfield (Mass.) Republican*, the *Hartford Journal*, and the *Chicago Daily News* before settling in New Jersey. Willis Fletcher Johnson, *George Harvey "Passionate Patriot"* (Boston: Houghton Mifflin, 1929), 12–30.
19. Ibid., 272 and 284, JD, *The Wilson Era: Years of Peace* (Chapel Hill: University of North Carolina Press, 1944), 19.
20. Johnson, *George Harvey*, 94.
21. Quoted in Bragdon, *Woodrow Wilson*, 338.
22. For instance, Wilson refused to vote for William Jennings Bryan in 1896 (he voted the Gold Democratic ticket), and in ensuing years made no secret of his distrust of Bryan's "radicalism." In 1897 and again in 1907 he published laudatory articles on Grover Cleveland, interpreting him in ways most pleasing to conservative Democrats ("Mr. Cleveland As President," *Atlantic Monthly*, Mar. 1897, 289–300, and "Grover Cleveland, Man of Integrity," *New York Times*, magazine section, Mar. 17, 1907, *PWW*, 17: 73–8). His "Democracy and Efficiency," *Atlantic Monthly*, Mar. 1901, 289–99 was no less pleasing to men of that persuasion.
23. Editorial note, *PWW*, 8: 316.
24. "Edmund Burke: The Man and His Time," Aug. 31, 1893, ibid., 342.
25. Ibid., and "After-Dinner Speech," June 30, 1904, ibid., 15: 147–8.
26. For a general discussion of Wilson's political views see editorial note, ibid., 8: 313–18 and Niels AAge Thorsen, *The Political Thought of Woodrow Wilson* (Princeton: Princeton University Press, 1988), 37–8, 143–44, and 157–60.

27. *Harper's Weekly*, Mar. 10, 1906, 30. For yet other press responses to Harvey's speech see clippings, reel 511, WWP.
28. See p. 44.
29. A Jeffersonian Democrat [Mayo Hazeltine], *NAR*, 182 (Apr. 1906): 490–1.
30. *LD*, Apr. 14, 1906, 557–8.
31. Address on Thomas Jefferson, Apr. 16, 1906, *PWW*, 16: 365, 367–8.
32. Medical authorities who have studied this incident concur that Wilson suffered a retinal hemorrhage at this time. Some see it as the result of hypertension; others believe that it was caused by a cerebral vascular disease and that Wilson suffered a stroke. SA, "*Brother Woodrow*," 256, n. 24 and Heckscher, *Woodrow Wilson*, 151.
33. WW to GH and GH to WW, Dec. 16 and 17, 1906, *PWW*, 16: 531–33.
34. William Inglis, "Helping to Make a President," *Collier's*, Oct. 7, 1916, 14.
35. Clipping, *NYS*, March 1907, reel 511, WWP.
36. ASL, *Wilson*, 111.
37. "Credo," *PWW*, 17: 336.
38. Bragdon, *Woodrow Wilson*, 342–3 and 476, n. 12.
39. ASL, *Wilson*, 112.
40. Joseph Pulitzer to Frank Cobb, late Nov. 1907 in Don C. Seitz, *Joseph Pulitzer: His Life and Letters* (Garden City, N. Y.: Garden City Publishing Co., 1924), 327–8.
41. Johnson, *George Harvey*, 132–4 and *HW*, Jan. 25, 1908, 7.
42. Mayo W. Hazeltine, "Woodrow Wilson," *NAR*, 187 (June 1908): 846, 848–50. For Hazeltine's previous article, see pp. 48.
43. Quoted in RSB, *Wilson: Life and Letters*, 2: 277.
44. *Chicago Tribune*, Mar. 17, 1908, clipping, reel 16, WWP.
45. SA, "*Brother Woodrow*," 128.
46. *Constitutional Government*, chapter 3 and *Congressional Government*, chapter 5.
47. *Constitutional Government*, 44–7 and 70.
48. Wilson's Papers indicate that he began using a clipping service at least as early as 1902.
49. *NYT*, magazine section Nov. 24, 1907, 1 and WW to the editor of *NYT*, Nov. 24, 1907, *PWW*, 17: 521–3. The *NYT* published Wilson's letter on Nov. 27, 1907.
50. "The Banker and the Nation," Sept. 30, 1908, *PWW*, 18: 425–6 and 429.
51. *Rocky Mountain News*, Oct. 1, 1908, 1–2, and *Denver Daily News*, Oct. 1, 1908, 1–2.
52. Theodore Roosevelt to William Dudley Foulke, Dec. 1, 1908 and William Dudley, box 4, Foulke Papers, MDLC.
53. James Bryce to Edward Grey, vol. 27, Sept. 16, 1907, fol. 130, James Bryce Papers, Bodleian Library, Oxford.
54. Roosevelt made his well-publicized "muckrakers" statement on two occasions in 1906. The first, on March 17, at a Gridiron dinner; the second, in a similar speech a month later at the dedication of a new House Office Building. It is also worth noting that Wilson made no secret of his own irritation with many reformers. While believing and stating that all men

should be reformers, he told one Tennessee audience "your professional reformer is an unmitigated nuisance." Address to the Princeton Alumni of Tennessee, Nov. 9, 1907, *PWW*, 17: 484.

55. News report of a Press Club Banquet, Apr. 26, 1906, ibid., 16: 375.
56. Abstract of an address in New York to the Associated Press and American Newspaper Publishers, Apr. 28, 1910, ibid., 20: 400–1.
57. Will Irwin, "The American Newspaper: A Study of Journalism in its Relation to the Public," *Collier's*, Jan. 21, 1911–July 29, 1911.
58. Will Irwin, "The Voice of a Generation," *Collier's*, July 29, 1911, 23.
59. The above reference to Wilson's introducing a form of national journalism in World War I refers to his creation of the Committee on Public Information and, in particular, to its publication of the *Official Bulletin*.
60. Remarks in New York to the Friendly Sons of St. Patrick, Mar. 17, 1909, *PWW*, 19: 105–6, and an interview with Wilson, *New York Herald*, Mar. 19, 1909, ibid., 110–11.
61. WW to RB, Apr. 5, 1909, ibid., 19: 149.
62. Clippings, reels 511 and 514, WWP.
63. H. E. Baldwin to WW, June 3, 1910, reel 19, WWP.
64. Brougham to WW, Apr. 29, 1910, ibid.
65. "The Meaning of a Liberal Education," Jan. 9, 1909, *PWW*, 18: 593–4.
66. "Law or Personal Power," Apr. 13, 1908, quoted in Bragdon, *Woodrow Wilson*, 349.
67. "The Democratic Opportunity," printed in the *National Monthly* (Buffalo, N. Y.), Jan. 1910, *PWW*, 19: 471.
68. See address to a Democratic Dollar Dinner, Mar. 29, 1910, ibid., 20: 298–301.
69. HEA to WW, Mar. 28, 1910, reel 19, WWP.
70. R. S. Pieringer, "Principles, Not Men: The Institutional and Professional History of the *True American*, Published at Trenton, 1801–1913." (Senior Thesis, Princeton University, 1970), 132, in Trentoniana Collection, Trenton Public Library, Trenton, N. J.
71. Ibid., 134–5.
72. HEA to WW, Nov. 18, 1909, *PWW*, 19: 522, and Mar. 28, 1910, reel 19, WWP.
73. *HW*, May 15, 1909, 4.
74. ASL, *Wilson*, 141–2.
75. Quoted in ibid., 143.
76. See, e.g., Robert Bremner to WW, July 5, 1910, Joseph A. Dear to WW, July 8, 1910, and Chas. Willis Thompson to WW, July 9, 1910, reel 19, WWP.
77. ASL, *Wilson*, 142 and 148.
78. WW to WHP, July 16, 1910, *PWW*, 21: 6.
79. WW to GH, July 7, 1910, reel 532, WWP.
80. Clipping, *New York American*, July 8, 1910, 514, ibid.
81. Clipping, *TTA*, July 9, 1910, and HEA to WW, July 12, 1910, reel 18, ibid.
82. Quoted in ASL, *Wilson*, 152.
83. HEA to WW, July 17 and 18, 1910, reel 19, WWP.

84. Quoted in Bragdon, *Woodrow Wilson*, 393.
85. Ibid., 392.
86. OGV to WW, Aug. 22, 1910, *PWW*, 21: 59.
87. Quoted in Mulder, *Woodrow Wilson*, 267.
88. WW to GH, Aug. 3, 1910, reel 532, WWP.
89. GH to WW, Aug. 12, 1910, *PWW*, 21: 52–3, WW to Herbert Bowen, Aug. 12, 1910, reel 532, WWP, and HEA to WW, Aug. 23, 1910, *PWW*, 21: 62, 53, n. 2, and 54, n. 1.
90. News report of WW baccalaureate address in *NYT*, June 14, 1909, 5.
91. Quoted in ASL, *Wilson*, 127.
92. "Taken from the Proceedings of the N. J. State Federation of Labor," Aug. 16, 1910, box 5, folder 78, WW Corresp., NJSA, Trenton, N. J.
93. WW to Edgar Williamson, Aug. 23, 1910, *PWW*, 21: 59–61.
94. "A Proposed Democratic Platform," Aug. 9, 1910, ibid., 21: 45.
95. WW to GH, Sept. 10, 1910, reel 532, WWP.
96. JT, *Woodrow Wilson: As I Know Him* (Garden City, N. Y.: Doubleday, Page, & Company, 1924), 19–22 and Wilson's "Speech Accepting the Democratic Gubernatorial Nomination," Sept. 15, 1910, *PWW*, 21: 94.
97. WW to GH, Sept. 21, 1910, reel 532, WWP.

Chapter 4 Wilson's Gubernatorial Campaign and the Press

1. Irving S. Kull, *New Jersey: A History* (New York: The American Historical Society, 1930), 3: 1044.
2. N. W. Ayer & Son's, *American Newspaper Annual and Directory* (Philadelphia: N. W. Ayer & Son, 1910), 549–63.
3. The New Jersey circulation of the *Philadelphia Record* was discussed in JK to JT, Jan. 7, 1914, box 44, JT Papers.
4. Joseph A. Dear to WW, Sept. 16, 1910, box 69, WWPP.
5. The *Evening News* statement is quoted in ASL, *Wilson*, 170; the *TTA* is from a clipping, Sept. 16, 1910, reel 514, WWP.
6. Clarence Hughson Baxter to WW, Sept. 22, 1910, *PWW*, 21: 158.
7. Robert Gunn Bremner to WW, Sept. 17, 1910, ibid., 133 and clipping, *Passaic Daily Herald*, Sept. 16, 1910, reel 514, WWP.
8. Dekler to WW, Sept. 19, 1910, reel 20, ibid.
9. *NYT*, Sept. 15, 17 and 18, 1910, 8, and especially Sept. 16, 1910, 3, and *New York Evening Post*, Sept. 16, 1912, clipping, reel 514, WWP.
10. OGV to WW, Aug. 22, 1910, *PWW*, 21: 58–9.
11. Pulitzer to Frank Cobb, Aug. 6, 1910, quoted in W. A. Swanberg, *Pulitzer* (New York, Charles Scribner's Sons, 1967), 385–6.
12. *New York World*, Sept. 18, 1910, clipping, reel 514, WWP.
13. Quoted in ASL, *Wilson*, 170.
14. Clippings, reel 514, WWP.
15. *HW*, Sept. 24, 1910, 4.
16. "The Progress of the World," *ARR*, 42 (October 1910): 393 and Shaw to WW, Oct. 11, 1910, reel 21, WWP.

17. "The Nomination of Dr. Woodrow Wilson," *Outlook*, Sept. 24, 1910, 141.
18. Bok to WW, Sept. 16, 1910, box 69, WWPP.
19. Quoted in ASL, *Wilson*, 171.
20. Johns to WW, Sept. 19, 1910, reel 20 WWP.
21. *NYT*, Sept. 22, 1910, 8.
22. WW to David B. Jones, Sept. 25, 1910, quoted in RSB, *Wilson: Life and Letters*, 3: 84–5.
23. *Trenton Daily State Gazette*, Sept. 17, 1910, reel 514, WWP.
24. JK, *Political Education of Woodrow Wilson*, 63.
25. Interview, "Dr. Wilson Declares He Never Had Wall Street Connections," *Trenton Evening News*, Sept. 16, 1910, *PWW*, 21: 100.
26. The material Nugent distributed was headlined "DEMOCRATIC MATTER," and his speech to the editors appeared in a boilerplate dated Sept. 15, 1910, reel 514, WWP.
27. Regarding the financing of the campaign, James Smith later said that he had contributed $50,000 to the campaign and had collected $3,500 more from Wilson's friends at Princeton. George Harvey collected another $10,000 from a number of wealthy entrepreneurs. Altogether Wilson's managers collected about $119,000 for his campaign. ASL, *Wilson*, 187–8.
28. GH to WW, Oct. 4, 1910, *PWW*, 21: 243.
29. WW to GH, Oct. 5, 1910, ibid., 245.
30. For example, see GH to WW, Oct. 10, 1910, Oct. 14, 1910, and Oct. 25, 1910, in ibid., 292, 327, and 433.
31. During the campaign, editors and publishers often began their letters to him by thanking him for his "kind letter," etc. See, for instance, F. L. Chrisman, the proprietor of the *Montclair Herald* to WW, Oct. 4, 1910, reel 21, WWP.
32. HEA to WW, Sept. 29, 1910, reel 21, WWP. Edgar Williamson, the publisher of the *Labor Standard* (Orange, N. J.) also wrote to him about the opposition's "dirty tactics." Edgar Williamson to WW, Oct. 24, 1910, ibid.
33. Enclosed in HEA to WW, Sept. 19, 1910, box 69, WWPP and interview, "Lie Nailed by Woodrow Wilson, Uses Plain Language in Stating Labor Views," *TTA*, Sept. 29, 1910, *PWW*, 21: 179–81.
34. HEA to WW, Oct. 1, 1910, and Oct. 2, 1910, ibid., 219 and 225–6.
35. David W. Hirst, *Woodrow Wilson, Reform Governor: A Documentary Narrative* (Princeton: D. Van Nostrand Company, 1965), 84–5.
36. SA, "*Brother Woodrow*," 163.
37. A record of Wilson's speeches and commentary about them can be found in Charles Reade Bacon, *A People Awakened: The Story of Woodrow Wilson's First Campaign* (Garden City, N. Y.: Doubleday, Page & Company, 1912). It contains the daily dispatches that reporter Bacon sent while touring with Wilson for the *Philadelphia Record*. Other news reports of Wilson's campaign appearances can be found in *PWW*, 21.
38. *Jersey City Jersey Journal*, Oct. 3, 1910, in *PWW*, 21: 228 and 476.
39. Quoted in A. R. Groh, "Wilson Campaigning Methods Surprise to Friends and Foes," *Philadelphia Record*, Oct. 30, 1910, Magazine Section, p. 1, clipping, reel 515, WWP.

40. Ibid.
41. Bacon, *People Awakened*, 112, 150, and 165.
42. Quoted in JK, *Political Education of Woodrow Wilson*, 72.
43. A. R. Groh, "Wilson Campaigning Methods Surprise to Friends and Foes."
44. Ibid.
45. *NYT*, Oct. 5, 1910, 10 and clipping, *Trenton Evening Times*, Oct. 6, 1910, reel 515, WWP.
46. *Philadelphia Inquirer*, Nov. 2, 1910, 2.
47. Some pro-Wilson newspapers, like the *Newark Evening News*, tried to hold an even balance between the two candidates in their news reports and reserved their enthusiasm for the editorial columns (*Newark Evening News*, Oct. 8–Nov. 10, 1910). Other newspapers were, in effect, cheerleaders for him. The *Trenton True American* was the most obvious practitioner of this style of campaign journalism. Although pledging itself to deal fairly with both friends and opponents during the campaign, it was quick to stray from that principle. During the month of October, e.g., it published 32 front page articles about Wilson and only nine about Lewis and nine editorials on Wilson (positive, of course) and only three on Lewis (two of those coming during the first two days of his campaign while the third one entitled "LEWIS'S HANDICAP," matched his progressive promises against the antiprogressive record of his party for many years). In the week before the election, the *True American* went all out for Wilson with a final surge. Aside from front page and editorial support for him it filled its inside political pages with 14 articles for Wilson and only three for Lewis (*TTA*, Oct. 1–Nov. 8, 1910).
48. *Trenton Evening Times*, Oct. 6, 1910, clipping, reel 515, WWP. In the United States, the term "Bourbon" refers to the extreme conservative Democrats, usually in the South. Originally it referred to the rulers of France from 1589 to 1793 and from 1814 to 1830. In the latter stages of their rule, they too were known as extreme conservatives.
49. Hirst, *Wilson, Reform Governor*, 86.
50. Quoted in ASL, *Wilson*, 190.
51. GH to WW, Oct. 10, 1910, *PWW*, 21: 293.
52. WW to GH, Oct. 11, 1910, ibid., 297.
53. ASL, *Wilson*, 190.
54. Quoted in ibid., 188.
55. JK, *Political Education of Woodrow Wilson*, 72–4.
56. Heckscher, *Woodrow Wilson*, 214.
57. Hirst, *Wilson, Reform Governor*, 101–3.
58. Walter Dear to WW, Oct. 27, 1910, reel 21, WWP.
59. Clippings, reel 515, ibid.
60. *Woodbury Constitution*, Nov. 2, 1910, 4.
61. *Newark Evening News*, Oct. 5, 1910, 6.
62. *New York American*, Sept. 16, 1910, reel 514, WWP.
63. For example, see the *New York Tribune*, Nov. 4, 1910, 6; Nov. 5, 1910, 6; and Nov. 7, 1910, 6.
64. *Trenton State Gazette*, Sept. 17, 1910, clipping, reel 514, WWP and *Woodbury Constitution*, Oct. 26, 1910, 4.

65. See, e.g., reports of his various campaign speeches, *PWW*, 21: 196, 253–6, 456, 468, and 521.
66. *Long Branch Record*, Oct. 13, 1910, clipping, reel 515, WWP.
67. *Woodbury Constitution*, Oct. 12, 1910, 4.
68. See pp. 63.
69. The union spokesman, David L. MacKay, was associated with the Central Association of Building Trades in Manhattan (MacKay to WW, Oct. 13, 1910, *PWW*, 21: 323). Wilson and MacKay exchanged several letters about the candidate's views toward unions, but MacKay remained unconvinced that he was a friend of labor. ASL points out that Wilson's views on labor, such as those in question in this instance, were based on misinformation and that Wilson, when pushed, admitted he had obtained all of his information from "those who do employ labor on a grand scale." Quoted in ASL, *Wilson*, 127.
70. Quoted in *PWW*, 21: 335, n. 2. See also, ibid. 16: 14–15. Wilson made this and other similar criticisms of organized labor in the context of also criticizing trusts as well as labor unions and, in the case of his baccalaureate address, people in professional life who had "too narrow a sense of duty" as well as college students who cheapened their diplomas by getting by doing "as little work as possible." On such occasions, he was attempting to stress the need for individuals to serve society to the best of their ability. See *PWW*, 16: 14–15 and 19: 245–6.
71. *Labor World*, Sept. 29, 1910, 4.
72. Ibid., Oct. 20, 1910, 1.
73. Quoted in *If Wilson Only Could and Would* and *The Labor Record of Woodrow Wilson: The Aristocratic Candidate of Democratic Bosses and Their Wall Street Allies*, has been one of sustained opposition to labor's welfare. They appeared over the signature of Luke McKenney, who claimed to be the secretary of the Progressive Voters of Labor. Oct. 6 and 12, 1910, reel 21, WWP. See also, *PWW*, 21: 335–6, n. 2.
74. For instance, one labor leader, John H. M'Lean made a public statement about the Republicans' circulating these pamphlets and the secretary of the International Association of Machinist Local No. 87 wrote to Wilson about them. See "Labor Speaks Up For Wilson," *Newark Evening Times*, Oct. 27, 1910, 1, reel 515, WWP, and William Blackburn to WW, Oct. 15, 1910, *PWW*, 21: 335.
75. Lewis T. Stevens to WW, Nov. 5, 1910, reel 21, WWP.
76. See "Race Prejudice is Appealed to by the Republican Machine," *TTA*, Nov. 7, 1910, 1. In his *Woodrow Wilson*, p. 399, Bragdon stated unequivocally that the Republicans circulated these pamphlets.
77. Williamson to WW (two letters), Oct. 24, 1910, reel 21, WWP.
78. Oct. 25, 1910, *PWW*, 21: 425–6, and Oct. 29, 1910, ibid., 466–70.
79. *American Labor Standard*, Nov. 18, 1910, clipping, reel 515, WWP.
80. Delahunty to WW, Oct. 7, 1910, reel 21, ibid.
81. Editorial, *Industrial News*, Nov. 17, 1910, enclosed in Delahunty to WW, Nov. 16, 1910, reel 23, ibid.
82. *NYT*, Oct. 3, 1910, 3.

83. See, e.g., "Labor Men Cheer Wilson's Name at Big Mass Meeting," *TTA*, Oct. 14, 1910, 1, "Lewis Refused to Protect New Jersey Labor Against the Cruelty of 'Blacklist,'" ibid., Oct. 21, 1910, 1, "Labor Leader Denounces Lewis," ibid., Oct. 28, 1910, 1, "Labor Man Scores Heavily in Speech for Woodrow Wilson," ibid., Nov. 4, 1910, 1, "Labor Men Out for Dr. Wilson," *Newark Evening News*, Oct. 26, 1910, 2, and "Labor Speaks Up for Wilson," ibid., Oct. 27, 1910, 1.
84. "RAILROAD MEN GREET WILSON: Give Democratic Nominee One of the Most Novel Welcomes of Campaign, HEART-WARMING ENTHUSIASM," *Newark Evening News*, Nov. 5, 1910, *PWW*, 21: 560.
85. "Railroad Men Strong for Wilson," *TTA*, Nov. 5, 1910, 1.
86. "Labor is Still Against Wilson," *Newark Evening News*, Oct. 24, 1910, clipping enclosed in Williamson to WW, Oct. 24, 1910, reel 21, WWP, and "Refuse Gov-Elect Congratulations," *Newark Star*, Nov. 12, 1910, clipping, reel 23, ibid.
87. ASL, *Wilson*, 200.
88. JK, *Political Education of Woodrow Wilson*, 105.
89. Pulitzer to WW, 9 Nov. 1910, *PWW*, 21: 595.
90. Emma Lou Thornbrough, "American Negro Newspapers, 1880–1914," *Business History Review* 60 (Winter 1966): 466–8.
91. Ibid., 487.
92. There were only a few small black newspapers published in New Jersey. They were weeklies like the *Jersey City Appeal*, the *Orange Union*, and the *Red Bank Echo*, copies of which could not be located.
93. William T. Ferguson to WW, Oct. 7, 1910, *PWW*, 21: 275, ibid., n. 2 and William Monroe Trotter to WW, Nov. 15, 1910, ibid., 22: 50.
94. William T. Ferguson to WW, July 28, 1910, ibid., 21: 28.
95. *New York Age*, Oct. 20, 1910, 4.
96. Dorsey to WW, Sept. 22, 1910, *PWW*, 21: 156 and William T. Ferguson to WW, Oct. 7, 1910, ibid., 275.
97. Appended note on Edward E. Lee to WW, Nov. 12, 1910, reel 23, WWP.
98. JK, *Political Education of Woodrow Wilson*, 82.
99. WW to GH, Aug. 8, 1910, *PWW*, 21: 40.
100. See WW to Robert Gunn Bremner (editor and publisher of the *Passaic Daily Herald*), Sept. 22, 1910, *PWW*, 21:153. In this case, Bremner forwarded four precise suggestions to Wilson. In another revealing letter Bremner wrote, "I enclose clippings with hesitation, for I know you are overburdened with such matter, but as I wrote to you about a month ago and I received such a kind reply, I do this to show how we stand today." Bremner to WW, Sept. 17, 1910, ibid., 133.

Chapter 5 Governor Wilson and the Press, 1910–11

1. Campaign statements, Nov. 3, Oct. 12, and Oct. 3, 1910, *PWW*, 21: 523, 306, and 232–3.

2. Campaign speech, Nov. 3, 1910, ibid., 524.
3. *Hoboken Observer*, Dec. 10, 1910, reel 515, WWP.
4. ASL, *Wilson*, 211.
5. St. John to WW, Nov. 7, 1910, *PWW*, 21: 581–3.
6. JK to WW, Dec. 6, 1910, reel 25, WWP.
7. James Norton to WW, Dec. 6, 1910, ibid.
8. JK to WW, Dec. 15, 1910, ibid.
9. Joseph Dear to WW, Dec. 19, 1910, ibid.
10. HW to WW, Dec. 17, 1910, reel 25, ibid.
11. Editorial, *Hoboken Observer*, Dec. 10, 1910, reel 515, ibid.
12. Editorial, enclosed in JK to WW, Dec. 6, 1910, reel 25, ibid.
13. *Philadelphia North American*, Dec. 20, 1910, ibid., 22: 231.
14. The *Newark Star*, Nov. 6, 1910, 6; Dec. 22, 1910, 1; Jan. 19, 1911, 1, and Jan. 20, 1911, 1 and 8. The *Star* was especially irate about a so-called "secret" planning meeting Wilson held in New York City that included several Republican editors. Pro-Wilson newspapers explained that there was nothing secret about the meeting. Its purpose was to gather a variety of viewpoints, and Democratic, Republican, and independent editors either attended or were invited to attend. *Newark Evening News*, Jan. 19, 1911, 1.
15. Charles Eaton (editor of the *Stanhope Press*) to WW, Jan. 21, 1911, box 1, WW Corresp., NJSA.
16. Clippings, reel 516, WWP.
17. "Wilson As An Advertisement," *Jersey City Jersey Journal*, Dec. 16, 1910, clipping, reel 516, WWP.
18. JK, *Political Education of Woodrow Wilson*, 95.
19. "The Governor's Chorus," the *Star*, Jan. 20, 1911, p. 8.
20. *Labor Standard*, Feb. 24, 1911, enclosed in Williamson to WW, Feb. 27, 1911, reel 26, WWP.
21. News report, *TTA*, Aug. 22, 1910, 10.
22. Record's column for Apr. 22, 1911, cited above, is quoted in full in Hirst, *Wilson Reform Governor*, 297–8. For editorials of similar opinion see, e.g., the *Newark Evening News*, Apr. 21, 1911, 6, and the *New York World*, Apr. 10, 1911, 10.
23. "NEW JERSEY'S REVOLUTION," *New York Tribune*, 23 April 1911, 8.
24. For example, see the *Woodbury Constitution*, Apr. 26, 1911, 4 and the *NYS*, Apr. 14, 1911, 6.
25. JK, *Political Education of Woodrow Wilson*, 264.
26. "Governor Tells Plans to Editors," *Trenton Evening News*, 27 Feb. 1910, 2, and "Wilson Outlines Legislative Plans to State Editors," *TTA*, Feb. 28, 1910, 1.
27. "Seeing the Governor: Easiest Thing in the World in the Case of Mr. Wilson," untitled clipping, n.d. (Winter, 1911), reel 516, WWP.
28. "Governor Meets Newspaper Men," *TTA*, Apr. 4, 1911, 2 and Charles Willis Thompson, *Presidents I've Known and Two Near Presidents* (Indianapolis: Bobbs-Merrill, 1929), 304.
29. Ibid., 277.

30. *PWW*, 22: 398 and "Take Politics From Ambush Says Wilson," *NYT*, Feb. 1, 1911, 8 (italics mine).
31. Delos F. Wilcox, "The American Newspaper: A Study in Social Psychology," *Annals of the American Academy of Political and Social Science*, 16 (July 1900): 87.
32. Irwin to LaFollette, Jan. 29, [1911–12], box B71, LaFollette Family Papers, MDLC. Hereinafter cited as LaFollette Collection.
33. Hearst to Dent H. Roberts, May 3, 1914, Letters 1912–19, box 24, folder 4, Phoebe Hearst Papers, BANC MSS 72/204c, Bancroft Library, University of California, Berkeley.
34. Hazel Dicken-Garcia, *Journalists Standards in Nineteenth-Century America* (Madison: University of Wisconsin Press, 1989), 109–15.
35. "Newspaper Men and Legislation," *TTA*, Feb. 20, 1911, 4.
36. Untitled clipping, Feb. 3, 1911, reel 516, WWP.
37. *TTA*, Feb. 1, 1911, 1.
38. John Lathrop to WW, Feb. 1, 1911, reel 26, WWP.
39. DL to WW, Nov. 9, 1910, *PWW*, 21: 608 and "WILSON CAPTURES WASHINGTON FOLK," clipping, Feb. 3, 1911, reel 516, WWP.
40. "CORRESPONDENTS AT EVENING MEAL," *TTA*, Mar. 15, 1911, 1.
41. "Newspaper Man is Rebuked by Wilson," *Trenton Evening Times*, Feb. 9, 1911, Feb. 1 and 10, 1911, 6.
42. RSB, *Wilson: Life and Letters*, 4: 229.
43. JK, *Political Education of Woodrow Wilson*, 264.
44. For numerous examples of friendly journalists writing to Wilson offering him their advice, etc., see reels 23, 24, 25, and 26, WWP.
45. Dear to WW, Nov. 26, 1911, *PWW*, 22: 97.
46. Scudder to WW, Dec. 20, 1910, reel 25, WWP. See also, William W. St. John to WW, Dec. 8, 1910, ibid.
47. For example, see Edward C. Potter (New York manager of the American Press Association) to WW, Dec. 16, 1910 and Matthew Ely (editor of the *Hoboken Observer*) to WW, Dec. 29, 1910, reels 25 and 26, ibid.
48. Pulitzer to GH, Nov. 14, 1910, box 9, Joseph Pulitzer Papers, MDLC. Hereinafter cited as Pulitzer Papers.
49. Pulitzer to George Johns, Dec. 5, 1910, and Pulitzer to Frank Cobb, Nov. 2, 1910, ibid.
50. Pulitzer to GH, Nov. 14, 1910, ibid. For Pulitzer's early interest in Wilson, see JD, *The Wilson Era*, 3.
51. Pulitzer to Frank Cobb, Dec. 20, 1910, box 9, Pulitzer Papers.
52. Pulitzer to Frank Cobb, Dec. 8, 1910, ibid.
53. Armistead to WW, Feb. 17, 1911, reel 27, WWP.
54. Two Washington correspondents, Louis Brownlow and Tom Pence, launched a Wilson for President movement on their own. While seeking shelter from a rainstorm in a street side doorway early in January 1911 and discovering they both favored Wilson for the Democratic nomination, they decided to write and place items promoting that idea. "So there began, without authorization, without funds, without any deliberate preparation, the newspaper pre-convention campaign for Woodrow Wilson for the

Democratic nomination for President in 1912," Brownlow recollected years later. Brownlow, "Wilson's Personal Relations," *Lectures and Seminar at the University of Chicago*, 90–1. Copy, reel 537, WWP.

55. *HW*, Nov. 19, 1910, 4.
56. Ibid., Feb. 4, 1911, 4.
57. GH, "The Political Predestination of Woodrow Wilson," *NAR*, Dec. 1911, 321–30. For subsequent booming of Wilson in HW, see, May 6, 1911, 7 and 32; May 27, 1911, 4; June 3, 1911, 4; and July 29, 1911, 6.
58. WW to MAHP, Mar. 5, 1911, *PWW*, 22: 479.
59. GH, "The Problem, the Solution and the Man," *NAR*, 193 (Apr. 1911): 481–93.
60. WW to MAHP, Apr. 2, 1911, *PWW*, 22: 532.
61. Edwin Camp to WW, Oct. 27, 1910, reel 21, WWP.
62. Armistead to WW, Feb. 17, 1911, reel 22, ibid.
63. Harkrader to WW, Nov. 17, 1910, reel 23, ibid.
64. C. Vann Woodward, *Origins of the New South 1877–1913* (Baton Rouge: Louisiana State University Press, 1951), chapter 14.
65. Edward L. Ayers, *The Promise of the New South: Life After Reconstruction* (1992; reprint, New York: Oxford University Press, 1993), 413.
66. ASL, *The Higher Realism of Woodrow Wilson*, 281; Woodward, *Origins of the New South*, chapter 14; and I. A. Newby, *The South: A History* (New York: Holt, Rinehart, and Winston, 1978), 359–70. Newby points out that, aside from the urban progressives, there was an identifiable number of agrarian progressives. Less respectable and more demagogic than the urban progressives, they appealed to tenant farmers and other marginalized groups.
67. Quoted in Joseph L. Morrison, *Josephus Daniels Says . . . : An Editor's Political Odyssey From Bryan to Wilson and F. D. R., 1894–1913* (Chapel Hill: University of North Carolina Press, 1962), 220. See also, pp. VII–IX.
68. JD to George Creel, Feb. 10, 1941, reel 48, JD Papers. Daniels served as Chief Clerk, Department of Interior, 1893–95; Secretary of Navy, 1913–20; and Ambassador to Mexico, 1922–41.
69. JD, *Wilson Era*, 4.
70. "From the day it was my pleasure to accompany you to Chapel Hill and hear your inspiring address to our University boys, it has been my hope and belief that you would be called to the great work upon which you are to enter next Tuesday," Daniels to WW, Feb. 25, 1913, reel 65, JD Papers.
71. JD, *Wilson Era, Years of Peace*, 15–17.
72. Quoted in RSB, *Wilson: Life and Letters*, 3: 197–8.
73. ASL, *Wilson*, 315.
74. WW to MAHP, Apr. 30 1911, *PWW*, 22: 597–8.
75. "News Reports of Two Speeches in Atlanta," Mar. 10, 1911, ibid., 22: 490; "Wilson Against Class Warfare," *TTA*, Feb. 24, 1911, 4; "Gov. Wilson For Progress," *NYS*, Apr. 30, 1911, 10; and "Not Radical, Says Wilson," ibid., July 15, 1911, 2.
76. Quoted in JK, "Woodrow Wilson, Governor," *Independent*, May 11, 1911, 986.

77. *Norfolk Virginian Pilot*, Apr. 30, 1911, *PWW*, 22: 592–3.
78. ASL, *Higher Realism of Woodrow Wilson*, 282. The leading southern progressive newspapers are listed in ibid., 295, n. 96.
79. John Milton Cooper, *Walter Hines Page: The Southerner as American* (Chapel Hill: University of North Carolina Press, 1977), 206.
80. Hendrick, *Life and Letters of Walter Hines Page*, 1: 104–6.
81. WW to WHP, Feb. 10, 1911, *PWW*, 22: 414, and WW to MAHP, Feb. 19, 1911, ibid., 439, and WW to William B. Hale, Feb. 10, 1911, ibid., 414.
82. Quoted in RSB, *Wilson: Life and Letters*, 3: 191.
83. Walter McCorkle to WHP, Nov. 4, 1908, folder 669, WHP Papers.
84. WW to WHP, Feb. 10, 1911, *PWW*, 27: 413–14, and William F. McCombs, *Making Woodrow Wilson President* (New York: Fairview Publishing Co., 1921), 40–1.
85. WHP to WW, Feb. 15, 1911, *PWW*, 27: 433.
86. McCorkle to Page, Feb. 11, 1911, folder 669, WHP Papers.
87. WW to MAHP, Mar. 26, 1911, *PWW*, 22: 518–19.

Chapter 6 The Wilson Presidential Movement: Publicity and Opposition

1. WHP to McCorkle, Mar. 3, 1911, folder 669, WHP Papers and FPS, "How Woodrow Wilson Won His Nomination," *Current History* 20 (July 1924): 562–3.
2. WHP to McCorkle, Apr. 1, 1911, folder 1015, WHP Papers.
3. FPS to WHP, Apr. 28, 1911, ibid., and FPS, "How Woodrow Wilson Won the Nomination," 563–4.
4. Ibid., 562.
5. Ibid.
6. FPS to WHP, Apr. 22 and 28, 1911, folder 1015, WHP Papers.
7. FPS to RSB, Mar. 10, 1927, reel 83, RSB Papers.
8. WW to MAHP, May 7, 1911, box 33, folder 7, WWCP.
9. FPS, "How Woodrow Wilson Won the Nomination," 564–5.
10. See, news reports of the tour, *PWW*, 23: 3–102 and continuous coverage of the tour in *BS* and *TTA*.
11. EAW to WW, May 11, 1911, *PWW*, 23: 30–1.
12. FPS to WHP, May 12, 1911, folder 1015, WHP Papers.
13. Nelson to HW, May 20, 1911, box 10, HW Papers.
14. FPS to WHP, May 21, 1911, folder 1015, WHP Papers.
15. WW to MAHP, May 21, 1911, *PWW*, 23: 80.
16. For example, see reports quoted in *PWW*, 23: 41, 53 and FPS, "Woodrow Wilson in the West," *LD*, May 20, 1911, 988–9.
17. WW to MAHP, May 13, 1911, *PWW*, 23: 49–50.
18. Barclay made notes of Wilson's comments soon after their conversation (RSB, *Wilson: Life and Letters*, 3: 225–6). However, Wilson continued to be equivocal about his intentions in later conversations.

19. William Bayard Hale, "Woodrow Wilson: Possible President," *World's Work*, May 1911, 14339–53.
20. Hale portrayed Harmon as an old-fashioned, honest man, unfettered by passionate ideas and convictions. "Judson Harmon and the Presidency," ibid., June 1911, 14446–59.
21. Hale to Olga Unger Hale, Mar. 9, 1911, William Bayard Hale Papers, Yale University Library, New Haven, Conn.
22. JK, "Woodrow Wilson, Governor," *Independent*, May 11, 1911, 986–9, and "A Virginia Democrat," *HW*, May 6, 1911, 7 and 32, and editorial comments in ibid., May 27, 1911 and June 4 and 3, 1911, 4.
23. *Raleigh News and Observer*, June 1, 1911, 1; May 28, 1911, 1; May 30, 1911, 1, 2, and 4; May 31, 1911, 1; and June 2, 1911, 1, 4, and 10; and Daniels to Wilson, June 9, 1911, *PWW*, 23: 139.
24. WW, address, June 2, 1911, ibid., 126–7.
25. Ibid., 117–18 and 125.
26. ASL, *Wilson*, 327–8.
27. WHP to McCorkle, June 17, 1911, folder 669, WHP Papers.
28. "Governor Wilson is Home Again," *TTA*, June 5, 1911, 1 and 2. For his visit with Democrats in Washington, see "Gov. Wilson Home Again," *BS*, June 5, 1912, 2.
29. Quoted in ASL, *Wilson*, 118.
30. Quoted in ibid., 318.
31. McKee Barclay, "Wilson at Bryan's Home," *BS*, May 28, 1911, 2 and "Harvey and Bryan Discuss National Politics," *TTA*, June 1, 1911, 1.
32. FPS to WHP, May 7, 1911, folder 1015, WHP Papers.
33. Barclay to WW, Aug. 14, 1911, WWPP.
34. Watterson to Desha Breckinridge (president of the *Lexington Herald*), Aug. 22, 1911, box 1, HW Papers.
35. WW to HW, July 24, 1911, box 14, HW Papers.
36. Russell to WW, July 20, 1911, box 17, folder 55, WW Corresp., NJSA.
37. Seely to WW, Sept. 14, 1911, and enclosure, box 5, folder 76, ibid.
38. "A Little Presidential Primary," *World's Work*, Aug. 1911, 14716–20.
39. Hale, "Woodrow Wilson—A Biography," ibid., Oct. 1911, 14940–53, ibid., Nov. 1911–Mar. 1912, 64–77, 229–35, 297–310, 466–72, and 522–34.
40. For example, see *HW*, May 27, 1911, 4; June 3, 1911, 4; July 29, 1911, 6; and Johnston, "A Talk with Governor Wilson," ibid., Aug. 19, 1911, 11–12.
41. "For President: Woodrow Wilson," ibid., Nov. 11, 1911, 4–5; "The Voice of the South," ibid., Nov. 18, 1911, 32; "The Voice of the West," ibid., Nov. 25, 1911, 19; "The Voice of the East," ibid., Dec. 2, 1911, 20; and "For Government by the People," ibid., Dec. 9, 1911, 20–1.
42. Miller to WW, Sept. 21, 1911, box 83, WWPP.
43. FPS to RSB, Mar. 10, 1927, and RSB interview with FPS, Nov. 2, 1927, reel 83, RSB Papers, and WW to WHP, June 7, 1911, *PWW*, 23: 135.
44. FPS, "How Woodrow Wilson Won His Nomination," 568–9 and RSB, *Wilson: Life and Letters*, 3: 233.
45. JK, *Political Education of Woodrow Wilson*, 148.

46. McCombs to WW, Sept. 20, 1911, Sept. 21, 1911, and Sept. 26, 1911, *PWW*, 23: 341, 352, and 360, and McCombs, *Making Woodrow Wilson President*, 42.
47. ASL, *Wilson*, 335.
48. McAdoo to WW, Nov. 15, 1910, *PWW*, 22: 51; RSB, *Wilson: Life and Letters*, 3: 234–5; ibid., 312.
49. "Memorandum Concerning Colonel House," Aug. 26, 1926, reel 53, RSB Papers, and "Colonel House," Sept. 13, 1926, and Charles Seymour, *The Intimate Papers of Colonel House* (Boston: Houghton Mifflin Company, 1926–28), 1: 34–61.
50. See pp. 264–5 n. 54.
51. *Raleigh News and Observer*, Sept. 1, 1912, 1.
52. "Two Tarheels Who Hold Leverage in Big Campaign—Josephus Daniels and Tom Pence," ibid., Sept. 1, 1912, 1, reprint of an article from the *New York Evening Post*, and JD, "Wilson and the Newspapermen," ms. of a syndicated article, 1924, box 732, JD Papers.
53. For an example of Wilson's recognition of the "spontaneous effort" of his friends, see WW to James Alfred Hoyt, Jr., June 22, 1911, *PWW*, 23: 171.
54. WGM, *Crowded Years: The Reminiscences of William G. McAdoo* (Cambridge, Mass.: Riverside Press, 1931), 117.
55. WW to Dodge, June 20, 1911, *PWW*, 23: 160–1.
56. Letters from a wide variety of Wilson's well wishers, news reports of Wilson's speeches from June to Dec. 1911, and his interviews can be found in *PWW*, 23.
57. Address in Denver, Sept. 30, 1908, ibid., 18: 424–34. For examples of his earlier criticism of special interests, see ibid., 21: 209–11 and 330.
58. Interview, "Wilson on America's Money Trust," *TTA*, Sept. 11, 1911, ibid., 23: 312, and address, "Money Monopoly is the Most Menacing Wilson's Warning," June 15, 1911, ibid., 157.
59. Robert D. Heinl, "Down Washington Way," *Leslie's*, June 29, 1911, 730.
60. Quoted in *Leslie's*, editorial, July 13, 1911, 33.
61. *NYS*, July 15, 1911, 4, 7, and Oct. 19, 1911, 6.
62. "Governor Wilson Losing Ground," *Leslie's Weekly*, July 13, 1911, 33 and "Let Republicans Beware," ibid., Oct. 12, 1911, 403. See also the continuing reports of Robert D. Heinl (*Leslie's* Washington correspondent) from July to Dec. 1911 in ibid.
63. *NYT*, Sept. 1, 6. Wilson made his comments about the Monetary Commission in an interview with Henry Beach Needham, "Woodrow Wilson's Views," *Outlook*, Aug. 26, 1911, 944–6.
64. McCombs to WW, Aug. 21, 1911, *PWW*, 23: 287.
65. McCombs to WW, Sept. 13, 1911, ibid., 325.
66. McCombs to WW, Sept. 23, 1911, ibid., 355–6.
67. "WHAT A TIMES MAN THINKS OF WILSON," *TTA*, Oct. 14, 1911, 8.
68. William Garrot Brown to WW, Oct. 30, 1911, *PWW*, 23: 513–16.
69. WW to William Garrot Brown, Nov. 7, 1911, ibid., 542–3.
70. William Garrot Brown to WW, Nov. 10, 1911, ibid., 547–8.

71. The commission plan of government provided for the election of usually five commissioners, who were considered experts in the concerns of the departments they would head, to administer a municipality. Since it challenged the sinews of political machines, the bosses fought it. In this case, Nugent united with the Republican minority in the Assembly and had the measure amended to require 40 percent (later reduced to 30 percent) of the number of votes cast for assemblymen in the recent election before a municipality could adopt the plan. The amended bill also stipulated that any city adopting the plan would also adopt the initiative, referendum, and recall. ASL, *Wilson*, 265–6 and 279.
72. *NYS*, Aug. 31, 1911, 11.
73. "INSULTING TOAST TO WILSON," *NYS*, July 27, 1911, 11; "NUGENT'S BARROOM JIBE MAKES COMMENT," *TTA*, July 27, 1911, 4; "'Get Out or Be Kicked Out'—That's Democracy's Word to Chairman Nugent," ibid., July 28, 1911, 1. See also ASL, *Wilson*, 280–1.
74. Nugent showed up at the meeting with a group of thugs and kidnapped one of the attendees in order to prevent a quorum, but after he left and as the meeting was about to adjourn another committeeman arrived, a quorum was declared, and the meeting proceeded. Ibid., 281.
75. *NYS*, Nov. 8, 1911, 1. Progressive newspapers like the *Trenton True American* led the editorial chorus in making this point. In Essex County, 40,516 Democrats voted in 1910 compared with 23,360 in 1911. For the Republicans, 35,577 voted with 1910 compared with 30,648 in 1911, thus giving them a 7,288 majority in the latter election. See, "New Jersey Democratic Totals," *TTA*, Nov. 18, 1911, 1.
76. Ibid., Nov. 18, 1911, 1.
77. Both the *Boston Transcript* and the *New York Tribune*, two Republican newspapers, made generous comments about Wilson and the elections. See "The Elections: Their Significance," *Outlook*, Nov. 25, 1911, 708.
78. Quoted in "Wilson in His Home State, Newspaper Views as to the Effect of Defeat on His Boom Vary," *NYT*, Nov. 9. 1911, 3.
79. *Trenton Daily State Gazette*, Nov. 20, 1911, 1 and Nov. 9, 1911, 6.
80. *NYT*, Nov. 8, 1911, 12.
81. Ibid., Nov. 9, 1911, 12.
82. See pp. 22–3, this book.
83. Quoted in Frank M. O'Brian, *The Story of the Sun* (New York: D. Appleton and Co., 1928), 230.
84. *NYS*, Dec. 5, 1911, 1. Information about the terms for the pensions specifying there were two separate categories for eligibility had been published in a number of journals. See, e.g., Joseph Jastrow, "The Advancement of Teaching," *NAR*, Oct. 1907, 215 and Henry S. Pritchett (President of the Carnegie Foundation for the Advancement of Teaching), "Mr. Carnegie's Gift to the Teachers," *Outlook*, May 1906, 124.
85. Henry Smith Pritchett to WW, Dec. 29, 1910, *PWW*, 22: 283.
86. WW to MAHP, Dec. 10, 1911, ibid., 23: 590.
87. Published in *Newark Evening News*, Dec. 6, 1911, *PWW*, 23: 565–6.
88. Quoted in ASL, *Wilson*, 350.

89. *Trenton Daily State Gazette*, Dec. 7, 1911, 6.
90. See JCH to WW with enclosure, Jan. 22, 1906, and WW to JCH, Jan. 26, 1906, *PWW*, 16: 286–8.
91. JCH to President Taft, Jan. 1, 1912, box 18, JCH Papers. See also ASL, *Wilson*, 349–50.
92. WW to MAHP, Dec. 10, 1911, *PWW*, 23: 590.
93. *NYS*, Jan. 7, 1912 and Jan. 8, 1911, 1.
94. Quoted in JD, *The Wilson Era*, 32.
95. JK, *Political Education of Woodrow Wilson*, 173.
96. *NYS*, Jan. 9, 1912, 1.
97. *Newark Evening News*, Jan. 9, 1912, *PWW*, 24: 16–17.
98. Ibid., 17.
99. "An Address in Washington at a Jackson Day Dinner," Jan. 8, 1912, ibid., 16.
100. Quoted in JD, *The Wilson Era*, 35.
101. WW to MAHP, Dec. 10, 1911, *PWW*, 23: 590.

Chapter 7 The Press and Wilson's Preconvention Campaign

1. Clipping of a speech by Urey Woodson (proprietor of the Greenville, Ky. *Muhlenberg Echo*) to the Kentucky Press Association, Paducah, Ky., 1931, box 906, JD Papers.
2. ASL, *Wilson*, 361–2. The description of this entire and often recounted episode can be found in ibid., 359–80.
3. In a letter to her cousin, Colonel Watterson's brother-in-law, Wilson's wife explained that he "never for a moment dreamed" he had offended Harvey when departing from the Manhattan Club (EAW to Robert Ewing, Jan. 12, 1912, *PWW*, 24: 41). Evidence supporting her account can be found in an invitation Wilson extended to Harvey after the incident occurred to speak to "the boys of the Press Club of Princeton University." Since the Club's leaders were "abashed at the idea of approaching you directly . . . I am glad to act as their sponsor," Wilson wrote. The letter would not have been written by someone who felt his relations with Harvey were strained (WW to Harvey, Dec. 27, 1911, *PWW*, 23: 630).
4. WW to Harvey, Dec. 21, 1911, ibid., 603 and Harvey to WW, Jan. 4, 1911, ibid., 652.
5. WW to Harvey, Jan. 11, 1912, ibid., 24: 31, and Harvey to WW, Jan. 17, 1912, ibid., 45.
6. Wilson's brother-in-law called it a "deliberate . . . frameup." SA, "*Brother Woodrow*," 172–3. Others close to Wilson shared that opinion as have his biographers. Heckscher called it "a trap" (*Woodrow Wilson*, 241) and Link, "Harvey's Scheme," *Wilson*, 365.
7. Watterson to Thomas F. Ryan with copies to Harvey and Hemphill, Jan. 9, 1912, reel 1, HW Collection.
8. Hemphill to Watterson, Jan. 15, 1912, reel 1, HW Papers.
9. Hemphill, Jan. 5, 1912, Scrapbook—Clipped Articles, JCH Papers.

10. Hemphill to Taft, Jan. 1, 1912 (Hemphill's Scrapbook—Clipped Articles, JCH Papers). The intrigue can be followed through Hemphill's correspondence with Watterson and Harvey between Jan. 5 and Jan. 22, 1912 in box 18 of Hemphill's Papers and Hemphill's role in escalating speculation about a Wilson-Harvey break can be traced in the clipped articles from Jan. 5–Jan. 31, 1912, in scrapbooks also kept in the Hemphill Papers.
11. Statement issued to the press Jan. 17 and 18, 1912 and also issued in *HW*, Jan. 20, 1912, in ibid., 24: 45.
12. *NYT*, Jan. 18, 1912, *PWW*, 24: 45–7.
13. Stated in reference to several newspapers' comments in "Democracy Awaits Its Leader," *LD*, Feb. 10, 1912, 252.
14. Clipping, Jan. 17, 1912, Hemphill Scrapbooks, JCH Papers.
15. Hemphill to Col. H. A. McLong, Jan. 22, 1912, box 18, ibid.
16. The *New York Evening Post* published the Wilson–Harvey letters on Jan. 30, 1912 and the other newspapers on Jan. 31, 1912.
17. Watterson to Harvey, Feb. 28, 1912, copy, box 18, JCH Papers.
18. Watterson to Hemphill, Feb. 15, 1912, ibid.
19. Thanks to ASL, there is a convincing path of evidence pointing to Harvey as the guilty party. *Wilson*, 363–77.
20. See p. 78.
21. J. C. Tebbetts to Hemphill, Mar. 29, 1912, box 19, JCH Papers.
22. D. A. Tompkins to Hemphill, May 7, 1912, ibid.
23. Legal brief, *Ambrose E. Gonzales and J. C. Hemphill v. D. A. Tompkins, George Stephens, W. H. Wood, and First National Bank of Charlotte, N. C.*, June 14, 1912, box 19, ibid.
24. JD claimed it was Pence who initiated this counter movement by contacting Sen. Benjamin Tillman about it ("Wilson and the Newspapermen," ms. of a syndicated article, 1924, box 732, JD papers). James Kerney supports that claim (*Political Education of Woodrow Wilson*, 170). However, ASL attributed the source to Sen. Lee S. Overman, who told Sen. Tillman that Watterson had omitted the Ryan factor from his published statement and the latter related it to the newspapermen (ASL, *Wilson*, 374). While either Sen. Overman or Pence may have been the source, Tom Pence seems the most probable one since he set out to push the idea.
25. "Governor Wilson's Candidacy: A Poll of the Press," *Outlook*, Feb. 1912, 307.
26. Judson Harmon was the first Democrat to declare his candidacy and the first to establish a press bureau. Hugh L. Nichols headed it at first; Charles A. Cottress, later. Fred Dubois headed Champ Clark's press bureau, and Thomas M. Owen was in charge of Oscar W. Underwood's. Arthur Wallace Dunn, "Campaigning for the Nomination," *ARR*, Apr. 1912, 429–30.
27. George Kibbe Turner, "Manufacturing Public Opinion: The New Art of Making Presidents by Press Bureaus," *McClure's Magazine*, July 1912, 319.
28. Louise Overacker, *The Presidential Primary* (New York: Macmillan, 1926), 12–13 and 236.
29. "Demand for Press Agents in Politics," *Fourth Estate*, Mar. 2, 1912, 19..

30. Stephan Ponder, *Managing the Press: Origins of the Media Presidency, 1897–1933* (New York: St. Martin's Press, 1998), 3; Wm. David Sloan and James D. Startt, *The Media in America: A History*, 4th ed. (Northport, Ala.: Vision Press, 1999), 282.
31. RSB, *Wilson: Life and Letters*, 3: 270–5; ASL, *Wilson*, 394–95; and Russell B. Nye, *Midwestern Progressive Politics* (1959; New York: Harper & Row, Publishers, Torchbook edition, 1965), 265.
32. EWS to R. F. Paine, Feb. 28, 1906, quoted in Gerald Baldesty, *E. W. Scripps and the Business of Newspapers* (Urbana: University of Illinois Press, 1999), 125.
33. EWS to Chas. H. Wheeler, Oct. 11, 1914, box 16, EWS Papers.
34. Baldesty, *EWS*, 93–106.
35. EWS to Judge Ben S. Lindsey, Jan. 4, 1912, box 14, EWS Papers and EWS to Amos Pinchot, Apr. 10, 1912, box 11, Amos Pinchot Papers, MDLC. Hereinafter cited as Pinchot Papers.
36. WW to WGM, Nov. 10, 1911, box 517, WGM Papers.
37. EWS to Amos Pinchot, Apr. 10, 1912, box 11, Pinchot Papers.
38. *Cleveland Press*, Jan. 22, 1912, 3 and Jan. 23, 1912, 6.
39. H. R. Rickey to John Hannon, Feb. 12, 1912, box B72, La Follette Collection.
40. For example, see "A Poll of the Press," *Outlook*, Feb. 10, 1912, 307–8 and Erman J. Ridgway, "Weighing the Candidates," *Everybody's Magazine*, May 1912, 582.
41. *Camden Courier*, ibid., and *Trenton Daily State Gazette*, Apr. 18, 1912, 6.
42. Ibid., Apr. 18, 1912, 6. See also, ibid., Mar. 4, 1912, 6; Apr. 4, 1912, 5; and Apr. 13, 1912, 8.
43. Unsigned copy, letter to WW, Jan. 20, 1912, box 6, file 92, WW Corresp., NJSA.
44. WW, *A History of the American People* (New York: Harper & Brothers Publishers, 1902), 5: 212–14.
45. Ibid., 140–1, 203, 238–9, and 267.
46. Quoted in Bragdon, *Wilson: The Academic Years*, 247.
47. "Wilson is Target of G. F. Williams," *NYT*, Feb. 2, 1912, 2.
48. Ibid.
49. Introductory comment, ibid.
50. "Yellow Journalism's Evils," *Editor and Publisher*, Aug. 19, 1911. For the extent of yellow journalism, see W. Joseph Campbell, "Yellow Journalism and Urban America, 1900: What Explains the Contagion?" (Paper presented at the annual meeting of the American Journalism Historians Association, Portland, Ore., 1999), 4 and 12.
51. Arthur Brisbane to Col. Watterson, Sept. 29, 1911, box 1, HW Papers.
52. Quoted in W. A. Swanberg, *Citizen Hearst: A Biography of William Randolph Hearst* (New York: Galahad Books, 1961), 101.
53. Ibid., 230–1 and 267–8. The Independence party (also called the Independence league) originally was the Municipal Ownership League.
54. Quoted in Edmund De Coblentz, ed., *William Randolph Hearst: A Portrait in His Own Words* (New York: Simon & Schuster, 1952), 38.

55. Swanberg, *Citizen Hearst*, 91.
56. Hearst described his journalism as "striking" rather than "sensational" in a 1906 interview. Quoted in ibid., 247.
57. Quoted in Frank P. Glass to RSB, Jan. 5, 1925, reel 76, RSB Papers, and FPS to RSB, Nov. 2, 1927, reel 83, ibid.
58. Quoted in "Hearst and Wilson," *Trenton Daily State Gazette*, Sept. 28, 1911, 6.
59. "'GOV. WILSON A FEDERALIST, NOT A DEMOCRAT'—W. R. HEARST," *New York American*, Mar. 14, 1912, 2.
60. For Lewis's literary and journalistic career see Louis Filler, "Wolfville," *New Mexico Quarterly Review*, 13 (Summer 1943): 35–47 and for his attitude toward life, see Alfred Henry Lewis, "What Life Means to Me," *Cosmopolitan*, Jan. 1907, 295–97.
61. Alfred Henry Lewis, "The Real Woodrow Wilson," *Hearst's Magazine*, May 1912, 2265–74.
62. Ibid.
63. Ibid., and Ferdinand Lundberg, *Imperial Hearst: A Social Biography* (New York: Equinox Cooperative Press, 1936), 212–14.
64. JK, *Political Education of Woodrow Wilson*, 184.
65. Quoted in ASL, *Wilson*, 387.
66. *Collier's*, Mar. 16, 1912, 8.
67. W. H. Porterfield to EWS, Feb. 24, 1912, box 32, EWS Papers.
68. News reports of Wilson's speeches in Sterling, DeKalb, Peoria, and Springfield, Illinois, Apr. 6 and 7, 1912, *PWW*, 24: 290, 292, 299, and 230. See also, ASL, *Wilson*, 410–12. Wilson mentioned Hearst in this same manner again in his Massachusetts campaign. See his address in Boston, Apr. 27, 1912, *PWW*, 24: 363.
69. *Nation*, Feb. 15, 1912, 147.
70. ASL, *Wilson*, 383, 385, n. 166, and 387.
71. Clark won California, Illinois, and Massachusetts. Underwood won Georgia and Charles Murphy, the Tammany Hall boss hostile to Wilson, controlled the New York delegation.
72. Lewis, "The Honorable Champ" *Cosmopolitan*, Nov. 1911, 760–5. Lewis also praised Oscar W. Underwood to whom Hearst also gave some support. See, Lewis's "Underwood—House Leader," ibid., Dec. 1911, 109–14.
73. See, John Temple Graves, "Speaker Clark," *Independent*, Nov. 2, 1911, 959–63, and the *New York American* quoted in "The Democratic Presidential Candidates: A Poll of the Press," Outlook, May 11, 1912, 107.
74. Interview, "The Views of Champ Clark," by John E. Lathrop, *Outlook*, May 11, 1912, 73.
75. John P. Scripps to EWS, Mar. 14, 1912, and Mar. 27, 1912, box 33, EWS Papers.
76. EWS to James G. Scripps, Apr. 11, 1912, and EWS to Gilson Gardner, Mar. 12, 1912, box 14, ibid.
77. EWS to W. H. Porterfield, Feb. 28, 1912, ibid.
78. Quoted in "Progress of the Democratic Candidates," *LD*, May 18, 1912, 1021–2.

79. WGM to WW, Apr. 3, 1912, box 517, WGM Papers.
80. *NYT*, Mar. 1–June 30, 1912. Scripps's *Cleveland Press* made an even more severe departure from news about Wilson. In January it reported Wilson favorably and made strong editorial statements in his favor, and from January 30 to February 5, it featured a seven part biographical–promotional series on Wilson and his family. After that there was abundant news about Roosevelt and Taft but little on Wilson until a strong editorial on his behalf on May 18. *Cleveland Press*, Jan. 1–June 30, 1912.
81. Poe to J. H. Patten (General Counsel, Farmers' Educational and Co-operative Union), Mar. 12, 1912, box 6, file 105, WW Corresp., NJSA.
82. *Atlanta Constitution*, June 1, 1912, 2.
83. Frank P. Glass to RSB, Jan. 5, 1926, reel 26, RSB Papers.
84. Woodward, *Origins of the New South*, 476–7, and ASL, *Wilson*, 415–16.
85. ASL, "The Underwood Presidential Movement of 1912," *Journal of Southern History 9* (May 1945): 237.
86. Ibid., 236. The editor of the *Atlanta Journal* explained this publicity tactic in detail to Wilson's press secretary. James R. Gray to Walker Measday, May 24, 1912, box 7, folder 106, WW Corresp., NJSA.
87. *Montgomery Advertiser*, May 13, 1912, 4.
88. Historians discovered that Ryan contributed $35,000 (about one-third of his total campaign expenditure) to Underwood's campaign and another $50,000 to Harmon's campaign. Ryan did not contribute to Wilson's campaign, though at one point he was willing to do so until Wilson refused to deal with him. Previously, Ryan had made a small contribution to Wilson's gubernatorial campaign. Evans E. Johnson, "The Underwood Forces and the Democratic Nomination of 1912," *The Historian* 31 (Feb. 1969): 177 ASL, "Underwood Presidential Movement," 236, n. 28; and ASL, *Wilson*, 187, n. 37 and 376, n. 119.
89. Graves to Underwood, May 5, 1912, and E. W. Barrett to Underwood, May 9, 1912, Oscar W. Underwood Papers, Alabama Department of Archives and History, Montgomery, Ala. Underwood claimed he had "no knowledge whatever of the arrangement" and had he known about it he would have repudiated it (Underwood to Graves, May 10, 1912, ibid). His refusal to abandon the Tennessee campaign lends credence to his claim.
90. Hearst to Underwood, May 5, 1912, ibid. See also, Johnson, "The Underwood Forces and the Democratic Nomination of 1912," 180–1. The editor's effort to design campaigning that would defeat Wilson in specific states, implies that there was some basis for McAdoo's charge that the campaigns of the other candidates were working in coalition against Wilson (WGM to JD, Mar. 26, 1912, box 669, JD Papers). Comments to this effect often appeared in the press.
91. George Green, "The Florida Press and the Democratic Presidential Primary of 1912," *Florida Historical Quarterly* 44 (1966): 170.
92. *Tampa Morning Tribune*, Apr. 1 and 12, 1912, and the *Tallahassee Semi-Weekly True Democrat*, Apr. 2 and 12, 1912, quoted in ibid., 179.
93. WGM to WW, Apr. 3, 1912, box 517, WGM Papers.

94. ASL "The Democratic Pre-Convention Campaign of 1912 in Georgia," *Georgia Historical Quarterly* 39 (1945): 144–50.
95. Ibid., 150–1.
96. Watson founded the *People's Party Paper* in 1891 and served as its editor in chief until 1898. In 1894 he founded a campaign daily, the *Daily Press*, that ceased publication within a year. He founded *Tom Watson's, Magazine* (subsequently *Watson's Magazine*) in New York in 1905 and served as its editor until its demise a year later. Then he founded a weekly, the *Jeffersonian*, in 1906 in Thomas, Ga. and a monthly *Watson's Jeffersonian Magazine* (again, subsequently *Watson's Magazine*) in 1907 in Atlanta. Woodward C. Vann, *Tom Watson: Agrarian Rebel* (New York: Rinehart & Company, 1938), 490–1.
97. *Watson's Magazine*, Dec. 1905, 154, quoted in ibid., 369.
98. Representative quotations published in the *Jeffersonian*, Oct. 26, 1911–Apr. 11, 1912.
99. Ibid., Apr. 18, 1912, 1, 8, 9, and 10. The incident involving Washington is covered in Louis R. Harlan, et al., eds., *The Booker T. Washington Papers* (Urbana: University of Illinois Press, 1972–84): 11: XIX and 1–10. See also *American National Biography*, s. v. "Washington, Booker T.
100. *Jeffersonian*, Apr. 18, 1912, 8.
101. Woodward, *Tom Watson*, 420.
102. ASL, *Wilson*, 388 n. 178.
103. *Atlanta Constitution*, May 1, 1912, 6.
104. Ibid., May 3, 1912, 6.
105. *Jeffersonian*, May 9, 1912.
106. Woodward, *Tom Watson*, 429.
107. James E. Gray to WW, July 12, 1912, reel 29, WWP.
108. *Atlanta Journal*, May 26 and June 16, 1912, quoted in ASL, "Democratic Pre-Convention Campaign in Georgia," 158, n. 67.
109. Editorial quoted in full in *Trenton Daily State Gazette*, May 6, 1912, 1.
110. EWS to John P. Scripps, May 27, 1912, box 14, EWS Papers.
111. *Collier's*, May 8, 1912, 8.
112. Quoted in "The Democratic Presidential Candidates," *Outlook*, May 11, 1912, 107.
113. Wilson's supporters often cited Clark's intemperate statements. For example, *Collier's*, May 30, 1912, 8, and "One of the Democratic Candidates," *Independent*, June 13, 1912, 1336–7.
114. Quoted in "Progress of the Democratic Candidates," *LD*, May 18, 1912, 1022.
115. *Trenton Daily State Gazette*, Apr. 11, 1912, 6, and Apr. 25, 1912, 6.
116. WGM to WW, May 29, 1912, box 517, WGM Papers.
117. *New York World*, May 30, 1912, quoted in RSB *Wilson: Life and Letters*, 3: 330–1.
118. Cobb to WW, June 6, 1912, reel 27, WWP.
119. Quoted in *Collier's*, Apr. 13, 1912, 8.
120. Daniels to the People of North Carolina, n. d., box 669, folder "Elections—1912—March–May," JD Papers.

121. Morrison, *Josephus Daniels Says*, 271.
122. WW to Daniels, June 11, 1912, *PWW*, 24: 471.

Chapter 8 Wilson and the Press at the Democratic Convention and Afterward

1. *New York World*, June 5, 1912, 9.
2. Ibid., June 7, to June 15, 1912, 8, 9, and 10.
3. Grasty to WW, July 1, 1912, box 90, WWPP.
4. Delker to WW, June 22 and 26, 1912, reels 27 and 28, WWP.
5. Pence to WW, 15 June 1912, *PWW*, 24: 475.
6. For example, see Joseph E. Davis (Western manager of Wilson's campaign) to Wilson delegates, June 14, 1912, reel 27, WWP.
7. *Charlotte Daily Observer*, June 27, 1912, 1.
8. *Chicago Daily News*, June 28, 1912, 1.
9. *NYT*, June 30, 1912, 6.
10. Harold A. Williams, *The Baltimore Sun, 1837–1987* (Baltimore: Johns Hopkins University Press, 1987), 135.
11. *BS*, June 25, 1912, 1. See also, Frank Kent (the *Sun*'s managing editor) to RSB, reel 78, RSB Papers. Kent gave Baker a full account of the article and how it was obtained.
12. *BS*, July 1, 1912, 6.
13. WW to Grasty, July 2, 1912, box 90, WWPP.
14. Grasty, "Notes [on his role at the convention]," n.d., box 89, ibid.
15. Quoted in Gerald W. Johnson et al., *The Sunpapers of Baltimore* (New York: Alfred A. Knopf, 1937), 309.
16. Huston Thompson, "Why Wilson Disliked Reporters," *Dearborn Independent*, Apr. 3, 1926, 5 and 26–7, clipping in box 254, Raymond Clapper Papers, MDLC. Hereinafter cited as Clapper Papers.
17. *BS*, June 30, 1912, 1.
18. News reports, *NYT*, June 29, and July 2, 1912, *PWW*, 24: 505–7 and 516–19.
19. Ibid., 24: 516.
20. Ibid., 523–4.
21. Ibid., 525–6.
22. News report, July 3, 1912, ibid., 528.
23. EWM, *The Woodrow Wilsons*, 166.
24. Ibid., 167.
25. Thompson, "Why Wilson Disliked Reporters," 27, clipping, box 254, Clapper Papers.
26. EWM, *The Woodrow Wilsons*, 168.
27. *New York World*, July 3, 1912, 1.
28. *Montgomer Advertiser*, July 3, 1912, 4, and the *Atlanta Constitution*, July 3, 1912, 6.
29. Quoted in "The Effect of Woodrow Wilson's Nomination," *LD*, July 18, 1912, 45.

30. Ibid., 46.
31. *San Francisco Chronicle*, July 3, 1912, "Effects of Woodrow Wilson's Nomination," 46.
32. Bagley to WW, July 3, 1912, box 7, WW Corresp., NJSA.
33. Robert Underwood Johnson to WW, July 3, 1912, reel 28, WWP.
34. Gray to WW, July 29, 1912 and Suter to WW, July 17, 1912, reel 29, ibid.
35. Hale to General Wilbur F. Sadler, July 4, 1912, box 90, WWPP.
36. Doyle to WW, Aug. 28, 1912, reel 30, WWP.
37. News report, "Wilson Here; Dines At A Lunch Counter," *NYT*, Aug. 4, 1912, *PWW*, 24: 587–9.
38. WW to MAHP, Aug. 11, 1912, box 33, folder 7, WWCP.
39. WW to Louis Wiley, Sept. 5, 1912, *PWW*, 25: 107.
40. Juergens, *News From The White House*, 63. Roosevelt, moreover, made a habit of denying statements in the press that he had made. H. W. Brands, *T. R.: The Last Romantic* (New York: Basic Books, 1997), 507.
41. WW to MAHP, Aug. 25, 1912, *PWW*, 25: 55.
42. *New York Age*, July 11, 1912, 4.
43. Regarding Trotter and the National Independent Political League, see p. 89.
44. Trotter to WW, July 18, 1912, *PWW*, 24: 558.
45. Statement by Waldron, the *Crisis*, Sept. 1912, 216–17.
46. WW to OGV, Aug. 23, 1912, *PWW*, 25: 52–53.
47. OGV to WW with enclosure, Aug. 28, 1912, ibid., 25: 60–1.
48. Waldron statement, 217.
49. Quoted in ASL, *Wilson*, 499.
50. Ibid., and RSB, *Wilson: Life and Letters*, 3: 383–4.
51. JD to WW, Aug. 24, 1912, reel 30, WWP.
52. "A Talk in New York to Editors of Foreign-Language Newspapers," Sept. 4, 1912, *PWW*, 25: 94–7.
53. Notes for a Talk before the Platform Committee at the Democratic National Convention, June 26, 1912, American Federation of Labor Papers, Pres.' Office, Speeches and Writings, box 49, folder 7, State Historical Society of Wisconsin, Madison, Wisc. Hereinafter cited as AFL Papers.
54. Marc Karson, *American Labor Unions and Politics, 1900–1918* (Carbondale: Southern Illinois University Press, 1958), 71.
55. Quoted in ASL, *Wilson*, 471.
56. Sara Hunter Graham, *Woman Suffrage and the New Democracy* (New Haven: Yale University Press, 1996), 9 and 73.
57. *Woman's Protest*, July 1912, 4.
58. Inez H. Irwin to Maud Wood Park, Mar. 29, 1910, quoted in ibid., 54.
59. WW to Foss, Aug. 17, 1912, reel 30, WWP.
60. Richard Lloyd Jones to WW, July 13, 1912, reel 29, ibid.
61. OGV to Susan W. Fitzgerald, Aug. 14, 1912, box 92, WWPP, and *PWW*, 24: 29, n. 1.
62. O'Brian, *The Story of the Sun*, 203, and George Britt, *Forty Years—Forty Millions: The Career of Frank A. Munsey* (New York: Farrar & Rineha, 1935), 1–19.

63. Munsey to HW, Nov. 22, 1909, box 10, HW Papers.
64. Munsey, published lecture, *Journalism*, delivered at Yale University, Jan. 12, 1903, 4, 18–20, and 25.
65. Robert Davis to Frank Munsey, July 26, 1912, letter file, 1910–20, Robert Hobart Davis Papers, Manuscripts and Archives Section, New York Public Library. Hereinafter cited as Davis Papers.
66. Aug. 20, 1912, ibid.
67. Three of Munsey's newspapers, the *Baltimore News*, the *Boston Journal*, and the *Washington Times* were examined from Jan. to June 1912 for the treatment his press accorded Wilson during the preconvention campaign.
68. Milton A. McRae to WW, July 6, 1912, reel 28, WWP.
69. EWS to R. F. Paine, Aug. 9, 1912, series 1, subseries 1.2, box 14, folder 9, EWS Papers.
70. For example, Gilson Gardner, the Scripps' NEA correspondent in Washington, D. C. was for Roosevelt as was Negley Cochran, the editor of Scripps's non advertisement newspaper, the *Day Book* (Chicago). Both men exerted influence throughout "the concern" (Gardner to T. Roosevelt, July 1, 1912, series 1, reel 148, Theodore Roosevelt Papers, MDLC. (hereinafter cited as Roosevelt Papers), and Negley Cochran to James G. Scripps, Apr. 1, 1918, box 3, folder "Scripps, James G.," Negley Cochran Collection, Local History Department, Toledo-Lucas County Public Library, Toledo, Ohio (hereinafter cited as Cochran Collection)).
71. EWS to John S. Scripps, Aug. 15, 1912, series 1, subseries 1.2, box 14, folder 9, EWS Papers. See also, EWS to R. F. Paine, Aug. 9, 1912, ibid; and EWS to H. N. Rickey, copy to Cochran, July 20, 1912, box 3, folder "Scripps, James G.," Cochran Collection.
72. Alphonse Chrostowski to WW, July 14, 1912, translation of his editorial of July 11, 1912, enclosed, reel 29, WWP.
73. See Milton A. McRae to WW, July 6, 1912, reel 28, ibid., and Robert Davis to Frank Munsey, July 26, 1912, letter file, 1910–20, Davis Papers.
74. Garrett Droppers to WW, Aug. 21, 1912, *PWW*, 25: 50.
75. Roy Dee Keehn to WW, July 29, 1912, ibid., 24: 574. Keehn was the general counsel for Hearst's *Chicago Examiner* and *Chicago American*, ibid., n. 1.
76. The *Chicago Tribune* reported Wilson's "character assassin" remark, Apr. 6, 1912, quoted in ASL, *Wilson*, 410–11.

Chapter 9 Wilson's Election Campaign of 1912 and the Press

1. The Democrats had majorities in both houses of Congress for a short while during Cleveland's second administration, but they were more nominal than real. Mowry, "Election of 1912," in Arthur M. Schlesinger, Jr. ed., *The Coming to Power* (New York: Chelsea House, 1972), 292.
2. Robert H. Wiebe, *The Search for Order, 1877–1920* (1967; reprint, New York: Hill and Wang, 1999), 217.
3. *Philadelphia Record*, Aug. 17, 1912, quoted in John Wells Davidson, ed., *A Crossroads of Freedom: The 1912 Campaign Speeches of Woodrow Wilson* (New Haven: Yale University Press, 1956), 56, n. 1.

4. For a discussion of the New Freedom, see Clements, *Woodrow Wilson*, 81–5.
5. Quoted in ASL, *Wilson*, 490.
6. For an explanation of the disservice the candidates did to one another's views, see John Milton Cooper, Jr., *The Warrior and the Priest: Woodrow Wilson and Theodore Roosevelt* (Cambridge: Belknap Press of Harvard University Press, 1983), 208–9.
7. Roosevelt to Sir Horace Plunkett, Aug. 3, 1912, Series 3A, reel 379, Roosevelt Papers, and Brands, *T.R.*, 718.
8. "Advertise the Presidential Nominees," *Fourth Estate*, July 13, 1912, 8. See also, "Demand for Press Agents in Politics," ibid., Mar. 2, 1912, 19; "How Press Agents Make Presidents," ibid., Apr. 13, 1912, 4; "Newspapers As An Aid to Political Candidates," ibid., Apr. 6, 1912, 6; Political Advertising," ibid., Nov. 16, 1912, 8; and George Kibbe Turner, "Manufacturing Public Opinion: The New Art of Making Presidents by Press Bureaus," *McClure's* Magazine, July 1912, 316–27.
9. Irwin, "The Power of the Press," *Collier's*, Jan. 21, 1911, 15.
10. Edwin E. Slosson, "The Place of Journalism in University Education," *Independent*, Nov. 23, 1911, 1128.
11. Irwin, "All the News That's Fit to Print," *Collier's*, May 6, 1911, 17–19, and OGV, "Some Weaknesses of Modern Journalism" *University of Kansas News-Bulletin*, Nov. 2, 1914, 5.
12. *San Francisco Chronicle*, Oct. 31, 1912, 6.
13. Copies of these and other campaign materials can be found in box 36, Albert Sidney Burleson Papers and box 34, Robert W. Woolley Papers, MDLC, Washington, D. C. Hereinafter cited respectively as Burleson Papers and Woolley Papers.
14. JD, *The Wilson Era*, 75.
15. Circular, "Has a Wilson and Marshall Club Been Formed in your Community yet?" Enclosed in Sen. T. P. Gore to Democratic Friends, Oct. 3, 1912, folder "Elections—1912—Oct.–Nov.," box 670, JD Papers.
16. JD to Louis D. Brandeis, Aug. 5, 1912, Louis Dembitz Brandeis Papers, University of Louisville, copy in MDLC. Hereinafter cited as Brandeis Papers.
17. R. W. Woolley to JD, Oct. 3, 1912, folder "Elections—1912—Oct.–Nov.," box 670, JD Papers and JD, *Wilson Era*, 78.
18. Address, St. Louis, Mo., Oct. 9, 1912, box 94, WWPP.
19. R. W. Woolley to JD, Oct. 1, 1912, folder "Elections—1912—June–Oct.," JD Papers.
20. R. W. Woolley to Louis D. Brandeis, Oct. 9, 1912, reel 29, Brandeis Papers.
21. Jana L. Hyde, "The Entertainment Media, 1900–present," in Sloan and Startt, *The Media in America*, 365.
22. "The 'Talker' as Spellbinder," *Talking Machine World*, Mar. 15, 1908, 35, and "Talking Machine in Politics," ibid., June 15, 1908, 1.
23. Ibid. See also, "Fifteen Columbia Records by Wm. H. Taft," ibid., Sept. 15, 1908, 1, "Ten Edison Records by William Jennings Bryan," *Edison Phonographic Monthly*, June 1908, 6–7, and "Making the Taft Records," ibid., Sept. 1908, 4.

24. Regarding Roosevelt's first recording experience, see "Roosevelt Records," ibid., Sept. 1912, 8.
25. The recordings were: "On the Third Party," "On the Trusts," "To the Farmers," "Democratic Principles," "On Labor," and "On the Tariff." Subj. file "Woodrow Wilson," Recorded Sound Reference Center, Library of Congress, Washington, D. C.
26. "Phonograph to give Wilson to all of U.S.," *NYT*, Aug. 9, 1912, 1, and "Records of Taft, Wilson and Roosevelt," *Talking Machine World*, Oct. 15, 1912, 26.
27. JD, *Wilson Era*, 71.
28. Huston Thompson, "Why Wilson Disliked Reporters," 5, clipping, box 254, Clapper Papers
29. David Nasaw, "Learning to Go to the Movies," *American Heritage*, 44 (Nov. 1993): 84–8, and Raymond Fielding, *The American Newsreel 1911–1967* (Norman: University of Oklahoma Press, 1972), 65.
30. Quoted in ibid., 73.
31. Ibid., 80–4.
32. Nasaw, "Learning to Go to the Movies," 90.
33. WW to MAHP, Aug. 25, 1912, *PWW*, 25: 55–6.
34. Fielding, *The American Newsreel*, 90, and Veronica M. Gillespie, "T. R. on Film," *Quarterly Journal of the Library of Congress* 34 (Jan. 1977): 42.
35. A Common Acquaintance, "Wilson–Taft–Roosevelt: The Candidates Compared—An Intimate Evening With Each," *World's Work*, Sept. 1912, 572.
36. "Theodore Roosevelt: The Picture Man," *Moving Picture World*, Oct. 22, 1910, 920.
37. "Teddy Roosevelt in Pictures," ibid., Oct. 19, 1912, 251.
38. "Governor Wilson At His Summer Home," *Moving Picture News*, July 6, 1912, 12, and "Phonograph to Give Wilson to all of U.S.," *NYT*, Aug. 9, 1912, 1.
39. "Campaign Pictures," *Motography*, July 6, 1912, 25.
40. "Phonograph to give Wilson to All of U.S.," and the TV documentary, "The American Experience: Woodrow Wilson," Part 1, PBS (Channel 11, Chicago) Jan. 6, 2002.
41. "Governor Wilson in Universal Films," *Universal Weekly*, Oct. 5, 1912, 1.
42. "The Old Way and the New," Universal Film, Mfg., 1912, VBC 1424, Library of Congress Motion Picture Collection, Motion Picture, Broadcasting, and Recorded Sound Division, Library of Congress, Washington, D. C.
43. Huston Thompson, "Woodrow Wilson, Master of Dreams," *Dearborn Independent*, May 8, 1926, 23–4, box 254, Clapper Papers.
44. Charles Willis Thompson to his wife, Oct. 6, 1912, *PWW*, 25: 361, and Huston Thompson, "Woodrow Wilson: Master of Dreams," 12–13.
45. Thompson, *Presidents I've Known*, 292.
46. Oliver P. Newman, "Woodrow Wilson Grieves Because Some People Think He's a 'Stiff, Old Ass,'" *Toledo News-Bee*, Nov. 6, 1912, 8.
47. *New York Journal of Commerce and Commercial Bulletin*, July 3, 1912, 6.

48. *PWW*, 25: IX. August Heckscher claims that Wilson's campaign speeches of 1912 "rank with the greatest platform accomplishments of American political history." *Woodrow Wilson*, 258.
49. RSB, *Wilson: Life and Letters*, 3: 393.
50. Ibid., 392.
51. *New York World*, Nov. 4, 1912, 10. For a comprehensive editorial extolling the virtues of candidate Wilson, see *BS*, Nov. 4, 1912, 6. The above composite profile of the pro-Wilson press during the campaign is based on a cross section of 26 newspapers from July to November 1912, and on "Forecasting the Verdict of November Fifth," *LD*, Oct. 5, 1912, 545–7; "Tariff Ideas of Roosevelt and Wilson," ibid., Sept. 14, 1912, 408–9; "The Trusts and the Candidates," ibid., Nov. 2, 1912, 769–71; and "Trust Remedies of Roosevelt and Wilson," ibid., Sept. 28, 1912, 499–501.
52. R. F. Paine to EWS, Aug. 8, 1912, Series 1, Subseries 1, box 32, folder 11, EWS Papers.
53. J. C. Harper to EWS, Aug. 23, 1912, folder 7, ibid.
54. Rickey and Howard related their impressions of Wilson to Milton A. McRae, McRae to EWS, Aug. 31, 1912, folder 10, ibid.
55. Ibid.
56. Oliver Knight, ed., *I Protest: Selected Disquisitions of E. W. Scripps* (Madison: University of Wisconsin Press, 1966), 449. In the end, Gardner wrote a series of six favorable articles on Roosevelt and the Bull Moose party.
57. *Cleveland Press* and *Toledo News-Bee*, Aug. 9–Oct. 15, 1912.
58. James G. Scripps to N. D. Cochran (and to all Scripps editors), Oct. 15, 1912, folder "Scripps, James G.," box 3, Cochran Collection.
59. Harold Cochran to N. D. Cochran, Oct. 16, 1912, folder "Harold to N. D. Cochran 1906–15," ibid., and Vance H. Trimble, *The Astonishing Mr. Scripps: The Turbulent Life of America's Penny Press Lord* (Ames, Iowa: Iowa State University Press, 1992), 322–3.
60. For example, see *Toledo News-Bee*, Oct. 19–Nov. 4, 1912.
61. Reported by Robert Davis to Frank Munsey, July 26, 1912, Davis Papers.
62. *San Francisco Examiner*, Sept. 13, 1912, 1 and 15–16.
63. Enclosed in a letter from John Temple Graves to JT and forwarded to WW, Sept. 16, 1912, reel 30, WWP.
64. Graves to WW, Sept. 24, 1912, box 92, WWPP.
65. *New York American*, Oct. 10, 1912, and Woolley to JD, with article enclosed, Oct. 9 [10], 1912, folder "Elections—1912—Oct.–Nov. 11" ibid.
66. *New York American*, Oct. 14, 1912, 20.
67. *New York Evening Journal*, Nov. 2, 1912, 12, and *San Francisco Examiner*, Nov. 4, 1912, 20.
68. WW to Hapgood, Oct. 12, 1912, *PWW*, 25: 449.
69. *Grand Rapids Herald*, Oct. 4, 1912, 6.
70. *Milwaukee Sentinel*, Oct. 23, 1912, 6.
71. *Milwaukee Free Press*, Nov. 1, 1912, 4.
72. M. J. Wade to JD, Nov. 4, 1912, box 670, JD Papers.
73. For instance, see *St. Louis Globe-Democrat*, Oct. 12, 1912, 8, and Jim Allee Hart, *A History of the "St. Louis Globe-Democrat"* (Columbia: University of

Missouri Press, 1961), 188–9. The above criticism of Wilson was based on a cross section of 20 newspapers from July through November 1912, and "The Trust and the Candidates," Nov. 2, 1912, 769–71. Also consulted were: *the American Review of Reviews, Collier's, the Independent, Leslie's Illustrated Weekly Newspaper, Munsey's Magazine*, and the *Outlook*.

74. E. Leake ed. (editor of the *Woodland Daily Democrat*) to JD, Oct. 5, 1912, and *Los Angeles Tribune* Oct. 2, 1912, clipping enclosed in Robert Woolley to WGM, Oct. 9, 1912, box 94, WWPP. Also, *Salt Lake City Herald Republican*, Oct. 22, 23, 25, 28, and 30, 1912, clippings in reel 512, WWP. Wilson discussed this matter with Col. House. See, EMH Diary, Oct. 12, 1912.
75. Little is known about the validity of Park's comments nor about how they came into the possession of the *Los Angeles Tribune*. The *Herald Republican*'s handling of Park's charges and subsequent statements concerning them hint at entrapment. It reported that Wilson could not recall Park, but upon checking records, he remembered that he had rejected some of Park's work because it was confusing. Thereupon, the newspaper produced a letter Wilson wrote recommending him for a position at the Kansas State Agricultural College saying he was a promising scholar (*Herald Republican*, Oct. 22, 1912). Bearing in mind the newspaper's explanation that Park was Wilson's "favorite student," Wilson's recommendation for Park is curious. It comprised only two sentences of a total of five and a half lines in length. How can the brevity of the letter be explained? How did the newspaper manage to obtain it? What was the context of Wilson's alleged original comments? Did he make them once or often?
76. Mary's first husband, Thomas Hulbert, a mining engineer, died in 1889. The following year she married Thomas Peck, a manufacturer in Pittsfield, Mass., but her second marriage was difficult from the start, and in 1911 she brought suit for divorce against her husband. It was granted in 1912. For accounts of Wilson's relationship with her see, Heckscher, *Woodrow Wilson*, 161–2 and 185–90, and especially Phyllis Lee Levin, *Edith and Woodrow: The Wilson White House* (New York: Scribner, 2001), 124–32.
77. WW to MAHP, Sept. 29, 1912, box 33, folder 7, WWCP.
78. White, *Wilson*, 269.
79. For example, see "Roman Catholic Churches' Recent Attentions to Gov. and Mrs. Wilson," and "As to Woodrow Wilson and the Knights of Columbus," *Jeffersonian*, Oct. 31, 1912, 3 and 8.
80. WW to WGM, Oct. 22, 1912, box 517, WGM Papers.
81. J. C. Monaghan to WW, Aug. 30, 1912, reel 30, WWP. See also, *PWW*, 25: 64, n. 1.
82. For instance, see JK to Michael J. Drummond Aug. 13, 1912, reel 30, WWP.
83. *Chicago Defender*, Oct. 5, 1912, 7.
84. *Cleveland Gazette*, Oct. 5, 1912, and *Washington Bee*, Aug. 3, 1912, 4, *Chicago Broad Ax, Chicago Defender, Indianapolis Freeman, New York Age*, and *Savannah Tribune*, July–Nov., 1912.
85. The African American editors were still irate about the Brownsville, Texas incident of 1906 in which some black soldiers stationed there became

involved in a fight with some white townspeople that resulted in several of the latter being shot. One was killed. Only about a dozen soldiers were involved, but at the subsequent investigation their comrades refused to testify. President Roosevelt responded by ordering three companies of the soldiers involved, either directly or indirectly, in the affair to be dishonorably discharged (Brands, *T.R.*, 587–8). These editors also held Roosevelt responsible for the exclusion of southern African American delegates from the Progressives' convention in August. ASL, "The Negro as a Factor in the Campaign of 1912," *Journal of Negro History* 32 (Jan. 1947): 96.

86. Regarding the incident in New York City, see p. 168. Taft made the above reference to Washington in 1911. Harlan, *Washington Papers*, 11: 347.
87. Moore to BTW, May 13, 1912, reel 63, BTW Papers.
88. Spencer, *Booker T. Washington*, 166, and William Calvin Chase to Emmett Jay Scott, April 28, 1911, and Chase to BTW, Apr. 17, 1912, Harlan, *Washington Papers*, 11: 118–19 and 519–20. It is also notable that one of Washington's friends reported that the *New York Age* received $2,005, a large sum of money for an African American newspaper, from the Republican National Committee and another $200 from the New York State Committee during the campaign (Charles W. Anderson to BTW, Nov. 8, 1912, ibid., 12: 49–50). For Washington's influence with the black press in general, see August Meier, "Booker T. Washington and the Negro Press," *Journal of Negro History* 38 (Jan. 1953): 67–90.
89. BTW to Charles Dewey Hillis (Taft's secretary), July 16, 1911, and Hillis to BTW, July 17, 1911, Harlan, *Washington Papers*, 11: 270–1.
90. Quoted in August Meier, "The Negro and the Democratic Party, 1875–1915," *Phylon* 17 (1956): 189. See also, Stephen R. Fox, *The Guardian of Boston: William Monroe Trotter* (New York: Athenaeum, 1970), 168.
91. For the connection between the *Crisis* and the NAACP see, "The Crisis and the NAACP," *Crisis*, Nov. 1915, 25–6.
92. Manning Marble, *W. E. B. DuBois: Black Radical Democrat* (Boston: Twayne Publishers, 1986), 77.
93. W. E. B. DuBois, *The Autobiography of W. E. B. DuBois: A Soliloquy on Viewing My Life from the Last Decade of Its First Century* (1962; reprint, New York: International Publishers, 1968), 263–4, and David Levering Lewis, *W. E. B. DuBois: Biography of a Race 1868–1919* (New York: Henry Holt & Co., 1993), 423.
94. *Crisis*, Nov. 1912, 29.
95. "Scheda Democratics" and "La Lotta Elettorale," *Il Progresso Italo-Americo*, Nov. 2, 1912, 2.
96. "Wilson Talks With Brandeis on Trusts and Immigration Greets Foreigners," *TTA*, 29 1912, Aug. *PWW*, 25: 59. Also, after the election Wilson responded to a Polish correspondent thanking him for his support during the campaign and saying, "The Polish vote was certainly most extraordinary." WW to Nicholas L. Piotrowski, Dec. 11, 1912, *PWW*, 25: 586.
97. Editorial notes, *L' Italia*, Oct. 30, 1912, reel 30, *Chicago Foreign Language Press Survey*, Chicago Public Library Omnibus Project, Works Project

Administration, Chicago, Ill., 1942. See also, "To Se Votate Per Roosevelt," *L' Italia*, Oct. 20, 1912, 6, and "L' Esito Dell 'Elezioni Coi Proiettori Elettrici," ibid., Nov. 3, 1912, 1.

98. Frederick C. Luebke, *Bonds of Loyalty: German-Americans and World War I* (De Kalb: Northern Illinois University Press, 1974), 31 and 45.
99. Carl Wittke, *The German Language Press in America* (Lexington: University of Kentucky Press, 1957), 214–15, and *Deutscher Anzeiger* (Freeport, Ill.), Oct. 30, 1912.
100. Fritiof O. Ander, "The Swedish-American Press in the Election of 1912," *Swedish Pioneer Historical Quarterly* 14 (1963): 103–26.
101. For the cultural and socialist inclination of these newspapers, the record of eastern and southern European foreign-language newspapers published in Chicago was consulted and included: *Bollettino Della Camera Di Commercio* and *L 'Italia* (Italian), *Dziennik Zwiazkowy Zgoda and Narod Polski* (Polish), *Soko* (Serbian), *Proletetarec* (Slovene), *Radnicka Straza* and *Znaje* (Croatian), *Loxias* (Greek), and *Rovnost Ludu* (Slovak). See reels 9, 28, 30, 55, and 62 of the *Chicago Foreign Language Press Survey.* For the socialist commitment of foreign-language newspapers published in this country see Dirk Hoerder, ed., *The Immigrant Labor Press in North America, 1840s to 1970s: An Annotated Biography*, 3 vols. (New York: Greenwood Press, 1987): 1: 27 and 32, 2: 15 and 313–40; and 3: 7, 17–25, 325–41.
102. George E. Reedy, *From "the" Ward "to the" White House: The Irish in American Politics* (New York: Charles Scribner's Sons, 1991), 92–3. In some cases (for instance in Cincinnati, Philadelphia, and Pittsburgh) the Irish political machines supported the Republican party.
103. Ibid., 102–3; Edwin M. Levine, *The Irish and the Irish Politician* (Notre Dame, Ind.: University of Notre Dame Press, 1966), 136–8; and William V. Shannon, *The American Irish* (New York: Macmillan, 1963), 329.
104. *Dictionary of American Biography*, s. v. "Ford, Patrick"; *Dictionary of National Biography*, s. v. "Ford, Patrick"; and "The Long Arm of Patrick Ford," *LD*, Oct. 18, 1913, 724–6.
105. *Irish World and American Industrial Liberator*, Nov. 2, 1912, 4. See also, July 13, 1914, 4, and Oct. 2, 1912, 4.
106. See p. 63.
107. *Trades Union Advocate* (Trenton, N. J.), Feb. 16, 1912, 1.
108. Ibid.
109. Campaign pamphlet, *Wilson and Labor*, 1912, in box 34, Woolley Papers.
110. Gompers, "Labor's 1912 Political Program," *American Federationist*, Oct. 1912, 804–7.
111. Gompers, "The Presidency in the Pending Campaign: The Duty of the Hour," ibid., Nov. 1912, 889–94.
112. "Woodrow Wilson As A Free Trader," *Utica Advocate*, July 20, 1912, 3; "Democratic Tariff Blundering" and "The Apologetic Candidate," ibid. Sept. 21, 1913, 3; and "Stand By Taft," ibid., Oct. 19, 1912, 4.
113. Thompson, "Progress of the Campaign," *New York Freeman's Journal and Catholic Register*, Sept. 21, 1912, 8
114. "While the Political Pot Boils," *Catholic Universe*, Oct. 25, 1912, 4.

115. Quin O'Brian, "The Church Not a Political Football," *Catholic Union and Times* (Buffalo), Oct. 31, 1912, 1.
116. One of the most enthusiastic pro-Wilson, non-denomination newspapers was *Unity* (Chicago), the official organ of the Congress of Religion. For example, see "Governor Wilson's Opportunity," Aug. 1, 1912, 341.
117. H. W. to JD, Nov. 2, 1912, editorial enclosed, box 670, JD Papers.
118. JD to Brother Editors, Oct. 19, 1912, enclosed in R. W. Woolley to JD, Oct. 21, 1912, ibid. Wilson's letter appeared in numerous newspapers and magazines. For example, see *LD*, Oct. 26, 1912, 729, and *NYT*, Oct. 27, 1912, 14.
119. JD to Brother Editors, Oct. 19, 1912, enclosed in R. W. Woolley to JD, Oct. 21, 1912, box 670, JD Papers.
120. DL, *True Story*, 60–1. Wilson did keep driving until the end. He issued his final public statement on the eve of the election. "A Statement to the Voters," *TTA*, Nov. 4, 1912, *PWW*, 25: 512–13.
121. E. W. McAdoo, *Priceless Gift*, 275; Lawrence, *True Story*, 523; and "Remarks of President Harold W. Dodds of Princeton University on the Occasion of the Placing of a Plaque on the Presidents' Box at Town Hall in Commemoration of Woodrow Wilson," Feb. 27, 1946, reel 537, WWP.
122. *New York Evening Post*, Nov. 6, 1912, 8.
123. In keeping with the trend among metropolitan newspapers of the time, most were listed as independent, but from beginning to end they were pro-Democratic and pro-Wilson.
124. A. B. Suter (editor and publisher of the *Grand Rapids Tribune*) to WW, Mar. 9, 1913, vol. 5, Burleson Papers. There is ample evidence in the form of letters from editors of small Democratic newspapers in the Wilson Papers to substantiate their advocacy of him in 1912.
125. JD to Albert Sidney Burleson, Apr. 12, 1913, reel 44, JD Papers.
126. For example, the *Sacramento Union* and the *Providence Journal* were two Republican newspapers that supported Wilson.

Chapter 10 On the Threshold of the White House

1. "Joke on Gov. Wilson," *Talking Machine World*, Nov. 15, 1912, 7.
2. "Mr. Wilson Jokes While Voting at Princeton Home," *TTA*, Nov. 5, 1912, *PWW*, 25: 518.
3. Charles Swem, unpublished ms., chap., "Attitude Toward Publicity and Newspapermen," pp. 1–2, box 87, folder 9, Swem Collection.
4. For example, Wilson informed Tumulty about his speaking confidentially to the editors of the *Newark Evening News*, WW to JT, Dec. 3, 1912, *PWW*, 25: 579.
5. H. V. Kaltenborn, *Fifty Fabulous Years, 1900–1950* (New York: G. P. Putnam's Sons, 1950), 72.
6. RSB, *American Chronicle: The Autobiography of Ray Stannard Baker* (New York: Charles Scribner's Sons, 1945), 273.

7. Arthur Bullard to Norman Davis, Apr. 3, 1927, box 6, Norman H. Davis Papers, MDLC.
8. Grasty to WW, Dec. 26, 1912, box 98, WWPP.
9. "Presidential Echoes," Feb. 25, 1912, quoted in the *Owensboro Messenger*, clipping, reel 518, WWP.
10. Quoted in Charles Willis Thompson, *Presidents I've Known*, 295.
11. DL, *True Story*, 64.
12. Thompson to Reuben Adiel Bull, Dec. 12, 1912, *PWW*, 25: 588.
13. EWM, *Priceless Gift*, 275.
14. WW to McCombs, Nov. 30, 1912, *PWW*, 25: 572.
15. EWM, *The Woodrow Wilsons*, 189.
16. Thompson, *Presidents I've Known*, 295. A watered down news report about this incident appeared in the press. See, "Wilson Says he will Use Fists on Photo Man," *TTA*, Nov. 22, 1912, *PWW*, 25: 556.
17. EWM, *The Woodrow Wilsons*, 192.
18. Quoted in Juergens, *News From the White House*, 135 and DL, *The True Story*, 344.
19. *NYT*, Feb. 4, 1913, *PWW*, 27: 96.
20. Ibid., 25: 617, n. 2.
21. EMH Diary, Feb. 14, 1913.
22. Thompson, *Presidents I've Known*, 298–301.
23. Ibid., 297.
24. For the reporters' attitude toward Ellen Wilson, see DL, *The True Story*, 64–5.
25. Ibid., 71.
26. EMH Diary, Nov. 19, 6, 7, and Dec. 9, 1912, 14, 16, 22, 24, and 27, 1913.
27. EMH to WW, Jan. 3, 1913, *PWW*, 27: 11.
28. EMH Diary, Jan. 15, 1913.
29. Ibid., Jan. 5, 1913.
30. Ibid., Jan. 8, 1913.
31. House learned of Hearst's feeling slighted from Tom Pence. Ibid., Jan. 16, 1913.
32. Quoted in the *Grand Rapids Herald*, Nov. 4, 1912, 4.
33. Address to the New York Southern Society, Dec. 17, 1912, *PWW*, 25: 602; DL, *True Story*, 68–9; and Frank Kelly, *The Fight for the White House: The Story of 1912* (New York: Thomas Y. Crowell, 1961), 285–7. The story of Haman's hanging comes from Esther 3: 7.
34. "'Beware' Says Wilson To The Panic Makers," *Toledo News Bee*, Dec. 18, 1912, 9.
35. Quoted in "President-Elect Wilson's Dilemma," *LD*, Nov. 16, 1912, 887.
36. For example, see the *Baltimore News*, Oct. 3, 1912, 14.
37. *New York Age*, Feb. 27, 1913, 4, and *Washington Bee*, Nov. 2, 1912, 4.
38. *Crisis*, Dec. 1912, 76.
39. Alexander Walters to WW, Dec. 17, 1912, PWW, 25: 606–8.
40. *Irish World and American Industrial Liberator*, Nov. 16, 1912, 4.
41. Vierick to Theodore Roosevelt, Nov. 7, 1912, reel 156, Roosevelt Papers.

42. For example, see Charles Edward Russell, "Comment on Things Doing," *Changing Nation*, Nov. 9, 1912, 1 and cartoon, ibid., Nov. 23, 1912, cover.
43. Watson to Hon. W. J. Jelks, Dec. 21, 1912, folder 158, Thomas E. Watson Papers, Southern Historical Collection, Manuscripts Department, Library of the University of North Carolina at Chapel Hill.
44. H. C. Morrison, "The Old-Time Methodist Preacher," *Pentecostal Herald* (Louisville), Feb. 5, 1913, 1, enclosed in R. O. Alexander to WW, Feb. 8, 1913, reel 27, WWP.
45. *Toledo News-Bee*, Nov. 7, 1912, 8.
46. Brownlow, "Wilson's Personal Relations," *Lectures and Seminar at the University of Chicago*, 92, copy, reel 537, WWP.
47. See p. 15.
48. *Constitutional Government in the United States* (New York: Columbia University Press, 1908), 68.
49. *Leaders of Men*, T. H. Vail Motter ed. (Princeton, N. J.: Princeton University Press, 1952), 42.
50. "Hide-And-Seek Politics," *NAR*, May 1910, 585, 588, and 591–2.
51. Ibid., 598.
52. See p. 15.
53. See p. 53.
54. See p. 55.
55. "Address to the South Carolina Press Association," June 2, 1911, *PWW*, 23: 117.
56. "Address to the New York Southern Society," Dec. 17, 1912, *PWW*, 25: 594.
57. Robert T. Dallek, *Hail To The Chief: The Making and Unmaking of American Presidents* (New York: Hyperion, 1996), 139.
58. Richard Oulahan, chap. "The Stage at Washington," p. 4, unpublished ms., "Presidents and Publicity," box 1, Herbert Hoover Presidential Library, West Branch Iowa.

Bibliography

Manuscript Sources

Herbert Baxter Adams Papers, Special Collections, Milton Eisenhower Library, Johns Hopkins University.

American Federation of Labor Papers, State Historical Society of Wisconsin, Madison.

Ray Stannard Baker Papers, Manuscript Division, Library of Congress.

Albert J. Beveridge Papers, Manuscript Division, Library of Congress.

Henry Wilkenson Bragdon Collection, JHU Copy, Special Collections, Milton Eisenhower Library, Johns Hopkins University.

Louis Dembitz Brandeis Papers, University of Louisville, Microfilm Copy, Manuscript Division, Library of Congress.

Brisbane Family Papers, Manuscript Collections, Syracuse University Library.

James Bryce Papers, Bodleian Library, Oxford.

Albert Sidney Burleson Papers, Manuscript Division, Library of Congress.

Raymond Clapper Papers, Manuscript Division, Library of Congress.

Negley Cochran Collection, Local History Department, Toledo–Lucas County Public Library, Toledo, Ohio.

Josephus Daniels Papers, Manuscript Division, Library of Congress.

Norman Davis Papers, Manuscript Division, Library of Congress.

Robert Hobart Davis Papers, Manuscripts and Archives Section, New York Public Library, New York City.

William Dudley Foulke Papers, Manuscript Division, Library of Congress.

William Bayard Hale Papers, Manuscripts and Archives, Yale University Library.

Phoebe Hearst Papers, Bancroft Library, University of California, Berkeley.

Hemphill Family Papers, Special Collections Library, Duke University.

Hamilton Holt Papers, Department of Archives and Special Collections, Rollins College, Winter Park, Fla.

Edward M. House Diary, Edward M. House Papers, Manuscripts and Archives, Yale University Library.

LaFollette Family Collection, Robert Marion LaFollette, Sr., Manuscript Division, Library of Congress.

David Lawrence Papers, Seeley G. Mudd Manuscript Library, Princeton University.

William Gibbs McAdoo Papers, Manuscript Division, Library of Congress.

Richard Oulahan Papers, Herbert Hoover Presidential Library, West Branch, Iowa.

Walter Hines Page Papers, Manuscript Division, Houghton Library, Harvard University.
Amos Pinchot Papers, Manuscript Division, Library of Congress.
Joseph Pulitzer Papers, Manuscript Division, Library of Congress.
Joseph Pulitzer, Jr. Papers, Manuscript Division, Library of Congress.
Theodore Roosevelt Papers, Manuscript Division, Library of Congress.
E. W. Scripps Papers, Archives and Special Collections, Vernon R. Alden Library, Ohio University, Athens, Ohio.
Charles Swen Collection, Supplement to the Woodrow Wilson Collection, Seeley G. Mudd Manuscript Library, Princeton University.
Ida M. Tarbell Papers, Pelletier Library, Allegheny College, Meadville, Pa.
Joseph Tumulty Papers, Manuscript Division, Library of Congress.
Oscar W. Underwood Papers, Alabama Department of Archives and History, Montgomery, Ala.
Oswald Garrison Villard Papers, Manuscript Department, Houghton Library, Harvard University.
Booker T. Washington Papers, Manuscript Division, Library of Congress.
Thomas E. Watson Papers, Southern Historical Collection, University of North Carolina, Chapel Hill.
Henry Watterson Collection, University of Louisville, Microfilm Edition, Manuscript Division, Library of Congress.
Henry Watterson Papers, Manuscript Division, Library of Congress.
Woodrow Wilson Collection, Seeley G. Mudd Manuscript Library, Princeton University.
Governor Thomas Woodrow Wilson Correspondence, 1909–14, New Jersey State Archives, Trenton.
Woodrow Wilson Papers, Manuscript Division, Library of Congress.
Woodrow Wilson Papers Project, Seeley G. Mudd Manuscript Library, Princeton University.
Robert W. Woolley Papers, Manuscript Division, Library of Congress.

Special Collections

The Chicago Foreign Language Press Survey. Chicago Public Library Omnibus Project, Works Project Administration, 1942, Chicago Historical Society.
Trentonia Collection. Trenton Public Library.
Wilson Materials. New Jersey Historical Society, Newark, N. J.
Wilson Materials. Record Sound Reference Center, Library of Congress, Washington, D. C.
Wilson Materials. Special Collections and University Archives. Rutgers University, New Brunswick, N. J.

Newspapers

Atlanta Constitution, 1902, 1912–13.
Baltimore American, 1913.

Baltimore News, 1912–13.
Baltimore Sun, 1907, 1910–12.
Boston Evening Transcript, 1902, 1911–12.
Boston Globe, 1912.
Boston Journal, 1912.
Charlotte Daily Observer, 1902, 1912.
Chicago Daily News, 1912.
Chicago Daily Tribune, 1912.
Christian Science Monitor, 1912.
Cleveland Press, 1912–13.
Columbia (S. C.) The State, 1911
Dallas Morning News, 1912.
Denver Daily News, 1908.
Denver Rocky Mountain News, 1908, 1912–13.
Gary Tribune, 1912.
Grand Rapids Herald, 1912–13.
Hammond (Ind.) Lake County Times, 1912.
Houston Daily Post, 1912.
Jacksonville Florida Times-Union, 1912.
Kansas City (Mo.) Star, 1912–13.
Los Angeles Times, 1912.
Louisville Courier-Journal, 1911–12.
Madison Wisconsin State Journal, 1912.
Milwaukee Daily News, 1912.
Milwaukee Free Press, 1912.
Milwaukee Journal, 1912.
Milwaukee Sentinel, 1912.
Mobile Register, 1912.
Montgomery Advertiser, 1912.
Newark Evening News, 1910–12.
Newark Star, 1910–12.
New Orleans Daily Picayune, 1912.
New Orleans Times-Democrat, 1912.
New York American, 1907, 1910–13.
New York Evening Journal, 1907, 1910.
New York Evening Post, 1902, 1907, 1910, 1912.
New York Herald, 1908, 1910, 1912.
New York Press, 1910,1912.
New York Sun, 1902, 1907, 1910–13.
New York Times, 1902, 1904, 1907, 1910–13.
New York Tribune, 1902, 1910, 1912–13.
New York World, 1902, 1907, 1910–13.
Oklahoma City Daily Oklahoman, 1912.
Philadelphia Evening Bulletin, 1910, 1912.
Philadelphia Inquirer, 1910, 1911.
Philadelphia North American, 1911.
Philadelphia Press, 1907, 1908, 1910.

Philadelphia Public Ledger, 1912.
Philadelphia Record, 1910, 1911.
Phoenix Arizona Republican, 1912–13.
Pittsburgh Post, 1912.
Portland Oregonian, 1912.
Raleigh News and Observer, 1911–12.
Salt Lake Tribune, 1912.
Sacramento Union, 1912.
San Francisco Chronicle, 1912.
San Francisco Examiner, 1912–13.
Seattle Times, 1912.
St. Louis Globe-Democrat, 1912.
St. Louis Post Dispatch, 1913.
Toledo News Bee, 1912.
Trenton Daily State Gazette, 1911–12.
Trenton Evening Times, 1911.
Trenton True American, 1910–12.
Washington Post, 1912.
Washington Times, 1912.
Woodbury (N. J.) Constitution, 1910–11.

Special Interest Publications

African American

Baltimore Afro-American, 1912–13.
Boston Guardian, 1911–13.
Chicago Broad Ax, 1912–13.
Chicago Defender, 1912–13.
Cleveland Gazette, 1912–13.
Indianapolis Freeman, 1912–13.
New York Age, 1910–13.
Savannah Tribune, 1912–13.
Washington (D. C.) Bee, 1912–13.
Wichita Searchlight, 1912.

Business

New York Journal of Commerce and Commercial, 1912.
Wall Street Journal, 1910–12.

Ethnic

Deutscher Anzeiger (Freeport, Ill.), 1912.
Gaelic American (New York), 1912.
Irish World and Industrial Liberator (New York), 1912–13.
National Hibernian (Washington, D. C.), 1912.
Il Progresso Italo-Americano (New York), 1912.

Newspapers in the Chicago Foreign Language Press Survey
Bollettino Della Camera Di Commercio, 1911–12.
Dziennik Zwiazkowy Zgoda, 1910.
L'Italia, 1912.
Loxias, 1908–18.
Narod Polski, 1917.
Proletarec, 1906.
Radnicka Straza, 1907.
Rovnost Ludu, 1912.
Soko, 1912–13.

Labor
American Federationist (Washington, D. C.), 1910–13.
Iron City Trades Journal (Pittsburgh), 1912.
Labor Journal (Rochester, N. Y.), 1912.
Labor World (New York City and Jersey City), 1910.
National Labor Tribune (Pittsburgh), 1911–12.
Trades Union Advocate (Trenton), 1910–13.
Trade Unionist (Washington, D. C.), 1910–13.
Union Leader (Chicago), 1912.
Utica (N. Y.) Advocate, 1910, 1912.

Religious
Catholic Citizen (Milwaukee), 1912.
Catholic Union and Times (Buffalo), 1912.
Catholic Universe (Cleveland), 1912.
Christian Advocate (Chicago), 1912.
Christian Register (Boston), 1912.
Congregationalist (Boston), 1912.
Continent (Chicago), 1912.
Freeman's Journal and Catholic Ragister (New York), 1912.
Herald of Gospel Liberty (Dayton, Tenn.), 1912.
Indiana Catholic (Indianapolis), 1912.
Living Church (Milwaukee), 1912.
Methodist Review (New York), 1912.
The Pilot (Boston), 1912.
Providence Visitor (R. I.), 1912.
Unity (Chicago), 1912.
Western Watchman (St. Louis), 1912.

Socialist and Radical
Appeal to Reason (Girard, Kans.), 1912.
Chicago Evening World, 1912.
The Coming Age (Girard, Kans.), 1912.
The Intercollegiate Socialist (New York), 1913.
Milwaukee Leader, 1912–13.

New York Call, 1912–13.
Progressive Woman (Chicago), 1912–13.
Social Democratic Herald (Milwaukee), 1912.
Solidarity (New Castle, Pa.), 1910–12.
The World (Oakland, Calif.), 1911–12.

Suffragist and Antisuffragist
The Remonstrance, 1912–13.
The Suffragist, 1913.
Woman's Journal, 1911–13.
The Woman's Protest, 1912–13.

Trade Journals

Film
Moving Picture News, 1912–13.
Moving Picture World, 1911–13.
Universal Weekly, 1912.

The Press
Editor and Publisher, 1911–13.
The Fourth Estate, 1911–13.

Recorded Sound
Edison Phonograph Monthly, 1903–12.
Nickelodeon (Motography 1911–), 1910–18.
Talking Machine World, 1908, 1912.

Periodicals and Reform Journals

American Review of Reviews, 1902, 1905, 1907, 1910–13.
Collier's, 1911–12.
The Commoner (Lincoln, Nebr.), 1912–13.
The Crisis, 1910–13.
Current Literature, 1912.
The Forum, 1911–12.
Harper's Weekly, 1906–13.
Hearst's Magazine, 1911–13.
The Independent, 1902, 1909–13.
The Jeffersonian (Thomson, Ga.), 1912–13.
LaFollette's Weekly Magazine (Madison, Wisc.), 1912–13.
Leslie's, 1911–12.
Literary Digest, 1906–13.
Munsey's Magazine, 1912.

The Nation, 1907, 1909, 1913.
North American Review, 1911–12.
Outlook, 1902, 1905, 1907, 1910–12.
Princeton Alumni Weekly, 1900–02, 1907–10.
Saturday Evening Post, 1911–12.
Watson's Magazine (Thomson, Ga.), 1911–12.
Woman's Home Companion, 1912.
World's Work, 1908, 1911–1913.

Published Letters and Works

Baker, Ray Stannard. *Woodrow Wilson: Life and Letters*. 8 vols. 1927–39. Reprint, Potomac Edition, 6 vols., New York: Charles Scribner's Sons.
Harlan, Louis R. et al., eds. *The Booker T. Washington Papers*. 13 vols. Urbana: University of Illinois Press, 1972–84.
Hendrick, Burton J. *The Life and Letters of Walter H. Page*. 3 vols. 1922. Reprint, Garden City, N. Y.: Doubleday, Page & Company, 1924–25.
Knight, Oliver, ed. *I Protest: Selected Disquisitions of E. W. Scripps*. Madison: University of Wisconsin Press, 1966.
Link, Arthur S. et al., eds. *The Papers of Woodrow Wilson*. 69 vols. Princeton: Princeton University Press, 1966–91.
McAdoo, Eleanor Wilson. *The Priceless Gift: The Love Letters of Woodrow Wilson and Ellen Axson Wilson*. New York: McGraw Hill Company, 1962.
Seymour, Charles, ed. *The Intimate Papers of Colonel House*. 4 vols. Boston: Houghton Mifflin Company, 1926–28.
St. John-Stevas, Norman. *The Collected Works of Walter Bagehot*. 15 vols. London: The Economist, 1965–86.

Works by Woodrow Wilson

"The Author Himself." *Atlantic Monthly*, September 1891, 406–13.
"Cabinet Government in the United States." *International Review* 6 (August 1879): 146–63.
"A Calendar of Great Americans." *Forum*, February 1894, 715–27.
Congressional Government: A Study in American Politics. 1885. Reprint, New York: Meridian Books, 1956.
Constitutional Government in the United States. New York: Columbia University Press, 1908.
"Democracy and Efficiency." *Atlantic Monthly*, March 1901, 289–99.
Division and Reunion 1829–1889. 1893. Reprint, New York: Longmans, Green and Company, 1929.
"For Government by the People." *Harper's Weekly*, December 9, 1911, 20–1.
"Hide-And-Seek Politics." *North American Review*, May 1910, 585–601.
A History of the American People, 5 vols. New York: Harper & Row Publishers, 1902.
"A Language with a Style." *Atlantic Monthly*, September 1898, 363–74.

Leaders of Men. T. H. Vail Motter, ed. Princeton: Princeton University Press, 1952.
"A Literary Politician." *Atlantic Monthly*, November 1895, 668–80.
"Living Principles of Democracy." *Harper's Weekly*, April 9, 1910, 9–10.
"The Making of the Nation." *Atlantic Monthly*, July 1897, 1–14.
"Mere Literature." *Atlantic Monthly*, December 1893, 820–8.
"Mr. Cleveland As President." *Atlantic Monthly*, March 1897, 289–300.
"Mr. Goldwin Smith's 'Views' On Our Political History." *Forum*, December 1893, 489–99.
An Old Master and Other Political Essays. New York: Charles Scribner's Sons, 1893.
"On An Author's Choice of Company." *Century Magazine*, March 1896, 775–9.
"On Being Human." *Atlantic Monthly*, September 1897, 320–9.
"On the Writing of History." *Century Magazine*, September 1895, 787–93.
"Politics." *Atlantic Monthly*, November 1907, 635–46.
"Princeton in the Nation's Service." *Forum*, December 1896, 447–61.
"The Princeton Preceptorial System." *Independent*, August 3, 1905, 239–40.
"The Proper Perspective of American History." *Forum*, July 1895, 544–59.
"The Reconstruction of the Southern States." *Atlantic Monthly*, January 1901, 1–15.
The State: Elements of Historical and Practical Politics. Revised edition. Boston: D. C. Heath & Co., 1898.
"The States and the Federal Government." *North American Review*, May 1908, 684–701.
"The Tariff Make-Believe." *North American Review*, October 1909, 535–56.
"A Wit and a Seer." *Atlantic Monthly*, October 1898, 527–40.

Contemporary Articles and Books

"Advertise the Presidential Candidates." *Fourth Estate*, July 13, 1912, 8.
"After Exposure What?" *Nation*, March 22, 1906, 234.
"Animated Journalism." *World's Work*, October 1910, 13476–7.
Arnold, Cloe. "The Governor's Lady." *Delineator*, July 1912, 18.
Bacon, Charles Reade. *A People Awakened: The Story of Woodrow Wilson's First Campaign*. Garden City, N. Y.: Doubleday, Page & Company, 1912.
Barry, David S. "News-Getting at the Capital." *Chautauquan*, 1896, 282–6.
Bonaparte, Hon. Charles J. "Government by Public Opinion." *Forum*, October 1908, 384–90.
Bridges, Robert. "President Woodrow Wilson." *American Review of Reviews*, July 1902, 36–9.
——. "President Woodrow Wilson and College Earnestness." *World's Work*, January 1908, 9792–7.
——. "Princeton University: The Kind of Men Who Made It." *Outlook*, August 1902, 835–8.
Brooks, Sydney. "The Yellow Press: An English View." *Harper's Weekly*, December 23, 1911, 11.
Bryce, James. *The American Commonwealth*. 2 vols. London: Macmillan, 1888.

"Campaign Pictures." *Motography*, July 6, 1912, 25–6.

"The Carnegie Foundation for the Advancement of Teaching." *Popular Science Monthly*, June 1906, 570–1.

A City Editor. "The Newspaper's Contempt for the Public." *World To-Day*, March 1907, 262–6.

A Common Acquaintance, "Wilson–Taft–Roosevelt: The Candidates Compared—An Intimate Evening With Each." *World's Work*, September 1912, 569–75.

Cooper, Edward. "Sensational Journalism." *Living Age*, July 17, 1909, 187–90.

Crane, Burton L. "The Presidency of Princeton University." *Independent*, June 19, 1902, 1481–4.

"Demand for Press Agents in Politics." *Fourth Estate*, March 2, 1912, 19.

"The Democratic Presidential Candidates: A Poll of the Press." *Outlook*, May 18, 1912, 106–9.

"Disaffection of Mr. Hearst." *Harper's Weekly*, April 26, 1913, 3–4.

"Distorting the Nation's Conscience." *World To-Day*, December 1909, 1227–8.

Dunn, Arthur Wallace. "Campaigning for the Nomination." *American Review of Reviews*, April 1912, 429–30.

"Editor Now Also a Political Power." *Fourth Estate*, June 1, 1912, 3.

"Fifteen Columbia Records by Wm. H. Taft." *Talking Machine World*, September 15, 1908, 1.

"Following the Campaign: Wilson Versus Roosevelt." *Outlook*, October 5, 1912, 297–9.

A Friend of Princeton, "The Differences at Princeton." *Independent*, March 17, 1910, 574–6.

Gilliams, Leslie E. "Will Uncle Sam's Hostesses Be Three Bachelor Maids?" *To-Day's*, November 1912, 11.

"Government by Commission." *Independent*, November 30, 1911, 1221.

"Governor Wilson at His Summer Home." *Moving Picture News*, July 6, 1912, 12.

"Governor Wilson's Candidacy: A Poll of the Press." *Outlook*, February 10, 1912, 307–9.

"Governor Wilson in Universal Films." *Universal Weekly*, October 5, 1912, 1–2.

Griffin, Solomon Bulkley. "The Political Evolution of a College President." *Atlantic Monthly*, January 1902, 43–51.

Hale, William Bayard. "Judson Harmon and the Presidency." *World's Work*, June 1911, 14446–59.

——. *Woodrow Wilson-A Biography*. Parts 1–6. World's Work, October 1911, 14940–53; November 1911–March 1912, 64–77, 229–35, 297–310, 466–72, 522–34.

——. "Woodrow Wilson: Possible President." *World's Work*, May 1911, 14339–53.

——. *Woodrow Wilson: The Story of His Life*. Garden City, N. J.: Doubleday, Page & Company, 1912.

Harvey, George. "The Political Predestination of Woodrow Wilson." *North American Review*, March 1911, 321–30.

Harvey, George. "The Problem, the Solution and the Man." *North American Review*, April 1911, 481–93.

——. "Roosevelt or the Republic!" *North American Review*, October 1912, 433–48.

Hazeltine, Mayo W. "Woodrow Wilson." *North American Review*, June 1908, 844–50.

Heinl, Robert. "Down Washington Way." *Leslie's*, June 29, 1911, 730.

Hendrick, Burton J. "Woodrow Wilson: Political Leader." *McClure's Magazine*, December 1911, 217–31.

Hosford, Hester E. "The New Ladies of the White House." *Independent*, November 21, 1912, 1159–65.

——. "Woodrow Wilson." *Independent*, July 11, 1912, 68–79.

——. *Woodrow Wilson and New Jersey Made Over*. New York: Knickerbocker Press, 1912.

"How Press Agents Make Presidents." *Fourth Estate*, April 13, 1912, 4.

Hyde, William DeWitt. "The Issues of the Campaign." *Outlook*, October 5, 1912, 271–2.

Inglis, William. "Helping to Make a President." Parts 1–3. *Collier's*, October 7, 1912, 14–16, 37–41; October 14, 1916, 12–14, 40–1; October 21, 1916, 14–15, 20–1, 24.

"Intimate Moments With the Three Leading Presidential Candidates." *Current Literature*, October 1912, 397–9.

Irwin, Will. "The American Newspaper: A Study of Journalism in Its Relation to the Public." Parts 1–15, Colliers, January 21–July 29, 1911.

"Is Sane and Honest Journalism Possible?" *American Review of Reviews*, January 1910, 93–4.

Jastrow, Joseph. "The Advancement of Teaching." *North American Review*, October 1907, 213–24.

Johnston, Charles. "A Talk with Governor Wilson." *Harper's Weekly*, August 19, 1911, 11–12.

"Joke on Gov. Wilson." *Talking Machine World*, November 15, 1912, 7.

"Journalism for Public Service." *Fourth Estate*, May 18, 1912, 4.

Kerney, James. "Woodrow Wilson, Governor." *Independent*, May 11, 1911, 986–9.

Lathrop, John E. "The Views of Champ Clark." *Outlook*, May 11, 1912, 65–73.

Lewis, Alfred Henry. "The Honorable Champ." *Cosmopolitan Magazine*, November 1911, 760–5.

——. "The Real Woodrow Wilson." *Hearst's Magazine*, May 1912, 2265–74.

——. "Underwood-House Leader." *Cosmopolitan*. December 1911, 109–14.

——. "What Life Means To Me." *Cosmopolitan*, January 1907, 293–8.

——. "Wilson and His Pension Plea." *World To-Day*, February 1912, 1845–52.

Lissner, E. "Woodrow Wilson for President." *Harper's Weekly*, July 29, 1911, 6.

"A Little Presidential Primary." *World's Work*, August 1911, 14716–20.

"Making Taft Records." *Edison Phonographic Monthly*, June 1908, 6–7.

"The Moral Menace of Yellow Journalism." *Current Literature*, April 1908, 414–15.

"The Moving Picture in Politics." *Talking Machine World*, October 15, 1908, 66.
"Moving Picture Movement." *Independent*, January 11, 1912, 108–10.
Munsey, Frank. *Journalism*. New Haven: Yale University Press, 1903.
Needham, Henry Beach. "Woodrow Wilson's Views." *Outlook*, August 26, 1911, 939–51.
"Newspapers as an Aid to Political Candidates." *Fourth Estate*, April 6, 1912, 6.
"The Newspaper's Contempt for the Public: An Interview with the City Editor." *World To-Day*, March 1907, 262–6.
"Offenses Against Good Journalism." *Outlook*, February 29, 1908, 479.
Pennypacker, Samuel W. "Sensational Journalism and the Remedy." *North American Review*, November 1909, 587–93.
"Political Advertising." *Fourth Estate*, 6 April 1912, 6.
"The Political Transformation of Woodrow Wilson." *Current Literature*, February 1912, 153–7.
Pomeroy, Eugene Cowles. "Our Next President." *Forum*, November 1912, 513–25.
Pritchett, Henry S. "Mr. Carnegie's Gift To The Teachers." *Outlook*, May 19, 1906, 120–5.
"Records of Taft, Wilson and Roosevelt." *Talking Machine World*, October 15, 1912, 26.
Ridgway, Erman J. "Weighing the Candidates." *Everybody's Magazine*, May 1912, 579–92.
"Roosevelt Records." *Edison Phonographic Monthly*, September 1912, 8.
Sedgwick, Ellery. "The Man with the Muck Rake." *American Illustrated Magazine*, May 1906, 111–12.
Slossom, Edwin E. "The Place of Journalism in University Education." *Independent*, November 23, 1911, 1127–31.
——. "Princeton University." *Independent*, March 4, 1909, 458–77.
Stockbridge, Frank Parker. "How Woodrow Wilson Won His Nomination." *Current History* 20 (July 1924): 561–72.
——. "With Governor Wilson in the West." *World's Work*, August 1911, 14713–16.
"The 'Talker' As Campaign Orator." *Talking Machine World*, April 15, 1908, 1.
"The 'Talker' As Spellbinder." *Talking Machine World*, March 15, 1908, 35.
"Talking Machine in Politics." *Talking Machine World*, June 15, 1908, 1.
"Teddy Roosevelt in Pictures." *Moving Picture World*, October 19, 1912, 251.
"Ten Records by William Jennings Bryan." *Edison Phonographic Monthly*, June 1908, 6–7.
"Theodore Roosevelt: The Picture Man." *Moving Picture World*, October 22, 1910, 920.
Turner, George Kibbe. "Manufacturing Public Opinion: The New Art of Making Presidents by Press Bureaus." *McClure's*, July 1912, 316–27.
Villard, Oswald Garrison. "Some Weakness of Modern Journalism," *University of Kansas News-Bulletin*, November 2, 1914, 1–19.
"A Virginia Democrat." *Harper's Weekly*, May 6, 1911, 7, 32.
Wilcox, Delos F. "The American Newspaper: A Study in Social Psychology." *Annals of the American Academy of Political and Social Science* 16 (July 1900): 59–92.

Williams, Jesse Lynch. "Woodrow Wilson: The New President of Princeton." *McClure's*, October 1902, 534.
"Wilson As Viewed in the Roosevelt Camp." *Current Literature*, August 1912, 127–8.
"Woodrow Wilson and the New Jersey Governorship." *American Review of Reviews*, November 1910, 555–62.
"Woodrow Wilson, A Presidential Possibility." *Current Literature*, October 1910, 381–4.
"Woodrow Wilson: The First Lay President of Princeton." *Century Magazine*, November 1902, 161–2.

Selected Secondary Articles and Books

Ander, Fritiof O. "The Swedish-American Press in the Election of 1912." *Swedish Pioneer Historical Quarterly* 14 (1963): 103–26.
Axson, Stockton. *"Brother Woodrow": A Memoir of Woodrow Wilson*, Arthur S. Link et al, eds. Princeton: Princeton University Press, 1993.
Ayers, Edward L. *The Promise of the New South: Life After Reconstruction*. New York: Oxford University Press, 1993.
Baker, Ray Stannard. *American Chronicle: The Autobiography of Ray Stannard Baker*. New York: Charles Scribner's Sons, 1945.
Baskerville, Barnet. *The People's Voice: The Orator in American Society*. Lexington: University of Kentucky Press, 1979.
Bekken, Jon. " 'No Weapon So Powerful': Working-Class Newspapers in the United States." *Journal of Communication Inquiry* 12 (Summer 1988): 104–19.
Billington, Monroe. "Thomas P. Gore and the Election of Woodrow Wilson." *Mid-America; An Historical Review* 39 (1957): 180–91.
Bragdon, Henry Wilkinson. *Woodrow Wilson: The Academic Years*. Cambridge: Belknap Press of Harvard University Press, 1967.
Brands, H. W. *T. R.: The Last Romantic*. New York: Basic Books, 1997.
Britt, George. *Forty Years—Forty Millions: The Career of Frank A. Munsey*. New York: Farrar and Rinehart, 1935.
Carlson, Oliver. *Brisbane: A Candid Biography*. New York: Stackpole Sons, 1937.
Clements, Kendrick A. *Woodrow Wilson: World Statesman*. Boston: Twayne Publishers, 1987.
Coblentz, Edmond D., ed. *William Randolph Hearst: A Portrait in His Own Words*. New York: Simon and Schuster, 1952.
Cooper, John Milton, Jr. *Walter Hines Page: The Southerner as American*. Chapel Hill: University of North Carolina Press, 1977.
——. *The Warrior and the Priest: Woodrow Wilson and Theodore Roosevelt*. Cambridge: Belknap Press of Harvard University Press, 1983.
Crews, Kenneth D. "Woodrow Wilson, Wisconsin, and the Election of 1912." *Presidential Studies Quarterly* 12 (1982): 369–76.
Crowe, Charles. "Tom Watson, Populists, and Blacks Reconsidered." *Journal of Negro History* 55 (April 1970): 99–116.

Dallek, Robert T. *Hail to the Chief: The Making and Unmaking of American Presidents*. New York: Hyperion, 1996.

Daniels, Josephus. *The Wilson Era, Years of Peace: 1910–17*. Chapel Hill: University of North Carolina Press, 1944.

Davidson, John Wells, ed. *A Crossroads of Freedom: The 1912 Campaign Speeches of Woodrow Wilson*. New Haven: Yale University Press, 1956.

Dicken-Garcia, Hazel. *Journalistic Standards in Nineteenth-Century America*. Madison: University of Wisconsin Press, 1989.

Diner, Steven J. *A Very Different World: Americans of the Progressive Era*. New York: Hill and Wang, 1998.

DuBois, W. E. B. *The Autobiography of W. E. B. DuBois: A Soliloquy on Viewing My Life from the Last Decade of Its First Century*. New York: International Publishers, 1968.

Endres, Kathleen L. and Therese L. Lueck, eds., *Women's Periodicals in the United States*: Social and Political Issues. Westport, Conn.: Greenwood Press, 1996.

Farrar, Hayward. *The Baltimore Afro-American 1892–1950*. Westport, Conn.: Greenwood Press, 1998.

Fielding, Raymond. *The American Newsreel 1911–1967*. Norman: University of Oklahoma Press, 1972.

Filler, Louis. "Wolfville." *New Mexico Quarterly Review* 13 (Summer 1943): 35–47.

Fleming, Thomas. *New Jersey: A Bicentennial History*. New York: W. W. Norton; Nashville: American Association for State and Local History, 1977.

Fox, Stephen R. *The Guardian of Boston: William Monroe Trotter*. New York: Athenaeum, 1970.

Gardner, Gilson. *Lusty Scripps: The Life of E. W. Scripps, 1854–1926*. New York: Vanguard Press, 1932.

Gatewood, Willard B. "James Calvin Hemphill: Southern Critic of Woodrow Wilson, 1911–1912." *The Georgia Review* 13 (Winter 1959): 378–92.

——, ed. "The President and the 'Deacon' in the Campaign of 1912: The Correspondence of William Howard Taft and James Calvin Hemphill, 1911–1913." *Ohio History* 74 (1965): 35–54.

Geitz, Henry, ed. *The German-American Press*. Madison: German American Cultural Society, 1992.

Gillespie, Veronica M. "T. R. on Film." *The Quarterly Journal of the Library of Congress* 34 (January 1977): 39–51.

Goldman, Eric F. "Public Relations and the Progressive Surge." *Public Relations Review* 3 (Fall 1978): 52–62.

Graham, Sara Hunter. *Woman Suffrage and the New Democracy*. New Haven: Yale University Press, 1996.

Graybar, Lloyd. *Albert Shaw of the "Review of Reviews": An Intellectual Biography*. Lexington: University of Kentucky Press, 1974.

Green, George N. "The Florida Press and the Democratic Presidential Primary of 1912." *Florida Historical Quarterly* 44 (1966): 169–80.

Hart, Jim Allee. *A History of the St. Louis Globe-Democrat*. Columbia: University of Missouri Press, 1961.

Hearst, William Randolph, Jr. and Jack Casserly. *The Hearst: Father and Son*. Niwot, Colorado: Roberts Rinehart Publishers, 1991.

Heckscher, August. *Woodrow Wilson*. New York: Charles Scribner's Sons, 1991.

Hirst, David W. *Woodrow Wilson, Reform Governor: A Documentary Narrative*. Princeton N. J.: Van Nostrand, 1965.

Hoerder, Dirk, ed. *The Immigrant Labor Press in North America, 1840s–1970: An Annotated Bibliography*. 3 vols. New York: Greenwood Press, 1987.

Hofstadter, Richard. *The Progressive Movement, 1900–1915*. Englewood Cliffs, N. J.: Prentice-Hall, 1963.

Hofstadter, Richard and Wilson Smith. *American Higher Education: A Documentary History*. 2 vols. Chicago: University of Chicago Press, 1961.

Hudson, Robert V. *The Writing Game: A Biography of Will Irwin*. Ames: Iowa State University Press, 1982.

Jablonsky, Thomas J. *The Home, Heaven, and Mother Party: Female Anti-Suffragists in the United States, 1868–1920*. Brooklyn, N. Y.: Carlson Publishing, 1994.

Johnson, Evans C. "The Underwood Forces and the Democratic Nomination of 1912." *The Historian: A Journal of History* 31 (February 1969): 173–93.

Johnson, Gerald W. *An Honorable Titan: A Biographical Study of Adolph S. Ochs*. New York: Harper & Brothers, 1946.

Johnson, Gerald W. et al. *The Sunpapers of Baltimore*. New York; Alfred A. Knopf, 1937.

Johnson, Willis Fletcher. *George Harvey: "A Passionate Patriot."* Boston: Houghton Mifflin, 1929.

Juergens, George. *News From The White House: The Presidential–Press Relationship in the Progressive Era*. Chicago: University of Chicago Press, 1981.

Kaltenborn, H. V. *Fifty Fabulous Years, 1900–1950*. New York: G. P. Putnam's Sons, 1950.

Karson, Marc. *American Labor Unions and Politics, 1900–1918*. Carbondale: Southern Illinois Press, 1958.

Kelly, Frank K. *The Fight for the White House: The Story of 1912*. New York: Thomas Y. Crowell, 1961.

Kerney, James. *The Political Education of Woodrow Wilson*. New York: Century, 1926.

Knock, Thomas J. *To End All Wars: Woodrow Wilson and the Quest for a New World Order*. New York: Oxford University Press, 1992.

Kuehl, Warren F. *Hamilton Holt: Journalist, Internationalist, Educator*. Gainesville: University of Florida Press, 1960.

Kull, Irving, S. *New Jersey: A History*. 4 vols. New York: American History Society, 1930.

Lawrence, David. *The True Story of Woodrow Wilson*. New York: George H. Doran, 1924.

Leonard, Thomas C. *The Power of the Press: The Birth of American Political Reporting*. New York: Oxford University Press, 1986.

Levin, Phyllis Lee. *Edith and Woodrow: The Wilson White House*. New York: Scribner, 2001.

Levine, Edward M. *The Irish and Irish Politicians*, Notre Dame, Ind.: University of Notre Dame Press, 1966.

Lewis, David Levering. *W. E. B. DuBois: Biography of a Race, 1868–1919*. New York: Henry Holt, 1993.

Link, Arthur S. "The Democratic Pre-Convention Campaign of 1912 in Georgia." *Georgia Historical Quarterly* 39 (1945): 143–58.

——. *The Higher Realism of Woodrow Wilson and Other Essays*. Nashville: Vanderbilt University Press, 1971.

——. "The Negro as a Factor in the Campaign of 1912." *Journal of Negro History* 32 (January 1947): 81–9.

——. "The Underwood Presidential Movement in 1912." *Journal of Southern History* 11 (May 1945): 230–45.

——. *Wilson: The Road to the White House*. 1947. Reprint, Princeton: Princeton University Press, 1965.

Luebke, Frederick C. *Bonds of Loyalty: German Americans in World War I*. DeKalb, Ill.: Northern Illinois Press, 1974.

Lunardini, Christine A. and Thomas J. Knock. "Woodrow Wilson and Woman Suffrage: A New Look." *Political Science Quarterly* 95 (Winter 1980–81): 655–71.

Lundberg, Ferdinand. *Imperial Hearst: A Social Biography*. New York: Equinox Cooperative Press, 1936.

McAdoo, Eleanor Wilson, *The Woodrow Wilsons*. New York: Macmillan, 1937.

McAdoo, William Gibbs. *Crowded Years: The Reminiscences of William G. McAdoo*. Cambridge, Mass.: Riverside Press 1931.

McCombs, William. *Making Woodrow Wilson President*. New York: Fairview, 1921.

Marble, Manning. *W. E. B. DuBois: Black Radical Democrat*. Boston: Twayne, 1986.

Marcosson, Isaac F. *"Marse Henry," A Biography of Henry Watterson*. New York: Dodd, Mead, 1951.

Meier, August. "Booker T. Washington and the Negro Press: With Special Reference to the *Colored American Magazine*." *Journal of Negro History* 38 (January 1953): 67–90.

——. "The Negro and the Democratic Party, 1875–1915." *Phylon* 17 (1956): 173–91.

Miller, Sally M., ed. *The Ethnic Press in the United States: A Historical Analysis and Handbook*. Westport, Conn.: Greenwood Press, 1987.

Mitchell, Edward P. *Memoirs of an Editor: Fifty Years of American Journalism*. New York: Charles Scribner's Sons, 1924.

Morreale, Joanne. *The Presidential Campaign Film: A Critical History*. Westport, Conn.: Praeger, 1993.

Morrison, Joseph L. *Josephus Daniels Says . . . : An Editor's Political Odyssey from Bryan to Wilson and F. D. R., 1894–1913*. Chapel Hill: University of North Carolina Press, 1962.

Mowry, George. "The South and the Progressive Lily White Party of 1912." *Journal of Southern History* 6 (May 1940): 237–47.

Mulder, John M. *Woodrow Wilson: The Years of Preparation*. Princeton: Princeton University Press, 1978.

Nasaw, David. *The Chief: The Life of William Randolph Hearst*. Boston: Houghton Mifflin, 2000.

Nasaw, David. "Learning to Go to the Movies." *American Heritage*, November 1993, 78–92.

Newby, I. A. *The South: A History*. New York: Holt, Rinehart and Winston, 1978.

Nye, Russell B. *Midwestern Progressive Politics*. 1959. Reprint, New York: Harper & Row, Torchbook Edition, 1965.

O'Brian, Frank M. *The Story of the Sun*: *New York, 1833–1928*. 1928. Reprint: Westport, Conn.: Greenwood Press, 1968.

O'Connor, Richard. *The German-Americans: An Informal History*. Boston: Little, Brown, 1968.

Osborn, George C. "The Influence of Joseph Ruggles Wilson on His Son Woodrow Wilson." *North Carolina Historical Review* 32 (1955): 519–43.

——. *Woodrow Wilson: The Early Years*. Baton Rouge: Louisiana State University Press, 1968.

Overacker, Louise. *The Presidential Primary*. New York: Macmillan, 1926.

Park, Robert E. *The Immigrant Press and Its Control*. New York: Harper & Brothers, 1922.

Peterson, Theodore. *Magazines in the Twentieth Century*. Urbana: University of Illinois Press, 1956.

Pollard, James E. *The Presidents and the Press*. New York: Macmillan, 1947.

Ponder, Stephen. *Managing the Press: Origins of the Media Presidency*. New York: St. Martins, 1998.

Puttkammer, Charles W. and Ruth Worthy. "William Monroe Trotter, 1872–1934." *Journal of Negro History* 43 (October 1958): 298–316.

Reedy, George E. *From the Ward to the White House: The Irish in American Politics*. New York: Charles Scribner's Sons, 1991.

Reid, Edith Gittings. *Woodrow Wilson: The Caricature, the Myth and the Man*. London: Oxford University Press, 1934.

Ritchie, Donald A. *Press Gallery: Congress and the Washington Correspondents*. Cambridge: Harvard University Press, 1991.

Robinson, Judith. *The Hearsts: An American Dynasty*. Newark, Del.: University of Delaware Press, 1991.

Sarasohn, David. *The Party of Reform: Democrats in the Progressive Era*. Jackson, Miss.: University of Mississippi Press, 1989.

Schlesinger, Arthur M. Jr., ed. *The Coming to Power: Critical Presidential Elections in American History*. New York: Chelsea House, 1972.

——, ed. *History of American Presidential Elections, 1789–1968*. 4 vols. New York: Chelsea House in Association with McGraw-Hill, 1971.

Schudson, Michael. *Discovering the News: A Social History of American Newspapers*. New York: Basic Books, 1978.

Sedgwick, Ellery. *The Happy Profession*. Boston: Atlantic Monthly Press Book, Little, Brown and Company, 1946.

Seitz, Don C. *Joseph Pulitzer: His Life and Letters*. Garden City, N. J.: Garden City Publishing Company, 1924.

Shannon, William V. *The American Irish*. New York: Macmillan, 1963.

Shore, Elliott, Ken Fones-Wolf, and James P. Danky. *The German-American Radical Press: The Shaping of a Left Political Culture, 1850–1914*. Urbana: University of Illinois Press, 1992.

Sloan, Wm. David and James D. Startt. *The Media in America: A History*. 4th ed. Northport, Ala: Vision Press, 1999.

Solomon, Martha M., ed. *A Voice of Their Own: The Woman Suffrage Press, 1840–1910*. Tuscaloosa: University of Alabama Press, 1991.

Spencer, Samuel R., Jr. *Booker T. Washington and the Negro's Place in American Life*. Boston: Little, Brown and Company, 1955.

Steffens, Lincoln. *The Autobiography of Lincoln Steffens*. New York: Harcourt, Brace, 1931.

Swanberg, W. A. *Citizen Hearst: A Biography of William Randolph Hearst*. New York: Galahad Books, 1961.

——. *Pulitzer*. New York: Charles Scribner's Sons, 1967.

Talese, Gay. *The Kingdom and the Power*. 1966. Reprint, New York: World Publishing, 1969.

Tebbel, John and Sarah Miles Watts. *The Press and the Presidency: From George Washington to Ronald Reagan*. New York: Oxford University Press, 1985.

Thompson, Charles Willis. *Presidents I've Known and Two Near Presidents*. Indianapolis: Bobbs-Merrill, 1929.

Thornbrough, Emma Lou. "American Negro Newspapers, 1880–1914." *Business History Review* 40 (Winter 1966): 467–90.

——. "The Brownsville Episode and the Negro Vote." *Mississippi Valley Historical Review* 44 (June 1957–March 1958): 469–93.

Thorsen, Niels Aage. *The Political Thought of Woodrow Wilson, 1875–1910*. Princeton: Princeton University Press, 1988.

Trimble, Vance H. *The Astounding Mr. Scripps: The Turbulent Life of America's Penny Press Lord*. Ames, Iowa: Iowa State University Press, 1992.

Troy, Gil. *See How They Ran: The Changing Role of the Presidential Candidate*. Cambridge: Howard University Press, 1996.

Tumulty, Joseph. *Woodrow Wilson As I Know Him*. Garden City, N. J.: Doubleday, Page, 1924.

Villard, Oswald Garrison. *Fighting Years: Memoir of a Liberal Editor*. New York: Harcourt, Brace, 1939.

——. *Prophets True and False*. 1928. Reprint, Freeport, N. Y.: Books for Libraries, 1969.

——. *Some Newspapers and Newspaper-men*. New York: Alfred A. Knopf, 1923.

Watterson, Henry. *"Marse Henry,"* An Autobiography. 2 vols. New York: George H. Doran, 1919.

Weisenburger, Francis P. "The Middle Western Antecedents of Woodrow Wilson." *Mississippi Valley Historical Review* 23 (December 1936): 379–90.

White, William Allen. *Woodrow Wilson: The Man His Times and His Task*. Boston: Houghton Mifflin, 1924.

Wiebe, Robert H. *The Search for Order, 1877–1920*. 1967. Reprint, New York: Hill and Wang, 1999.

Williams, Harold A. *The Baltimore Sun, 1837–1987*. Baltimore: Johns Hopkins University Press, 1987.
Winkler, John R. *William Randolph Hearst: A New Appraisal.* New York: Hasting House, 1955.
Wittke, Carl. *The German Language Press in America*. Lexington, Ky.: University of Kentucky Press, 1957.
——. *The Irish in America*. Baton Rouge: Louisiana State University Press, 1956.
Wolseley, Roland E. *The Black Press, U. S. A.* 2nd ed. Ames, Iowa: Iowa State University Press, 1990.
Woodward, C. Vann. *Origins of the New South, 1877–1913*. Baton Rouge: Louisiana State University Press, 1951.
——. *Tom Watson: Agrarian Rebel.* New York: Rinehart, 1938.

Miscellaneous Sources

The American Experience: Woodrow Wilson. Documentary. January 6, 2002. Public Broadcasting System, Channel 11, Chicago.
Campbell, Joseph. "Yellow Journalism and Urban America, 1900: What Explains Contagion?" Paper presented at the annual meeting of the American Journalism Historians Association, Portland, Ore., October 1999.
The Old Way and the New. Universal film, 1912. Motion Picture Collection. Motion Picture, Broadcasting, and Recorded Sound Division, Library of Congress, Washington, D. C.
Pieringer, R. S. "Principles, Not Men: The Institutional and Professional History of the *True American*, Published at Trenton, 1801–1913." Senior Thesis, Princeton University, 1970.

Index